THE LIGHTHOUSES
OF HAWAI'I

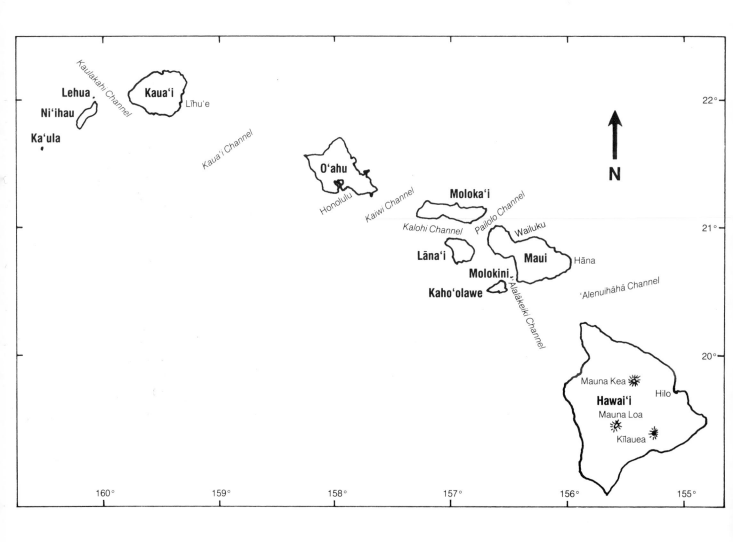

THE LIGHTHOUSES
OF HAWAI'I

Love Dean

A Kolowalu Book
University of Hawaii Press
HONOLULU

For Betty Bruce and Sue McMillan

Printed in the United States of America

91 93 94 95 96 97   5 4 3 2 1

Library of Congress Cataloging-in-Publication Data

Dean, Love.

The lighthouses of Hawai'i / Love Dean.

p.   cm. — (A Kolowalu book)

Includes bibliographical references and index.

ISBN 0–8248–1319–7

1. Lighthouses—Hawaii—History. I. Title.

VK1024.H3D43   1991

387.1'55—dc20   90-11214

CIP

Preparation of the maps was supported in part
by Friends of the Library of Hawaii.

CONTENTS

Foreword   VII
Preface   IX

Introduction   I

Part I: Lighthouses of O'ahu   5
 1. Honolulu Harbor   6
 2. Barbers Point   17
 3. Diamond Head   26
 4. Makapu'u Point   38
 5. Ka'ena Point and Other Lights along
    O'ahu's Shores   54

Part II: Lighthouses of Maui County   59
 6. Maui   60
 7. Molokini, Kaho'olawe, and Lāna'i   82
 8. Moloka'i   89

Part III: Lighthouses of Hawai'i County   III
 9. The Island of Hawai'i   112

Part IV: Lighthouses of Kaua'i County and Ka'ula   137
 10. Kaua'i   138
 11. Lehua and Ka'ula   154

Part V: Lighthouse Tenders   161
 12. The *Kukui* and Other Lighthouse Tenders
     in Hawai'i   162

     Epilogue   171

     Lighthouse Keepers in Hawai'i   173
     Notes   179
     Glossary   203
     Index   209

EXECUTIVE CHAMBERS

HONOLULU

JOHN WAIHEE
GOVERNOR

It is a pleasure to join in this celebration of Hawaiian lighthouses.

Hawaiians long have recognized the importance of light to lead sea-farers to safety. It is said that Kamehameha the Great, caught in stiff night winds, was guided to shore by a large fire. Ancient Polynesians used signal fires to aid returning voyagers.

More recent history chronicles the prominent role Hawaiians played in the development and maintenance of the more formal light-houses. Kamehameha III built a nine-foot high, wooden tower in Lahaina in 1840 to serve as a beacon through the Lahaina Roadstead. Ten major lights and over 100 other lighted aids are in use today, some of which can be seen from 25 miles at sea.

Now technology has taken on the role so diligently observed by those light keepers of old. We are indebted to those stalwart souls who ensured the continuous operation of lighthouses in Hawaii during the worst of conditions so that today we have a vigorous commercial and recreational ocean industry and safe sea travel throughout the seven seas.

I welcome this new opportunity to learn more about another facet to Hawaii's colorful history as a maritime outpost. We are indebted to the author who has researched and compiled this information.

FOREWORD

Hawai'i, surrounded by the sixty-eight million square miles of the Pacific Ocean, is the most geographically isolated land on earth. Add to this isolation waters that are among the roughest in the world, with rocky shorelines that offer notoriously few safe anchorages, and one can quickly appreciate the importance of the lighthouses of Hawai'i.

The number of vessels that have gone aground or been wrecked on the shores of the Islands is legion. With the erection of some 176 lighted aids to navigation since the first one was established in 1840, losses have markedly decreased, but Hawaiian waters continue to take a steady yearly toll. From the volcanoes that might have served as fiery beacons for the first voyagers to Hawai'i to the modern, automated lights of today, lighthouses continue to play a vital role in safely guiding the lifeline of ships that sustain America's only "ocean state."

Few of man's architectural institutions integrate the functional and the symbolic more fully than lighthouses. In ancient Hawai'i during annual Makahiki times, "the bonfires of Puea [a deity] were lighted along the coast . . . visible to all the fishermen far and near. These beacons guided their actions. . . ." Today, as always, lighthouses conjure up in sea-weary mariners welcome feelings of sanctuary, safety, and warmth. Lighthouses are an international language as well, an all too rare, but long-standing and irrefutable example of international humanitarianism.

Lighthouses, each with its own distinctive signature, have come to symbolize the maritime history of a country. And they provide a constant reminder of a sometimes-savage sea, evoke the drama of a mariner's life, and recapture the raw loneliness of the lightkeeper. The dependability of the lights and the lightkeeper are the stuff of countless stories, songs, and sagas all over the world. The history of the lighthouses of Hawai'i, as one will see in this excellent work, is as colorful and dramatic as one would expect from the legendary islands of Hawai'i.

TOMMY HOLMES

Hawaii Maritime Center

PREFACE

Lighthouses played a particularly important part in my life for fourteen years. I lived, cruised, and worked on boats from Maine to the Dry Tortugas and spent many anxious moments with a chart in one hand and binoculars in the other, looking for navigational aids. I also experienced many moments of joy when, after hours of nothing but water and darkness, the loom of a light appeared and it turned out to be the light I was looking for; my boat was right on course.

On land, I like to visit lighthouses and when I moved to Hawai'i my goal was to see every lighted navigational aid in the Islands, by land or by sea. The scenery, I knew, would be spectacular, and I thought this would be an exciting and enlightening way to explore the Islands. I didn't realize at the time that there are 176 lighted aids in Hawai'i! One hundred and one of these aids are visible under five nautical miles, seventy-five can be seen over five nautical miles, including ten primary seacoast lights visible a minimum distance of seventeen nautical miles. I began to wonder how, when, and why all these lights were established.

I was soon reading whatever I could find about lighthouses in Hawai'i. There is little published history about many of the beacons, but what I read made me want to know more. As I began researching, I realized that the historical records of lighthouses in the Islands are so scattered that it might be an enjoyable and worthwhile project to bring the pieces together in a book.

There was more history than I expected, just as there were more lights, and this book does not attempt to cover all of either. Part of the history was anticipated—the interrelatedness of the development of aids to navigation and the development of commerce in Hawai'i. The part that was not anticipated was the legendary and historical importance to ancient Hawaiians of the sites on which the lighthouses were later built. This background added a dimension to the story that I found particularly fascinating.

I hope this book will stimulate further research on the lighthouses of Hawai'i and especially on the builders and the keepers of the lights. At the end of the text I have listed the names of the keepers, the dates, and the lighthouses on which they served. This is not a complete list and there are great gaps that need to be filled. In some cases dates may be wrong and names misspelled. Documenting the navigational aids and the lightkeepers and their families is an ongoing research project. I ask readers who have information about the people and the aids in this book, or who find inaccuracies, to contact me. There is much historically valuable information on this subject that has yet to be discovered and recorded.

The information I have gathered on existing navigational aids in Hawai'i was obtained through the cooperation of the Aids to Navigation Branch of the Fourteenth District of the U.S. Coast Guard in Honolulu. The tours I made of the light stations on the Islands would not have been possible without the hospitality of the Aids to Navigation team. In particular I would like to thank Admiral William Kozlovsky; Commander R. W. Brandes; Commander

Henry W. Motekaitis; Lieutenant Mike Swegles; Lieutenant (jg) Brad Nelson; Warrant Officer John Haley; Petty Officers David Santos, Scott Hartvigsen, Rick McKersie, and Bill Souder; Seaman David Goff; and the entire ANT team. For architectural information and drawings of the lighthouses I relied on James Morita and Neil Kawamoto, with the U.S. Coast Guard Shore Maintenance Detachment.

The guidance of archivists and librarians has been essential in researching records, letters, and official documents that reveal the history of the lighthouses. Richard Thompson, at the State Archives of Hawaii, helped me locate much of the information concerning the establishment of the lighted aids before 1900. In working with the Hawaiian Collection at Hamilton Library, University of Hawaii at Mānoa, I have relied on the help of Dr. Nancy Morris, Dr. Chieko Tachihata, Dr. Michaelyn Chou, and Eleanor Au. Agnes Quigg helped me with microforms and Mabel Suzuki guided me through government publications and the University's historic map collection. Charles Okino, State of Hawaii, Survey Division, located survey maps, land deeds, and harbor charts for me.

There are many people on the Big Island, Maui, Moloka'i, O'ahu, and Kaua'i who not only aided me with my research, but befriended me; I especially want to thank Karen and Keith Baxter, Carla Mauri, Carol Karakawa, Lynne McCory, Tamara Horcajo, Hokulani Holt-Padella, Gail Bartholomew, Mary Pinho, Jean Greenwell, Sister Eligia Eiholzer, Sri TenCate, Stewart Wastell, Tony Oliver, Helen Chapin, Barbara Dunn, Dave Lyman, Tommy Holmes, and Dr. Alfred Morris. Personal interviews have given me a better insight into the lightkeepers' lives and I am deeply grateful to all who shared their time and experiences with me. Carol Edgecomb Brown is one who has shared both memories and photographs. I have indeed been fortunate to have had the encouragement and guidance of Eileen D'Araujo at University of Hawaii Press. My lighthouse mentor is F. Ross Holland, Jr.

INTRODUCTION

On the island of Maui there is a thirty-nine-foot light tower at the edge of the harbor of Lahaina with a plaque that reads, "On this site in 1840 King Kamehameha ordered a nine foot wooden tower built as an aid to navigation for the whaling ships anchored off Lahaina." The significance of this simple statement goes far beyond the event mentioned; it marks the beginning of the history of Hawaiian lighthouses.

Before Western contact, Hawaiians did not need permanent navigational aids. Those who set out in boats to fish or to travel to neighboring villages or islands knew the coastlines and all the landmarks well. An open fire to guide them safely to shore was used only at night or during storms.

All over the world, a fire kindled upon a headland was the first type of navigational aid used by mariners. It soon became obvious that the higher a fire could be placed, the farther out to sea it could be seen. At some ports on the Mediterranean Sea, towers were built on which wood was kept burning day and night. In the day the smoke could be seen from the sea, and at night the fire's glow was visible.[1]

The tallest lighthouse ever built was constructed on the island of Pharos, off Alexandria, Egypt, in about 247 B.C. Our word *pharology*, derived from Pharos, means the scientific theory and treatment of signal lights and lighthouse construction. The Pharos lighthouse survived for more than 1,600 years and served as an important navigational aid for early Mediterranean seafarers.[2]

While mariners were sailing the Mediterranean Sea, Polynesians were exploring the Pacific Ocean.

Explorations starting from Samoa, reached the Marquesas and perhaps even as far as Tahiti, distances of about 2,000 miles. Later they sailed north from Samoa to Tokelau and the Ellice Islands. During one period of dramatic ocean voyages, Polynesians sailed east to Easter Island and north to the Hawaiian Islands. No one knows what prompted these extraordinary long-distance voyages, but settlements were made at both locations. Traditional Hawaiian chants and stories indicate that Polynesians continued to make the 3,000-mile voyages between the Hawaiian Islands and Tahiti for perhaps two hundred years.[3]

In Europe, while the Roman Empire was expanding and sea trade increasing, new lighthouses were built at important ports. In all, the Romans built thirty lighthouses from the Black Sea to the Atlantic Ocean before the Empire collapsed in the sixth century.[4]

One of the first events in modern times that gave impetus to the development of navigational aids occurred in England in 1565. In the first English statute relating to aids to navigation, a central authority called Trinity House was made responsible for the erection and preservation of sea marks.[5] Although Trinity House was charged with establishing and maintaining lighthouses throughout Britain, during the colonial period in America each of the thirteen colonies was responsible for its own aids to navigation.[6]

The first lighthouse in the American colonies was built in 1716 by the Massachusetts Bay Colony on Little Brewster Island in Boston Harbor. By the end of the eighteenth century, there were twenty-four lighthouses in the United States—all of them built to direct ships into harbors. Oil lamps without reflectors were used and each of the lights showed the same characteristic—a steady glow referred to as "fixed."

Before 1781 all lighthouses had fixed lights and were difficult to identify. Some displayed two or more lights, so that mariners could identify the lighthouse with certainty and thereby know their vessel's location. Then a revolving light was invented that produced periods of light and dark rather than a steady glow. The period of the revolution could be set differently for different lights. The specially timed sequence of light and eclipse provided a means of identifying each light, its place, and purpose. By 1800 the total number of lightships and lighthouses in the world was 175, yet only twelve lighthouses had revolving lights; by 1819 there were thirty-five. In the daytime, lighthouses could be identified by the architectural design of the structure, or the towers might be painted with a particular pattern, such as stripes or bands.[7]

While lighthouses on both sides of the Atlantic Ocean were becoming more technically sophisticated, especially after the Fresnel lens was developed in 1822, for many years no lighthouses existed on Pacific Ocean coasts. Neither the Spanish government, nor, later, the Mexican government, erected any type of permanent lighted navigational aids along the west coasts of North and South America. The first lighthouses were established there by the United States. Between 1852 and 1858, the U.S. Light House Board erected sixteen lighthouses along the California, Washington, and Oregon coasts.[8]

The beacon erected by Kamehameha III at Lahaina in 1840 was the first permanent lighted navigational aid, not only in the Hawaiian Islands, or Sandwich Islands as they were then called, but in the Pacific.

As shipping and trade increased around the world in the late nineteenth century so did the building of lighthouses. Not only had the architectural engineering of lighthouses progressed to the point that light towers could be erected successfully on rock outcroppings, coral, and even shifting sand bars in the open sea, but the illuminants and lighting apparatuses were continually being improved.[9]

In Hawai'i the navigational lights were established for both commercial vessels trading with the Islands and for transpacific shipping that used the Islands as a provisioning and refueling destination. The goal of lighting harbors and coasts in Hawai'i was an ambitious one and progress was slow. The beacon at Lahaina Roadstead was the only navigational light in the Islands for nineteen years. By the time the U.S. Light House Board assumed responsibility for the navigational aids in Hawai'i in 1904, eighteen lighted beacons had been established; in 1917 there were fifty-eight lighted aids, and by the 1980s the number had tripled.

There are some special beacons in Hawai'i, such as two of the highest lighted navigational aids in the world. The absence of fog in the Islands allowed the builders to select many sites at elevations that would have been impractical elsewhere. The lighted aid off Ni'ihau on Lehua is 704 feet above sea level and the Ka'ena Point Light on O'ahu is 931 feet above sea level. The Makapu'u Point Lighthouse on O'ahu is the only lighthouse in the United States with a hyperradiant lens; this was the largest type of lens ever built. The lighted beacon at Ka Lae on the island of Hawai'i is the farthest south of any U.S. light, and the lighted beacon on Lehua is the farthest west.

Interesting as these facts are, it is the story of the people who worked together to establish the beacons and keep them burning that makes the history of Hawaiian lighthouses compelling. Their ethnic and cultural backgrounds covered a wide spectrum, as did their values and goals. During the time that the lights were being established the government changed from a monarchy to a republic, and then the Islands became a territory of the United States and finally a state. But no matter what the politics, bureaucracy always had to be dealt with. It spite of the difficulties encountered, the navigational aids were established and vigilantly maintained and kept burning.

The goal of lighting the harbors and coasts of the Hawaiian Islands was attained. The record of how this was accomplished is an integral part of the maritime history of Hawaiʻi.

PART I

Lighthouses of O'ahu

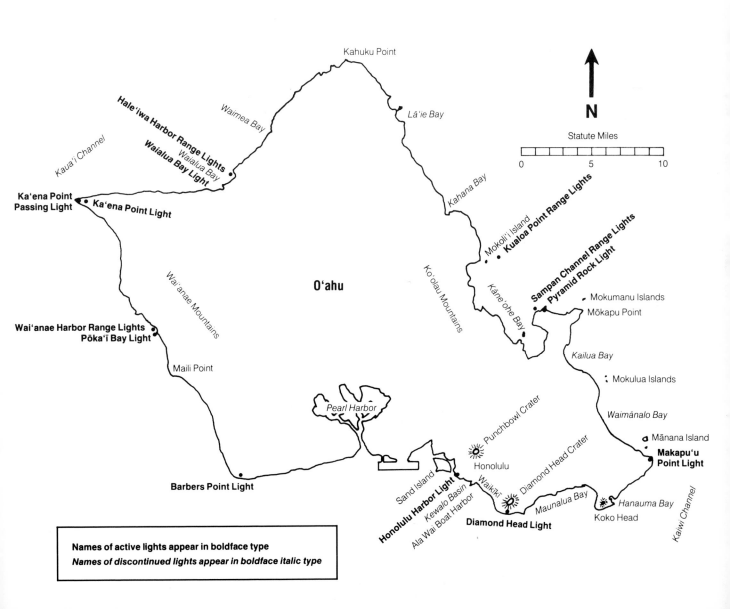

Kahuku Point

Waimea Bay

Lā'ie Bay

Hale'iwa Harbor Range Lights

Kaua'i Channel

Waialua Bay

Waialua Bay Light

Kahana Bay

N

Statute Miles

0   5   10

Ka'ena Point Passing Light

Ka'ena Point Light

Mokoli'i Island

Kualoa Point Range Lights

Wai'anae Mountains

O'ahu

Ko'olau Mountains

Kāne'ohe Bay

Sampan Channel Range Lights
Pyramid Rock Light

Mokumanu Islands

Mōkapu Point

Wai'anae Harbor Range Lights
Pōka'ī Bay Light

Kailua Bay

Maili Point

Mokulua Islands

Waimānalo Bay

Pearl Harbor

Punchbowl Crater

Mānana Island

Honolulu

Makapu'u Point Light

Diamond Head Crater

Sand Island

Honolulu Harbor Light

Kewalo Basin

Waikīkī

Maunalua Bay

Hanauma Bay

Kaiwi Channel

Ala Wai Boat Harbor

Diamond Head Light

Koko Head

Barbers Point Light

Names of active lights appear in boldface type
Names of discontinued lights appear in boldface italic type

Chapter 1

HONOLULU HARBOR

The island of Oʻahu, as seen at night from the deck of an approaching vessel, presents a dazzling display of shimmering lights as it seems to rise out of the dark sea. After thousands of miles of nothing but water, it is like an enchanted island conjured up in the mind of an ocean-weary sailor. But as the vessel sails closer to the island, some apprehension dims the mariner's joy, and the search begins for navigational aids to guide the ship safely to shore.

Landfall beacons must first be located and identified to determine the vessel's position. Closer to shore there are dangers to be avoided, and so a visual search must be made for aids that warn of reefs and shoals. Finally, the lights that will guide the vessel to a protected harbor must be found.

The *Coast Pilot,* an invaluable mariners' guide, warns that primary seacoast lighthouses have sometimes been wrongly identified, even though each one has its unique characteristic. Mariners have on occasion confused the Makapuʻu Point Light with the Diamond Head Light and have run aground on the reef west of Koko Head.[1]

To anyone unfamiliar with the island, finding Honolulu Harbor among the myriad lights along the southern shore of Oʻahu can be a challenge. The *Coast Pilot* cautions vessels sailing toward the harbor from the west at night not to mistake the glow on the land east of Pearl Harbor for the lights of Honolulu. Coming from the east, the brightness of the area north of Diamond Head could be mistaken for Honolulu, or the city lights between Koko Head and Diamond Head might be confused with the ones on Waikīkī Beach.

Amidst the flashing of white, yellow, red, and blue shore lights, the Honolulu Harbor entrance light flashes green, making it easier to identify. This light is located on the southeast point of the channel and is not displayed from a lighthouse of traditional architecture, but from the top of a pole, ninety-five feet above the water.

Coming into the harbor during the day is less confusing than at night. The famous 193-foot Aloha Tower, with its square clock tower, is the most distinctive landmark. It was once a lighthouse for Honolulu Harbor and continues to display the signals controlling incoming and outgoing traffic. Inland is the unique 500-foot-high hill called Punchbowl, and northwest of the tower is a pineapple-shaped water tank almost 200 feet high. These landmarks seen during the day are unusual and distinctive, but navigational markers are essential for safe entry into the harbor, day or night.[2]

The present channel leading into Honolulu Harbor passes directly over the site where the first Honolulu Harbor lighthouse, built in 1869, once stood. No other lighthouse looked quite like this one. The building sat high on pilings in the middle of the channel and could be reached only by boat. It gave the impression of being put together on a whim with leftover pieces of boats and buildings. Seen from the entrance to the harbor, the structure appeared rather squat, tapering only slightly to the

The first Honolulu Harbor Lighthouse (also known as the Harbor Wink) as seen from the entrance to the harbor. The illustration adorned an 1869 chart of Honolulu Harbor. (Survey Division, Department of Accounting and General Services, State of Hawaii)

level of the lantern floor. The lantern, with its glass sides and metal roof, was the only thing that made the building recognizable as a lighthouse during the day. The glass panes required daily cleaning, and Captain McGregor, the keeper, would often be seen waving at the vessels that passed on both sides of the lighthouse as they entered and left Honolulu Harbor.[3]

Although it was a busy port, Honolulu did not have any lighted navigational aids until 1869. Before

that time, various ingenious ways were devised to bring foreign vessels into the harbor. The present-day entrance channel, which over the years has been widened and dredged many times, is an enlargement of the original natural passage into the harbor —a break through the coral reefs that was created by the fresh water emptying into the ocean from Nu‘uanu Stream. The coral polyps that form the reefs cannot live and grow in fresh water and so the reef did not develop where the fresh water flows toward the sea, creating a natural channel into the harbor.[4]

The once-narrow passage was difficult to see unless one knew it was there. Hawaiians easily maneuvered their canoes through the cut and beached them inside the harbor at a canoe landing known as Pākākā.[5] But Westerners, once they discovered Honolulu Harbor in the last part of the eighteenth century, faced difficulties in entering the harbor with their deep-draft sailing vessels. It was almost impossible to sail through the cut between the reefs because of prevailing winds and the narrowness of the passage. At first, foreign vessels were rowed in by their own tenders.

As the sandalwood trade and other commerce developed, more and more foreign ships came to Honolulu. In the early 1800s, Hawaiians in their double-hulled canoes towed vessels into the harbor. But no ships entered at night. If a ship arrived after dark it would either lie to offshore in deep water until daylight or anchor outside the reef and fire a gun to signal for assistance. In the morning several canoes would arrive to tow the ship into the harbor under the guidance of a pilot. Because vessels did not enter the harbor after dark or come in under their own power, and because a pilot's services were always used, a lighthouse was unnecessary.

Between 1840 and 1850, when Honolulu Harbor was developing into a major provisioning port for whaling ships, Hawaiian brute strength was used to tow vessels into the harbor. Ships anchored near the entrance to the channel, and at low tide two hundred to four hundred men assembled on an exposed reef extending out from shore. The men, hauling on a long hawser fastened to the ship, pulled inland up a path on the reef and brought the ship into the harbor. About 1850 the reef was paved with white coral stones and converted to an ox path. Twenty or more oxen, substituting for the men, did the hauling.[6]

The first clamor for a lighted aid in the harbor began about 1851.[7] On March 12 of that year, Mr. Crabb, president of the Chamber of Commerce, at the urging of merchants, ship owners, and sea captains, began petitioning the minister of Interior for a lighthouse to be established for Honolulu Harbor.[8]

"An act to Provide for Lights for the Harbor of Honolulu" was passed by the House of Representatives and the House of Nobles on June 20, 1851, and signed by King Kamehameha III on July 11. It empowered the minister of Interior to "construct a lighthouse on the promontory commonly known as Diamond Head or Leahi" and also to "construct a lighthouse, or to moor a light boat . . . near the mouth of the channel of Honolulu Harbor."[9] Nothing was done to implement this act, and neither of these lights was established or even mentioned again by the government for another seventeen years.

During 1862–1863, however, the subject of a lighthouse was raised in the private sector. A series of meetings was held to collect money for a monument to Captain James Cook. At one meeting held in March 1863, Captain Richards, of the British ship *Hecate,* suggested that a lighthouse erected near the entrance to Honolulu Harbor would be the most appropriate monument. The subscribers could not come to any agreement and no action was taken.[10]

"Cook's Lighthouse" was not an entirely new idea. In 1837 Captain Bruce of the British ship *Imogene* had stated that he favored a lighthouse as a memorial to the famous explorer. Several months later a notice for a meeting appeared in the *Sandwich Island Gazette* inviting "Shipmasters, residents and strangers who felt an interest in the erection of a lighthouse at Oahu . . . to meet at the Pagoda Rooms, Monday, October 23rd, at 7:30 p.m." At the meeting it was moved, "that a subscription fund be opened for the erection of a lighthouse on Diamond Head or such other point on the Island of Oahu as may be deemed most eligible to the name of the illustrious Cook."[11] But "Cook's Lighthouse" did not win popular support in 1837—nor in 1863.

The first extant government documents regarding plans for establishing a lighthouse for Honolulu Harbor are dated 1869. The land needed for a beacon was acquired by the Department of the Interior from J. I. Dowsett and J. K. Sumner, both prominent Honolulu residents. Sumner was a lawyer and Dowsett was involved in almost every type of business on the island. Dowsett owned a fleet of whaling ships, a few schooners and small steamers involved in interisland trade, ranches, and sugar plantations. Sumner and Dowsett also owned adjoining pieces of land about a mile from the port's wharves. The land was located near the harbor's entrance on the inner edge of the western reef. Sand had accumulated on the reef at this point, forming a small island.[12]

Surveys were made of the island, and Robert Sterling, superintendent of public works, received two bids for construction of the light. Thomas Hughes, of Honolulu Iron Works, estimated the total cost, including iron pilings, at $2,141. L. L. Gilbert bid to construct an all-wooden structure and whitewash it for $360, or give it three coats of paint for an additional $82. Gilbert's lower bid was accepted.[13]

Wooden pilings were driven into the reef upon which the structure holding the light was built. The keeper's residence was similarly constructed, and the two were joined by a wooden footbridge. Lanterns and fittings were installed in April 1869, and the keeper (Captain McGregor) lit the lamps for the first time on August 2, 1869.[14] Thereafter "light dues" of three dollars were charged all vessels entering the harbor from abroad. Vessels engaged in the island coastal trade paid ten cents per ton annually for the privilege of visiting all ports that had a lighthouse.[15]

The *Hawaiian Gazette* published a "Notice to Mariners" on August 4, 1869; the light was described as being twenty-six feet above sea level and visible "from the deck of an ordinary vessel at the distance of nine nautical miles."

Mariners and businessmen who had campaigned for a light were well satisfied, but Honolulu's newspaper, *Pacific Commercial Advertiser,* on August 2, 1869, was derisive, calling it, "an infantile structure which more resembles a birdcage than a lighthouse." It was dubbed the "Harbor Wink."

The Harbor Wink, no matter what the press thought of it, was an important addition to harbor facilities. The light from the whale oil lamps was magnified and concentrated by a fourth-order Fresnel lens, an appropriate size for a harbor light.[16]

The lighthouse soon served a double function. The minister of finance announced that a light tower had been erected on the "Esplanade," an open space of ground and public walk created along the shore from harbor dredgings. This light, when used in conjunction with the harbor light, formed a range marking the channel, "thereby enabling vessels to work into the harbor with perfect safety at any hour of the night."[17]

The tower on the Esplanade was discontinued about a year later, and in its place a light was attached to the top of the Custom House, twenty-eight feet above sea level. This light, which was just an ordinary kitchen lamp, was draped with red cloth (changed later to green cloth) to give it a color and thus distinguish it from the town's white lights. It could be seen five miles at sea. The Harbor Wink and the Custom House light became the range lights for vessels entering the harbor.[18]

Henry Whitney, in his *Hawaiian Guide Book for Travelers,* gives a description of the harbor in 1875.

It is always safe except in a Kona or south storm, which rarely occurs except during the winter months, from December to March. . . . The channel, which ought never to be taken, even by a war vessel, without a pilot, is a narrow passage through the coral reef, averaging 550 feet in width, by three-quarters of a mile in length, from the spar-buoy to the light-house. This light may be seen from a steamer's deck eight miles off. There are 22 feet of water on the bar at mid tide, the rise and fall being about thirty inches, twice each day. Sailing vessels are generally towed into the harbor by a government steam-tug, whose charges vary from thirty to seventy-five dollars, according to the tonnage of the vessel. On leaving port, vessels seldom have to wait for a wind, as the trades blow fresh and fair nine months of the year.[19]

The lighthouse was in the center of the harbor entrance channel, and ships passed on either side. The cargo sought by most of the vessels was sugar. The sugar industry, which dominated the lives, economy, and politics of the Islands, was given a tremendous boost in 1875 when the Reciprocity Treaty was ratified; it allowed sugar to be sold duty free in the United States and goods from the United States to be sold duty free in Hawai'i. Twelve years later the treaty was renewed.[20]

As commercial use of the harbor continued to increase, a survey was made by the Hawaiian government to determine the feasibility and cost of widening and deepening the channel into the harbor. By 1892 work was under way to remove the shallow bar near the entrance. A year later the channel had been deepened to thirty feet. The operation proved so successful that the government hoped eventually to deepen the entire harbor to a uniform depth of twenty-eight to thirty feet.[21]

The Honolulu Harbor Light Station on September 15, 1902, showing Young Brothers boathouse with the keeper's dwelling directly behind. The keeper's house and the lighthouse were joined by a pier. (L. E. Edgeworth album, Bishop Museum)

Eight years later, after the Hawaiian Islands formally became a territory of the United States, the territory, with its own money, once again had part of the harbor dredged, at a cost of $61,058. There were also plans to build a new lighthouse, but no further funds were available. If Honolulu Harbor was to continue to grow and serve the shipping needs of the people of Hawai'i and the United States, the harbor and the navigational aids required maintenance and improvement. Hawai'i was in a period of economic depression and did not have the financial resources necessary for lighthouse or harbor improvements, nor, for that matter, were these concerns any longer the territory's responsibility.[22]

In 1902 Prince Jonah Kūhiō Kalaniana'ole was elected to Congress as a delegate from the Territory of Hawaii. Kūhiō had not been a delegate long when he was informed that the territorial government's funding of appropriations for lighthouses in Hawai'i would be discontinued after December 31, 1903. He went immediately to the U.S. Navy Department for help, but discovered that harbors and navigational aids were not within the navy's jurisdiction. He was sent to the Light House Board, but the board could do nothing because Congress had not allocated money specifically for Hawaiian navigational aids.[23]

Kūhiō knew that if he could not obtain funds, none of the lights in Hawai'i could continue functioning. When he explained the situation to the Speaker of the House, he was informed that there was a $25,000 emergency fund that would cover such a contingency. But the clerk of the Appropriations Committee told him that Hawai'i was ineligible because it was an "insular possession." The fact that Hawai'i was a territory seemed to make little difference.[24]

Time was running out. Kūhiō continued working toward getting the needed funds allocated. At almost the last minute, the comptroller of the U.S. Treasury decided, on December 23, 1903, that "the appropriations for the Light-House Establishment . . . could be extended for the maintenance of the light-houses and buoys" of Hawai'i. Five days later President Theodore Roosevelt, by proclamation, ordered that the lighthouse service of the Territory of Hawaii be taken over by the U.S. Lighthouse Service under the Department of Commerce and Labor. By January 4, 1904, the Hawaiian Islands became a subdistrict of the Twelfth United States Lighthouse District, which extended from the Mexican border in the south, north through California to the Oregon border. The navigational lights in Hawai'i continued burning. The Light House Board paid the lightkeepers and made "such inconsiderable and inexpensive repairs as were absolutely necessary . . . to keep the light-houses from falling down."[25]

Kūhiō began another campaign for appropriations to dredge and improve Honolulu Harbor. This time President Roosevelt offered to help and talked with the Speaker of the House and the chairman of the Appropriations Committee. Kūhiō took his plea directly to the floor of the House of Representatives, emphasizing to the congressmen that, unlike other ports that had access to rail transportation, Honolulu was totally dependent on shipping and that two of the largest and newest steamers servicing Hawai'i might have to bypass Honolulu because the draft of their vessels was so deep they could not enter the harbor.[26]

Kūhiō also explained to the Light House Board that a new lighthouse was needed for the harbor; the old one was so decayed "that the blast of a fog horn could cause it to collapse."[27] (Fortunately, there was never any fog in Honolulu Harbor.) The Board agreed with Kūhiō and recommended an appropriation of $40,000 for a new lighthouse and range lights "in place of those . . . which are in an advanced state of decay, and which are not only unsightly, but unsafe."[28]

There was more good news. An appropriation was made by Congress to reimburse the territory for the money spent on maintaining the navigational aids in the Islands after Hawai'i became a territory. Governor George R. Carter of Hawai'i had written George B. Cortelyou, secretary of the U.S. Department of Commerce and Labor, about this matter, enclosing a statement of the actual lighthouse expenses and the monthly pay of lighthouse keepers.[29]

In the listing of lightkeepers, William Williams was named as the keeper of the Honolulu Light. His salary of $100.00 a month was the highest for that position in the islands. Most keepers in Hawai'i were paid $15.00 to $28.00, and some as little as $8.00 a month. The average salary of keepers in the United States was $46.14 a month.[30]

Reimbursement of all the lightkeepers' salaries and lighthouse expenses was based on the monthly expenditure figure of $501.90 multiplied by the number of months that had elapsed between April 30, 1900, when Hawai'i became a territory, and January 1, 1904, when the Light House Board took over, a period of forty-four months. The total amount reimbursed in 1906 was $23,292.69, slightly more than the amount claimed.[31]

Appropriations were also made for the improvements needed in Honolulu Harbor and for a new lighthouse. A temporary light was erected while the work in the channel got under way. Over the years a large man-made island had been built up in the center of the harbor; the first segment, called Quarantine Island, was formed by dredging operations during the monarchy.[32] By 1907 the harbor had been deepened to thirty-five feet and widened to twelve hundred feet. The dredgings were used to enlarge the area of Quarantine Island to thirty-six acres, and the name was changed to Sand Island.[33]

Work was also in progress on the new harbor entrance light. The site selected for the lighthouse was on the west side of the inner end of the channel just as it curved leading into the harbor. Originally this area was covered by four to six feet of water at high tide; on the bottom were twelve to sixteen feet of mud, sand, and broken coral overlying a reef of coral rock.[34]

Preparations for constructing the lighthouse began in 1906, with the purchase of cement, wooden cylinders, iron, and steel. A workshop, office, and blacksmith shop were built on Sand Island, and a trestle was erected from the Sand Island wharf to the site of the lighthouse. Test borings were made for the twenty-four foundation pilings, and then the wooden forms were driven in place and the concrete poured. The completed pilings were each three feet in diameter.[35]

The lighthouse structure erected on top of the pilings was also built of reinforced concrete. It included a keepers' dwelling combined with the light tower at the top of the building.

> The structure is rectangular in plan, one and a half stories high . . . The main floor contains quarters for two keepers, each provided with kitchen, living room, two bedrooms, and a bathroom. There are ample closets and pantries for each keeper. The main entrance and hall are approached from outside by a flight of concrete steps, and there are steps in the rear of the structure for both sets of quarters. The roof is framework, covered with metal tiles. Atop the keepers' quarters is the square tower supporting: an occulting fourth-order lens, revolving on ball bearings, and arranged to show

a characteristic of "fixed white, 4 seconds; eclipse, 2 seconds" . . . with a focal plane 38 feet 7 inches above mean high water. . . . The illuminant is incandescent oil vapor used in a 34-millimeter Welsbach mantle.[36]

As the new lighthouse was being built, the temporary light was kept burning by "Bill" Williams. Williams had been appointed keeper of the Harbor Wink in 1871 when Captain McGregor left to command the steamer *Kilauea*. Williams, born in Cape Cod, Massachusetts, in 1838, went to sea as a young man. For a time he was a miner in California and also served in the U.S. Army. In 1865 Williams came to Hawai'i. One of his first jobs was taking care of the Armory in Honolulu and all of the equipment belonging to the volunteer Citizens' Guard. Six years later he was appointed keeper of the Honolulu Harbor Light. He was tending the temporary light when he died. On February 27, 1908, the *Evening Bulletin* reported, "Grief and regret is generally expressed this morning among the old timers on the waterfront with whom 'Billy' had so long associated and was such a favorite. All flags on the boats in the harbor are at half mast." Williams had been a lightkeeper for thirty-six years.

On February 15, 1910, the new Honolulu Harbor Lighthouse was completed, and Harry W. Flint tended the light, which could be seen eleven nautical miles from shore.[37] The Harbor Wink was but a memory. Steamers using the widened and deepened channel depended on the new forty-three-foot lighthouse as their navigational guide. Many of the ships were transporting cargoes of the newest product for export from Hawai'i—pineapples. In 1912 the first million-case pack of canned pineapples was shipped. Sugar, pineapples, and the growing need for imports kept Honolulu Harbor a bustling port.[38]

The opening of the Panama Canal in 1914 stimulated transpacific shipping and increased the number of vessels using Honolulu Harbor. In 1916 the

Sixty-fourth Congress passed the River and Harbor Act, which provided for a new channel extending westward from Honolulu Harbor basin. The Reserved, or Kapalama, Channel was to be 35 feet deep, 800 feet wide, and 1,000 feet long.[39] Plans were also under way for building one of the most unusual lighthouses ever built, one that would serve many diverse uses.

The territorial Board of Harbor Commissioners wanted a permanent waterfront terminal that would be equal to facilities in the largest mainland cities. This terminal was to combine freight and passenger facilities for piers 8, 9, and 10, and a tower, to be built in conjunction with the piers, would contain offices for the harbor master, pilots, and customs officials; atop the tower would be a light for mariners.[40]

The harbor commissioners considered this to be the "most important project ever handled in Honolulu Harbor." The project was financed under the Territorial Loan Fund Act of 1915. The builder, National Construction Company, began work on March 15, 1916. A few items on the materials list included 6,000 barrels of cement, 4,000 lineal feet of steel conduit, 10,000 feet of copper wire, 1,400 gallons of egg-shell-white paint for the exterior, and 15 gallons of soft green paint for the cupola.[41]

The multipurpose facility was constructed on land built up over the years from dredgings, which had changed the shoreline considerably. The last vestiges of an old fort, begun by the Russians in 1815 and later completed under the Hawaiian monarchy, disappeared in 1857 when its stones became part of the 2,000-foot seawall built to retain the dredgings for the new land of the Esplanade.[42]

The location chosen for the Aloha Tower was at Pākākā, which had been the ancient canoe landing and later the site for James Robinson's wharf and boat business. In 1827 when Robinson had completed building his shipyard, known as Robinson &

Company, it was the only one in the Islands— indeed, the only one in the Pacific at that time. One hundred years later, in the same area of the harbor, the Aloha Tower would welcome ships from around the world.[43]

The entire complex covered a six-acre area. Precast concrete cylinders, designed to carry a load of a quarter ton per square foot, supported the decks and superstructure. Piers 8, 9, and 10, with 1,760 linear feet of berthing space and 221,000 square feet for cargo, were completed at a cost of $480,000.[44]

The steel frame for the tower, built by Honolulu Iron Works, cost $161,063. The twelve-story tower itself, costing $190,000, contained offices for the harbor master and his assistants on the third floor and for the harbor pilots on the fourth floor. The tenth floor housed the mechanical works of the much-touted clock, which had faces on all four sides of the tower. The eleventh floor served as a pilot's lookout, with balconies all around; in the front of each balcony was carved the word *Aloha*. Each "Aloha" was to be lighted up at night, as were also the clock faces. The other floors, furnished with the most modern equipment, were to be rented out to private businesses or individuals. One of the first to rent was Arthur Reynolds, the tower's architect.[45]

The tenth floor was often referred to as the "missing floor" because it could not be reached by the elevator or by the building's stairway. The only entrance was by way of stairs from the pilot's lookout. The clockworks, the elevator machinery, and water tanks were located on this floor. Two nights before the Aloha Tower was to be officially turned over to the Board of Harbor Commissioners, the water tanks overflowed! Water flooded over the new walls and through the elevator shaft. Fortunately no damage was done, and when the electrical wiring for the elevator dried out, all was well (though the elevator's erratic functioning has always been the butt of humor and complaint). Water usually had to be pumped up to the tanks at the 160-foot level. The overflow was caused by excess pressure during the night. Prevention of future mishaps was achieved by simply turning off the main water line at night.[46]

The clockworks were unharmed by the flooding and continued functioning with an accuracy within a variation of thirty seconds per month. The Howard Clark Company of Boston took out a large advertisement in the *Honolulu Advertiser*'s May 30, 1926, edition to describe the seven-ton clock, the largest clock movement ever made by their company. H. F. Wichman & Company of Honolulu designed the clock faces, with their solid cast bronze frames and dials. The clock was run mechanically by means of weights, and when it needed rewinding an electrical motor was tripped on. The motor also controlled the exterior electric lights and the siren blast that sounded at 7:00 A.M., noon, and 4:00 P.M., except on Sundays. The siren could also be operated manually to welcome airplanes as well as ships, or to be used as a warning signal for tsunamis, fires, or other dangers.[47]

It was the siren's blast that opened the dedication ceremonies for the Aloha Tower, the tallest building in Honolulu. Governor Wallace R. Farrington and Mayor John H. Wilson presided, the Royal Hawaiian Band played, a giant lei was presented, and after the speeches, there were guided tours of the skyscraper and dancing on the piers.

Scant attention was given to the lighthouse function of Aloha Tower. The last lines of the *Honolulu Advertiser*'s article read:

> On top of the tower the harbor light, which is now located on Sand Island, is to be installed, and the light on Sand Island done away with. The light will be known as Honolulu Light, and will be visible to ships at sea for many miles. The light will be a flashing white light of welcome, not a red light of warning. It will indicate to the ships that pass in the night that here lies at

the Crossroads of the Pacific—"the loveliest fleet of islands anchored in any ocean."[48]

The old occulting light illuminated with an oil-wick lamp was replaced by an electric 500-watt incandescent lamp set within a dioptric lens with a mirror reflector. A self-winding time switch and rotary switch controlled the flasher, causing the white light to flash on for two seconds and off for three. The light was projected across a 180-degree arc seaward and could be seen for twenty miles. Many residents, who never had the opportunity to stand on the deck of an incoming vessel and see the light's flash, were unaware that Aloha Tower served as a lighthouse.[49]

But no one could miss seeing the forty-foot mast on the top of the tower. It held a "time ball" four feet in diameter, which was dropped to the bottom of the mast at noon each day. Most important for shipping was a yardarm jutting out from the building. On this yardarm, an orange ball and cone were attached by a long line for signaling messages to ships. When both ball and cone were run up the yardarm, the harbor was closed to all traffic. Right-of-way was signaled to incoming shipping when the ball alone was displayed, and the cone by itself gave the right-of-way to outgoing vessels. The siren's blast three times a day was soon stopped by complaints from irritated and irate residents, but it was occasionally used as a signal of welcome to incoming ships.[50]

On December 7, 1941, when the Japanese attacked Pearl Harbor, low-flying planes bombed Pier 2 and machine-gunned Pier 31 in Honolulu Harbor. Aloha Tower was unscathed except for a stray bullet that pierced a window in the harbor master's office. After the attack three ships that had been standing by off the channel were towed into their berths. The business of the harbor continued, but the light in the

The beacon atop Aloha Tower was blacked out during World War II and the building camouflaged. After the war, and for the next twenty-five years, Aloha Tower operated as Honolulu Harbor's lighthouse. (Hawaii State Archives)

Aloha Tower did not shine that night. Police and military personnel were ordered to shoot out all visible lights. All lighted navigational aids were blacked out during the war. The tower was closed to the public and camouflaged with netting and green and brown paint. Machine guns along with some artillery were set up on each side of the harbor channel, and an ammunition bunker was built on Sand Island.[51]

In 1948 the reopening of the Aloha Tower was a great celebration. Camouflage paint was sandblasted from the exterior of the building, and the tower served once again as a lighthouse. The elevator took visitors to the top as many as ten times a day.

The view in some ways was the same as it had been in 1926: the calm, clear blue waters of the harbor and the white foam of the breakers over the reefs; vessels rounding Diamond Head; docks filled with ships; a small pilot boat keeping pace with a large commercial tanker, ready to take the pilot aboard. But many changes could also be seen: the increased activity and number of buildings on Sand Island, the development of Kapalama and Kalihi basins, and the new pier under construction to be known on completion as Diamond Head Terminal.[52]

There was no longer a lighthouse in the channel. The position of keeper had been abolished once the automatic harbor light was established in Aloha Tower. The keeper's dwelling became the home of the depot manager, who was in charge of lighthouse equipment. The light tower, though it no longer showed a light, remained on the charts as a daymarker until 1934, when the old station was demolished to make way for dredgers once again widening the channel.[53]

By the late 1960s the Aloha Tower was surrounded by many taller buildings, and the navigational light at the top was lost amidst the dazzle of the lighted city at night. The Coast Guard made arrangements to have a rotating beacon installed eighty feet above ground on the 220-foot television tower being built by station KHVH. The flashing green 7.5-second light was ninety-seven feet above water and had a range of twenty miles.[54]

In 1975 a new Honolulu Harbor light was established at the top of a ninety-five-foot, red-and-white metal pole erected at the end of Pier 2, but the characteristic and intensity of the light were retained. The pole is now white, but at night the same flashing green light guides vessels to Honolulu Harbor.[55]

As a lighthouse, the Aloha Tower is no longer needed, but the building itself continues as a landmark and a symbol of Hawaiian hospitality—a warm greeting and farewell that is familiar around the world.

Chapter 2

BARBERS POINT

West of Honolulu's sheltered harbor, the low coastal plain gradually becomes more arid, less hospitable. The southern Wai'anae Mountains create a rainshadow over the area, and it is only with the arrival of winter's kona storms that a green lushness appears for a short time. The weathered limestone coastline curves a bit south and then northwest forming what the Hawaiians called Kalaeloa, which means "the long point."[1]

The coral reef off Kalaeloa was the scene of the first recorded wreck of a European ship in the Hawaiian Islands that claimed human lives. The date was October 31, 1796; the ship was the *Arthur,* and the captain was Henry Barber.

Captain Barber had become involved in the fur trade three years before his disastrous shipwreck. His route from England on the brig *Arthur* was a complicated one. First he sailed to India, then to Australia with supplies for the penal colony. From there the *Arthur* continued on to the northwest coast of North America to collect sea otter hides. Barber then set out for Canton by way of the Hawaiian Islands, where he stopped to replenish his ship's supplies.[2]

The brig left Honolulu Harbor with an offshore breeze at six o'clock in the evening of October 31, 1796. The plan was to stop briefly on Kaua'i to pick up a supply of yams before continuing on to Canton. Almost two hours later, the *Arthur* was sailing west, but much too close to O'ahu's south shore. It

is not known why Barber, who should have been fairly familiar with the waters, would allow his vessel to continue on such a dangerous course. Perhaps the wind shifted, or dropped, or an onshore current was making the *Arthur* crab toward the coast. Perhaps the helmsman was not aware of the ship's position as the *Arthur* approached the shallow reef off Kalaeloa.

At 8:00 P.M. the *Arthur* struck the shoals. Caught in the swell, the ship scraped shoreward across the reef and then was trapped by waves. Breakers drove the brig onto the rocks. Six men, of a crew of twenty-two, drowned. The *Arthur* was a total wreck.[3]

How Barber transported his surviving crew and cargo of furs to Canton is not known, but he probably left on one of the many ships that stopped in the Hawaiian Islands on their way to China. In 1807 he was once again seen on the Northwest Coast, but what happened to him after that is unknown. He never again returned to Hawai'i, but the point off which the *Arthur* wrecked became known as Barber's Point. (In 1968 the apostrophe was officially deleted from the name by the U.S. Board of Geographic Names.)[4]

The location of the reef off Barbers Point was well known to early mariners calling at Honolulu, but as commerce increased, this dangerous point needed to be marked in some way. In 1855 the French whaleship *Marquis de Turenne* arrived from Havre to take on supplies. After leaving Honolulu Harbor en route to the whaling grounds, the ship went aground on the Barbers Point reef and it, too, was totally wrecked.[5]

Evidence of the wreck was still visible in 1880 when William Dewitt Alexander made a survey of the area to determine the best location for a lighthouse:

> I examined the coast for some miles in the neighborhood of Barber's Point, selected a site for a light house and marked the spot by a pile of stones and a staff with a red and white flag. I also fixed the position by triangulation and corrected our chart of that locality. It is the SW point of Oahu, known as Lae loa where there are several pieces of . . . the French whaleship *Marquis de Turenne,* which was wrecked about a mile off the point in 1855. A shoal with only 6 to 10 feet of water on it is said to extend 2 or 3 miles south by west from the point, and it should be sounded. In fact it is a question whether the light house might not be placed on a shallow spot or "okohola" whale's back, as the natives call it, a mile or more offshore. The best guide is old Moke, who lives in Honolulu not far from the Catholic Church and ought to accompany the sounding party. The best landing place in the neighborhood is at Koolina about 2 miles N.W. of the point under the lee of the land. . . . Distance to Honolulu light house about 14 nautical miles.[6]

Alexander was surveyor general of the Hawaiian Government Survey Bureau, a position he held for almost thirty years. Born in Honolulu, he graduated from Yale and returned to the Islands in 1857, where he was a teacher and later president of Punahou School before joining the survey bureau. During the years 1882–1886, under Alexander's direction, nearly all the harbors and roadsteads in the Hawaiian Islands were charted. Most of the charts were compiled by Lieutenant George Edward Gresley Jackson, a retired navigator for the British navy, and were published by the British Admiralty.[7]

Alexander did much of the surveying on the Islands himself and wrote extensively on the work of the bureau. In describing Oʻahu's coast and the Barbers Point area he wrote:

> The islands of Kauai and Oahu have fringing coral reefs, though there is little coral around the other islands of the group. The Oahu Reef is found on its southern and northeastern shores. . . . (The southern) reef is about two miles broad westward of Pearl Harbor where it has been elevated to some ten feet above sea level forming a level plain whose surface is characteristically pitted with holes varying from one to fifteen feet in diameter and depth.[8]

This was the location selected for the Barbers Point Lighthouse. The next step was for the superintendent of public works to obtain the needed funds for materials, labor, and construction. An appropriation was passed in 1880 that provided $7,500 for lighthouse expenses and included $2,500 for a new lighthouse on Barbers Point.[9]

Some of the monies appropriated were used as a deposit for the Fresnel lens, lamps, and lantern ordered through W. H. Crossman & Brother, Commission Merchants in New York. On February 11, 1881, the contracted manufacturer in Paris, L. Santter Lemonnier, announced that the lens and lamps for the Barbers Point Lighthouse would be ready by the twentieth of the month, but if they were to furnish the lantern also, it would take a month more. The metal and glass lantern, which would contain and protect the lamp and lens at the top of the light tower, had to be made to exact specifications.[10]

The lantern was not ready in March even though Crossman reported that his company "did all in our power to expedite the . . . shipment of the goods, but it was impossible to have these French Manufacturers work any faster than they have." Once the shipment arrived in New York, Crossman

> at once gave instructions to our Custom House Broker to have these goods shipped in Bond via rail to San

Francisco and thence by steamer to Honolulu . . . but were informed that the U.S. Government had lately withdrawn the privilege of shipping goods in Bond via the continent. We are therefore compelled to ship them by steamer to the Panama Railroad, then to Panama, and thence by steamer to Honolulu. The goods are now going aboard the steamer *Acapulco* which will sail June 2.[11]

The Fresnel lens and kerosene lamps finally arrived, but lighthouse funds were exhausted and the plans for Barbers Point were postponed. The lens for the lighthouse was put in storage.

Requests were made in 1882 and in 1884 for an additional appropriation of $3,000 for the Barbers Point Light, but they were turned down.[12] It wasn't until 1887 that funds were finally made available for constructing the tower. During the last week of the last month of the year, there was a flurry of activity concerning the lighthouse. In December, J. A. Hassinger, chief clerk for the minister of the Interior, wrote to John Ena, secretary of the Inter-Island Steam Navigation Company, asking him if the company felt the lighthouse at Barbers Point was a necessity. Without waiting for a reply, Hassinger also wrote to Cecil Brown, agent and attorney for James Campbell: "I am directed by the Minister to say that it is proposed to build a lighthouse at Barber's Point in the near future, and to ask if permission can be obtained to erect the necessary buildings at a proper locality for this purpose upon the lands of Mr. Campbell."[13]

The next day a letter arrived from Inter-Island Steam Navigation Company stating that they considered the lighthouse at Barbers Point "to be a matter of greatest necessity." A few days later Hassinger received an answer from Cecil Brown saying that James Campbell would deed the government a piece of land, "say ½ acre," at Barbers Point.[14]

After seven years of talking about building a light at Barbers Point, something finally seemed to be happening. Bids were accepted for the tower and for the keeper's house. Peter High was awarded the contract to build the light tower for $1,892 and the keeper's dwelling for $309, with plans supplied by the superintendent of public works.[15]

The lightkeeper chosen was A. Alona. Lorrin A. Thurston, minister of the Interior, wrote him: "Your appointment to commence on the 9th of April 1888 and your pay shall be Twenty Dollars a month. You are required to report to the Minister of the Interior, from time to time, the condition of the Light House under your charge, and to make requests to this office for oil and other supplies."[16]

Thurston described the light to the 1888 Legislative Assembly:

> The tower supporting the metal lantern is of stone laid in cement mortar with suitable platforms inside and outside on iron frames. The whole structure being made in as durable a manner as possible. The light is 42 feet above mean tide. The location selected is on the shore at Puhilele, about ¼ of a mile west from Kalaeloa. A coral ledge, about 6 feet above mean tide, here forms the shore, and the reef extends about 5,000 feet to 6 fathoms water. It would have been preferable to navigators to have placed the light at the extremity of the shoals, but the vastly increased cost of construction and maintenance prevented, and it is considered that the purpose will be well served by the structure as it is. A small frame house has been added for the use of the light keeper and a water cistern built for his use. Cost $2,848.00.[17]

The fourth-order Fresnel lens projected a fixed white light, showing from all points of the compass, to a distance of ten miles. As a daymark, the white coral tower with its red-painted metal lantern was quite visible and identifiable from seaward.

The first complaint about the effectiveness of the light came from Captain A. S. Baker of the USS *Philadelphia* in 1894. "The Barber's Point Light should be increased. If necessary the structure should be raised. The light should be seen for 15 miles and should show a red sector from the edge of the reef off Diamond Head."[18]

No action was taken to improve the light until after the United States assumed responsibility for the Hawaiian navigational aids in 1904, and the first repair made was not to the lighthouse but to the roof of the keeper's dwelling. The keeper, W. Hatton, had been appointed in 1902; he received a salary of twenty-five dollars a month.[19]

By 1904 the light station site comprised two acres. Six years later three more acres were acquired by condemnation. The 1910 survey map shows some of the changes that had taken place over the years. An assistant keeper's dwelling stood close to the light tower, and a separate oil house had been built. At the edge of a thick growth of *kiawe* (algaroba) trees were the keeper's dwelling, a storeroom and barn, the laundry, and the water tank.[20]

Kiawe, which grew abundantly throughout the light station acreage and beyond, was considered to be one of the most valuable trees introduced to Hawaiʻi, providing both animal fodder and firewood. Barbers Point was a major source of firewood for Honolulu after 1880, and there was continuous logging of the kiawe trees in the lighthouse area.[21]

The light tower, standing grandly by the shore, was well in front of the wooded area. New lamps were supplied to the station in 1905, and the Light House Board recommended replacing the fixed white light with a flashing red light, "increasing its range and intensity and making it more clearly distinguishable from the plantation lights in the vicinity."[22]

Although the area around the light station was becoming more populated, the color and characteristic of the light were not changed to make it more distinguishable from the surrounding household lights until 1912. The first improvement came when the old wick lamps were replaced and a concrete cap was placed on the tower to allow room for a new incandescent oil-vapor lamp.[23]

Further improvements to the property were reported in 1915. A new keeper's dwelling was built west of the tower.

> The concrete piers for the footings are laid upon solid coral formation which has an average elevation of 3 feet above high water, the whole forming an excellent foundation. The dwelling is a single frame building of four rooms, bath, pantry, storeroom and two closets. It has plastered interior, shingled roof, is fitted with complete plumbing and water systems and is screened on all exterior openings. Completed June 26, 1915. Amount expended $3,198.96.[24]

More than three and a half miles of 1½-inch pipe were laid to supply water to the station's new distribution tanks, at a cost of $2,299. For the first time the keepers now had indoor plumbing and did not have to rely on their cistern for water.

Frederick Edgecomb, an engineer with the Lighthouse Service, inspected the light station on February 15, 1916. He reached Barbers Point by traveling on the Oahu Railroad and Land Company train to "Gilbert Number 2" and then walking three miles along a rough coral road to the light station. The nearest post office was six miles distant at Ewa Mill. The station was fenced in; on the property, besides the light tower, there was a concrete oil house, a two-room storehouse, and two keepers' dwellings. The buildings were painted brown with white trim and had brown metal roofs. The keepers had recently whitewashed the tower, and Edgecomb reported that the station was well maintained.

The most important improvement made at Barbers Point was the change in the light's characteristic. The fixed white light, difficult to distinguish from the surrounding plantation lights, had been changed to group flashing. A newly installed double-flash lens revolved every five seconds around the lamp. It produced one flash for 0.1 second, with an eclipse of 1.1 seconds, followed by another 0.1-second flash and an eclipse of 3.7 seconds. The light could be seen twelve miles at sea.[25]

Marking the shoals and reefs off Barbers Point has been a boon to mariners. There have only been two ship groundings of any consequence since the light was established. The first occurred in the early morning hours of August 31, 1906, when the *Sheridan* struck a small uncharted coral reef off Barbers Point. The *Sheridan* was an army transport ship arriving in the islands from Manila. As soon as it was light, the 132 passengers were brought ashore. It was hoped that at high tide the *Sheridan* could be hauled off the reef, but this was impossible. The stranded vessel couldn't be budged until all the freight was off-loaded and tons of coal were dumped overboard. According to the *Hawaiian Annual*

> special helpers, with some 500 tons of wrecking gear, were sent from the coast. . . . Fortunately the weather held good with the exception of a couple of threatening days when matters looked critical. All being in readiness October 2nd she was hauled off into deep water, and on being towed toward port by the *Iroquois,* she was beached off Pearl Harbor to avoid capsizing. On the 6th she was hauled off again and brought safely to port.[26]

The second grounding occurred on August 5, 1920, when the freighter *West Eldura* ran up on a part of the Barbers Point reef that was charted. The *West Eldura* was en route from Manila to New York with a cargo of sugar. It took four days for vessels from the Inter-Island Steam Navigation Company to haul the freighter off the reef.[27]

Smaller boats have been stranded off Barbers Point, but they were successfully refloated at high tide. Sometimes storms blew fishing boats up on the reef, where they were wrecked. In 1919 Manuel Ferreira, the keeper at Barbers Point Lighthouse,

helped rescue seven Japanese fishermen who had been aboard a 60-foot sampan that smashed to pieces on the reef off Barbers Point. After getting the men ashore safely, Ferreira brought the fishermen to his home, gave them dry clothing, and fed them. He was commended for his actions by the Bureau of Lighthouses.[28]

Mrs. Ferreira's work in an emergency also impressed lighthouse authorities. When both her husband and his assistant were stricken with influenza at the same time, Mrs. Ferreira took over their duties. With a six-year-old son tagging along, she took care of all the housekeeping chores during the day, and at sunset she became the lightkeeper, keeping the light burning while the men were in the hospital. The kerosene-vapor lamps in those days were temperamental. They were difficult lamps to light and to keep burning, even for those who performed the job regularly. The wicks had to be trimmed and the kerosene fuel pressure maintained by laboriously pumping the fuel from the tanks by hand. She also had to wind the revolving mechanism on the light every three hours during the night. These counterweights were heavy. As the weight descended, it operated the machinery that revolved a panel around the lens. This gave the "flash" to an otherwise steady beam of light. Once the weight had descended, it had to be raised to keep the assembly functioning. Mrs. Ferreira did it all, night after night, without mishap.

When the superintendent came to inspect the light, he was so impressed with Mrs. Ferreira's work that he suggested she remain as the lightkeeper until her husband and the assistant were well enough to resume their duties. Mrs. Ferreira may have felt complimented, but she declined the honor. A substitute keeper soon arrived on the scene.[29]

Perhaps the story told most often about Manuel Ferreira concerns the time he helped save the *Bianca.* On January 14, 1923, the *Bianca,* despite threatening weather, left Honolulu Harbor en route to the Orient. The five-masted schooner cleared the reefs off the channel entrance and was sailing south by west to avoid Barbers Point when the storm struck. Torrential rains began to flood the streets of Honolulu. The storm was so severe that it unroofed houses, knocked down trees, and did much flood damage to the outlying plantation districts. One person was killed at Waikīkī.[30] On the ocean, the waves built rapidly, and the *Bianca* could not make headway or hold course. The schooner's decks were awash, and before the sails could be furled the wind ripped the canvas to ribbons.

Ferreira was at his post keeping the light burning when he saw the *Bianca*'s sudden plight. The anchors put out to keep the vessel in deep water were not holding, and the wooden-hulled schooner was being blown ever closer to the jagged coral off Barbers Point. There was neither a telephone nor a radio at the lighthouse on which Ferreira could call for help; the closest phone was three miles away. Ferreira ran most of way over the dirt road, which the heavy rains had turned into mud. He called the naval authorities, and they responded quickly. Tugs were promptly sent out to aid the *Bianca*.

The storm hampered the tugs' rescue efforts. Even after the *Bianca* was towed back into Honolulu Harbor, the wind was so strong and the waves so huge that the tow lines severed and the *Bianca* was almost blown up on Sand Island. After the storm abated and damage could be assessed, it was found that the *Bianca* had suffered only the loss of sails, thanks to Ferreira's prompt action.[31]

By 1930 Barbers Point Light was considered inadequate, and inspectors found that the tower showed signs of deterioration. In 1933 an allotment of $20,000 was made for the construction of a reinforced concrete tower and general improvement of the station. Work began immediately. Among the improvements was installation of gasoline-driven

When the forty-foot stone tower was erected on Barbers Point in 1888 it was the tallest lighthouse in the Islands. As the surrounding area developed, the light became difficult to identify at night. In 1933 construction began on a seventy-two-foot-high reinforced concrete cylindrical tower. (Courtesy of Carol Edgecomb Brown Collection)

engine-generator units at the station to produce electricity for the light tower and the keepers' houses.[32]

The old light, of 44,000-candlepower intensity, was replaced by an automatic electric light with 700,000 candlepower, but the original fourth-order Fresnel lens was still used. The light, atop the cylindrical concrete seventy-two-foot tower, could be seen fifteen miles at sea. The new light was put into operation on December 29, 1933. The total cost was $19,304.[33]

The old tower, flawed and unstable, proved easy to topple. Workmen cut into the soft coral foundation, in the same way a tree is felled, and the last of the old Hawaiian lighthouses crashed to earth.[34]

As an engineer and assistant superintendent of the lighthouse district, Frederick Edgecomb had been very much involved in establishing the new light on Barbers Point. His daughter, Carol Edgecomb Brown, remembers visiting the new lighthouse with her father: "There were the keepers' dwellings with grass around to play on and even a few trees. The narrow sandy beach was inviting and the ocean was usually calm enough for us to explore shallow pools in the rocks and to look for crabs and shells. On one historic day I can recall the great excitement in the group of spectators as we gathered to watch the old light tower fall into oblivion on the sand as the new tall lighthouse took its place."[35]

The improvements to the light were something Fred Robins could appreciate. Robins came from a lightkeeping family. Both his grandfather, Edward, Sr., and his father, Edward, Jr., were lightkeepers. Fred Robins was sixteen years old when he signed up with the U.S. Commerce Department in 1922, the youngest man in the service at the time. His first assignment was at Barbers Point. The station was much too isolated and lonely for the young man, but he stuck it out for two years before he quit. After serving with the Merchant Marine, he rejoined the Commerce Department and was reassigned to Barbers Point in 1930. Robins watched the new tower being constructed and the old one as it tumbled down. He had served on the old tower; now he was to be the assistant keeper of the new Barbers Point Light for three years.[36]

In 1939 Samuel Apollo Amalu, at 62, was spryly climbing the ninety-five pie-shaped steps to the top of the light. Amalu joined the lighthouse service in

1906. He had served on the Kawaihae, Kīlauea, and Makapuʻu lights, as well as at Barbers Point Light Station once before, when he lived alone on the point for four years. Amalu liked being a lightkeeper because he was his own boss and it was the kind of job that called for all types of skills and ingenuity. Amalu considered himself a gardener, a mechanic, a carpenter, a painter, and a "gasoline engineer." He believed that a lighthouse keeper had to be a jack of all trades. When he first took the job it paid $61.50 a month; in 1939 he was receiving $165.00 a month, less $20.00 a month for housing.[37]

Nothing was deducted for housing when Fred Robins returned to Barbers Point in 1953. After leaving Barbers Point twenty years before, he had served in lighthouses on Kauaʻi and Molokaʻi. Now he was Boatswain's Mate First Class serving with the U.S. Coast Guard and head keeper at Barbers Point. When the Lighthouse Service was consolidated with the Coast Guard system in 1939, keepers were given the choice of remaining as civilians or joining the Coast Guard. In 1941 had Robins joined the Coast Guard.

Robins, his wife, Annie Naʻauao, and their baby son, Roy, loved living at Barbers Point in the 1950s. The Robinses already had three grown children. Their second daughter, Anna Mae, had been born in 1932 when the family was stationed there earlier. In 1958, Anna Mae, her husband Edward Kaʻanehe, a longshoreman, and their three children came to live with her parents at Barbers Point. Anna Mae was thrilled that her children could experience lighthouse living. "I listen to them talk about things that happened to them when they were growing up, and the life we shared at Barbers Point is one of their happiest memories."[38]

The light station in the 1950s was still quite isolated. When Halloween was celebrated there weren't any neighbors for the children to trick or treat, but there was a place that was even better to visit—the light tower. The children, dressed in their scary best, slowly ascended the darkened spiral staircase, higher and higher, to meet—who knew what? The ghost at the top of the tower surprised them and gave them treats. Down, down the stairs they came, and after gaining courage, they knocked at the back door of their own house. But the house didn't seem so familiar in the dark night of Halloween, and they wondered who would answer. A witch in their kitchen seemed strange, but she, too, was generous. Then out the back door and around to the front, and there was was another kind stranger who invited them in for cookies and milk.

"Lightkeepers' families know how to improvise," said Anna Mae. "My children had many things we did not, but I don't think they had any more fun." Anna Mae's children had bikes instead of the improvised scooters her father had helped build back in the 1930s. They sailed store-bought kites, not homemade ones, high above the coconut palms. The keeper's house, too, had been updated with many new conveniences, including a television set, a freezer, and an outdoor barbecue pit. But the tropical setting, the privacy, and the Pacific Ocean for a front yard were just as Anna Mae remembered from her childhood.

The routine but idyllic life ended at sunrise on December 7, 1964, when Fred Robins switched off the light in the tower for the last time. The Barbers Point Light was made automatic. No keeper would climb the spiral staircase to tend the light each night; electric timers had taken over.[39]

The area surrounding the light station had also moved into a new age. A highway had taken the place of the railway. Planes landed practically in the light station's back yard, and the light was an important navigational aid not only for ships, but for the Barbers Point Naval Air Station as well. Development along the island's northwest coast included a cement plant, a steel mill, and an oil refinery.

The Barbers Point Lighthouse as it stands today. (Scott Hartvigsen, photojournalist, Fourteenth U.S. Coast Guard District)

Beyond Camp Malakole Military Reservation, an L-shaped artificial harbor for barges was carved out of the coral shore in 1960–1961.[40]

Human activities continue to alter the land. By the late 1980s an industrial complex sprawled across Barbers Point. The light tower's territory diminished. A chain-link fence now defines a small bit of rock and dry grass around the light. A gigantic cement plant looms next door. On the other side a bit of parklike open space has been retained where tourists are entertained with luaus. Short, bushy kiawes and weeds almost cover old cement paths and cracked remains of the house foundation where the keeper once lived. But along the shore, palm trees still bow tousled fronds to the trade wind that blows across the beach. Their graceful slimness provides a tropical setting for the tall, slender Barbers Point tower. The Fresnel lens, and the iron and glass lantern that protected the lens, are both gone, but somehow the tower still looks complete.

On April 15, 1964, the fourth-order rotating light was replaced by a thirty-six-inch airway beacon that did not require a Fresnel lens. The focal plane of the light was eighty-six feet above the ocean and the light could be seen fifteen nautical miles. On April 30, 1985, Barbers Point Lighthouse was again improved by the installation of two high-intensity lights set in a Double Barreled Rotating Optic Directional Code Beacon (referred to as DCB-224).[41] The light's nominal range was increased to twenty-four nautical miles.

Atop the tower, as the barrels revolve, first one light is projected seaward, then there is darkness until the second light revolves into place. The revolutions are timed so that there is a light flash every 7.5 seconds day and night. At night, a mariner seeing this characteristic flash will know it is the light from Barbers Point. During the day the tall, white, tapering tower remains a familiar landmark.[42]

Chapter 3

DIAMOND HEAD

In the 1870s before anyone had given much thought to building a lighthouse at Diamond Head, the Hawaiian government, businessmen, and sea captains all seemed to agree on the importance of locating a lookout station on the slopes of this landmark crater. Honolulu merchants and shipping agents wanted to know if a ship was coming into port and have it identified as soon as possible.

Whenever a ship was sighted off O'ahu in the 1840s, young boys heralded its arrival by running through the town blowing on conch shells. After they had trumpeted the exciting news, they made sure the kerosene lamps on the streets were filled so that there would be lights in the evening for the strangers.[1]

Ship chandlers and agents, merchants, and townspeople prepared to cater to the ship's needs and to welcome the *malihini* (strangers). From the harbor, incoming ships could be spotted from the top of the Pagoda Building, which faced the water on Merchant Street. The two-story wooden house, built in 1838, had a stone basement and front and rear verandas. Its decorative cupola, along with a tall flagstaff protruding from the roof, provided a landmark for captains bringing their ships into port. The building also served as an observatory for anyone ashore who wished to identify incoming vessels.[2]

After dredgings created new land on the southeast side of the harbor, a simple wooden structure was erected in 1856 by contractor George Lucas for a lookout tower. A blast of the whistle on the Lucas Tower let the town know if there was an incoming vessel. If a ship displayed its national colors at the main, the lookout knew that mail was on board and would signal several short toots on the whistle. The sound brought practically the entire population of Honolulu down to the waterfront, for it might have been three weeks or three months since the last mail had arrived.[3]

In addition, in 1856 a telegraph station was situated on Punchbowl Hill. From this location the lookout, who would signal when he saw an approaching vessel, could see to windward a distance of about twelve miles from the port. Later, to spot ships as they rounded Koko Head, a station was located on the crest of the hill at Kaimukī. The man who acted as lookout used semaphore to signal the approach of steamers or sailing vessels from around Koko Head. In those days it was possible, with the use of binoculars, to see Kaimukī from the roof of the Hawaiian News Company building on Merchant Street; the company acted as a shipping exchange.[4]

The Kaimukī lookout station also used flags to give certain specific information: two small flags were raised to indicate a war steamer; a blue flag meant "sail ho"; and when a vessel had mail on board, a large blue flag with the letter M was raised in addition to the "sail ho" signal.[5]

After a ship was announced, the harbor pilot went out to meet the vessel and guide it into port. On May 14, 1857, the harbor pilot must not have arrived soon enough to suit the captain of the British ship *Pearl,* because the captain ordered more than the usual one gun to be fired to summon him. The *Pacific Commercial Advertiser* reported: "The steam frigate . . . fired two guns from her larboard and one from her starboard side . . . the latter was charged with shot, and probably well aimed, as it hit the pinnacle of Diamond Head, and bounded back into the gulch below. The natives, who were sitting on the beach watching the noble ship pass by, heard the ball fly over their heads with a whizzing noise."

Fortunately, no one was hurt. The lookout station on Diamond Head had not yet been built, but the man who was to become famous as its keeper arrived in Hawai'i at about this time. John Charles Peterson came to Honolulu aboard the schooner *Lizzie Wight.* He was born in Göteborg, Sweden, and arrived in the Islands when he was eighteen. Peterson first shipped out from Honolulu aboard a vessel going to Portland, Oregon; then he served on the schooner *C. M. Ward,* commanded by Captain James A. King.[6]

Peterson left his life as a mariner when he was appointed the first "Pilots' Watchman" on the newly built Diamond Head lookout station in 1878. He received a salary of fifty dollars a month and soon became known as Diamond Head Charlie. Peterson married a Hawaiian woman who died four months after giving birth to their only child, Melika.[7]

Father and daughter lived in the secluded small white cottage built on the rough slope of Diamond Head. The cottage had two bedrooms, a tiny pantry, and an observation room with an almost unlimited view of the Pacific. On one side of the house was a large water tank covered with a wooden roof for catching rain water. The house did not have a kitchen. Peterson did own a small kerosene stove, but he used it only in stormy weather; most of the time he cooked outdoors on an open fire. The Peter-

sons lived on canned goods and perhaps a few vegetables that could be raised. Meat was a rarity.

Once a month Diamond Head Charlie went down into town to collect his pay and purchase supplies to last until his next monthly visit. It was a solitary life on Diamond Head, but Peterson devoted himself to his job and raising his daughter. Melika, too, liked her life at the lookout station. As a young girl she attended school every day and preferred to return each evening to her home on Diamond Head rather than to live or board with friends in Honolulu.

Peterson considered himself on duty about seventeen hours a day. He became an expert at spotting ships and identifying them. He used a large telescope, which he placed either outdoors or in his observation room. With this aid he was said to be able to see a distance of at least thirty miles. The telescope had been presented to him by William G. Irwin, a banker, and other Honolulu businessmen.[8]

In 1891, C. N. Spencer, minister of the Interior, wrote to Peterson informing him that Diamond Head Station was to be included in the list of signal stations published by Lloyds of London. Peterson was sent a complete set of international code flags and code books. He was also instructed to telephone T. H. Davies & Co., the Hawaiian agents for Lloyds and immediately advise them when a foreign vessel was sighted.[9]

While Peterson spotted and reported incoming vessels from his post on Diamond Head, mariners used the prominent and distinctively shaped crater as a daytime landfall. The crater had been used as a landmark by foreign shipping since the late eighteenth century. When Captain Nathaniel Portlock viewed the unusual crater formation on his voyage aboard the English vessel *Queen Charlotte* in 1786, he named it Point Rose "after George Rose, Esq., secretary of the Treasury and the second worthy patron of our undertaking."[10] The name was not used for long. As soon as sailors discovered crystals in rocks

Diamond Head Charlie in 1907 using telescope beside his cottage on Diamond Head. *(Pacific Commercial Advertiser* photo, reprinted with permission of the *Honolulu Advertiser)*

near the crater's base, which they thought were diamonds, the word "diamond" became part of its name.

Charles Victor Varigny was prophetic in his description of Diamond Head when he first saw it in 1855. He was aboard the *Restless* and had come from France to be the secretary of the French Consulate in Honolulu. Varigny wrote that the vessel passed

Diamond Head, "a volcanic mountain prominently situated like a welcoming watchtower."[11]

The uniquely shaped hill has always held symbolic significance for Hawaiians. Five of their historic sacred temples were built on or close to this imposing natural phenomenon. Near the top ridge of the crater, facing the sea, stood the Ahi heiau where a navigational fire was tended.[12]

The Hawaiian name for Diamond Head was Lē'ahi, although a variety of spellings (and, hence, meanings) have been given. There are several plausible definitions; one suggests that the name might have been based on the phrase "Lae Ahi" (fire headland) or "Lei Ahi" (wreath of fire), which referred to the ancient Hawaiian practice of lighting a wood fire on the crest of Diamond Head to guide canoe fleets bound for the island.[13]

The historic heiau Pahu-o-Māui was located on the seaward lower slope of Diamond Head. This was the site chosen in the nineteenth century for the lookout station and later for the lighthouse. When the heiau still existed, fishermen came to this high place to look down into the clear waters offshore to locate schools of fish. It was here priests made offerings to the gods for calm seas and a bountiful catch.[14]

Though locating a lighthouse on Diamond Head seems obvious, the idea was satirized in the *Pacific Commercial Advertiser* on December 6, 1860. "Away back towards the days of chaos, a Hawaiian Legislature enacted a law authorizing and providing for the erection of a lighthouse on the highest peak of Diamond Hill, forgetting that its chalky cliffs and phosphorescent antecedents rendered it the very best of beacons out in that part of the world."

The idea of a light on Diamond Head, however, continued to be favored by sea captains and shipping firms. When Captain A. S. Baker of the USS *Philadelphia* was asked by James King, minister of the Interior, for his suggestions on improving Honolulu Harbor and vicinity, Captain Baker replied:

In my opinion the most necessary addition to the present system is the establishment on Diamond Head of a light, visible at least 18 miles. The characteristics of the light to be fixed white varied by flashes at intervals of 15 or 20 seconds and in order to give ample warning to incoming vessels that they are approaching the reef and therefore running into danger . . . the light should

show red from the edge of the reef off Barber's Point lighthouse to the lighthouse in Honolulu Harbor.[15]

From time to time delegations of mariners and members of the Hawaiian cabinet visited the slopes of Diamond Head to determine where the light should be located, but no two men could agree on details. Meanwhile, complaints became infrequent, but nonetheless insistent when they were made.

Complaints were loud and numerous after the findings of the naval court of inquiry in the case of the SS *Miowera* were made public. It was found that the stranding of the ship on the night of October 2, 1893, was due to the indistinct appearance of the land. The captain had taken a bearing on the high land to the north of Diamond Head, mistaking it for Diamond Head, which was itself obscured. The captain held his course, which brought him closer to the shore than he had supposed.[16]

As soon as the *Miowera* grounded, the wind and the swell pushed the stern higher, until the huge ship lay at full length upon the coral in fifteen feet of water. Efforts were immediately made to pull the vessel off the reef, but without success. Passengers were brought ashore and cargo off-loaded. After five days of strenuous effort on the part of vessels from the port, the ship seemed to be permanently lodged on the coral in about eleven feet of water. It was six weeks before the *Miowera* was successfully floated from her precarious position and towed to port.[17]

The naval court, after hearing all the testimony, made an important observation regarding the cause of the *Miowera* mishap: "As there is no light on the eastward or Diamond Head side of the [harbor] entrance there is no possibility of getting a reliable bearing if the outline of the land be even partially hidden."[18]

The *Miowera* grounding prodded the Hawaiian legislature into action. It was recommended that a light "be established at Diamond Head which should show a light to the west of the harbor entrance. That the light on Barber's Point be replaced with one sufficiently powerful to cut the Diamond Head Light off the entrance. That the leading light of the harbor be made more powerful and raised to clear intervening obstacles and as far as practicable escape the influence of the street lights."[19]

In 1894 funds were requested for the Diamond Head Lighthouse, but nothing was done. Again in 1895, Captain James King, minister of the Interior and himself a mariner, understanding well the need for a beacon on this landfall, asked the Hawaiian legislature to allocate funds for the light.[20]

And there the matter stood for two years, until the *China*, approaching O'ahu from the south, ran aground before reaching the harbor. The *China* was known as the most magnificent steamship in the Pacific at the time. The vessel had been registered under the Hawaiian flag since 1889. Some months after the grounding, an article in the *Pacific Commercial Advertiser* of December 4, 1897, commented, "It was said at the time the big liner *China* had her mishap . . . that the accident would have been averted had a light shown on Diamond Head. Captains coming from the south have been especially attentive to all plans for a light on the slope of the extinct volcano."

Something had to be done. There was much discussion, but no one took any action. According to a newspaper account of the same date,

Captain King became weary of hearing the pros and cons of the case, and after a few trips to the vicinity with Mr. Rowell, the Superintendent of Public Works, drove a stake for the site of the beacon. . . . There was ordered at once the material for the illumination and for the tower. The iron for the structure has arrived and so soon as some road is made to the slope point, work on the structure will begin. This metal tower will be forty feet high and when the light is capped upon it, the rays will be sent out from an elevation of 160 feet above

the level of the sea. The light will be seen without any trouble at all for 20 miles. . . . Electricity will be used and it is figured that Charles Peterson, the Diamond Head lookout, will be able to take care of the light as well as to continue his present excellent work.[21]

In 1897 King reported that the lighthouse site was about 250 yards west of the lookout station, on the bluff overlooking the sea. "The tower will be an open frame, arranged to obstruct the view from the signal tower as little as possible." The iron tower was being constructed locally at the Honolulu Iron Works.

The fixed white light was to be connected with the city system of the Hawaiian Electric Company. A third-order Fresnel lens, furnished by Barbier and Benard of Paris, was shipped on the *H. Hackfeld* from Liverpool about the middle of September 1897, together with three spare lamps and 100 extra white chimneys for the lamps, for use in case the electricity should fail. All the tools needed by the keeper were also included, as well as two kerosene tanks of seven-quart capacity.[22]

The lantern, also built by Barbier and Benard, was shipped in sections. The lantern room, which enclosed and protected the lens, had an interior diameter of ten feet. The lantern had a double copper roof, glass panels (including two spare panels), and the red glass that would cause the light to show red across dangerous areas within the range of the light. Evidently there was some breakage, for on the invoice someone had penciled through the words "careful packing" and so completely crossed out the charge for the service that it is unreadable. It must have been disappointing to be deprived of parts before the light was even completed. Many months would pass before replacements arrived from France.[23]

There were other frustrations. The open iron framework, designed by Superintendent Rowell, was similar to towers being built for lights in the

United States and Europe, but even as the metal tower was being erected on the site, the legislature began having second thoughts about the design and the construction material.

Civil engineers C. H. Kluegel and John Ouderkirk had examined the tower and reported that "the greatest stress will occur at the time of a violent wind . . . [and] we are of the opinion that this structure has ample strength for all the stresses to which it may be subjected." Even with this assurance the legislators wanted a masonry tower. A month later they had the engineers return to Diamond Head, this time to inspect the site. Kluegel reported that, although the ground was soft rock and there was some slope to the layers of rock, "the material is so gritty that there is no danger of its sliding. The supporting power of the material is fully equal to any load that may come upon it from the building of a stone tower 40 feet high, provided the foundation is excavated to a reasonable depth."[24]

King, in his report for 1898, wrote, "As the Legislature provided that before the completion of the light a stone tower must be erected instead of the iron tower already constructed, plans have been made and a tower of rubble masonry will be built occupying the same place as the iron tower."[25]

Bids were accepted for the masonry tower, and E. B. Thomas, with the lowest bid of $1,170, was awarded the contract.[26] It took a little over a year to complete the light. The stone for the tower came from quarries on O'ahu. The foundation was five feet in diameter, with walls two and one-half feet thick. The tower supported the ironwork for the watchroom and the lantern.

A description of the lighthouse in the April 28, 1899, edition of the *Pacific Commercial Advertiser* included the detail that a "bull's-eye arch" had been built in the tower so that Diamond Head Charlie's view in the direction of Barbers Point would not be obstructed.

When the lighthouse was completed, a Notice to

The 1899 Diamond Head Lighthouse was not only an important primary seacoast light, but was a distinctive daymark with its four-sided, whitewashed stone tower and stark-black lantern. This was the last primary lighthouse built by the Hawaiian government and it was in operation until 1918. (Aids to Navigation, Fourteenth U.S. Coast Guard District)

Mariners was published: "On and after July 1st, 1899, a light will be established at Diamond Head, on the South side of Oahu, Hawaiian Islands. Lat. 21° 15′ 8″ N., Long. 157° 48′ 44″ W. Elevation of light above sea level 145 ft. Visibility 15 miles. Stone tower 40 feet high white washed." The fixed white light with a red sector is described, and at the end of the notice is the name James A. King, Minister of the Interior. King probably derived a great deal of satisfaction from issuing that particular notice.[27]

King had proposed electricity as the illuminant for the light, but extant records do not indicate whether electricity or kerosene was originally used. The road to the lighthouse and lookout station, though still rough, was much improved. Diamond Head Charlie remained the pilots' watchman, and John M. Kaukaliu was appointed keeper of the light, at a monthly salary of seventy-five dollars. No house for the keeper had been built, and Kaukaliu lived in a private residence about a quarter of a mile from the lighthouse.[28]

Funds for lighthouse building and maintenance were dwindling. In 1902 members of a congressional committee came to the Islands investigating navigational aids. The testimony they later presented to the Congress, based on observations made during that trip, began:

> The coasts and harbors of Hawaii are woefully deficient in lighthouses. There is only one first-class light-house in the Territory. This is on Diamond Head. . . . There are a few other inferior lights established at different points, but they are wholly inefficient to meet the requirements and just demands of the rapidly increasing commerce of the Hawaiian waters.

Congress did not respond to this report. It wasn't until the lighthouse service was taken over by the U.S. Department of Commerce and Labor in 1904 that the Light House Board began work on navigational aids in Hawaiʻi. The board reported that the Diamond Head Light continued to be adequate, reliable, and trouble free. Only a few improvements were made at that time: a floor was built in the tower fourteen feet above the ground floor, which created an additional storage area, and windows were placed in two existing openings in the tower walls. Although there was still no keeper's dwelling, telephone lines were installed in the light tower, and the lookout station received a much-needed renovation.[29]

President Theodore Roosevelt, by executive order in 1906, acquired 157.5 acres of the territory's public lands on Diamond Head for military purposes. This land included the lighthouse property; however, it was not until 1910 that two acres of the military reservation of Fort Ruger, the tract on which the Diamond Head Lighthouse stood, was formally transferred to the Department of Commerce and Labor.[30]

After a survey of the site was made, fencing was erected around the lighthouse property and a water supply system was completed. An incandescent oil-vapor system was introduced in 1910 for illuminating the light. Kaukaliu continued as keeper, but the pilots' watchman at the lookout station was now Captain Niels C. Nielsen. Diamond Head Charlie died in 1907 at the age of sixty-seven after thirty years of service.[31]

In 1915 Kaukaliu was transferred to Barbers Point and Robert I. Reid, the keeper at Barbers Point, was transferred to Diamond Head. The light tower, though whitewashed regularly, had not had any extensive repairs for several years. Reid accompanied Frederick Edgecomb, an engineer with the lighthouse district, when he inspected the tower in 1916. The men noted that cracks in the cement work were becoming larger and the tower was showing signs of weakness.[32] Funds from general appropriations were finally made available in 1917 for the construction of a new lighthouse.

Plans were drawn up for a fifty-five-foot reinforced concrete tower to be erected upon the old foundation. Scaffolding was built around the old structure. The watchroom and lantern were then removed from the old coral-rock tower and mounted atop the new metal framework, and the light continued functioning. The old tower beneath the watchroom was dismantled, and a concrete tower was erected, up to and including the watchroom deck. A new cast-iron spiral stairway was provided and repairs and improvements were made to the watchroom lantern. The lighthouse was completed in 1918, at a cost of $6,109.

When the watchroom and Fresnel lens were secured atop the new tower, the focal plane for the incandescent light was 147 feet above sea level. The white light, with 7,300 candlepower, could be seen a nominal distance of eighteen nautical miles. The light's characteristic was changed from fixed to group occulting. An electrical circuit breaker controlled the light's signal: every 10 seconds an eclipse for 1.5 seconds, light for 2 seconds, a second eclipse for 1.5 seconds, then light for 5 seconds. Red-glass panels were installed at precise angles on either side of the lens on the glass walls of the lantern, causing the white light to show red over the areas of reefs and shoals.[33]

When Congress approved an appropriation of $50,000 in 1919 to be used specifically for the construction of keepers' dwellings, $5,000 was allocated for use at Diamond Head. Blueprints showing proposed location and general plans for the long-needed keeper's house were approved by the Bureau of Lighthouses on March 5, 1920. Detailed plans and specifications were drawn up showing the elevations for a double-wall, frame-construction dwelling, with plastered interior walls.[34]

Alexander Toomey and his family were the first to move into the completed house in 1921. Julia Toomey, as a child, would help her father polish the glass panes of the lantern. When she visited the

keeper's house forty-five years after she had moved away, it looked much different to her.[35] Though the one-story bungalow has changed over the years, it still retains the architectural features of the 1920s era. There are nine-foot ceilings and hardwood floors throughout the house, with arched openings over the doorways; there are bay and casement windows and French doors.

Being a lightkeeper's daughter, Julia lived near three other lighthouses in the islands while she was growing up, but she always considered Diamond Head Lighthouse the most beautiful. In 1924 the Diamond Head Light was automated, and the Toomey family was transferred to Makapu'u Point Light. Automation was made possible because of the development of highly efficient incandescent lamps and reliable electric-generating equipment that could be used in case commercial power failed.[36]

The keeper's house, with its spectacular view, did not remain empty for long. The charming bungalow, perched on the side of the famous Hawaiian landmark, became the residence of lighthouse superintendent Frederick Albert Edgecomb. Edgecomb, who was born January 3, 1887, in Groton, Connecticut, received a degree in civil engineering from Brown University in 1908. After graduation he worked for the war department as an engineer with the U.S. Department of Fortifications in New London. In 1911 Edgecomb transferred to the U.S. Lighthouse Service and was assigned to Hawai'i as an engineer. He worked as a construction foreman for many of the early lights built in the territory. After serving with the U.S. Army during World War I, Edgecomb returned to the Lighthouse Service in Hawai'i. In 1920 he was promoted to assistant superintendent of the Nineteenth Lighthouse District. No matter what his position, Edgecomb always took an active role in the development of lighted aids in the islands and a personal interest in the lightkeepers. In 1930 he became superintendent of the Nineteenth

Lighthouse District, the largest district in the Lighthouse Service.[37] He and his family moved to Diamond Head and spent the following nine years there until the Coast Guard assumed responsibility for the property. During the time Edgecomb served in the islands, 231 aids to navigations were established, including 96 lighted aids.

In 1939 the Coast Guard was placed in charge of the Diamond Head Light Station and maintained the light, the tower, the house, and the grounds. The light itself was equipped with a self-operated electric lamp exchanger, which automatically rotated a new lamp into position when needed. There was a self-winding electric control clock that turned the light on at sunset and off at sunrise, and just to be absolutely safe, a second clock cut in if the first one failed. And there was a backup automatic electric generator on standby in case commercial power failed. Diamond Head's automatic light was made as close to fail-proof as possible.[38]

Near the lighthouse, a keeper still remained on duty at the wide window of the lookout station at 3400 Diamond Head Road. With his telescope he could sight a ship approaching O'ahu, and when the vessel was identified, the keeper would phone another lookout who was stationed at the top of Aloha Tower; he in turn would notify the harbor pilot. Available records indicate that the territorial lookout station on Diamond Head was manned through 1940. The building, which was in poor condition, was later demolished.[39]

The buildings at the Diamond Head Light Station were considerably modified during World War II for Coast Guard use. The Coast Guard's radio station, which had been located on the sixth floor of the Aloha Tower, was housed in the former keeper's cottage, and another smaller building was erected to the east and seaward side of the tower. At the end of the war, the radio station was moved to Wahiawā, and the light was again manned until it was auto-mated in 1950. The smaller building, which had been constructed in keeping with the original keeper's house, became a guest cottage, and, with extensive redecorating, the keeper's home came into its own again. Since 1945, all of the commanders of the Fourteenth Coast Guard District have made their home there.[40]

Rear Admiral Benjamin Engel and his wife Ruth had lived in many places in the United States and in Puerto Rico before they moved to Diamond Head in 1967. Mrs. Engel said her first view of the Diamond Head house and setting left her speechless. Never before had there been a lighthouse next to her home, or had she lived in such a beautiful spot.[41]

When the Engels moved into the house it was almost completely furnished. It looked cool and tropical with bamboo and rattan furniture and colors to match the blue and green hues of the surrounding tropical foliage and ocean. Every family that had lived in the house had contributed something of their own, and the Engels added to the lanai. It was the perfect place for a party. One party in particular will probably always make the Engels chuckle. Mrs. Engel knew that the admiral occasionally invited additional guests and forgot to mention the fact, but at this party there seemed to be more than a few faces she did not recognize. And she was amazed that the admiral would invite so many people without telling her. The mystery was solved when Mrs. Engel, chatting with some of the unknown guests, learned that they were tourists who had come to explore Diamond Head Lighthouse and thought the Coast Guard was holding an open house as part of the tour.[42]

One of the most exciting times for residents at Diamond Head Light Station is during the biennial Transpac Yacht Race from Long Beach, California, to Honolulu. The finish line for this prestigious race is a line projected from the Diamond Head Light to the lighted buoy set approximately 300 yards offshore. The Transpacific Yacht Club applies to the Coast Guard for use of the light tower as an observation post. With a license in hand, members of the racing committee are on duty day and night during the race to observe and record the finishing times of the yachts.[43] Diamond Head Road, which runs around the crater and is adjacent to the lighthouse, is jammed with cars and crowds during this race. It is an unforgettable experience to watch some of the most splendid yachts in the world, under full sail, broad-reaching in the trade winds and heading for the finish line.

On the ocean side of Diamond Head Road is an iron gate that opens onto lovely, bright plantings along the cement sidewalk leading to the light tower. On the right, a thick, high hedge of aralias creates a graceful green wall of privacy from the road. Tall old trees throw cool shadows over the well-kept lawn and flower beds. The bungalow is just west of the light tower. The guest house seems to have been built as close to the seaward edge of the property as possible, although all of the buildings, including the tower, are sitting in dramatic cliff-hanging positions. The light tower itself is only fifty-five feet high, and one can run up the spiral staircase without even puffing.

It is the view from the top that takes the breath away. The viewer's eyes are at a level with the focal plane of the light, 147 feet above the Pacific. There is almost a straight drop down to the ocean and on either side an unimpeded panoramic scene of the south and east shores of Oʻahu and the mountains beyond. "The view," says Coast Guardsman Aaron Landrum, "makes this one of my favorite lights to work on." Landrum is a machinery technician with the Aids to Navigation Team (ANT), which inspects all primary seacoast lights, including Diamond Head, every three months.[44] The team is the modern equivalent of the traditional lightkeepers of the past.

On July 18, 1988, Landrum and Electrician's Mate Glenn Aikin arrived at the lighthouse to make their quarterly inspection. It is the ANT team's job to make sure that all the lights in the Hawaiian Islands are maintained and functioning at all times. The records kept of work done on the light stations read very much like nineteenth- and early twentieth-century logs of lightkeepers at any U.S. light station: "painted exterior of lighthouse, 100%"; "replaced lamp and cleaned lamp changers"; "polished brass lens and railings, swept out entire light, cleaned glass, walls and decks"; "painted interior of light." The repetition of jobs completed year after year has a monotonous ring, yet Landrum says he has the "best job in the islands!"[45]

The Fresnel lens at Diamond Head has a section that opens. This allowed the lightkeeper to stand outside the lens and reach inside to the center pedestal and attend the incandescent oil vapor lamp. In 1988 Glenn Aikin reached through this same opening to tend the 1,000-watt electric lamp (the term *light bulb* may be used by laymen, but the ANTs say, "Bulbs are only for planting!"). The primary lamp burns continuously day and night. It is mounted in a rotating two-place 120-volt lamp changer. If the primary lamp goes out, a second 1,000-watt lamp automatically rotates into place. The primary position is marked in red, so the Coast Guardsman can immediately tell if the light with the red mark is the one functioning. If not, he knows it has burned out and it is the replacement lamp that is burning.

Encircling the lens is a metal platform. The original high glass domelike lantern with a metal roof encloses and protects the lens and platform from the elements. Attached to the inside wall of this enclosure is the red rectangular glass panel that creates the red sector when the white light shines through it.

From the inside platform a door leads to the outside balcony that encircles the lantern. The backup system for the Diamond Head Light is attached at

The Diamond Head Light Station is the only station on O'ahu, and one of two in the Islands, where the keepers' dwellings have been preserved (the other is at Kīlauea on Kaua'i). The original 1921 Diamond Head lightkeeper's cottage has served as home for the commandant of the Fourteenth U.S. Coast Guard District since 1945. In 1980 the station was placed on the National Register of Historic Places. (Aids to Navigation, Fourteenth U.S. Coast Guard District)

the seaward railing. It looks very small compared with the Fresnel lens, but, in case commercial power should fail, it does the same job of projecting Diamond Head's light characteristic. The auxiliary light also has a red sector. The white light from the backup system can be seen for only eight nautical miles and the red sector for six nautical miles, compared with the main white light, which can be seen for seventeen nautical miles and the red sector for fourteen nautical miles. The backup system is powered by two six-volt batteries. It has a 250-mm plastic lens with a 2.03-watt lamp mounted in a six-place, 12-volt lamp changer. The six tiny lamps (each about the size used inside the star at the top of a Christmas tree) are arranged in a circle and rotate

like a ferris wheel; if one burns out a ratchet mechanism clicks the next one into place. Thus, when darkness descends, mariners are always assured of seeing the same unmistakable Diamond Head Light characteristic that was first shown from the concrete tower in 1918.[46]

Aikin does most of the work checking the electrical input and output, the lamps, and the Aids to Navigation (ATON) equipment while Landrum watches, for Landrum's tour of duty is almost over and he is training Aikin to take his place. Neither man paid much attention to lighthouses before they were assigned to the ANT team; now both are lighthouse buffs. Landrum not only knows the names and locations of all the lighted aids in the Hawaiian

ANT team member Glenn Aikin servicing the six-place lamp changer on Diamond Head's backup light. Backup systems such as this one have been in use on automated primary lighthouses in Hawai'i since 1971. (Jeff Crawley, photojournalist, Fourteenth U.S. Coast Guard District)

Islands, but has worked on most of them for two years as well as helping to maintain the unlighted aids. "I'm from North Carolina," Landrum says, "way back in the country. I never saw a lighthouse before I came to Hawai'i. These lights are the most beautiful things I've ever seen. I have no idea what the value of the Diamond Head lens is, but to me it's priceless."

Both the lens and the lighthouse are an important part of Hawai'i's maritime history. It was the last primary seacoast light built by the Hawaiian government and was the pride of the Islands. The Diamond Head Light continues to guide ships to O'ahu and it has become one of the best-known lighthouses in the world.

Chapter 4

MAKAPU'U POINT

The road to Makapu'u Point Lighthouse is narrow, twisting, and full of potholes and outcroppings of rocks. At its beginning, toward the southeast off Kalaniana'ole Highway, there is a wide swing gate with a tamper-proof lock on it to keep vehicular traffic out. Hikers and other trespassers, of good or bad intent, have only to walk around the gateposts to gain access to the road. There is a long, gentle incline before the road begins to curve along the rocky cliffs and disappears from view above the ocean.

When the lighthouse was first built in 1909, there was no road around the island. The lightkeepers and their families traveled five miles down from the light through the thorny kiawe growth on the flats and up across the Koko Head saddle to connect with the eastern extremity of the road that ran between Honolulu and Kuli'ou'ou. Transportation was by foot or horseback. Supplies needed to sustain the people and the light were hauled up by mule-drawn wagon.[1]

In the 1930s the trip to the light station could be made by automobile from Honolulu in less than two hours over fourteen miles of well-paved highway. A two-mile narrow side road led from the highway to the crest of the Makapu'u ridge.[2] In the 1990s the same narrow road that cuts off from Kalaniana'ole Highway to the light station has been minimally asphalted, but is little more than dirt and dust, bumps and ruts, for almost a mile. As it winds up the hill it is barely wide enough for the U.S. Coast

Guard truck. The switchbacks cut out of the sides of the cliff are just as narrow, sharp, and tough to negotiate as they ever were.

At the end of the road, the lighthouse is nowhere in sight. Another locked gate guards a snaking foot trail made safe by a post and rail fence curving along the rim of the cliff. Round the last bend, past the protecting cliff, the wind assaults the visitor, and the lighthouse comes into view.

In photographs that show only the tower, the Makapu'u Point Lighthouse looks squat and stubby; but seen in its natural setting, solidly set on the cliff's edge, the proportions are exactly right. There is no need on this high bluff for a tall, tapering lighthouse like the one on Barbers Point. The Makapu'u tower, just large enough to contain and support the lighting equipment, is as round and sturdy as the surrounding boulders.

The story of the establishment of this light is like that of many lights—government procrastination until maritime mishaps caused an uproar from commercial interests. The Hawaiian government was first petitioned to place a light on Makapu'u in 1888. On October 9 of that year, a group of shipowners, shipmasters, and others interested in commerce between the Islands and foreign ports wrote to Lorrin A. Thurston, minister of the Interior, emphasizing the importance of having a lighthouse placed on Makapu'u Point. The petitioners wanted to prevent a repetition of the unfortunate accident that had befallen the American bark *S. N. Castle* one month

Makapuʻu Lighthouse is accessible by land only along a track that is too narrow for a vehicle. Equipment needed in 1987 for major renovations to the tower was brought in by a U.S. Marine Corps CH-53D Sea Stallion. (Seaman Melissa C. Youngberg, Aids to Navigation, Fourteenth U.S. Coast Guard District)

earlier. The sailing ship had begun regular runs between San Francisco and Honolulu with passengers and cargo at the beginning of the year. On the night of September 6, 1888, the captain, misjudging the vessel's position, ran the ship aground on the reefs north of Kāneʻohe Bay. Anchors were immediately set out, but the vessel could not be kedged off until noon the next day.[3]

Many believed that the grounding could have been prevented if a light had been showing from Makapuʻu. The petition emphasized that a lighthouse on this point would prove of great benefit to vessels attempting to make the passage between Molokaʻi and Oʻahu by night: "Under present circumstances vessels are frequently compelled to lay-to until daylight when approaching this Channel, with the risk of being detained outside for some days by reason of any change in the weather. Should Your Excellency think favorably of this petition, we would respectfully suggest for Makapuu, a Flash-light, 2nd class, placed at an elevation capable of being seen 20 miles."[4]

The petition was signed by twenty-six captains of vessels regularly using this sea route, three shipowners, three officers of companies owning ships, six shipping agents, twenty-one underwriters, the Honolulu harbor master, and two Honolulu harbor pilots. One of the petitioners was the shipping agent for the Pacific Mail Steamship Company, whose ship *Manchuria* was one of the largest steamers calling at the port of Honolulu.

No immediate action was taken; however, Thurston in his 1890 annual report, requested that a lighthouse be built at Makapuʻu Point: "It seems important that this should be done, as a light at this point will mark the main highway of the most important lines of trade with Honolulu."[5]

As a consequence of the minister of the Interior's report, Superintendent W. E. Rowell, of the territorial Department of Public Works, was contacted. The construction of lighthouses was the responsibility of this department, and the superintendent was instructed by Thurston to write to Chance Brothers and Company, of Smethwick, England, manufacturers of lighthouse apparatus, asking the cost for lamps, a lens, and a lantern. In October 1890 the company, in response to Rowell's query, replied, "We think in your clear atmosphere, so free from fogs, a 3rd Order Revolving (flashing) Light with a large burner would be amply sufficient and this arrangement will also be cheaper for your stone tower."[6]

By 1901 the proposed lighthouse was in the planning stage, but the Department of Public Works reported that the third-order light would be fixed, rather than flashing, as suggested. The light would show red sectors on either side of the white light to warn mariners of the reefs along the shore. A small masonry tower was suggested: "The point is high, and good stone for building is abundant in the vicinity. The estimated cost is $10,000."[7]

The territorial government took no further action because it was anticipated that the United States would soon be assuming responsibility for navigational aids in the Islands. When the U.S. Light House Board did take over the territory's lighthouse service, appropriations were barely adequate to keep the existing lighthouses from falling down. No funds were appropriated for new construction. Furthermore, the House Committee on Interstate and Foreign Commerce wanted more information on Makapu'u Point's importance to commercial shipping. In response, the Light House Board reported that all Honolulu-bound shipping traffic, from both east and west, passed Makapu'u Head, adding that "there is not a single light on the whole northern coast of the Hawaiian Islands to guide ships or warn them of their approach to land after a voyage of several thousand miles." The board recommended passage of H.R. Bill No. 5294 for the establishment of a lighthouse at Makapu'u Point and requested an appropriation of $60,000.[8]

It was not until 1905 that the House of Representatives again took up the Makapu'u question, but by that time the Makapu'u light was only one item on a long list of lighthouse priorities. Highest on the list were appropriations needed to maintain and improve existing lights, and for the establishment of

other lighthouses besides Makapu'u. The legislative process for all these items took time.

On January 9, 1906, the first session of the Fifty-ninth Congress heard the report on Makapu'u Point Lighthouse.

> Makapuu Point is the extreme southeastern point of the island of Oahu. To the east of it is the Kaiwi Channel, which passes between the islands of Oahu and Molokai, which are about 25 miles apart. The harbor of Honolulu, the principal harbor of the central Pacific Ocean, is on the southern coast of Oahu, a short distance west of Makapuu Point. . . . There is no light on the entire northern coast of the Hawaiian Islands to guide ships or warn them as they approach those islands. The lack of such a light not only renders navigation at times very dangerous, but in bad weather or at night often compels them to slow down and await clear weather or daylight. With the increasing importance of the commerce between the United States and the Hawaiian Islands, and the commerce passing the Hawaiian Islands and stopping at Honolulu, it will be very greatly to the advantage, speed, and safety of vessels that this much-needed aid to navigation be provided.[9]

The bill was passed and an appropriation for $60,000 was made on June 30, 1906.

In the predawn hours of August 20, 1906, the *Manchuria* ran aground off Makapu'u Point. It was raining and visibility was almost zero. The 13,600-ton steamer had been cautiously under way at slow speed. Although Captain J. W. Saunders made allowances for the current that flows toward land along this part of O'ahu, he had mistaken Rabbit Island for Bird Island and was heading much closer to shore than he realized. By the time the captain and crew heard the breakers it was too late. The engines were thrown in reverse, yet the ship continued its forward thrust. The captain was unable to maneuver the vessel away from the shallow ledge between Rabbit Island and Waimānalo Landing.

The *Manchuria*'s bow ran up on Pāhonu Ledge so smoothly, it was said, that sleeping passengers did not even wake. When asked later by a board of inquiry why his ship had gone aground, Captain Saunders attributed the mistake not only to the poor visibility, but to the lack of a lighthouse on Makapu'u.[10]

The fifty-seven cabin passengers were transported ashore and, according to newspaper reports, "sumptuously housed at the best hotels." The two hundred steerage passengers were also brought ashore, but housed less elegantly. All bills were paid by the owners of the *Manchuria*, the Pacific Mail Steamship Company, whose Honolulu agent in 1888 had signed the petition for a lighthouse on Makapu'u.

Excitement over the grounding was high throughout the island. Everyone wanted to see what was happening to the *Manchuria*, as day after day all the resources of the art of salvage were used to save as much as possible of the $2,500,000 invested in the floating palace. An article in *The Friend* lightheartedly reported:

> The quiet even tenor of life in this Pacific of the Common Place was invaded . . . effectively by the telephone message that awakened all Honolulu early Monday, August 20th. The *Manchuria* is ashore off Rabbit Island. . . . A procession of vehicles such as Honolulu alone can create steamed, gasolined, trotted, jogged, and toiled over the Pali and transformed sleepy Waimanalo into a center of hustling activity.[11]

The owners of the ship hired Captain John Metcalf, a salvage expert, to take charge of the operation and direct the rescue work. Once Captain Metcalf had assessed the situation, six heavy anchors were set out from the *Manchuria*. Coal and bags of flour were jettisoned from the steamer, much to the benefit of local salvagers. Cargo, reportedly valued at $300,000, was off-loaded. When the ship was light-

ened of all freight, portions of the reef obstructions were blasted out for a passage.[12]

At noon on September 16, the *Manchuria* was hauled off Pāhonu Ledge by the *Restorer*, the *Manning*, and the *Iroquois*, and towed into Honolulu Harbor. Thorough inspection of the steamship revealed that the *Manchuria*'s propeller blades were crumpled and the starboard side of the bilge keel was badly damaged, but the ship had never been in danger of sinking. By October 8, the *Manchuria*, seaworthy once again, departed for San Francisco.[13]

Once the *Manchuria* was off the reef, life in Honolulu became quiet again, but the pleas for a Makapu'u lighthouse could still be heard. W. M. Gifford, president of the Honolulu Chamber of Commerce, wrote, "Such an accident has been feared for many years and has many times been narrowly averted. . . . Until this light is completed every vessel approaching Honolulu from the Pacific Coast will be exposed to the danger of a similar disaster." An article in *Paradise of the Pacific* concluded, "A lighthouse at Makapuu Point . . . is needed . . . and doubtless, in view of the Manchuria mishap the $60,000 Congressional Appropriation will be used at once."[14]

First, land had to be acquired for the lighthouse site. Oscar L. Strauss, secretary of the U.S. Department of Commerce and Labor, sent a cablegram to Governor George R. Carter: "President proposes issuing executive order reserving lighthouse purposes at Makapuu tract about ten acres do you approve?" Carter responded: "Approve reservation Makapuu lighthouse—Territory owns only portion of the same which is under lease."[15]

The lease was with the Waimānalo Sugar Company. The rest of the land surveyed for the lighthouse site was owned by the estate of Bernice Pauahi Bishop. President Theodore Roosevelt issued an Executive Order on January 12, 1907, declaring that an area of 9.82 acres be reserved for lighthouse purposes. In addition to this public land, 7.906 acres were acquired on August 7, 1907, and another 11.1 acres on April 29, 1908, making the area of the entire site 28.826 acres.

The summit of Makapuʻu is 647 feet above the ocean. The jagged slopes were formed of layer upon layer of lava flows. On the shoreward edge of the sea cliff there is a wave-cut terrace, carved by the incessant pounding of the waves onto the shore. Between the summit and the terrace, a site was selected for the lighthouse about 395 feet above the water. Dynamite was used to make a trail across the steep lava-rock incline, and a shelf to accommodate the lighthouse was blasted out of the side of the cliff.

At the same time, a road was being constructed through the lighthouse reservation from the Kuli-ʻouʻou road to the site for the keepers' dwellings. The three keepers' houses were located about twelve hundred feet uphill from the lighthouse in a slight depression in the ridge, which offered some protection from the strong, almost constant trade winds that blow across Makapuʻu. The houses were built for permanence, with fourteen-inch-thick walls of lava rock gathered from the property. They had white-painted trim and red-shingled roofs. Each contained a living room, two bedrooms, a kitchen, two clothes closets, a bathroom, and a front porch—luxurious living compared with earlier keepers' quarters in the Islands.

Fresh water, pumped up to the lighthouse reservation from the pumping station at Waimānalo Landing four miles away, was stored in a ten-thousand-gallon tank. The tank, constructed of redwood and held together by iron hoops, was located about five hundred feet north on a hill one hundred feet above the keepers' dwellings. It supplied all the water for the houses, the barn, and the tower by gravity.[16]

A fence enclosed a three-quarter-acre paddock and a red-roofed, gray barn for the station's mules and horses, which were needed for transportation of personnel and supplies. There was also a small com-bination shop and storeroom, as well as a reinforced concrete oil house that could hold 360 five-gallon kerosene oil cans.

The small lighthouse world of Makapuʻu was slowly taking shape. The circular tower was complete by October 1908, but sat unusable and agape awaiting the lens and lantern, which had not yet arrived. The delay was due to a change in plans. The original suggestion in 1901 was for a third-order lens. Later designs called for a second-order and then a first-order lens. Captain C. W. Otwell, U.S. Army Corps of Engineers, kept insisting on a powerful light for Makapuʻu. As a result of his insistence, the Light House Board decided to use a "hyperradiant" lens.

Great improvements had been made in the design of Fresnel lenses in the late 1800s. The Scottish lighthouse builder Thomas Stevenson (father of Robert Louis Stevenson) had introduced a first-order lens with an inside diameter of six feet. His nephews, David and Charles, designed the largest lens ever manufactured—the hyperradiant lens. The U.S. Light House Board purchased one of these lenses, which had been built in 1887, from Barbier and Company in Paris. The lens was displayed at the Chicago World's Fair in 1893, where the Light House Board had built a full-size lighthouse containing an exhibit of illuminating apparatus and scale models of various innovative light towers built in the open sea. The Light House Board later reported: "Some idea may be had of the interest taken in lighthouse building by the fact that the exhibit was one of the most popular at the fair."[17]

The hyperradiant lens made an impressive display. After the exhibition the lens was placed in storage. It soon became obsolete with the invention of illuminants of high intensity, such as incandescent oil vapor, which increased the candlepower of the light so greatly that a lens as large as the hyperradiant was no longer necessary. When a first-order lens was needed at Makapuʻu, the Light House

Board probably decided that rather than purchase a new lens, they would use the hyperradiant lens they had already acquired. The hyperradiant lens at Makapu'u is the only one that was ever used in the history of U.S. lighthouses.[18]

The lens had an inside diameter of 8 feet, 8.7 inches and a height of 12 feet, and weighed, as shipped with its pedestal, about fourteen tons. Because of its size, new designs for the lantern and the occulting mechanism had to be drawn up and the parts manufactured.[19]

The thirty-five-foot tower, designed to house the lens, was solidly secured to its perch by a foundation of reinforced concrete blocks set eight feet below the surface of the ledge. The walls at the base were twenty-seven inches thick, tapering to twenty inches at the parapet. The diameter of the tower was twenty feet at the base and eighteen feet, six inches at the top. The smooth, natural gray concrete walls of the tower appeared white against the background of the dark and broken volcanic rock. The wind whirled outside and inside the incomplete structure for almost a year.[20]

In 1908 the tower was visited by a lone news reporter, who described the magnificent view from the lighthouse site: "Waimanalo valley, stretching green and fresh from the island dotted bay, is backed by the somber pali walls rising from 2,000 to 3,000 feet sheer above the canefields, while depressions in the crest of the mountain ranges mark very distinctly the openings of both Nuuanu and Kalihi valleys."[21]

Another visitor to the station was Theodore Kelsey, who kept a diary of his trek around O'ahu from May to August in 1909.

> There are kiawes at the foot of the beautiful valleys on one side and on the other . . . the ocean until you ascend Makapuu Point where there are three houses and the beginning of a lighthouse. . . . I met the light keeper, Kaiwi, coming up the trail and he showed me

the cave where the Kilo Kupua lay in wait for single men. Farther on there is a larger cave which was also used by the Kupua amid the ruins of an old heiau. I crept into the second cave and discovered a pole and what I took for a finger bone.[22]

Makapu'u Point, with its awesome beauty, was an important place in ancient Hawaiian legends. It was the stepping-off point for the goddess Pele when she left O'ahu forever. It was named for Makapu'u, a *kupua* (a supernatural being who possessed several forms), who was said to have eight bright eyes. Makapu'u arrived on O'ahu from Tahiti long before Pele; she decided to stay on the island's high southeast point, which, according to legend, she described as, "back pelted by wind and by tide," and where she could "see the cloud drifts of Tahiti."[23]

The Hawaiian word *makapu'u* is usually translated as "bulging eye" (*maka,* eye, and *pu'u,* hill or bulge). But what made the eyes of Makapu'u so memorable was not that they were bulging, but that there were eight of them. Nevertheless, the figurative comparison to the lighthouse built on this site with its especially large "bulging eye" lens is tempting and often repeated.

The gigantic lens has to be "experienced" rather than "seen" to be believed. One set of stairs leads to a platform encircling the lens; another special staircase terminates within the lens itself. The keepers tended the lamps by working inside the lens surrounded by the 1,188 prisms that optically turn the world topsy-turvy and color it with rainbows. There are 624 pieces in the top section above the central belt, 288 pieces in the bottom section, and 288 pieces in the central belt, including twelve large center pieces.[24] Inside this optic one has the weird sensation, not that the lens is so gigantic, but that one has suddenly become very small.

The magnificent lens and lantern were set in place, but only after backbreaking and hair-raising operations. The precious pieces, carefully packed, were brought by ship to the precarious landing beneath the sheer cliffs of Makapuʻu. Block and tackle raised the brass framework, the sections of finely polished glass prisms and the large center pieces for the lens, and the glass panes and cast-iron framework for the lantern. The lantern had twenty-four sides; the glazed portion was sixteen feet in diameter and twelve feet high.[25]

Seldom are the energies, anxieties, difficulties, and frustrations involved in such an undertaking documented. One has to imagine the problems of securing a boat in such turbulent waters, where wave action would have made every move precarious. The cliff that looks sheer from above actually tapers outward toward the sea; it must have been an engineering nightmare to haul each piece up from the rocking boat and keep it from crashing into the protruding rocks with the wind constantly blowing toward the cliff at its usual fifteen to thirty knots. There is no record of how many directions were shouted, how many loads were hauled up, or how many days it took to off-load the parts and assemble them upon the Makapuʻu tower. The feat was accomplished.

The lamp was installed inside the lens. It was an incandescent oil-vapor (i.o.v.) lamp and created a light, through the lens, of 29,000 candlepower. According to a Bureau of Lighthouses report, "When it seemed that the ultimate results from kerosene as a lighthouse illuminant had about been obtained, a new development, the incandescent oil-vapor lamp, became available. This type of lamp, burning vaporized kerosene under a mantle . . . produced a very brilliant light on a moderate consumption of oil."[26]

On October 1, 1909, George A. Beazley, first assistant keeper, and George Mansfield, second assistant, watched as lampist Palmer of the U.S. Engineer's office lit the lamp. The light sent its sig-

nal twenty-five miles out to sea. The head keeper, John McLaughlin, who had been serving on the Nāwiliwili Light on Kauaʻi, was expected to report for duty the next day and missed the auspicious occasion. The occasion, however, was not missed by the Matson steamship *Hilonian,* the first vessel to pass the light after it was turned on at dusk. The officers of the steamship remarked that the light was brilliant and that they saw it when they were still far out at sea.[27]

The characteristic of this light was occulting. A white light showed for a duration of seven and a half seconds, with an eclipse period of one and a half seconds. The eclipses were formed by a revolving chariot carrying three copper screens between the light and lens. The chariot revolved on ball bearings in a V-groove raceway or track. The mechanism was run by weights that would keep the machinery operating for three and a half hours; but, just to be on the safe side, the keepers cranked the weights up every three hours. The weights were wound from the service room directly below the watch room. The watch room contained the oil and air pressure tanks and the air pump. An electric bell, for calling relief keepers, was connected from the watch room to each dwelling.[28]

The keepers kept the light station in perfect condition, making repairs as soon as they were needed. Some part of the roadway always required attention. The tower, which was originally left its natural gray color until the cement cured, was painted white in 1914. When it became a problem to obtain fresh water from Waimānalo, the Department of Commerce and Labor began proceedings in 1912 to acquire the right-of-way for a pipeline for a permanent water supply from a mountain spring to the station. After the right-of-way was granted, the keepers completed the new water system in 1916. A 2,600-gallon lava-rock tank was constructed four hundred feet west above the dwellings, and the men laid a two-inch pipe to the spring about 7.8 miles from the station at an elevation of 585 feet above sea level. The keepers also added their individual touches to the landscaping around their cottages, but vegetable gardening proved impossible in the small patches of soil in the rugged, rocky terrain.[29]

Even with the light to tend and all the daily jobs, large and small, there was still time to enjoy life. When Diamond Head Light was automated in 1924, Alexander Toomey and his family were transferred to Makapuʻu. His daughter Julia remembers the good times she had with her father. The family took trips to Mākaha or enjoyed all-day drives around the island. Some weekends Toomey invited as many as forty of Julia's schoolmates up to the light station to play, and the children never wanted to go home. The beach, reached by a steep trail down the cliff from the lighthouse, was Julia's favorite place. The family fished and swam there. If they caught a lot of fish when Toomey was working and could not join them, their dog, Sport, "would run up the cliff to get my father and he would haul the fish up. . . . He was a good father."[30]

And then tragedy struck. On April 9, 1925, Toomey and John Kaohimaunu, the other assistant keeper, were getting ready to light the lamp for the night. Alcohol was used for heating the oil-vapor lamp. After the men had drawn off what was needed to fill the alcohol lighter, only a small quantity was left in the tank, but fumes filled the tank and the room. When the match was struck, the fumes exploded and filled the room with fire. Toomey was in the midst of the blaze and his clothing was immediately afire. The explosion blew the bottom out of the twenty-five-gallon tank and charred the inside of the lighthouse, but no damage was done to the lens or casing. Kaohimaunu, though burned, was near the door and managed to escape. Toomey, "charred black and crinkled," somehow managed to get back to his home. He died at noon the next day.[31]

In the May 1925 edition of the *Lighthouse Service Bulletin,* a publication circulated throughout the Bureau of Lighthouses, the editor wrote:

Mr. Toomey has been connected with the Lighthouse Service since July 1, 1908. He was a loyal and faithful employee and was one of the most competent keepers in the nineteenth district, having just been recommended for promotion to principal keeper at Kilauea Point Light Station, one of the important stations in the district. His courageous sense of duty was shown after the explosion. When he was taken from the light station to the hospital following his injury, he refused to permit his wife to accompany him and insisted that she remain at the lighthouse, which would necessarily be without a keeper for a considerable time, while Keeper Akana took the two injured assistants to Honolulu. After having called his wife and children about him and with them repeated the Lord's Prayer, his last words to his wife were, "Stand by the light and keep it burning." These words were made the text of an eloquent sermon delivered by the Reverend Akana, of Kawaiahao Church, Honolulu, at the funeral of Mr. Toomey on April 11.[32]

Toomey was forty years old at the time of the accident. Soon after the tragedy, Toomey's wife, Minnie Ululani Ua, gave birth to their daughter Violet. Then three months after her husband's death, Minnie Ululani Ua "died of a broken heart." Their daughter Julia was fifteen.[33]

The Bureau of Lighthouses, in its yearly reports, had been listing the number of deaths and partial or permanent disabilities sustained by keepers while in performance of duty. The service wanted Congress to make provision for these men and their families. In its report for 1925 was the statement that when compared with that of all other branches of the Department of Commerce, the number of men killed or injured in the Lighthouse Service indicated the hazardous nature of the field work. The report went on to say, "It is believed that the authorized maximum compensation for disability on account of injury is too low and that congressional action is desirable to provide a more adequate scale."[34]

In 1925 by an Act of Congress, disability retirement within the Lighthouse Service was provided for the first time. In 1926 the benefits of the Public Health Service were extended to lightkeepers located at isolated points who previously had been unable to avail themselves of these services. Congress also eliminated the ration allowance for keepers and increased their salaries.[35]

Samuel Apollo Amalu was one of the keepers who saw all of the changes in the Lighthouse Service from the time it first took over Hawaiian navigational aids. Amalu became a keeper in 1906 and was originally stationed at the Kawaihae Light Station on the island of Hawaiʻi. After several moves, in 1925 he was transferred to Makapuʻu, where he remained until 1929. Amalu's grandson Sammy long remembered his summers and holidays at what he called "that wild and almost forbidding spot at the end of nowhere." It was lonely for Sammy, but the loneliness stimulated his imagination. "The bare hills became festooned with castles. Caves became dark dungeons." Sammy felt that his grandfather must have understood, "for out of the kindness of his heart and the generosity of his soul he reached down and was able to make a child of nine less lonely. He peopled each day with wondrous goblins and griffins. He scented each night with tales of wonder."[36]

Keeper Amalu was at Makapuʻu in 1927 when the latest wonder in navigational aids was erected at the station—a radio beacon. The Lighthouse Service began experimenting with the use of radio in navigational direction finding in 1917, and by 1921 the first radio beacon was established at the Sea Girt Light Station on the New Jersey side of New York Harbor. The service described the use of radio beacons and their application in the navigation of ships as "per-

U.S. Lighthouse Service personnel at Makapuʻu Point Light Station, 1930. *Left to right:* 2nd Assistant Keeper John Enos, Keeper Manuel Ferreira, Superintendent Frederick A. Edgecomb, 1st Assistant Keeper Frank Pate. Edgecomb came to Hawaiʻi in 1911 as an engineer with the U.S. Lighthouse Service. By 1930 he had been promoted to superintendent of the Nineteenth District, a position he held until 1939 when he received a commission as commander in the U.S. Coast Guard, Aids to Navigation Branch, and served as captain of the Port of Honolulu. In 1942 he was transferred to Long Beach, California, where he was placed in command of the Eleventh Coast Guard District. In 1946 he retired after thirty-five years of dedicated service to the improvement of aids to navigation. (Courtesy of Carol Edgecomb Brown Collection)

haps the most important development in lighthouse engineering in the past half century."[37]

The beacon established at Makapuʻu was the first in the Hawaiian Islands. Two eighty-foot galvanized steel towers were erected on the promontory behind the light to carry the 180-foot antenna. A wooden frame building, 20.0 by 25.5 feet, was constructed to house the radio equipment, engines, and generators. The building had a concrete floor with independent concrete foundation blocks under the heavy generators.

Makapuʻu now had its own electrical generating plant. Operating the automatic radio beacon transmitters during the night were two direct-connected diesel engines. Each engine operated for one week and then alternated with the other, leaving one engine always in reserve. During the daytime, electricity was produced by one of three gasoline-powered generators.[38]

When electrical power was added for the radio beacon, it also became a source of power for the light. Three 500-watt incandescent electric lamps replaced the three incandescent oil-vapor mantles that used kerosene; however, the oil-vapor system was retained and kept in working order in case of emergency. With the use of electric lights, the candlepower was increased from 50,000 to 150,000, making the Makapuʻu light visible at sea for a distance of twenty-eight nautical miles.[39]

The Makapuʻu radio beacon signal could be picked up under normal conditions by a ship two hundred miles away. The signal consisted of a group of four dashes broadcast on 290 kilocycles for 60 seconds alternating with 120 seconds of silence.[40]

There had also been other changes at the light station. A combination garage and storeroom replaced the barn, and a one-ton truck replaced the mules and horses. Soil had been brought in for lawns around the keepers' houses, and flowers added bright borders in the yards. Even a few trees had been planted and struggled to stand upright in the constant wind.[41]

The duties of the keepers were also changing. In 1929 Manuel Ferreira was head keeper at Makapuʻu. With the introduction of electricity, Ferreira and the assistant keepers spent most of their time, not in the watch room of the light tower, but in the radio house. It was there that the keeper on duty took the night shift. He sat in front of an instrument board and pushed a test button at regular intervals.

This set into operation the gauges that indicated the amperage the navigational light was consuming. Any lessening of the current flowing to the lamp would dim its brilliance. If this was indicated, the keeper took immediate action to locate the cause of the trouble and make repairs.[42]

The keepers, using the station's receiving set, also checked the radio beacon signals to make sure that they were being broadcast automatically at the correct time. The accuracy of the clocks controlling the broadcasts was checked against navy time radio signals received by the Makapuʻu station.[43]

The keepers took day as well as night shifts, for although the light and radio beacon operated automatically, all the equipment was constantly checked and maintained. The standard equipment for the station included a transmitter, automatic code machine, emergency power supply in addition to regular sources, master control and synchronizing clocks, radio monitoring receiver, and a warning device for failure of equipment.[44]

The radio frequency, characteristic, range, latitude, and longitude of the radio beacon signal from Makapuʻu were listed, along with a description of every light and buoy in the Hawaiian Islands, in a navigational reference book, *Light List,* published yearly by the Lighthouse Service, Department of Commerce. Once the Makapuʻu radio beacon was established, it was used by nearly all the ships coming to the islands of Hawaiʻi from the west coast of the United States to help them verify their position. Celestial navigation was still used to determine a ship's latitude and longitude, but when weather conditions prevented the navigator from taking sightings of the sun, moon, or stars, the Makapuʻu signal could be relied upon. In addition, it would give a navigator a second bearing by which he could check his dead reckoning position. The signal could also be used as a landfall or leading mark for ships approaching the islands.[45]

If a navigator could take bearings on two radio beacons, the position of the ship could be determined even more easily and accurately. This was not true only for ships, but also for airplanes. Air flights to Hawai'i were increasing rapidly. Early interisland flights were made by Major H. M. Clark of the Fort Kamehameha Aero Squadron in 1918 between O'ahu and Moloka'i. On July 3, 1919, two army seaplanes carried the first interisland mail between Pearl Harbor and Hilo. That same year, the U.S. Navy shipped four seaplanes, nine pilots, and forty mechanics to Hawai'i. By 1923 the naval air station was established at Pearl Harbor. Five years later a U.S. Army plane made the first flight from the Pacific coast to the Hawaiian Islands, and the light from Kīlauea Point Light Station was the pilot's first landfall.[46] The lighthouses were proving to be useful navigational aids for planes as well as for ships.

The Kīlauea Point Light Station on Kaua'i was the site of the second radio beacon in the Hawaiian Islands. The operation of this beacon, established in 1930, was synchronized with the one at Makapu'u. In clear weather Makapu'u broadcast its group of four dashes on 290 kilocycles from twenty minutes to thirty minutes after the hour and from fifty minutes to the hour mark every hour of the day and night. The Kīlauea station, operating on 300 kilocycles, radioed its signal of two dashes at ten minutes after the hour until twenty minutes after, and again from forty until fifty minutes after the hour.

In clear weather, during each station's period of broadcast, its characteristic signal was sent out continuously for the first minute, then there was silence for the next two minutes. This pattern was repeated a total of three times during the ten minutes of broadcast, leaving the final minute of broadcast silent.

When weather conditions were poor, a different schedule was followed. Kīlauea transmitted its two-dash group for one minute; the next minute Maka-pu'u transmitted its four-dash signal for one minute; then there was one minute of silence followed by the Kīlauea/Makapu'u sequence once again, broadcast over their respective channels. This pattern was repeated continuously until the weather improved and the clear-weather broadcast schedule could be resumed.[47]

Continual broadcasting of the Makapu'u radio signal could be requested for certain periods of time for special navigational purposes of ships or planes. In January 1934 the U.S. Navy air squadron, under the command of Knefler McGinni, was the first to make such a request and to use the Makapu'u signal for navigational purposes. The second flight request was made by Captain C. T. P. Ulm, commanding the twin-engine plane *Star of Australia*.[48]

The purpose of Ulm's 1934 flight was to survey a commercial air route between the Pacific coast and Honolulu and between Honolulu and Australia. At 3:41 in the afternoon of December 3, the *Star of Australia* took off from Oakland, California, with Ulm in command; George Littleton, copilot; and Leon Skilling, navigator.

At 10:30 P.M. (8:00 P.M. Honolulu time) Ulm broadcast, "Everything O.K." During the night he contacted several vessels that were on the plane's flight path, and from position reports made at 12:50 A.M., it was determined that *Star of Australia* was 1,370 miles from the Oakland airport. An hour later the USCG *Itasca* intercepted a message from the freighter *Maliko* which said, "Ulm is cutting over our stern now"; at that time *Maliko* was about 350 miles east of Honolulu. The report was a mistake. It was not *Star of Australia* that had been seen; "It was a bright star." Still, everything about the flight seemed to be all right. At 4:03 A.M. the *Itasca* determined that the plane's position was 480 miles east of Honolulu.

The first emergency call came at 7:30 on the morning of December 4. Ulm reported he was flying at twelve thousand feet and in bad weather, "I don't know if I'm south or north of the islands." He said he was running short of gas and asked for the radio beacon. He was told that the beacon at Makapuʻu Point had been broadcasting since midnight. "I must get the beacon soon," Ulm said. "Have no position. Must be badly lost."

At 7:45 A.M., Ulm was desperate, "Very little gas left. Need the beacon badly. Please shake them up on the beacon." It was again reported that the beacon was working on 290 kilocycles. Ulm pleaded, "Would like help. Will you get bearings on us." The navy sent out three planes, with the fliers given orders to divide and circle both sides of the island. The objective was to try and contact Ulm's plane by radio rather than sight. Once radio contact was made, the pilots could give Ulm his bearings and bring him in to Wheeler Field.

The hoped-for contact was not made. Between 9:20 and 9:24 A.M., Ulm sent this message: "We are going into the water. We are turning into the wind now and going into the water. Plane will float two days. Come and get us. On the water now." Ulm sent out an SOS and added, "Plane will float two days. Using radio on the surface."

The search began. Army and navy planes, U.S. Coast Guard vessels, and all other ships in the area began searching the seas east, west, north, and south for the missing fliers. Destroyers and submarines covered an area three hundred to four hundred miles north of the Islands. At the time, this was the most gigantic search operation in the history of aviation disasters.

No trace of the fliers or the *Star of Australia* was ever found. As hope was abandoned, an editorial that appeared in the *Herald* of Auckland, New Zealand, concluded, "It was not a thoughtless adventure, but a definitely planned enterprise undertaken for practical reasons; misfortune having attended it, there has been a magnificent and selfless

effort by the Americans to succour the airmen in their distress."[49]

But the frantic radio message sent by Ulm— "Turn on the beacon. We are desperate"—still seemed to linger in the air. Frederick Edgecombe, lighthouse district superintendent, had ordered the Makapuʻu signal broadcast beginning at midnight on December 3. He had also ordered that one of the keepers stand by the station's receiver continuously to make sure the beacon was operating faultlessly. On December 15, 1934, the *Honolulu Star-Bulletin* commented on the radio beacon:

> That it did operate without fail was proved when every radio station within range heard the beacon's signals. It was kept operating continuously after the first day in the event of it being useful to the surface aircraft and vessels in the search. . . . If Ulm had the correct type of equipment, the Makapuu beacon would serve him like a "homing device" and allow him to set a course directly for Oahu no matter how far he had flown off his original course.[50]

The radio beacon at Makapuʻu was used successfully day and night in foul and fair weather by navigators on ships and planes for the next thirty-eight years, but its use began to drop off as other navigational aids were developed. LORAN, an acronym for LOng RAnge Navigation system, was developed during World War II. In the late 1950s, the original Loran-A was replaced by a new system with greater range and accuracy called Loran-C.

In 1972 the Fourteenth U.S. Coast Guard District, which included the Hawaiian Islands, took a "user survey" to determine if there was a continuing need for the radio beacon at Makapuʻu. Captain F. Hedeman, who was running a forty-five-foot pleasure fishing sampan said, "The Kilauea and Makapuʻu beacons have been extremely helpful to me in my trips between the islands both at night and in rain conditions. They are much needed navigational aids." Others agreed and several comments emphasized the affordability of RDF (Radio Direction Finder) receiving equipment for the small boat operator: "RDF only practical item because of price"; "No room or dollars for more sophisticated navigational equipment." Nevertheless, most navigators were not using the radio beacon at Makapuʻu, and it was discontinued on November 1, 1973.[51]

Discontinuing the radio beacon was the first step toward automating the lighthouse. Commercial electricity had already taken the place of diesel and gasoline generators, and Coast Guardsmen had replaced the civilian lightkeepers. The last civilian keeper at Makapuʻu was Joseph Pestrella. He and his family were transferred from Cape Kumukahi Light Station after Kīlauea volcano on the island of Hawaiʻi erupted in 1960 and lava demolished their home.[52]

The Pestrellas shared life at Makapuʻu with two Coast Guard families. Here the parents did not worry about lava flows, but rather how to keep the younger children from falling over the edge of the cliff and how to get the older children to and from their various schools, which were all far from Makapuʻu. The only problem presented by nature was the wind—it was so strong that washed clothes had to be tied to the clothesline, flags were shredded within weeks, and parents said they had to "buckle down the babies."[53]

The road did present a challenge to vehicle brakes and tires. Cars and trucks got a constant workout going up and down the hill with children, provisions, mail, garbage, and lighthouse supplies. Tourists and friends coming to visit the light station had to go through certain formalities. First, a liability release had to be signed, and second, before turning in on the approach road, where the sign warned, "Proceed At Your Own Risk," a phone call to the station was an absolute necessity, for there was room for only one car at a time on the narrow road from the highway.

Occasionally, unexpected visitors did arrive. It was just after dawn one morning when Pestrella received word that the Coast Guard had given up their night-long search for a seaman who had jumped ship while his vessel was offshore Makapuʻu. A few minutes later, the seaman walked into Pestrella's home. Bleeding from repeated attempts to pull himself ashore onto the wave-battered rocks, the man had somehow managed to climb the almost vertical cliff during the night.[54]

Hiking in the Makapuʻu area is rough even during the day, so Boatswain's Mate Ronald Cianfarani, when he was stationed at Makapuʻu, was very surprised one afternoon to meet a barefoot, bikini-clad young woman who had climbed the steep, rocky hill to the lighthouse from Makapuʻu Lookout. Another surprising visitor for Cianfarani and his wife Barbara was Jack Lord, who arrived at Makapuʻu along with the entire "Hawaii 5-o" cast and camera crew to film a scene of high adventure at the light station.[55]

But visitors were few and far between. Companionship was found almost completely with the other Coast Guardsmen and their families living at the station.

Coast Guardsmen Cianfarani, Steve Sullivan, and Ed Gillespie were the last keepers of Makapuʻu Lighthouse, and Makapuʻu was the last lighthouse on Oʻahu to be automated. "We're closing the station today," Cianfarani said, watching as the flag was lowered at 2:00 P.M. on January 4, 1974. Cianfarani, Barbara, and their five-year-old son Greg had lived at the station for two years. Their twin daughters were born while the Cianfaranis were stationed at the light. The family explored the mountain and the World War II bunkers together; climbed down the cliff to the tide pools, where they snorkeled and gathered cowries; spent hours on the hilltop watching whales, porpoises, stingrays, and turtles swimming in the clear offshore waters; doing all the things lightkeepers and their families had done at Makapuʻu for sixty-five years. "We will miss the place," Cianfarani said, "and the peace and quiet. Greg hasn't had anyone his own age to play with for two years, but he will miss it, too. To him, the hilly retreat has been a wonderland of discovery."[56]

The automatic light at Makapuʻu was monitored with an alarm system located at the Coast Guard Joint Rescue Coordination Center in Honolulu. In the event of an equipment failure, an alarm would sound and the emergency backup system would automatically switch on and keep the light operating until the ANT team arrived and corrected the failure. Normal response time was usually one hour or less.[57]

Unbeknownst to almost everyone, Makapuʻu light station was again occupied for a short while sometime during the year 1974–1975. While federal tax evasion trials were being held involving reputed underworld boss Wilford "Nappy" Pulawa, prosecution witnesses were brought to Makapuʻu for their safety. One man who was familiar with the operation told reporter James Dooley:

> The security was terrific. There was only the one lonely, winding road. . . . There were marshals up on the cliffs surrounding the place—sharp shooters with high-powered rifles. There were helicopter evacuation plans. You had to go through this elaborate routine to get out there—switching cars in Hawaii Kai, communicating by radio. . . . Then you'd get up there and there would be this luau going on.[58]

Evidently the greatest fear during this operation was that one of the witnesses would fall off the cliff.

The isolation of the station may have been perfect for securing government witnesses, but it leaves the light station vulnerable to vandals. The large sign reading, "U.S. Government Property No Trespassing Violators Will Be Prosecuted," mounted on the chain-link fence did nothing to protect the historic buildings. Someone using a high-powered rifle shot at the priceless Fresnel lens. The glass in one section of the lantern was shattered and the prisms of the lens pierced.

Four years after the last keepers left their homes at Makapuʻu, the lava-rock houses that were built for permanence fell victim to vicious acts of destruction. All windows were smashed, screens ripped, and doors torn from their hinges. When a reporter from the *Honolulu Star-Bulletin* examined the houses, he reported on August 13, 1978, what he had found: "The fine old, hardwood floor has been pocked with ugly holes. . . . Porcelain washbasins and toilets have been smashed with a sledge hammer. An axe has been thrown not once but a dozen times into a wooden wall. Wiring has been yanked out in dozens of places."

In 1987 the Coast Guard declared forty acres at Makapuʻu Point as surplus, including the area where the houses were located; only the land around the light tower was retained. The forty acres were turned over to the state of Hawaii. On June 13, 1987, about fifteen members of a Hawaiian family and their supporters staged a land-ownership protest and moved into one of the houses. Land ownership is a continuing issue in the Hawaiian community, especially in regard to lands acquired by the federal government at the time of annexation of the Islands. The protesters occupied the Makapuʻu site for over a month before they were evicted. An editorial in the *Honolulu Star-Bulletin* commented on July 25, 1987:

> The confrontation at the Makapuu Point lighthouse fortunately ended without bloodshed, although there might have been. Several of the Hawaiian activists who had been squatting on state land were armed, and there was no advanced assurance that they would not offer

violent resistance. . . . But disputes over land occupancy must be settled in court. Whatever the merits of the family's claim, illegal occupation of the property was an unacceptable way to pursue it.

Soon after this incident the keepers' dwellings were razed by the state.

On their quarterly inspection tour, Aids to Navigation Team members Aaron Landrum and Glenn Aikin arrived at Makapu'u Light on July 18, 1988. Before going to the tower the men took the path up the hill that once led to the three keepers' homes. There was nothing left but rubble piled among the thorny kiawe shrubs. On the other side of the path, one thing was left intact that suggested the happy life once shared here—the round cement kiddies' pool the Coast Guardsmen built for their children. No trace of lawns or gardens remained. Large stands of prickly pear, pencil cactus, and night-blooming cereus covered the land.

The light tower, sitting boldly near the edge of the cliff, looked as it did in 1909. The tower and five thousand square feet of surrounding land had been listed on the National Register of Historic Places. The windward view from the tower extends along the mountains from Makapu'u Beach past Lanikai to Kāne'ohe Bay. Just offshore are four islets. It was off the largest one, Rabbit Island, that the *Manchuria* went aground, hastening the building of Makapu'u Lighthouse. The island of Moloka'i, about twenty-five miles to the east, is also visible.

The men worked on the main light from within the huge lens. According to Landrum, "Makapu'u's four-place lamp changer is the last one in use in any of the light stations. When this one goes, a DCB-224 will be installed, just like the one at Barbers Point." Each lamp is 1,000 watts, 120 volts, and if the primary lamp burns out, the next lamp automatically rotates into position. The light's characteristic is occulting ten seconds. The light is on for eight

Machinery Technician Aaron Landrum supervises Electrician's Mate Glenn Aikin as he checks the lamp inside the Makapu'u hyperradiant lens. The four-place lamp changer was the last one in use in Hawai'i; the giant hyperradiant lens is the only one in use in the United States. (Jeff Crawley, photojournalist, Fourteenth U.S. Coast Guard District)

seconds followed by a two-second eclipse. This signal is repeated continually. The light's range is nineteen nautical miles.[59]

When the day comes that the DCB-224 is installed, the magnificent lens will no longer be needed, but it will remain in place. In the future the historical lens and tower will be opened to the public on a limited basis for educational and recreational purposes under a licensing agreement between the U.S. Coast Guard and the Hawaii Maritime Center. The center is a private, nonprofit organization formed in 1984 when the Aloha Tower Maritime Center and the Friends of the *Falls of Clyde* merged. The center's offerings include the Aloha Tower; the Kalākaua Boat House, which is the center's shoreside museum on Pier 7; the museum ship *Falls of*

Clyde; the now world-famous voyaging canoe *Hōkū-le‘a;*[60] and the tuna clipper *Blue Fin.* Makapuʻu Lighthouse, representing another unique and important part of Hawaiian maritime tradition, is an invaluable addition to the center's destination out- ings. Lighthouse buffs and all who cherish the maritime heritage of Hawaiʻi and want to learn more about the past, present, and future of navigational aids in the Islands will want to travel the road to Makapuʻu.[61]

Chapter 5

KA'ENA POINT

AND OTHER LIGHTS

ALONG O'AHU'S SHORES

After the first lighthouse was established on O'ahu at Honolulu Harbor in 1869, there are no records of any other lighted navigational aids being built on the island until 1885, when the governor of O'ahu, J. O. Dominis, wrote out the "Rules and Regulations" for two lighted aids on northwestern O'ahu at Waialua.

> The outside of the light boxes are to be kept painted white, so as to be useful as day signals, (Note: They have been painted on the outside with red and green. This is a mistake and Mr. Cox will repaint them). The lights are always to be lighted at sunset of the evening before the expected arrival of the steamer, and also at any other time for any other vessels, if duly notified beforehand either by telephone or letter. The colored glasses are to be wiped with a clean dry cloth (one that is perfectly free of any grease) and the reflectors should be cleaned with chamois skin and a little French chalk or whitening (on no account must brick dust or knife polish be used). Care must be taken before attempting to light the lamps, to see that the glassware is dry and perfectly free from any spots of rain or water; otherwise the chimneys, upon heating, will break.[1]

The steamer *Waimanalo* left Honolulu for Waialua twice a week, calling at other landings along the way. The agent for the steamer requested the minister of the Interior Department to order the two lights to be lit on Mondays and Thursdays after sunset; "if the *Waimanalo* should not have arrived before such time, it would facilitate traffic and be a great convenience to passengers, who would thus avoid staying overnight on board the steamer."[2]

These lights must have been discontinued before 1902, as no mention is made of them in the Department of Public Works report on lighthouse expenses submitted to the U.S. Light House Board. The only lighthouses listed on O'ahu were Honolulu Harbor, Barbers Point, and Diamond Head. Recommendations for the establishment of other lights were made in 1903 by the board, including a lighthouse at Ka'ena Point.[3]

Ka'ena Point

Although a light was needed at Ka'ena Point to mark the extreme westernmost end of O'ahu, no action was taken until 1919 when the Bureau of Lighthouses decided to establish an unattended acetylene gas light somewhere on the point. The area was surveyed and a suitable site was found about 480 feet from the extreme tip of the point. Before construction of the tower began, 1,315 linear feet of light wooden track was laid from the main road to the lighthouse site to make it easier to bring in building materials and supplies across the sand. A sixty-five-foot white pyramidal tower built of reinforced concrete was completed in 1920 at a cost of $2,479.84. The automatic, flashing white, three-second light was visible for ten miles.[4]

In the 1930s when Frederick Edgecomb, superintendent of the lighthouse district, went to inspect the Ka'ena Point Lighthouse, he sometimes brought his family with him. Edgecomb's daughter Carol remembers those trips to the "rugged, isolated tip of Oahu with its solitary light tower." The trip was made by train.

> It was an all day excursion with a picnic lunch. After the train deposited us on the sand, we were totally alone with the small unimpressive light tower as the only evidence of civilization around us. There was no water to drink, no shelter of any kind, no trees, no shade or protection from the intense Hawaiian sun. There the ocean meets itself in a rush of waves coming from opposite directions. . . . I remember the violent, rugged beauty of that enchanting spot and then of coming home late, tired, thirsty, sunburned, but happy after our unique adventure under the sun.[5]

The literal translation of Ka'ena is "the heat."[6] The sun's light and heat radiate off the sand dunes along this western coast throughout the year. A short distance inland, steep cliffs rise abruptly from the flat coastal area. Along the coast low, rolling dunes are covered in some places with *naupaka,* a spreading, succulent shrub found on many coasts in Hawai'i. But Ka'ena Point is also the habitat of rare endemic plants, including an *'akoko, Chamaesyce celastroides* var. *kaenana.* These plants help to bind the soil, protecting it from wind erosion. Their destruction in recent years by motorcycles and other vehicles has caused the dunes to be blown seaward, with a great deal of sand lost in the ocean.[7] Deep tire

The Ka'ena Point Passing Light shown here was undermined by shifting sands and replaced in 1990 with a solar-powered light atop a pole. The Ka'ena complex, which includes the navigational aid, is on the National Register of Historic Places. (Electrician's Mate Glenn Aikin, Fourteenth U.S. Coast Guard District)

tracks crisscross the low sandy hill on which the concrete light tower stands. The surrounding vegetation is sparse, and in places the wind has blown the sand away from the lighthouse foundation, laying it bare.

The lighthouse itself is the victim of more vandalism than any other navigational aid in the Hawaiian Islands. The concrete tower constantly has to be repainted to cover graffiti. The light itself was extinguished eleven times between 1980 and 1985 because of vandalism. The lens has been smashed or damaged by gunfire. The batteries that power the light are repeatedly stolen.

Vandals and illegal vehicular traffic have also caused great damage to the surrounding light station property, which is in the center of a primary archaeological site. Archaeologists working in the area discovered an ancient fishing site, burial grounds, and eroding midden deposits that include bird bones, sea urchin spines, kukui nuts, marine shells, and charcoal. Two partial human skeletons were excavated by state park archaeologists in 1982, because the bones were being exposed by erosion and off-road-vehicle traffic.[8]

Ka'ena is significant for its legendary associations as well as archaeological prehistory. One of the most famous legends about the point locates it as the place where the demigod Māui stood when he attempted to unite Kaua'i and O'ahu by casting his magic fishhook out into the ocean, hoping to hook Kaua'i. His hook did take hold of the island, but when Māui gave a tug on the line, only a huge boulder fell at his feet. The boulder, called Pohaku o Kaua'i, lies offshore not far from the lighthouse.[9]

The land around the light, though trampled and despoiled, may still be recognized in the words from an ancient chant:

> Ka'ena, salty and barren,
> Now throbs with the blaze of the sun;
> The rocks are consumed by the heat,
> Dappled and changed in their color:
> The sand-holes sink, the coral forms heaps.[10]

Because of the archaeological and legendary significance of Ka'ena Point, as well as the rare endemic plants found in the area, the point and surrounding land, together known as the Ka'ena Complex, were placed on the official lists of both the State and National Registers of Historic Places in 1988.

The light became known as the Ka'ena Point Passing Light when a new lighted aid was installed atop the Ka'ena Point Tracking Station in 1987. The original light was retained to aid interisland traffic passing the westernmost point of O'ahu. The new light was established because the navy requested the Coast Guard to increase the range of the Ka'ena Point Light from eight miles to fifteen miles as a navigational aid for their submarines. The tracking station, high on the cliffs behind the point, was chosen as the site for the needed new light because commercial power was available and the light would be protected from vandalism. Two DCB-24 optics weighing a total of 470 pounds were mounted on an unused radar pedestal on the top of the building. This optic became the new Ka'ena Point Light.[11]

Ka'ena Point Passing Light's characteristic was changed from a white flashing 3-second light to a 2.5-second white flashing light, which can be seen seven miles. The Ka'ena Point Light on the tracking station building is 931 feet above sea level. Its flashing white 10-second light has a range of twenty-five miles, and is one of the primary seacoast lights on O'ahu.[12]

Pearl Harbor

Other navigational lights have also been established on O'ahu through the years. In 1887 the Reciprocity Treaty between Hawai'i and the United States included an agreement that the United States was to have exclusive rights to enter the harbor of "Pearl River," just west of Honolulu Harbor, and to establish and maintain a coaling and repair station there for the use of vessels of the United States.[13]

Although the United States acquired treaty rights to Pearl Harbor, nothing was done at the time to improve the channel or the harbor, and it remained much as it had always been—an oval inland lake, six by three miles, lying east to west. An island and peninsulas divided the lake into "lochs." The lake was separated from the ocean by low-lying coral land about two and a half miles wide, rimmed by a coral reef. A passage, about one-third of a mile wide, curved through the four miles from ocean to lake. The entrance to the passage was obstructed by a bar, and borings were taken in 1895 to find out if the area could be dredged. It was determined that the bar was not coral, but sand over coral rubble, and that it would be possible to deepen the channel; however, because the United States was not using Pearl Harbor at the time, dredging was unnecessary and navigational aids were not needed.[14]

It was not until 1902 that dredging was again considered and the United States government began proceedings for the condemnation of lands necessary for the establishment of a naval station and army post at Pearl Harbor. To facilitate navigation, the Public Works Department of the Territory of Hawaii began deepening the entrance channel and constructed two sets of range lights in 1903.[15]

In 1909 the Light House Board requested an appropriation of $80,000 for beacons and buoys for Pearl Harbor, explaining that it was essential to mark the harbor's entrance and entrance channel, "on account of the set of the current, which is across the channel . . . and the prevailing northeasterly winds." The appropriation was not made; instead, the Army Corps of Engineers was responsible for the work done at Pearl Harbor. In February 1910, Major E. Eveleth Winslow, district engineer, reported that a forty-five-foot lighthouse and keeper's dwelling had been completed at the entrance of Pearl Harbor. The cost for this light station was $40,000.[16]

No further improvements were made in the harbor's beacons until after 1917, when Congress appropriated the $80,000 first requested in 1909. The project called for marking the entrance channel with steel towers supported by reinforced concrete piers or piles erected in the water near the channel's edge. All the bids received were higher than the amount of money appropriated and had to be rejected. In 1919 a revised system was suggested by the navy that included electric lights on towers at the outer reaches of the channel, and seventeen acetylene gas lighted buoys and eleven unlighted buoys marking the sides of channel. Since the time these aids were established in 1920, periodical improvements and addi-

The former beacon at Hospital Point, Pearl Harbor, was one of the few concrete, boxlike structures erected in Hawai'i. (Aids to Navigation, Fourteenth U.S. Coast Guard District)

tions have been made to the lights marking Pearl Harbor entrance, the entrances into the west, east, and southeast lochs, and the channels in the harbor. By the 1980s there were twenty-four lighted beacons in Pearl Harbor.[17]

Kāne'ohe Bay

Another area that has been dredged and marked with navigational aids is Kāne'ohe Bay on the east side of O'ahu. This is the largest estuary in the Islands. The mouth of the bay extends over 4.6 miles from Kualoa Point on the northwest to Mō-kapu Peninsula on the southeast. The greatest extent inland is 3 miles. Before channels were dredged, the bay was quite shallow, with numerous islets, living coral reefs, and sand shoals.[18]

In pre-contact times the Kāne'ohe area was the

most populated part of the island. The ancient Kāne'ohe *ahupua'a* (land division)[19] was the property Kamehameha I retained for himself in 1795 when he conquered O'ahu. Mōkapu Peninsula was called Mokukapu (sacred district) because Kamehameha I met there with his chiefs. Kualoa Point, on the other side of the opening to the bay, was a *pu'uhonua* (place of refuge). It is said that when a chief was at Kualoa, masts were lowered on all passing canoes as a gesture to the chief's sacredness.[20]

At least twelve heiau existed in the Kāne'ohe area, two going back to the beginning of the twelfth century. The lands around the bay were once among the most productive on O'ahu, and the waters of the bay provided ample supplies of fish from the bay itself and from the many fishponds made by the Hawaiians along its shore.

The bay is still used for fishing and for recreational purposes, but there have been many changes as a result of dredging. The most extensive dredging activities began in 1939. In 1941 the Pyramid Rock Light was built on the northwestern point of Mōkapu Peninsula, which was southeast of the deepened Sampan Channel leading into the bay. Range lights, needed to mark the channel, were first erected in 1943.[21]

Dredging operations continued through the 1950s, and some of the spoils were used to fill some of the ancient Hawaiian fishponds for modern housing subdivisions. The front range light for Sampan Channel was erected on top of the remaining section of a rock wall built to enclose a pond. The light, mounted on a concrete pole, displays a quick-flashing red light thirty-eight feet above the water. The rear range light is located in the backyard of a private residence. It is a pyramidal skeleton tower that places the fixed red light eighty feet above sea level.[22]

Working with the ANT team, Ralph Craig has been servicing the Sampan range lights for many years. "When I first started going to the range lights, the area used to be just brush; now condominiums are being built there and we can drive instead of hike to the trail that leads to the front range light. The trail runs along the rim of one of the walls of an ancient fishpond that is now owned and maintained by Bishop Estate. It is about a quarter of a mile long. The width of the wall varies from about two to five feet. The front range is built on one of the wider sections. There are a few bad spots in the walls where the sea rushes in, but most of the walls enclosing the pond are in fairly good shape."[23]

There is nothing aesthetic or romantic about the Sampan front range light. It is as simple as the first lighted aid established on the Islands—a light attached to a pole. Yet to see this modern aid on the ancient rock wall evokes a sense of the history of human activity in Kāne'ohe Bay.

PART II

Lighthouses of Maui County

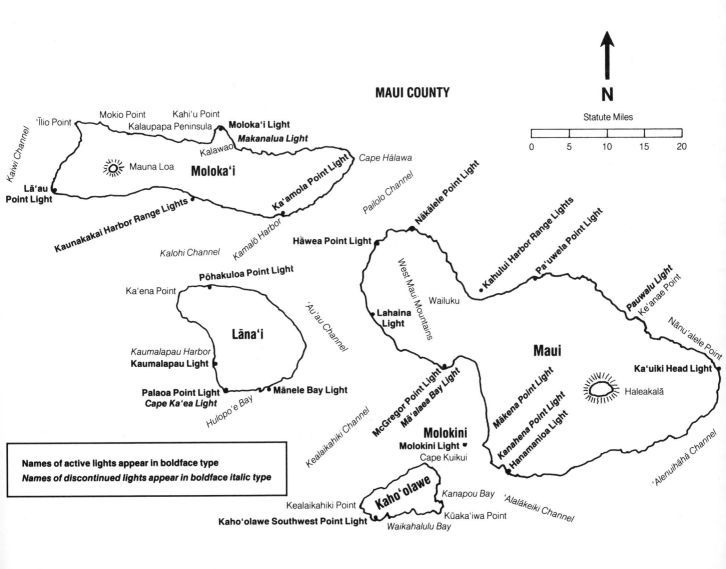

MAUI COUNTY

N

Statute Miles

0   5   10   15   20

'Īlio Point

Mokio Point

Kahi'u Point

Kalaupapa Peninsula

Moloka'i Light

Makanalua Light

Kalawao

Mauna Loa

Moloka'i

Cape Hālawa

Ka'amola Point Light

Pailolo Channel

Nākālele Point Light

Lā'au Point Light

Kaunakakai Harbor Range Lights

Kamalō Harbor

Hāwea Point Light

Kalohi Channel

West Maui Mountains

Kahului Harbor Range Lights

Pa'uwela Point Light

Pauwalu Light

Ke'anae Point

Nānu'alele Point

Pōhakuloa Point Light

Ka'ena Point

Wailuku

Lāna'i

'Au'au Channel

Lahaina Light

Maui

Ka'uiki Head Light

Kaumalapau Harbor

Kaumalapau Light

Haleakalā

Palaoa Point Light

Cape Ka'ea Light

Mānele Bay Light

Hulopo'e Bay

McGregor Point Light

Mā'alaea Bay Light

Mākena Point Light

Kanahena Point Light

Hanamanioa Light

Kealaikahiki Channel

Molokini

Molokini Light

Cape Kuikui

Kealaikahiki Point

Kaho'olawe

Kanapou Bay

'Alalākeiki Channel

'Alenuihāhā Channel

Kaho'olawe Southwest Point Light

Kūaka'iwa Point

Waikahalulu Bay

Names of active lights appear in boldface type
Names of discontinued lights appear in boldface italic type

Chapter 6

MAUI

Lahaina

In the early 1800s Hawaiians sang "of forest trees on the unresting sea."[1] The "trees" were the tall masts of ships that arrived in ever-increasing numbers each year at Honolulu Harbor and Lahaina Roadstead. The island of Maui offered no deep, protected harbor such as Honolulu's; however, on the western shore of the island off the village of Lahaina, ships found shelter from the strong trade winds. F. D. Bennett, in recording his whaling voyage experiences in the 1830s, described the anchorage as

> an extensive and usually tranquil sheet of water. Two projecting points of land give it some title to the name of a bay, but it can be regarded as little better than a roadstead. It is exposed to westerly gales, that blow dead on the land, and the anchoring it affords is rocky and treacherous. A barrier reef (limited to this point of the coast) is raised at a short distance from the shore; but the single aperture it offers is not broader than will admit a boat, and the water it protects is shallow.[2]

On November 26, 1778, Captain James Cook sighted the island, but adverse winds and currents prevented a landing.[3] And so it was that Jean-Francois Galaup de La Pérouse in 1786 became the first European to set foot on Maui. Although La Pérouse's frigates, *Boussole* and *Astrolabe,* also encountered strong winds and currents off Maui, a precarious anchorage was found on the south coast of the island in what is now called La Pérouse Bay. After

going ashore and exchanging gifts with the villagers, La Pérouse sailed west by northwest from this bay and dropped anchor off Lahaina on May 28, 1786.[4]

Russian, English, and American mariners engaged in exploration and the fur trade with China began to hear about the roadstead and to use Lahaina as a provisioning port. With favorable winds, ships could arrive or leave the anchorage at any time. No permanent navigational aids marked the area, but beacon fires were sometimes lit at night. Captain George Vancouver, with two vessels under his command, the *Discovery* and the *Chatham,* arrived off Maui in March 1793. The ships' first anchorage at night was off what Vancouver described as, "the low isthmus that unites the two lofty bodies of land which compose the island." The next day a chief named "Tomohomoho" came aboard with orders to conduct Vancouver's vessels to the more protected anchorage at Lahaina. Tomohomoho recommended that the ships should get under way immediately in order to arrive before dark, but in the event of any delay, he told Vancouver that directions had been given for fires to be lit, which would guide the ships to Lahaina.[5]

The protected anchorage, a plentiful supply of food, and the availability of fresh drinking water helped make Lahaina a favored stopover for mariners. As the Pacific whaling industry increased, so did Lahaina's popularity. It became a fall and spring destination for refitting and reprovisioning.[6] Because of the increasing number of vessels using

Lahaina, there was a great need for a permanent light to mark the roadstead at night.

In 1840 the first lighted navigational aid in the Hawaiian Islands was built on the waterfront of a section of Lahaina known as Keawaiki, which means literally "the small passage."[7] The name refers to a narrow break through a coral reef that lies about 850 feet from shore. In times of southerly gales, waves break along the entire stretch, making the entrance extremely dangerous. Many seamen lost their lives in attempting to go through the small passage at such times.[8]

The only extant description of the Keawaiki Light written at the time it was established is found in a letter dated November 14, 1840, from Jonah Kapena, Lahaina, to Paulo Kanoa, Honolulu. The correspondence, translated from Hawaiian, describes the light as a "tall looking box-like structure, 9 feet high . . . built on a suitable position facing the landing." Its placement was such that the Lahaina landing might be visible

> to those vessels, boats, and canoes that may come in port at nights, because there are quite a number of boats wrecked by the waves. . . . Therefore was this lighthouse erected with two lights projecting one above the other and having two glass windows on the eastern and two on the southern sides, in a position facing the landing. Two openings on the western and two on the northern sides were doors with real wooden enclosures where the lights are inserted to their positions. On the fourth day of November 1840 the light was turned on, and it is burning every night. . . . The salary that will be paid to the keeper of this lighthouse is $20 a year.[9]

By 1846 Lahaina was reaching its peak of activity as a whaling port. Four hundred twenty-nine whaleships used the roadstead that year, while 146 anchored in Honolulu Harbor.[10] In the village there were dozens of European-style stone and wooden buildings, as well as native-style grass houses.[11] As a child, Harriet Baldwin Damon lived on the main street, where there were Chinese stores and a doctor's office. She often visited the waterfront where small boats brought in passengers and cargo. She wrote:

> In landing at Lahaina when the tide was high, passengers could clamber up and down the coral steps, but when the tide was low with the bow of the boats dipped into sand, all passengers young and old, heavy and light, women and children, coming or going were lifted by the native boatmen and carried through the water. . . . From the landing . . . across the main street was a hand pump, and during the season sailors were rolling constantly huge casks for water and steadily on for weeks that hand pump worked night and day.[12]

There was also a canal from which water could be drawn. A fee of $3 for water was collected along with other harbor dues paid by vessels using the roadstead. The anchorage and pilotage fee was $10; clearance fee, $1; and $1 was charged for the lighthouse. In the second six months of 1846 the government collected $2,110 in anchorage dues, $414 for water, and $210 in light fees.[13]

The establishment of a lighted beacon contributed to Lahaina's popularity with mariners, but as the town grew, the navigational light became almost indistinguishable from the other lights showing at night from the buildings on land. The first improvement in navigational aids for Lahaina may have been provided, not by the government, but by an individual, Edouard Duvauchelle.[14] Duvauchelle had good reason to want mariners to find their way ashore, for he owned a unique establishment on the main street, the Union Hotel, which functioned as a hotel, a saloon, a restaurant, a butcher shop, and—a lighthouse. The light he installed on the Union Hotel served the harbor until 1856 when the government, recognizing its responsibility, installed two powerful locomotive lamps by the Custom House.

Even though the lights burned only until twelve or one o'clock at night, they proved to be a great help to ships coming into the roadstead.[15]

The government also must have given some consideration to erecting a new lighthouse. The *Pacific Commercial Advertiser* commented on January 20, 1859, "By the by, what has become of that plan of putting up a lighthouse at Lahaina, about which we heard so much some months ago?"

Because of missing Department of Interior Public Works records before 1860, it is difficult to know just when a second lighthouse was built to replace the original nine-foot boxlike tower.[16] The structure was in deplorable condition when P. H. Treadway, sheriff of Lahaina, inspected it in 1865. He had been asked by F. W. Hutchinson, minister of the Interior, to repair the foundation.

Some idea of what the lighthouse looked like is given in Treadway's description of the building's condition. On examination he discovered that the foundation was constructed

> of a course of coral without any mortar, built out from the bank 30 feet into the sea, 10 feet high on the *makai* [ocean] side; the inside of these dry walls was filled in with small hard stone. . . . The building itself was an old slightly framed house, the principal supports . . . sills and studs were decayed, and when I proceeded with great care to raise the building to its original level, the foundation crumbled away. . . . The whole was in such a state that during a storm the entire establishment might fall to pieces, destroying the light (worth from four to five hundred dollars) and endangering vessels. . . . I did nothing to the building but secured it as well as could be done.[17]

In making suggestions for a new structure to replace the deteriorating one, the sheriff proposed alternative types of lighthouses; the first was a "storehouse of 20-feet width and 40-feet length and 10-feet high, strongly framed so as to support a light tower above the roof." Treadway estimated that the cost of the building would be $1,250. His second suggestion, to cost about $700, was for a tower tall enough to place the lights twenty-five to thirty feet above the upper bank. Treadway wanted the building to be substantially built, secured and braced by iron work and iron rigging.

In January 1866 the sheriff again wrote Hutchinson, "The late storm has knocked the whole center of the Lighthouse foundation out on the side . . . immediately fronting the sea. I shall have it laid up again as soon as I can get a man to do it."

The repaired lighthouse continued in operation, but plans were now under way to replace it with a light tower built above a storehouse, as Treadway had suggested. Final plans were sent to Honolulu, and lumber and other building materials were shipped to Lahaina aboard the *Kate Lee*.[18]

By October, Treadway was pleased with the progress made and reported, "The Light House will be quite a building and add to the appearance of the place near the landing when all is done." However, there were some problems: "We are in want of the stained glass now for our lighthouse window and the other material which I wrote you for. . . . If we have no drawback it will soon be done and will be a good light house at that."

The glass arrived, all of it broken, which must have been a great disappointment. The sheriff reported that "the stained is poor glass and badly warped and nothing was put between the layers . . . but the two pieces of green will be made to answer." Treadway also pointed out that at the "present prices of oil the appropriation will not pay the Keeper and pay for the oil if. . . . Sperm oil is used, but with Kerosene it will be ample."

Treadway was dedicated to completing the new lighthouse, no matter what the frustrations. When the wrong-size burners arrived and he was unable to find wicks for them, he borrowed lamps until he could put the new kerosene ones into operation.

Treadway wrote, "The lower part of the light house is ready to be occupied as a store house . . . and I expect to try the lights tomorrow night. The house looks very well both from seaward and shoreward."

The next day he managed to locate some proper-sized wicks and that night went out by boat to view the new lighthouse in operation. "I have just returned from a boat excursion. . . . The New Lights will be first rate if the burner does not burn out of oil too fast, for it will never do to have the lamp refilled in the night, an explosion would be sure sooner or later. . . . The lights are a decided improvement."[19]

The official announcement of the operation of the lighthouse was given on November 8, 1866.

> The old Light House at this port has been pulled down, and a new one erected on the old site, somewhat enlarged. The old house was 19 feet by 25 feet, the new one is 25 feet by 30 feet, and a light tower built on top, containing a light room and a sleeping room for the light-keeper. The lamps are altered to burn kerosene oil, instead of whale oil. A window has been made on the sea side of the light room, of 20 by 24 inch glass with green glass at the N.W. and S.E. ends. The colored glass stands at equal angles, side and front, and a vessel in two fathoms of water, will have two bright lights for about a half a mile each way, from directly in front of the Light House. At a greater distance it will show a colored light until both lights almost appear like one, or the green light like a reflection from the other light. The light towards Molokai is the brightest, so the lights now have the appearance of a large and small light close together. It will not be easy to mistake the lights when a person has seen them. . . . The lights stand about 26 feet above the water, and ought to be seen across the Lanai channel.[20]

The storehouse under the Lahaina Light was leased for twelve months at $96 to James Campbell and Harry Turton, the owners of a sugar plantation.[21] Sugar was becoming the dominant force in the Hawaiian economy. There were twelve sugar plantations in the Islands and four of them were on Maui.

While sugar production increased steadily, the number of whaling vessels, and free-spending whalers, using the Lahaina roadstead decreased. The town, according to a newspaper report in 1864, had a gloomy look, "even that which surrounds City Hall, the pride of the second city of Hawaii, is so dilapidated as to be a disgrace to the town if not the government."[22]

Treadwell kept trying to maintain the new lighthouse/storehouse. Red glass was substituted for the unwanted green in the light tower, and the storehouse was enlarged and repaired. Hutchinson reported in 1868 that the work was planned and supervised by Treadway, "to whom the department consider themselves much indebted for this and other assistance . . . a satisfactory light is now shown at that port . . . observable at a distance of 6 miles . . . building improved and enlarged and rented for $96 per annum. . . . Amount expended $432.44." Treadwell also improved the wharf "in a thoroughly substantial manner. It has proved itself a great accommodation and advantage to the commerce of that port, as well as a great convenience to passengers."[23]

Storms continued to take their toll, and eight months later the wharf and light were again in need of repair. The *Pacific Commercial Advertiser,* on December 12, 1868, quoted a "returning absentee" who described the "old familiar beacon light on the crumbling wharf" at Lahaina as being nearly extinguished "for want of oil."

The lighthouse often lacked for kerosene and repairs, but it never lacked for storehouse lessees. Treadway's idea to make the building commercially profitable for the government made the Lahaina Lighthouse unique. Each year he posted notices that the storeroom was for lease, and each year the lease was signed by Campbell and Turton until 1871, when

Colonel Z. S. Spalding and the West Maui Sugar Association secured the lease.[24]

In 1879 Thomas C. Forsyth suggested to Samuel G. Wilder, minister of the Interior, that rather than trying to repair the storeroom and the light tower, the structure should be torn down.

> The studding in the present building is good for nothing. It was old native lumber at the time the house was built and is all eaten up with ants and worms, and the shingles are rotten and worm eaten as well as the Battens on the roof . . . it would be better to build a new House and use what there is of the lumber in the old one on that than trying to repair the present Building, and that is my opinion of the matter.[25]

The building was extensively rebuilt, and then a December storm badly damaged the foundation. Repairs were made almost annually, but nothing was done to change the structure. In describing the Lahaina Light the *Hawaiian Annual,* from 1880 through 1891, repeats Treadway's 1866 description word for word; only the color of the glass varied. During one period both red and green glass were used. On one chart of Lahaina Roads the position of the lighthouse is shown with lines extending out from the colored lights indicating the extent and angle of their range. On one line is written, "Shows green north of this line," and on the other, "Shows red east of this line."[26] As a vessel approached the roadstead with a heading taken on the white light, the red would be kept on the vessel's starboard side and the green on the port side—even in those days the rule was "Red Right Return."

In 1893 the Hawaiian monarchy was overthrown. From Lahaina, Captain David Taylor wrote to James A. King, minister of the Interior:

> The present Keeper of the Lahaina Light House has refused to take the oath to support the Provisional Government should there be a change. I would like to have charge of the light, as I have now the charge of the wharf and am Harbor Master. I have had to look after the Lights very often lately myself, as the Keeper has been very careless in keeping the lights in proper trim.

Within two weeks Taylor was appointed keeper and wrote King: "Kukaia, the Light House Keeper, has delivered to me all the oil and other articles belonging to the Lahaina Light House. He claims that he has not received his salary for eight months. Enclosed you will find his vouchers for the same."[27]

During the political transitions from provisional government to a republic and the anticipation of annexation of Hawai'i to the United States, lighthouse communication and supply systems between Honolulu and Lahaina were unpredictable. Almost every month Taylor requested supplies of kerosene for the light: "I am completely out and had to buy a tin"; "Please send five cases of Kerosene oil. I had to borrow some oil lately for the lights and will have to return it." Whether it was because of the frustrations of trying to keep the lighthouse functioning under these conditions or for other reasons, Taylor resigned as keeper. His successor, George H. Dunne, facing the same situation, wrote, "Will you please send by return Steamer 5 cases of Kerosene Oil for the Lahaina Lighthouse."[28]

Dunne supplemented his eight-dollars-a-month salary as keeper by working as a notary public. This was one of the lowest keeper's salaries in the Islands. Dunne remained the keeper of the Lahaina Light during annexation and through the time that the U.S. Light House Board assumed the responsibility for the Hawaiian navigational aids.[29]

In the 1904 Light House Board report, the Lahaina Light was described as: "a fixed white light composed of two ordinary kitchen lamps of small power, with red and green sectors, estimated to be 20 feet above high water. The lights are shown from a white wooden pyramidal tower built on top of a wooden

Lahaina's lighthouses in 1906. The lighthouse on the left, completed in 1866, was the only one in the Islands with the light built above a storehouse. The government-owned property was leased by sugar companies on a yearly basis. It was replaced by the newly completed lighthouse on the right. (*Pacific Commercial Advertiser* photo, reprinted with permission of the *Honolulu Advertiser*)

storehouse. It is difficult to distinguish the light from the lights in town."[30]

The Lahaina roadstead continued to be the most important shipping destination on Maui, and the Light House Board proposed erecting a completely new lighthouse on the wharf. In 1905 building began. The *Maui News* on May 13, 1905, reported, "A splendid lens for the lantern was imported from Paris." The lens would replace the two ordinary reflector lamps formerly used.

The *Hawaiian Gazette* applauded the new structure.

> The old light . . . was so low it was hard to distinguish the lamps from the other lights of the town. . . . The new light . . . stands way above any other light in town. The fenders on either side of the light indicate the changes from white to red. As long as a ship keeps in the white light she may safely come into the buoy to anchor, but should she be in the red light to one side or the other, she must keep off shore for fear of the reef. The board fenders simply help the red light to be distinguished sharply from the white as otherwise the two colors would blend and the line of safety would be harder to ascertain. These fenders . . . were tested after the erection of the lighthouse. Captain Niblack went out and carefully sounded the entire section covered by the white light and in so doing found a shoal not before charted which required a reduction in the size of the white segment of the light.[31]

The wooden pyramidal skeleton tower was fifty-five feet tall, raising the focal plane of the light to sixty feet above high water. Just below the lens platform on the top of the tower was an enclosed workroom where the keeper could tend the lamp. The entire structure was painted white with lead-colored trimmings.[32]

The Lahaina Light served the roadstead well for the next ten years, but plans were underway to automate as many of the lighthouses in the islands as possible. The old light tower on the wharf continued

The thirty-nine-foot Lahaina Lighthouse is the tallest of eleven similarly designed concrete pyramidal beacons in the Islands. In the 1920s, when this photograph was taken, it was one of fifty-eight lighted aids in Hawai'i. (Aids to Navigation, Fourteenth U.S. Coast Guard District)

operating while a new reinforced concrete tower was being constructed on a land site near the shore. By 1917 the forty-foot concrete tower housing an automatic acetylene light was completed. The new tower was pyramidal in shape. A door at the base opened into the hollow lower section that served as a storeroom. A metal ladder on the outside led to a platform from which the light could be serviced. This type of concrete structure for supporting a light was beginning to be used throughout all the islands with variations in height and width. It was economical to build, withstood the elements well, and was easy to maintain. The light shown from the Lahaina tower was forty-four feet above high water, and the fixed red light could be seen seven miles at sea.[33]

Acetylene was the illuminant for the Lahaina Light until 1937, when electricity was brought in from the Lahaina Ice Company line. To turn the light on and off, a photoelectric cell was placed in the north window in the base of the concrete tower. A two-lamp changer was installed so that if one lamp burned out the other automatically revolved into place. There was also a battery-operated backup system that switched on in case of an electrical outage. The characteristic was a red flashing three-second light visible twelve miles at sea.[34]

The Lahaina Light, which today flashes red every 7.5 seconds, stands at the edge of the harbor in Lahaina's Historic District. A plaque on the lighthouse reads, "On this site in 1840 King Kamehameha ordered a nine foot wooden tower built as an aid to navigation for the whaling ships anchored off Lahaina." There are as many, if not more, pleasure boats at the roadstead today as there were whaling ships at the height of Lahaina's popularity in the 1860s. The establishment of a navigational light at the roadstead played a vital part in Maui's history and in the further development of lighthouses throughout the Hawaiian Islands.

Kanahena Point, Mākena, and Hanamanioa

In 1884 the Hawaiian government established another lighted beacon on Maui in addition to the one at Lahaina. It was located approximately twenty-three miles southeast of Lahaina near the southern tip of the island on Kanahena Point.[35] The Kanahena Point light marked a broad, low, lava point that projected seaward on the north side of La Pérouse Bay. The entire southwestern tip of Maui at Cape Hanamanioa is black lava, and a current sets strongly around the cape in a northwesterly direction.

The keeper assigned to the Kanahena light was J. Andersen. A keeper's house had not been built on the barren lava point, and Andersen and his family lived three miles northwest of the light in the village of Mākena.[36]

In 1886 a private beacon was erected at Mākena by Wilder's Steamship Company. The light marked an anchorage that offered good holding ground in twelve to fifteen fathoms of water. Mākena had been growing in importance since 1878 when Makee Sugar Company opened a mill there. Interisland vessels transporting sugar, freight, and passengers used the anchorage. When the light was established, Wilder's Steamship Company was in charge of maintaining and supplying the light, with the government paying for the supplies and fifteen dollars a month to the lightkeeper.[37]

Considerable confusion, especially for the Department of the Interior in Honolulu, was caused by the fact that there was a keeper living in Mākena who was in charge of the Mākena Point Light, and another keeper living in Mākena who was in charge of the Kanahena Point Light. On March 24, 1888, P. W. Simeona wrote to the Department of the Interior asking to be the keeper of the Kanahena Lighthouse at a salary of $400 a year. He complained, "There have been two nights when the lights were not lit. That foreigner [the lightkeeper] also sells pigs." Two weeks later Simeona again wrote to the department: "Your reply with regard to the lamp at Makena was received. That is a different lamp. That is right at the harbor of Makena. This lamp that I have reference to is right at Kanahena. . . . Makena is quite a distance from Kanahena . . . [Makena] is where Kukahiko . . . is taking care of the lamp. . . . This lamp which is located at Kanahena is the one which this foreigner is not looking after properly."[38]

Simeona did not get the job. Andersen remained keeper, and the "pig selling" business he was engaged in was explained several years later. In requesting a raise after twelve years of service, Andersen said that he had "by the raising of hogs and some other minor industries been enabled to live and support his family" on the pay of twenty dollars a month. He explained that

> owing to the overwhelming growth of Lantana, the raising of hogs is now impossible, and pasture for the horses used . . . in attending to the lighthouse has to be paid for at Ulupala Kua Ranch. The light house is situated on a lava flow some three miles from any available site for a house and necessitates that much of a journey in attending to the light. Wherefore I would respectfully Petition that the pay as Light House Keeper be raised to $30 per month.[39]

But in vain—he was still receiving twenty dollars a month six years later, and confusion still remained between the Mākena and Kanahena Point lights. Andersen is listed as the keeper at Mākena in the 1902 report of the Hawaii Department of Public Works, and the light at Kanahena Point is not even mentioned.[40]

In the 1904 report of the Light House Board, the Kanahene Point light was described as a fixed white light

composed of two orginary kitchen lamps, estimated to be 50 feet above high water. The light is shown from a pyramidal room built at the top of a square wooden trestle tower 40 feet high. The trestle is in bad condition. The light marks a low lava spit projecting into the sea. It was erected because of wrecks at this point. There is no dwelling for the keeper at this light-house. The keeper lives 3 miles away and is compelled to cross the rough trail over the lava flow.[41]

In 1905 the Board reported that the trestle tower was replaced with a thirty-four-foot mast. A platform for a "lens lantern" was constructed on top of the mast. The lens lantern was a glass prismatic lens cover that enclosed the lamp and focused the light's rays into a horizontal beam. The focal plane of the light remained at fifty feet above sea level, and the fixed white light was visible at night for a distance of ten miles. A service house was built at the base of the mast. It was given a red roof, and the house was painted white with lead-colored trim. A house for the keeper was not built, and Andersen and his family continued to live at Mākena.[42]

Andersen remained keeper of the Kanahena Point Light until his death in 1910. After her husband's death, Mrs. Andersen became keeper, and made the six-mile round trip each evening and morning until Charles K. Akana was appointed keeper in 1911. Available records seem to indicate that Mrs. Andersen was the only woman to serve officially as lightkeeper in the Islands.

The confusion between the Mākena Point Light and the Kanahena Point Light was finally resolved when both were taken out of service in 1918 and the Hanamanioa light established in their place. Here, an acetylene illuminated light was used with a lens lantern. A tapering four-sided reinforced concrete tower, similar to the one at Lahaina, was built to house light and lantern. The focal plane of the light, visible for ten miles, was seventy-three feet above the water. The signal was a "group flashing white ten-second light," meaning one second of white light was shown, then two seconds of eclipse, followed by one second of light and six seconds of darkness.[43]

The site chosen for the lighthouse is about five miles southeast of Mākena. The light marked Cape Hanamanioa on the southwest coast, one of the most inaccessible areas on Maui's shoreline. This bleak, lava-bound cape is the southeast point of La Pérouse Bay. Because it was impossible to reach this light by land with a vehicle, a wooden derrick was installed at the landing to facilitate the handling of acetylene tanks and lighthouse maintenance supplies.[44]

Mā'alaea Bay and McGregor Point

Many of the lighted beacons in the Islands in the 1880s were erected and maintained by Wilder's Steamship Company for the benefit of its own vessels. The beacon at Mā'alaea Bay was one of these private aids. The light was nothing more than an ordinary lantern hung from a post. The glass used in the lantern was red, to make the light distinguishable from the plantation lights on shore. When the Light House Board assumed responsibility for many of the private aids in 1904, the Mā'alaea Bay Light was replaced with a lens lantern that also showed a fixed red light. The lantern was suspended from a twelve-foot post erected on the westerly corner of the wharf landing. A year later the light was discontinued and a new beacon was built on the southwestern point of Mā'alaea Bay at McGregor Point, where one and a third acres of land had been acquired in 1903 by presidential proclamation.[45]

The point was named for Captain Daniel McGregor, who ran interisland ships engaged in what was called the Ko'olau trade, meaning trade with the windward side of the Islands. (It is likely that this is the same Captain McGregor who was the first keeper of the Honolulu Harbor lighthouse in 1869, and who resigned in 1871 when he was given command of the *Kilauea*.) Captain McGregor's destination one stormy night was the Mā'alaea landing. As he neared the bay, he knew he would not be able to anchor his ship at the usual place, for it was too exposed. He stationed crewmen off bow, port, and starboard to take soundings continuously as the vessel proceeded slowly through the dark night and slashing rain. Unable to see and groping along, guided only by the depth of the water beneath the hull, Captain McGregor ordered anchors dropped when the wind seemed to let up and the depth grew ominously shallow. With first light, the captain and crew realized what an excellent small cove they had blindly found. Their ship was close to shore and protected by high sea cliffs. The point was soon called McGregor Point and it became a more popular landing than the one nearby in Mā'alaea Bay.[46]

When the McGregor Point Light was completed, the old Mā'alaea Light was discontinued. The new one showed a fixed red light eighty feet above the water. The lens lantern was mounted on the top of a thirty-two-foot white mast. A small storage house at the base of the mast was painted the usual white with lead-colored trim and had a red roof. A one-story keeper's dwelling was built about one-sixth of a mile northwestward of the light. It also had a red roof, but the building was painted a light green (this was unusual, for it was the custom to paint all buildings at light stations the same color).[47]

The McGregor Point Light, completed May 1, 1906, was built on a site about forty-eight feet above sea level. This height above the water saved the new light from severe damage during a storm in August 1906, when huge tsunami waves destroyed the wharf at Mā'alaea where the old light had stood.[48]

By 1915 the thirty-two-foot wooden mast at McGregor Point had been replaced by a new twenty-foot reinforced concrete pyramidal tower. The focal point of the new light was seventy-two feet above sea level. The light operated automatically with acetylene and flashed white for 0.5 second every 1.5 seconds.[49] The last keeper at McGregor Point was James L. Cornwell.

Nākālele Point

By the time the McGregor Point Light was established, the south and west coasts of Maui seemed to be sufficiently well lit for mariners, but there were no lights along the other coasts. In 1908 the Light House Board decided to erect a forty-foot wooden mast with a temporary light "on the most northerly point of the westerly part" of Maui, at Nākālele Point. By 1910 a keeper's house had been completed with an elevated boxlike platform on the roof for the light. A tall tower was not required because the site was over 150 feet above the water. The fixed white light could be seen nine miles at sea. John M. Hanuna served on the Nākālele Point Light from 1910 until 1915, when John K. Mahoe took his place. In 1917 Luther K. Kalama was assigned keeper and remained at the station until it was automated in 1922. At that time its characteristic was changed from white fixed to white flashing.[50]

Ka'uiki Head

The Nākālele Point Light marked the northwest coast, but there were still no beacons along the north or east shores of Maui. The Light House Board felt it was particularly important to place a lighted aid at Kapueokahi (now Hāna) Bay, near the town of Hāna, on the east coast of Maui. The bay was actively used by fishermen, and vessels engaged in interisland commerce anchored outside the bay, while passengers and cargo were carried by small boats to and from the landing.

Pounding surf often builds up across the shoals and rocky shoreline of the bay. It was a precarious anchorage, open on the east and exposed to northeast winds that fight against the current. The bay, less than half a mile wide, lies between Ka'uiki Head and Nānu'alele Point. It was somewhere in this vicinity that the Light House Board wanted to establish a lighted aid.

One possible site was Ka'uiki Head, an extinct crater almost four hundred feet high on the south side of the bay entrance. Ka'uiki Head appears to be an island, but a narrow strip of land connects it with the shore near Hāna. In Hawaiian legend the crater was the home of the demigod Māui.[51]

History as well as legend is rooted on Ka'uiki Head. It was here that an early Maui king, Hua a Pohukaina, built a heiau called Honua'ula, to gain the favor of the gods in his expedition against the warriors of the island of Hawai'i. Evidence of the Honua'ula heiau could still be seen in 1908, when surveys were made of the area to determine the location for a lighthouse. The site finally chosen was not on Ka'uiki Head itself, but on the tiny islet of Pu'uki'i off its northeastern shore. The Territory of Hawaii ceded the island to the United States for use as a lighthouse station. The steep, rocky islet contains about an acre and a half of land. The forty-foot wooden mast built to support the light was located near the crest, placing the focal plane of the light ninety feet above the water. The characteristic of the light was fixed red. A small, one-story keeper's house was also built at the station.[52]

In 1909 festivities were held at Hāna to celebrate the completion of the new beacon. For some reason the light was officially named the Ka'uiki Head Light even though it was built on the islet of Pu'uki'i. An old hula dedicated to Ka'uiki was performed and rededicated to the new lighthouse.

He aloha no Ka'uili la
Auana i ke kai la meha manu ala

The Kaʻuiki Head Light Station was completed in 1909 on the islet of Puʻukiʻi. After the light was automated in 1914, the keeper's house was moved and is now part of a private residence near the Hāna Cultural Center. (National Archives)

> Beloved is Kaʻuiki
> Stretching out in the sea like a rising bird.[53]

Manuel Ferreira was in charge of the lighthouse. Ferreira was born in Hāna in 1885, and being keeper of the Kaʻuiki Head Light was his first job. Each evening before sunset he prepared the kerosene lamp for lighting. The lamp was attached to a carriage table top, and after the lamp was lit the entire unit was hoisted to the masthead. The light could be seen eight miles at sea, marking Kapueokahi Bay and warning mariners of the shoals and jagged rocks along the coastline.[54]

Behind the rugged seascape, lush tropical vegetation flourished. The wooden light mast didn't last long in that wet and rainy environment, and in a few years it had to be replaced. The Light House Board decided to automate the light. In 1914 a fourteen-foot pyramidal reinforced concrete tower was built. Acetylene replaced kerosene and a dioptric lens replaced the reflector. The characteristic was changed from fixed red to a two-second flashing white light, and the light's visible distance was increased to ten miles.[55]

Hāwea Point

The difficulties and expenses of maintaining manned lighthouses at a time when acetylene and electricity made possible the use of automatic lights prompted the Lighthouse Service to reevaluate all manned stations in the Islands. When new lights were needed in remote areas where electricity was not available, acetylene was used. The Hāwea Point Light, north of Lahaina, was one of the acetylene lens lantern lights established in the Hawaiian Islands between 1911 and 1912.

The site chosen for the light was in a remote area five miles north of Keka'a point. Ten acres were acquired for the light station by condemnation in 1911 and a sixteen-foot white pyramidal skeleton tower was erected to support an acetylene lantern. The focal plane of the Hāwea Point Light was seventy-five feet above sea level, and its characteristic was a one-second white flash every five seconds, distinguishing it from the Lahaina Light, which at the time showed two fixed lights, one white and the other red. The Hāwea Light flashed continuously, and at night it could be seen at a distance of ten miles.[56]

Kahului Harbor

By 1905 lighted beacons had been established along Maui's south, east, and west coasts, but there were no navigational aids on the north coast, and the Light House Board was particularly concerned about building some type of beacon to aid vessels using Kahului Harbor. Before annexation, the Hawaiian government had made various studies and considered several proposals regarding the type of navigational aids that should be established in the harbor.

The shallow harbor had been used by whaling ships and was known for many years as "Lyra Bay" after the American whaler *Lyra,* which struck the reef there in 1830 and was a total loss. By 1879, when vessels transporting sugar replaced the whalers, a landing was built to facilitate shipment of sugar, and navigational buoys were set out to mark the harbor entrance.[57]

In 1889, as use of the harbor increased, Lorrin A. Thurston, minister of the Interior, requested information about "replacing the lighthouse at Kahului." The wording of his letter seems to indicate that there was some type of lighted aid already in the harbor, but which Thurston felt was inadequate. He was informed that the steamship *Likelike* was leaving for Kahului and that when the captain, James A. King, returned he would offer suggestions regarding the location for a new light.[58]

Captain King proposed that a light should be placed on the most northern point of Maui about nine miles east of Kahului.[59] However, the owners and captains of the interisland steamers felt that the dangerous coral reef near the harbor needed marking more than the coastal approach to the harbor. The superintendent of Public Works, W. E. Rowell, suggested building the lighthouse directly on the reef close to the entrance of the harbor: "The coral will afford a good foundation. The depth of water on this reef hardly exceeds one fathom at high tide. A base of concrete with a stone tower will make a substantial structure and a light . . . with a visibility of ten miles will serve the purpose well."[60]

After considering the various suggestions, Thurston recommended that a stone tower be built on the reef near the entrance to the harbor. The light was to have a third-order Fresnel lens, and the height of the tower was to be such that the focal plane of the light would be forty feet above sea level.[61]

Rowell wrote to Chance Brothers and Company in England asking for their suggestions as to the type of lens to use at Kahului Harbor and inquiring whether lamps that burned unattended for eight days were available. The optical company replied:

> For Kahului Harbor either a third or fourth order light might be adopted. . . . With regard to the continuous burning of Kahului light . . . it is not practicable. . . . This could be done with gas, but even then we doubt the properties of trusting to it, unless the supply could be regulated and turned off and on from the shore. It is not advisable to leave a (gas) burner, or any oil burner, untended for more than 18 hours.[62]

Rowell received more encouraging information from the U.S. Light House Board. He was informed that "three, five, and eight day lanterns are made only in the shops of the Light House Establishment and at present they can be obtained no where else. The plans and specifications have not been published. So the Board proposes . . . to send you an eight-day lantern ready for use."[63]

All planning regarding the light came to a halt in 1900 because bubonic plague, carried by infected fleas and rats, broke out and spread through Kahului; the town was deliberately set afire and burned to the ground. If the town was to recover from this double disaster, commercial shipping had to be encouraged, and improvement of the harbor was essential to the rebuilding and growth of the town. At a congressional hearing in 1902, it was recommended that a lighthouse be established at Kahului at an estimated cost of $20,000.

> There is at present no light of any character on this coast of the island. . . . There is a dangerous coral reef close to the entrance of Kahului Harbor, where many vessels land, and the approach to the harbor at night is unsafe and dangerous. The only aid to commerce at this harbor at present is a single buoy, maintained . . . at the expense of the steamship companies. The plan for this new light house is to construct it with concrete, with a stone tower, with lens that would make the light visible 19 miles distant.[64]

No appropriations were requested by the Light House Board, however, until a study could be made of all the navigational aids on Maui. In the Board's 1905 report, two range lights at Kahului Harbor are described for the first time. These lights were erected and maintained by Wilder's Steamship Company. The main problem with the privately owned aids was that many vessels relied on them other than the steamers of the companies that controlled the lights; however, the lights were not shown every night, but only when the company's vessels were expected. The Light House Board recommended that beacon lights with lens lanterns be established in the place of the private aids and remain lit every night; in 1905 Wilder's Steamship Company's range lights were replaced.[65]

The increasing use of Kahului Harbor and its importance as a developing port encouraged the U.S. Congress to appropriate money for improving the harbor. It was dredged and a breakwater was constructed to protect the harbor from huge rollers that built up in periods of strong north winds and storms. In 1911 the breakwater was completed and an automatic acetylene light was placed on the east side of the harbor's entrance. This beacon was one of the first two such lights established in the Islands (the other, also built in 1911, was on the islet of Molokini). The Kahului Light was mounted on a red thirty-four-foot skeleton tower. It flashed on for 1.5 seconds every six seconds.[66]

By 1917 the breakwater had been extended and the docking area alongside the wharf had been dredged to a depth of twenty-four feet. In and out use of Kahului Harbor by commercial shipping increased from 74 steamers in 1904 to 170 steamers in 1915. A new Kahului beacon was erected twenty-five yards from the outer end of the breakwater on the east-side entrance of the harbor. The light was displayed from a thirty-two-foot pyramidal skeleton tower, painted black instead of red, but the light retained the same flashing white, 7.5-second characteristic. The breakwater light could be seen by vessels ten miles from the harbor.[67]

Pa'uwela Point and Pauwalu Point

In planning for a lighthouse on Maui's north coast, the Light House Board had first considered locating it on the coral reef near Kahului Harbor entrance, but it was finally decided that marking the coastal approach to Kahului Harbor was more important. The board proposed a lighthouse for the east side of the seaward approach to the harbor at Pa'uwela Point, the location suggested by Captain James King twenty-one years earlier.[68]

Almost three and one-half acres on the point were acquired by the United States in condemnation proceedings against the Haiku Sugar Company on March 17, 1910. The first light at Pa'uwela was put into operation in August 1910. It was a temporary, unattended, acetylene light displayed from a mast; however, a more substantial light tower and keeper's dwelling were under construction. The wooden tower was erected on the roof of the house built for the keeper and his family, a frame building with a living room, kitchen, and bedroom.[69]

The lighthouse stood about fifty feet from the edge of a sea cliff overlooking the ocean. Fresh water was obtained by collecting rain water off the roof of the house. The water was fed into two 3,000-gallon redwood tanks built about twelve feet from the east end of the dwelling. The quality of the water was fair except in times of stormy weather, when the salty winds turned it brackish.

The watch room atop the thirty-five-foot structure was reached by a wooden outside stairway. The illuminant for the one-wick lamp was kerosene; a standard lens and lantern, manufactured by Barbier, Benard, and Turenne, of Paris, was used on the light. On the west side of the tower stood a wooden

In architectural style the 1915 Pa'uwela Lighthouse echoes the early lighthouses built in New England, where the light was placed on top of the keeper's dwelling. (National Archives)

building six feet square built for the storage of thirty five-gallon cans of kerosene.

Lighthouse supplies could be brought to Pa'uwela by boat, but only if the weather and seas were calm, which was seldom the case for a strong, steady wind blows across this part of the northern coast. Supplies were therefore usually shipped to Kahului and trucked eleven miles east on the Hāna road. From the main road a one-and-a-half-mile dirt road snaked toward the sea cliffs through pineapple fields and pasture land. During heavy rains the dirt turned to mud, and the road became almost impassable.[70] Philip Kepilino, the keeper, made this journey many times. He was the first keeper at Pa'uwela and he remained at the light until it was automated in 1921.

Once the Pa'uwela Point Light was put into operation in 1911, plans were made for an additional coastal light east of Pa'uwela along the northern coast near the village of Ke'anae. This was another light that was difficult to reach. Frederick A. Edgecomb, foreman of the building project, wrote that he took a boat from Kahului to the landing at Ke'anae; then he walked, if he could not get a car, two and a half miles west on the Hāna road, "thence by dirt trail ⅗ mile to the lighthouse site."[71]

Eight acres of land at Pauwalu Point were purchased by the United States government on February 8, 1912. The location chosen for the light was approximately thirty-five feet from the edge of the sea cliffs, 104 feet above the water. The tower to support the light was built of cast iron and structural steel. The light could be reached for servicing by a ladder attached to the outside of the structure. The tapering, four-sided tower of openwork construction was built above a small cast iron service building, only three feet square. This building was used for storing the station's four acetylene gas tanks, along with fittings, gauges, wrenches, and other needed supplies. The tower and service house were both painted white, and in the daytime coastal vessels could see the structure quite distinctly against the rising mountain slopes and scant vegetation.

The lamp was supplied with fuel from a container of compressed acetylene. This container required replacement only every 524 days, making the services of a full-time keeper unnecessary. An acetylene lens lantern was used, but adapted so that the light, instead of showing a fixed white light, exhibited a white light that flashed once every three seconds. The light, with a focal plane 120 feet above high water, was visible a distance of ten miles. The Pauwalu Point Light was put into operation on April 8, 1912, but it was in use for only six years. Automating lights was economically important to the the Bureau of Lighthouses, but it was equally important to eliminate lights that no longer seemed to be needed. In 1918 the Pauwalu Point Light was discontinued.[72]

By 1936 all of the lights on Maui were automated: Ka'uiki Head on the east coast; Hanamanioa and McGregor Point on the south; Lahaina and Hāwea on the west; and Nākālele Point, Kahului (east and west breakwater and range lights), and Pa'uwela Point along the north coast.[73]

The main goal of the Bureau of Lighthouses, however, was not simply economy or automation, but establishing the most efficient, reliable, and effective types of aids for navigation. The development of a new type of light prompted the bureau to replace the automated light at Pa'uwela Point with one that would require a keeper. The *Maui News* reported on June 19, 1937:

> The new light, which fills a big need to the safe operation of vessels . . . was constructed under the supervision of Fred Jordon of the lighthouse service. . . . Throwing a beam of 560,000 candle power against 480 candle power of the old light, the new landfall beacon is known as an airways revolving beacon with green lens. . . . The green light is the latest development in lights . . . the green cannot be confused with white automobile lights. The structure . . . is a 72-foot reinforced concrete tower with a visibility of approximately 20 miles.

The light tower, erected sixty-four yards from the old 1910 light, was operated by electricity generated at the station. An engine house, oil house, combined storeroom and garage, and keeper's dwelling were also constructed. The *Maui News* explained: "The new light is the result of reports by mariners who have been after the lighthouse service for a number of years to have the old light replaced. . . . The old light frequently went out due to trouble with the burners. It generally stayed that way until reported by some ship's master who happened to pass the point."[74]

The new and distinctive revolving green light flashed four-tenths of a second every fourteen and six-tenths seconds. It was the brightest light on Maui. The tower stood 169 feet above high water. In 1939 President Franklin Roosevelt set aside the week beginning August 7 as "Lighthouse Week" in recognition of the "devoted, efficient, faithful and splendid work" of America's Lighthouse Service. The *Maui News* announced on August 5, that in celebration of the event, the public was invited to visit Pa'uwela Point, Maui's "principal light station, open daily from 8 A.M. to 4 P.M."

John Enos was the resident keeper, a position he held until U.S. Coast Guardsmen were assigned to the station during World War II and Enos was transferred to the Moloka'i Light Station at Kalaupapa. When the war was over, the relighting of Maui's navigational lights was a reassuring symbol that peace had, indeed, returned to the Islands. The event was noted in a *Maui News* editorial. "It is a pleasant sight to most of us here who remember the days of blackout—most of our doors and windows still show a maze of pin and tack holes where we nightly pinned up the blackout curtains—to see the mariners' safeguard, the green Pauwela light, flashing in the darkness, also those blinking lights at our harbor entrance."[75]

One of the keepers serving with Enos when he was stationed at the Moloka'i Light was Edward Marques. In 1946 Marques, who had worked at the Moloka'i station for ten years, became the keeper at Pa'uwela Point. When he arrived, the large Quonset hut that had served as a radio-transmitting center during the war was still in place and a new tower housed the light. This skeleton tower was forty-eight feet tall and was constructed of steel. The house

where the Marques family lived (Marques, his wife Helen, their grandson Wally, and their dog Buster) was the same one that was built in 1937. It had a living room, two bedrooms, kitchen, and a porch. At night, when the generators were running to produce electricity for the navigational light, the family also had light in their home. But Helen used a gasoline-powered washing machine and a kerosene refrigerator and stove. Rain water, collected from the roof, continued to supply their needs. These arrangements were not considered inconveniences. Marques and his wife liked everything about their home at Pa'uwela. After having lived for ten years at the Kalaupapa station with two other families, they enjoyed the privacy. The setting, as with every other lighthouse in the Hawaiian Islands, was magnificent. Moloka'i could be seen beyond the mountains of West Maui; a wall of sea cliffs curved along the coast, broken by a tiny bay just to the east. Across the bay cattle grazed on a high green plateau.[76]

The keeper's house was set back from the edge of a sea cliff that rose almost vertically 120 feet from the ocean. The trails down to the rock-bound shore were narrow, steep, and treacherous. Marques worried about his grandson falling over the cliff. Buster, the German shepherd, quickly learned that he could bark as effectively at passing vessels from the top of the cliff as from the shore. Wally, on the other hand, seemed to have more adventurous ideas, and Marques kept a close eye on the boy as he went about his work at the light station.

Marques' duties were extensive, for he was not only the keeper of the Pa'uwela Light, he was also responsible for seven other lights on Maui. Part of the "job description" issued by the Fourteenth Coast Guard District, which was agreed to and signed by Marques, read as follows:

Duties: I must exhibit the light; care for buildings, grounds, equipment and supplies, and make emergency repairs thereto; operate radio telephone equip-

The Pa'uwela Point Light Station as it was when Helene Marques rode her tricycle along the walkways there as a child in the 1950s. Today the area is a county park, and all that remains of the station is the skeletal tower with its automated DCB-24 optic. (Aids to Navigation, Fourteenth U.S. Coast Guard District)

ment; order, receive, store and account for supplies; make periodical and/or special written reports to the District Commander, and perform related duties as assigned. Operational inspections of the following aids to navigation are made quarterly and emergency servicing performed as required: Nakalele Point Light; Kahului Harbor Entrance Front and Rear Range lights; Kauiki Head Light; Hanamanioa Light; Hawea Point Light; and Lahaina Light.[77]

Some specific jobs at Pa'uwela included cleaning and maintaining the illuminating apparatus, operating and maintaining the standby power-generating equipment, and preparing and starting the illuminating apparatus one-half hour before sunset and extinguishing it one-half hour after sunrise. The job of starting the generators and turning on the light each evening was sometimes the most difficult, not for technical reasons, but because that duty required the keeper to be at the light before sunset every day of the year. For keepers at other lights this was no problem, but for Marques and the Coast Guardsmen who served after him at Pa'uwela it was a major problem, since they were also required to service the other lights on the island.

In 1930, front *(left)* and rear *(right)* range lights were constructed in Kahului Harbor to replace the first range lights established in 1922. The new skeleton towers were painted white and showed fixed red lights. In 1940 the day characteristic of the towers was changed to vertical red and white bands. The photographs shown were taken in 1958 after the towers (and the picket fence) had been freshly painted. (Aids to Navigation, Fourteenth U.S. Coast Guard District)

The only lights that were fairly easy to reach because they were just off a paved road were the ones at Kahului Harbor, fourteen miles from Pa'uwela, and Lahaina, thirty-eight miles away. These lights seldom needed emergency care because they were powered with commercial electricity. The lights that required attention more often than on a quarterly basis were the two lights operating with acetylene—at Nākālele Point, fifty-four miles from Pa'uwela, and Ka'uiki Head, forty miles away; and the two battery-operated lights at Hanamanioa, forty-five miles distant, and Hāwea Point, fifty miles from Pa'uwela.

The distance in miles does not give a true basis on

which to judge the time involved in transportation. The lights were far off the paved roadways—down rutted dirt roads, or across lava beds or over rocky hillsides where there was no road at all. Trails wound through fields of pineapple and sugarcane, and across pastures where gates had to be opened and closed while curious cows and truculent bulls looked on. And when the vehicle could go no farther, everything that was needed had to be carried, even sometimes through the water, if the footbridge at Ka'uiki Head had washed out.

Helen Marques always worried when her husband went to Hanamanioa Light because it was almost a two-mile walk from where the truck had to stop. The lava was rough, with loose stones and large holes. It was hard not to trip, not to slide. And if one fell or needed help there was no one to hear a call. Hanamanioa is a totally isolated place. "My wife came with me whenever she could. She would stand outside the truck and watch me until we couldn't see one another. Then as I walked further around the bend, I would look back and I could see her again and we would wave, but I would keep on walking to the light and soon she was out of sight." No matter how long Marques was at the light, when he returned, as he rounded that bend, he would see Helen still standing by the truck and they would wave. If Marques wasn't able to finish the work on Hanamanioa before he had to return to Pa'uwela to turn on that light, he would have to return the next day. The round trip, driving and walking, took about six hours.

The Marqueses' youngest daughter, Helene, was born in 1948. Some of her earliest memories are of waiting with her mother at Hanamanioa. She also remembers the fun she had riding her tricycle back and forth on the sidewalk that ran from the keeper's house to the other outbuildings at Pa'uwela Station. One garage had been converted to a recreation building, the other garage contained a storeroom

Ed Marques, keeper of the Pa'uwela Point Light Station from 1946 to 1962, often took his daughter Helene with him when he traveled to service the automated lights on Maui. (Courtesy of Helene Marques Kailipalauli)

and laundry, and there was a small shed for paints. Marques did a lot of painting. He said that a lightkeeper had to be a mechanic, a carpenter, a gardener. "You go to bed with a paint brush in your hand and wake up holding a hammer."[78]

Helene also remembers the magic-like flashing green of the light at night. The green was changed to white in 1959 when the light's intensity was increased to two million candlepower. The flashing white light was visible twenty-two miles.[79]

Marques' duties were increased to inspecting the unwatched aids every two weeks instead of quarterly, but extensive maintenance work was always performed by Coast Guard personnel from one of the tenders, such as the CGC *Planetree*. Marques began to have difficulty performing some of his manual work; arthritis was crippling his hands. "The hardest thing was climbing the ladder to the top of the light. Sometimes at night the alarm buzzer would go off, meaning the light was out, and up the ladder I'd go. The wind was always blowing hard, and if it was stormy the rain felt like it was slicing your face. It was hard holding on. Sometimes I thought I would fly away."[80]

Because of this disability, Marques retired in 1962. He had been a lightkeeper for twenty-six years. After twenty-seven years of retirement, Marques, at eighty-nine, clearly recalled his years at Pa'uwela. One of his best memories is of Helen and Helene waiting for him and waving to him as he walked back from the lonely Hanamanioa Light.

A civilian keeper's wife was often directly involved with lighthouse duties, but when the Coast Guardsmen became the lightkeepers, this opportunity for women seems to have disappeared. Elizabeth Hearn was an exception. Her husband, Robert Hearn, was assigned to Pa'uwela Point Light Station on January 29, 1962. Two years later the commander of the Fourteenth Coast Guard District recommended both Robert and Elizabeth for the International Institute of Communications Medal.

> Hearn and his wife personally attend Pauwela Point Light . . . every night of the year. In addition, this Coast Guardsman also has responsibility for the maintenance and operation of nine other lighted shore aids. . . . As a team, Hearn and his wife travel extensively and work together performing their tasks; always returning home before sunset to insure proper operation of the primary seacoast light at Pauwela Point. . . . Access to several of the lights . . . can only be gained by transiting miles of lava beds, and much of this on foot.[81]

When Robert was seriously injured in an automobile accident, Elizabeth took over for him. Though the official responsibility was delegated to the commanding officer of the Coast Guard tender, "the actual accomplishment of the light keeper's duty was performed in a highly satisfactory manner by Mrs. Hearn. No remuneration is afforded her for this work." The Pa'uwela station was considered by the Coast Guard as a "one man unit"; however, the commander ended his report by commenting that

> the only reason this unit is getting along so well is due to the assistance being furnished by the Officer in Charge's wife. Hearn's wife does a large majority of the administrative work, assists in some maintenance and provides necessary assistance during light attendant runs . . . has also acted as "Relief Keeper" during his authorized absences. Hearn has recently requested an extension of his tour of duty at this unit. It would be beneficial to the Coast Guard to grant this request if feasable.[82]

When the McGregor Point Light was reactivated, one more responsibility was added to the list of chores. The job became too time consuming even for Hearn and his wife. After reviewing "time away from station" reports submitted by Hearn, Commander C. W. Scharff recommended making the Pa'uwela Light automatic, thus relieving the keeper of the responsibility of returning to the light before sunset each day. This conversion was accomplished: "At 1200 local time, 1 September 1964 your station will discontinue functioning as a Light Station and commence operating as Pauwela Point Light Attendant Station."[83]

In 1965 Robert Hearn was responsible for servicing the primary seacoast light at Pa'uwela, seven secondary lights, and four harbor lights. He was also responsible for inspecting more than twenty private aids, and more were being built. To take care of this work load, a recommendation was made to assign two Coast Guardsmen to the light attendant station: "Although the present officer in charge is maintaining his station in a satisfactory condition it is doubtful that his replacement will be able to do so. The station is maintained in its present condition due to the direct assistance of the wife of the present officer in charge." Perhaps the greatest tribute given to the Hearns was that they exemplified "the 'old spirit' so prevalent among light keepers."[84]

Today, the keepers of Maui's lights are the members of the Aids to Navigation Team, who fly over from their base on Sand Island, Honolulu, to service the lights. Their four-wheel-drive truck is shipped to Maui for their annual maintenance of the aids. The lights, which are powered either by solar batteries or by commercial electricity with solar-powered back-up units, seldom have an outage. The main job is to scrape and paint, for the sea air and storms deteriorate the structures quickly. Getting to the lights is still almost the toughest part of the job, but sometimes for different reasons than in earlier days. One inspector reported in 1986 that the Hāwea Light "is very difficult to find because it is hidden down in a condominium complex." A helicopter takes the men to the Hanamanioa Light, but their truck takes them everywhere else.[85]

The same old, almost impassable, dirt trail leads to the Nākālele Light. The ground is covered with boulders and potholes of every size. The light is now exhibited from a twenty-one-foot pole, 142 feet above the ocean that pounds and reshapes the lava rocks. Beyond this wild coast across the Pailolo Channel are the mountains of Moloka'i. To the east of the light the concrete foundation piles for the old lighthouse can still be seen among the giant rock forma-tions. To the south the stark forms of the red cliffs are softened by casuarinas. The sparse green ground cover is grazed short by sure-footed cattle. Towering boulders and rocks of every size cover the ground and those who visit this primitive place have made interesting use of them. Rocks are piled in the manner of ancient altars; they are arranged in artistic designs; they are used to spell out the names of lovers, friends, and travelers. Rock graffiti have found full expression on Nākālele Point.

A surprising number of people also make their way down the dirt road through the pineapple fields to Pa'uwela. On March 30, 1981, the U.S. General Services Administration approved donation to Maui County of the land not needed for the lighthouse. The three and a half acres thus acquired was valued at $300,000. The county spent about $70,000 to improve the property and make it into a park. The rutted rough road off the Hāna highway leads down to a grassy area that is beautifully maintained. Many warning signs are posted: "Dangerous Cliff Area," "Approach At Own Risk," "Keep Away From Edge." But the ocean view pulls the visitor closer and closer to the cliff's edge, and the scene of vertical sea walls and high outcroppings is breathtaking. Somehow fishermen make their way down to the flat walls of rock to cast their lines from long poles.

Someone planted bougainvillea on one part of the cliff's edge, and the bright red and purple bracts cascade down the cliff like a waterfall. Cement foundations where the station's outbuildings once stood still remain. Morning glories stretch across their cracks and over ground stubbled with sisal plants. On one side of the light tower there is higher ground where an earlier lighthouse once stood. This slight rise offers the only protection from the wind. With the exception of one tall, straight palm, the trees all grow in the sweeping direction of the trades. Visitors to Pa'uwela Light always have to hold on to their hats!

Chapter 7

MOLOKINI, KAHO'OLAWE,

AND LĀNA'I

Looking west from Lahaina, beyond the cluster of anchored boats and across the 'Au'au Channel, is the island of Lāna'i. Across the 'Alalākeiki Channel to the south lies Kaho'olawe, and between Kaho'olawe and Maui is the tiny, crescent-shaped islet of Molokini. These channels are a playground for humpback whales, the official state marine mammal of Hawai'i. The humpbacks come from Alaskan and Siberian seas to winter in warm Hawaiian waters. They come to mate, give birth, and nurse their young. From October to February the whales arrive in ever-increasing numbers. Along the shores of the surrounding islands, or aboard boats, people watch these beautiful giants blow and breach, dive and cavort, until it is time for them to return to northern waters.

Molokini

The whales were beginning to leave in April 1988, when Coast Guardsmen Kenneth Savi and Ralph Craig arrived on Molokini. The men, members of the ANT team, were coming to the high islet for their annual paint, scrape, and service routine on the light. Both men agree that Molokini is one of the more difficult lights to reach, and Savi described his last experience there.

A marine helicopter transported us and the wind was blowing so hard—about 30 to 40 knots—that the pilot had to make three or four tries before he could place the back wheels in just the right place on the ledge. The ledge at the top is very narrow and the plane has to be balanced on its two back wheels with the nose sticking out over the cliff about one hundred and sixty feet above the water.[1]

The men made a fast exit through the rear door of the helicopter, quickly unloading their equipment, food, and water. As the craft was becoming airborne once again, a surge of air sent the lighter equipment and the cooler flying. Then an unexpectedly strong blast of wind caught the helicopter, forcing it back against the rocky ledge.

At the time we didn't know if it was damaged or not. We were scampering around gathering up equipment and trying to save the water and some food. The cooler had gone over the cliff, but we managed to save the water. It turned out the helo was damaged and they had to send a different one out for us that evening. The wind was still blowing and we were wondering if they'd be able to pick us up. We didn't have a tent or even a sleeping bag. There was just us on that rock with the geckos and spiders. It wouldn't have been too bad, but we were still happy to see the helo.[2]

It takes two men two days to scrape and paint the twenty-five-foot wood and steel skeleton tower and to service the light. After the helicopter drops them off at Molokini it usually goes to Kahoʻolawe, where it waits until it's time to pick the men up before dark. "Then it's back to Kahoʻolawe," said Savi, "where we stay in a Quonset hut and take drip-dry showers. The next day we finish up the work on Molokini. After that we usually work on the Kahoʻolawe light."[3]

The Light House Board first proposed a light for Molokini in 1905, estimating that it would cost $40,000 to erect the second-order light on the ridge. Congress, however, did not appropriate the funds. The Board repeated the request for this aid to interisland navigation every year until funds were finally made available five years later. On September 13, 1910, the entire island, of eighteen and one-half acres, was set aside for lighthouse purposes by a proclamation signed by Walter Francis Frear, governor of the Territory of Hawaii.[4]

Molokini is an extinct volcano with one side of the curving rim of the crater exposed and the rest below sea level. The area within the curve has been designated a marine life conservation district and is one of the most popular dive spots in the islands. Reef fish, many found only in Hawaiʻi, abound, as well as eagle and manta rays, spinner dolphins, white-tipped sharks, and turtles. There is a sheer deep drop-off on the southern, underwater side of the island. The exposed rim of the crater rises steeply above the water.

According to William Ellis' observations in the early 1800s, the islet "would render navigation of the strait exceedingly dangerous, were it not so much elevated above the sea as to be at all times visible from vessels passing between the islands. . . . [Molokini] is only visited by fishermen, who on its barren surface spread their nets to dry, and for this purpose it may be considered a convenient append-age to the adjacent islands." Henry Whitney never saw anyone on the islet and wrote in his 1875 Hawaiian guide book that the island was so bare "neither man nor beast can subsist on it."[5]

The site chosen for the light was on the high southwest crest of the crater. Difficult as it was to scale the steep slopes and raise the needed building material to the crest, the island's height and barrenness were assets for a lighthouse site. The first skeleton tower was only sixteen feet high, yet it placed the light 173 feet above water. The automatic white light flashed once every three seconds and could be seen ten miles at sea. It was illuminated by acetylene, and its performance record over the years was the best of any light in the islands—it flashed without a failure over two hundred million times! One who could attest to the reliability of the Molokini Light was Captain Loncke, a veteran shipmaster of the Inter-Island Steam Navigation Company and commander of its flagship, *Haleakala*. Captain Loncke declared that the most welcome sight for him, during the four trips he made every week through this channel, was the "never failing flash of the faithful Molokini." The light guided him safely through an extremely treacherous part of his run.[6]

In October 1925 the lighthouse tender *Kukui* left Honolulu to begin a search for five new lighthouse sites and to construct a new light tower on Molokini. Ralph Tinkham, superintendent of the Nineteenth Lighthouse District, said that work on the light would start immediately. "The framework in the present tower has deteriorated and we shall not only construct a new one, but shall also raise the height from 173 feet to 187 feet as complaints have been received from time to time that the light is hidden by a jutting piece of land to the north. The new light will raise it above this obstruction."[7]

The light marked the crest of Molokini for twenty-two years before it was replaced in 1947 with a twenty-five-foot skeleton tower. The new light was

The 1947, battery-operated Molokini Light was the third beacon to be built on the high barren islet off Maui. The earlier lights (1911 and 1925) had been illuminated with acetylene. (Aids to Navigation, Fourteenth U.S. Coast Guard District)

equally reliable until April 1989, when a storm, with winds over sixty miles an hour, toppled the tower and blew it over the cliff. The tower disappeared in the seas. Members of the ANT team were brought by helicopter to the island to establish first a temporary light and later a new lighted aid atop a metal pole erected on the high ridge. The characteristic of the light continued to be a flashing white light every two and one-half seconds, visible for seven miles.[8]

Kahoʻolawe

In legend, Molokini is the cast-off umbilical cord of Kahoʻolawe, the child of Wākea and Papa. Wākea is the ancestor of all Hawaiians and Papa was his wife. "She brought forth with flowing blood, Papa was weakened at the birth of the island Kanaloa [Kahoʻolawe]. It was both beautiful like the *punua* [young bird] and *naiʻa* [dolphin]. It was the child born of Papa."[9]

This child of Papa's has been a battered and abused child. The island looks desolate. Geological evidence suggests that water was once more abundant on Kahoʻolawe and that present-day gulches were gently sloping valleys. On the plateau there was fertile soil, and the island may have been green and even lush at one time. Archaeologists believe that people lived along the coast as early as A.D. 1150 and occupied inland sites on the central plateau in the late 1300s, where they raised sweet potatoes and other dryland crops.[10]

Sometime in the 1790s the English explorer Captain George Vancouver presented goats to a Maui chief. Some of the goats were released on Kahoʻolawe to multiply, and later sheep were introduced. Archaeologist J. Gilbert McAllister believes that these animals "cropped the grass and other herbage so closely that the sod cover was broken. This gave the entering wedge for the wind to exert its influence on the light top soil."[11]

By 1927, when a lighthouse was proposed for Kahoʻolawe, the ground was so exposed in the uplands that strong winds blew great clouds of dust off the island that could be seen far out to sea. The only vegetation to be found was in the protected gulches, where a few blades of grass clung to the slopes of the north and west coasts. The area selected for the light station was part of the land leased to the Kahoolawe Ranch. The land was set aside for lighthouse purposes by Executive Order 308 on December 13, 1927, and a proclamation declaring possession and use by the United States was signed by Calvin Coolidge on February 3, 1928.[12]

The twenty-three acres of land acquired for the light station were on the southwest coast near Kealaikahiki Point, "the way to foreign lands," a place of great importance in ancient times. This was a historical departure point for the ancient Hawaiians' long voyages into the South Pacific. The site chosen for the lighthouse is in the same area where signal fires were once kept burning, and according to McAllister, "It was this point that the Hawaiians used along with others to form a navigational triangle for trips to Tahiti, New Zealand, and other southerly areas."[13]

The forty-foot light tower built in 1928 was similar to the one erected on Molokini. The flashing white light was 140 feet above the water. At the time the light was built, the island was leased to Angus McPhee and Harry A. Baldwin, who used it for cattle grazing. The Kahoolawe Ranch Company remained in operation on the island until the outbreak of World War II.[14]

In 1941 parts of the island became a practice bombing target for use by the army and navy. In 1944 the entire island was used for bombing practice and the light was discontinued. In 1952 when the navy designated the light station as being outside the target area, the light was reestablished. Nevertheless, there were fears that there might be unexploded bombs nearby, and the Coast Guardsmen servicing the light were (and still are) careful to stay within the cleared bounds of the station and the path leading from the tower to the landing.[15]

In 1987 a new, rather stubby looking, twenty-foot white skeleton tower was built in approximately the same location as the old tower, 100 feet above the sea. The white flashing six-second light is visible seven miles. Northwest of the Kahoʻolawe Point

Light, the Kealaikahiki Channel separates Kahoʻolawe from Lānaʻi.

Lānaʻi

In legendary times Kaʻena, the northwesternmost
point of Lānaʻi, was known as the place where the
fish demigod ʻAiʻai marked a stone and then gave
the stone life as the first Hawaiian turtle. Another
famous legend tells the story of Kawelo, a prophet,
who kept a fire burning atop Keahiʻāloa Ridge
upland from Kaʻena Point. A similar fire was kept
burning on Molokaʻi across the Kalohi Channel by
the prophet Waha.[16] It is interesting to speculate
on the possibility that these fires on each side
of the channel may have served as navigational
aids.

Beacon fires would have been needed, for fierce
winds and strong coastal and channel currents make
navigation hazardous. Wrecks and debris from
wrecks have been washed ashore along the north
and east coasts for hundreds of years. One of the
earliest recorded shipwrecks on Lānaʻi, dated 1824,
was the British ship *Alderman Wood,* which went
aground and became a total wreck. In 1826 the
American ship *London* from New York was lost. The
vessel carried a considerable shipment of specie,
which was salvaged by the U.S. armed schooner
Dolphin. When archaeologist Kenneth Emory visited
Lānaʻi in the 1920s, he found much evidence of shipwrecks, not only along the beaches, but among
objects used by the residents, such as the boom
of a large schooner placed in the top of a rail
fence.[17]

Realizing the need for a navigational aid somewhere on the north and/or east shore of Lānaʻi,
Superintendent Ralph Tinkham, in 1925, dispatched
the *Kukui* to locate a suitable site for a lighthouse.
The point chosen was Laewahie on Shipwreck
Beach. The *Maui News,* reporting Tinkham's decision, commented:

The construction of a light at Wahie . . . will fill a
longfelt want according to local shipping men. At
present vessels bound through Auau Strait, between
Lanai and Maui, steer a course off Molokai coast
instead of a direct course which would bring them close
to the shores of Lanai and so place them in jeopardy
because of the sweep coming in from Pailolo Strait,
between Molokai and Maui towards Lanai. With a
light on Lanai ships will be enabled to steer a straighter
course and know their exact position off Lanai coast at
all times. This will mean a saving of time in steamer
schedules, also.[18]

For some reason the proposed light was not built.
Then, in 1930 Frederick A. Edgecomb, who had just
been appointed superintendent of lighthouses for the
nineteenth district, stated that one of the main
improvements in aids would be the construction of a
new light on the north shore of Lānaʻi. He selected a
site just west of Laewahie where there was one small
opening through the reefs at Pōhakuloa Point.[19]
This alluded-to light did not appear on the Light
Lists, nor is there any record of its being established
under the Lighthouse Service.

The first navigational light on Lānaʻi was privately built on the breakwater at Kaumalapau Harbor in 1924. The harbor was actually only a small
indentation in the southwest shoreline at the mouth
of the Kaumalapau gulch. There was no entrance
channel. Interisland vessels called at Lānaʻi on a
regular schedule, but most of the in and out boat
traffic consisted of barges that transported Lānaʻi's
pineapple crop to a cannery in Honolulu. James
Dole had bought most of Lānaʻi in 1922 from Harry
and Frank Baldwin for $1,100,000. From 1925 to 1926,
Dole spent about $500,000 for improvements in the
harbor, which mainly served shipping needs of the
pineapple industry. To create some protection for
vessels entering and leaving the harbor, the Hawaiian Pineapple Company built a breakwater on the
north side of the bight. On the seaward end of the
breakwater the company erected and maintained a

flashing, three-second red light. In 1925 the Bureau of Lighthouses took over this light and also established a lighted aid on the south side of the entrance. A flashing white light was installed on top of a small wooden building sixty-six feet above the water.[20]

Three and one-half miles south of Kaumalapau Harbor is Palaoa Point, where a light, established by the Bureau of Lighthouses, was first displayed on June 6, 1934. Called the Cape Ka'ea Light, it was a wooden skeleton tower, approximately thirty feet tall and painted white. It placed the automatically operated acetylene light ninety-one feet above water. The flashing one-second white light was visible nine miles. The light also had a red sector marking the rocks off the southwest point of Mānele Bay.

Mānele Bay, another bight along the southern coastline, is so shallow that it can be used only by small boats. In 1965 a breakwater was constructed on the south side of the harbor, and an entrance light, mounted on a pole above a small ten-foot-high white house, was erected at the end of the breakwater. The flashing white, four-second light could be seen four miles. The small boat harbor in the northwest corner of the bay was the first such harbor to be constructed in the islands with federal/state funds.[21]

Nothing was done to mark the dangerous north Lāna'i shore with a light until 1968. The U.S. Coast Guard chose Pōhakuloa Point as the site, the same location Edgecomb had selected in 1930. A metal pole was erected, which displayed a red-and-white-checkered diamond daymark and a light thirty feet above the water. The light had a flashing white, six-second characteristic with a red sector showing over the reefs.

The Pōhakuloa Light continues to be an important aid for interisland travel. Frequent extremely bad weather conditions in this area make navigation hazardous. The light still displays its original signal, but the diamond-shaped dayboard was changed to show black sectors at the top and bottom corners and white at the sides. For servicing, the lamp is

The Palaoa Point wooden pyramidal skeleton beacon, built in 1934, was typical of eleven automatic acetylene-lighted aids built throughout the Islands in the late 1920s and early 1930s. Known first as the Cape Ka'ea Light, it was serviced by the tender *Kukui*. The hoist on the shore to the right of the tower was used for unloading needed maintenance supplies, including acetylene tanks. (Aids to Navigation, Fourteenth U.S. Coast Guard District)

reached by a ladder with a "man hoop," a small platform with a waist-high railing at the top. This hoop acts as a safety rail for the person working on the light.[22]

The Pōhakuloa Light is located on the beach about fourteen miles from Lāna'i City. To reach it for servicing and maintenance, the ANT team must travel over dirt roads through pineapple fields. When it rains, the dirt turns to mud and the roads become almost impassable. For the last two miles to the light, the road is filled with large sharp rocks and huge sections of it have been washed out. The rocks are impossible to avoid and the ANT team must use extreme caution to prevent the truck's tires from being cut.[23]

The road to the Cape Ka'ea Light is almost as bad, with large eroded areas. The ANT team has recommended that the washed-out sections of the access roads be repaired and graded, but it is difficult to keep them in even fair condition. This light, now called the Palaoa Point Light, is still displayed atop a white skeleton tower, but its characteristic has been changed to a flashing white, six-second (instead of one-second) light visible six miles. The light still retains a red sector that flashes across the dangerous rocks off Mānele Bay.[24]

The Kaumalapau Light is another that is difficult of access. It is displayed from a small wooden building about ten feet high, erected on a concrete foundation. The white building, which serves as a locker for the solar-powered batteries, is at the top of a lava cliff. The Coast Guard ANT team keeps a photograph of the side of the cliff in the Kaumalapau Light file to show the formidable route that must be taken to reach the light for service and maintenance. There is little that can be done to make this light more accessible. The men on the ANT team have to park their vehicle at the barge docks and walk across the slippery rocks along the shoreline—surf permitting. The men wear hiking boots, for there is a thirty-foot, almost-vertical climb up to the light, and of course any needed equipment and supplies must be carried to the site. The climb is particularly perilous after a rain.[25]

The island of Lāna'i is very dry, but when it does rain, the men on the ANT team hope they won't be called to service the lights at Pōhakuloa, Palaoa, or Kaumalapau.

Chapter 8

MOLOKA'I

Kaunakakai and Ka'amola Point

The first navigational lights on the island of Moloka'i were established at Kaunakakai Harbor in 1880. The small anchorage was hardly worthy of being called a harbor, but all interisland trade and travel for Moloka'i arrived and departed from this point. The long and narrow island has no deep-water harbors.[1] This was no problem when trade and travel between the Islands were carried on by canoe. There were then direct canoe routes between several landings on Moloka'i and O'ahu, Lāna'i, and Maui. Some of the place names found in accounts of ancient interisland voyages are Kalaupapa on the north shore and, on the south, Kamalō and Kaunakakai. Kamalō was an important canoe landing because it was near the most populated area of the island. Kaunakakai was originally called Kaunakahakai, which means "beach landing."[2]

By 1875 the interisland steamer *Kilauea* was making monthly stops offshore Kaunakakai. Because of the abrupt shoaling, only barges or shallow-draft craft could enter the harbor. Cargo was transferred from larger vessels, anchored in deep water, to lighters, which then carried goods and passengers to shore.[3]

As use of the harbor increased, Rudolph William Meyer, a resident and businessman on Moloka'i, was asked by the minister of the Interior, H. A. P. Carter, to select sites for front and rear range lights to be established in the harbor. Meyer chose the locations and directed the erection of the aids. When they were completed, in 1880, Kaleimamo, who lived in Kaunakakai, became the keeper of the range lights, at a salary of eight dollars a month. The lights, although they were only ordinary kerosene lamps mounted on wooden spars, could be seen five to seven miles at sea.[4]

The lights were kept burning every night. With daylight, the keeper would lower the lamps, clean and fill them, trim the wicks, and see that all was in readiness for the coming night. In 1889 Samuel Kainali was the keeper of the harbor range lights. At times he had difficulty collecting his salary, and Meyer wrote to the minister of the Interior on his behalf. "Samuel Kainali has called upon me for his money, three months wages to March 31, 1889, at eight dollars a month." Fourteen years later, Keeper Joseph N. Uahinui was receiving the same salary and, although the beacons had been maintained, nothing further was done to mark Kaunakakai Harbor.[5]

In 1903, before the Light House Board assumed responsibility for the navigational aids in the Islands, a preliminary survey of existing beacons was made. The report to the board recommended that the red range lights in Kaunakakai Harbor be continued and that a stone light tower be built on the reef outside the entrance to the harbor.[6]

The reef was more than a mile offshore and no

further consideration seems to have been given to the lighthouse proposal; however, the existing front and rear range lights were replaced. Lanterns mounted on posts were used. The forty-foot front range light was erected on the "northerly side of the Kai O Kalohi Channel" and the color of the light was changed to fixed white. The forty-five-foot rear range light, built about 504 feet northeast of the front one, displayed a fixed red characteristic.[7]

In 1907 the front range light was lowered to thirty-six feet and a white, triangular daymark, with the apex up, was mounted below the light. A similar daymark, with the apex down, was placed on the rear range light. Aligning these two marks was helpful to vessels entering the harbor during the day.[8]

In 1912 the range lights were automated and mounted on wooden skeleton towers. The front tower was built on the roof of a house. The focal plane of the flashing white light was twenty-seven feet above high water. The tower for the rear range displayed an occulting white light, forty feet above high water. The same type of daymarks previously displayed were used on the new towers.[9]

Other improvements had been made in the harbor. The American Sugar Company had built breakwaters and a wharf for its own use, but the facilities were used by the public without charge. Sugar and cattle raising were the major industries of the island until the 1920s. When the sugar business began to decline, the American Sugar Company set up thousands of bee hives along the lee shore of West Moloka'i. The company was one of the largest honey producers in the world until 1937, when the bees became infected with a disease. Honey, cattle, and pineapples, shipped from Kaunakakai Harbor, then sustained the island's economy.[10]

As the pineapple business increased, wharves were extended at Kaunakakai and Kamalō. Kamalō, the small natural harbor east of Kaunakakai, was the only one considered safe during kona storms. It had been used by a sugar mill that operated in the area from 1870 to 1900. The entrance was marked by a buoy, but vessels anchored offshore while lighters carried people and goods to and from the wharf. As use of the wharf increased, a gas buoy with a light mounted on a cylindrical, skeleton superstructure flashed white every ten seconds at night. This was the only navigational aid marking the harbor until 1968, when a lighted beacon was erected on Ka'amola Point—an automatic light mounted on a twenty-three-foot steel pole. The solar panel that charged the battery for the light was also mounted on the pole. The light had a flashing white 2.5-second characteristic. For daytime identification the beacon displayed a red-and-white diamond-shaped dayboard. At night the Ka'amola Point Light could be seen for five miles.[11]

In 1986 the Ka'amola Point Light flashed white every four seconds and displayed a black-and-white diamond-shaped dayboard. In a Coast Guard Aids to Navigation inspection report made in June of that year, Lieutenant D. T. Noviello wrote, "I am not sure why we continue to mark this harbor. The pier is in shambles and there is no improved boat ramp. The road to the beach is either dirt or mud depending on the weather."[12] Four years later the situation had not changed.

The shallow harbor at Kamalō is used only by small boats, and Kaunakakai remains the main interisland barge harbor. Designed to serve the needs of Moloka'i, Kaunakakai harbor has 690 linear feet of pier and three acres of cargo area. A lighted buoy, flashing red, marks the entrance to the harbor. Fixed red range lights, displayed atop skeleton towers, are powered with commercial electricity.[13]

The Kaunakakai beach, a favored recreational spot by the people of Moloka'i for decades, has over the years become an eyesore, with makeshift huts, old cars and trucks, and trash. The County of Maui wants to improve the area, dredge the mud flats, increase the size of the harbor, and restore the tree-shaded walkway into town. The development of a Kaunakakai Beach and Lighthouse Park has been proposed, and perhaps someday will become a reality.[14]

Lā'au Point

Marking harbors, such as Kaunakakai, had been the primary objective of the Hawaiian government when considering where to establish navigational aids in the Islands. Erecting landfall lights to aid vessels approaching the Islands or sailing between the Islands was not considered necessary until trade with other nations expanded.

The Reciprocity Treaty in 1875 stimulated tremendous growth in commerce between the Islands and the United States. The Hawaiian sugar industry expanded rapidly and people were needed to work on the sugar plantations. Approximately ten thousand laborers, mostly Chinese, were brought to Hawai'i and most arrived during the four years after the Reciprocity Treaty was signed.[15]

It was the wreck of a ship transporting some of these workers that hastened the building of the first coastal light in the Islands—the Kalaeokalā'au Point Light (Lā'au Point Light) on Moloka'i. The *Hawaiian Annual* reported that on January 20, 1878,

> the American bark *H. N. Carleton,* with 380 passengers from Hongkong, went ashore on the west end of Molokai and became a total wreck. Schooner *Kinau* brought a number of the passengers and crew to port (Honolulu) on the 31st, and reporting the disaster, the U.S.S. *Pensacola* went to her assistance, and brought the balance of her passengers and crew to port.[16]

As commerce increased, more and more vessels on their way to and from Honolulu Harbor sailed through the twenty-five-mile-wide Kaiwi Channel separating O'ahu and Moloka'i. Diamond Head crater was used as a landfall on O'ahu, but there was no distinctive landmark on the Moloka'i side of the passage.[17] The west coast of Moloka'i between Lā'au Point on the south and 'Īlio Point on the north consists of only short stretches of sand and low bluffs, beyond which to the east the land rises gradually.

In 1880 an appropriation for $2,500 was made for a lighthouse on the west end of Moloka'i. Minister Carter again contacted Meyer and asked him to look for a suitable spot for the beacon and to locate the nearest landing place where building material and, later, lighthouse supplies could be landed.[18]

The site Meyer chose for the lighthouse was at Lā'au Point, the southwesternmost point of Moloka'i. It is a place of barren isolation; a place where no one would choose to stay for long; a place that quickly destroys any sentimental, romantic yearnings for the lightkeeper's life.

Even in Hawaiian myth, it was a place of struggle and defeat. It was named for a *lā'au,* or club, that was once imbued with supernatural power and given by the gods to Palila, a hero of Kaua'i. Palila, with his powerful club, leaped to the top of a hill on Moloka'i and from there attracted all the women of the island to him. The men of Moloka'i were furious. Consumed by jealousy and anger, they attacked Palila and defeated him when his club lost its power to the gods of Moloka'i. Palila, no longer desired by the women and defeated by the men, threw away his useless club and it landed on this southwestern tip of Moloka'i.[19]

The Hawaiians also tell of the time when the area was swallowed up by a tidal wave and the submerged peninsula remained beneath the sea, with only torn and fragmented pieces emerging from the swirling waters.[20] Boulders of black lava lie scattered about the barren earth that appears devoid of life. The swirling current sweeps around the point in a northerly direction, with a strong set toward the shore. Breakers build when the north wind battles against the riptide.

Meyer discovered an excellent location, set back from the low and rocky point, for a navigational light. He marked the spot by driving a five-foot wooden stake into the ground and surrounding it with a pile of stones. He reported to Carter:

> Nature has favored the place with a little projection about 25 feet above the level of the sea and by going 65 feet from the extreme point there is ample room for a structure 25 or 30 feet high or even more if desired. This would elevate the light to about 50 feet above sea level and can be distinctly seen from a distance of nearly ten miles. I was there at very low tide and could not discover any breakers further out than 400 feet in a westerly direction and 170 feet in a southerly one. Vessels can therefore come very near without danger, thus making a very high structure unnecessary.[21]

The tower for the light was originally to be built of stone. There were abundant stones in the vicinity, but they were not close to the site and would be extremely difficult to transport. So Meyer suggested erecting "a good substantial simple wooden structure, which in this locality being an exceedingly dry one, will stand for many years without repairs." In searching the surrounding coastline for a place where building materials and lighthouse supplies could be off-loaded, Meyer found a small spot along the shore about a mile and a quarter north of the point, where, during summer months, in good weather and at high tide, a boat could land.

> This is the spot where the Bark *Carlton* was wrecked . . . and as W. James Dowsett, who purchased the wreck, sends every now and then one of his vessels to this place, I beg to advise a consultation with this gentleman and some of his captains. . . . There is now a shed at this place which would serve as shelter for the workmen. From the landing to the building spot the ground is very rough . . . and on this account the material has to be carried by men . . . nor can it be rafted for the shoreline is rocky.[22]

Meyer suggested having the structure built in Honolulu and then sending "the framer with sufficient native help to put it up." In the meantime Meyer wanted to suspend a lantern from a thirty-foot spar, as had been done in 1880 for the Kaunakakai lights.

The latter suggestion was not acted on, but Carter did write Meyer thanking him for the very clear and explicit manner in which he "collated the necessary preliminaries required for the work."[23] Carter, and others in government, knew from past experiences that Meyer was a man on whom they could depend.

In the matter of lighthouses, Carter relied on Meyer not only for locating a suitable site but also for choosing the keeper. Several men applied for the position: W. Benjamin B. Macy, Joseph Bishaw, and William Louis Richards. However, Carter told them that Meyer was making the selection. Meyer suggested hiring either Kaleimamo, who was already attending the Kaunakakai lights at a salary of eight dollars a month, or Kuimeheua. "The two natives were born near . . . La'au. I have known them for many years as good and reliable men." He believed it would be better to hire a Hawaiian as keeper because

> foreigners will soon get tired of the place on account of the extreme isolation and the difficulty with which the necessities of life can be obtained. . . . The nearest settlement is Kaunakakai about twenty miles distant, with no habitations between. Water is scarce and brackish and has to be brought about three or four miles; this difficulty, however, may be partly overcome by having a good iron tank for catching rain water. Fresh meat cannot be had, but fish of the best kind is in abundance. . . . Firewood is at present easily found, the whole coast is strewed with driftwood, the remains of a wreck. A good Hawaiian appears to me to be more at home in such a place; he would raise a few potatoes,

melons and pumpkins . . . and then with the great abundance of fish he would make an excellent living where foreigners would fare rather hard.[24]

Meyer had assessed the situation accurately, especially regarding the water, which in the future would cause severe problems; but when the time came to select the keeper, he was told whom to hire.

The land proposed for the lighthouse belonged to Kulikolani, a woman of Hawaiian royal lineage. On March 14, 1881, Meyer, writing on behalf of Kulikolani, informed Carter that she was willing to lease the land to the government.[25]

With the land acquired, H. Hackfeld and Company began construction, not of a wooden tower as Meyer had suggested, but of a stone tower. Native workmen were hired for the arduous task of gathering the stones and transporting them to the lighthouse site. By December 1881 the light station was completed and the minister of the Interior had leaflets prepared describing the Lā'au Point Light. These were sent to the minister of foreign affairs for distribution to the representatives of other nations.[26] The Notice to Mariners stated:

> On and after the FIRST of January, 1882, there will be exhibited on the extreme Southwest Point of the Island of Molokai . . . a fixed white Fresnel Light of the Fourth Order, showing from all points of the compass. The Light is fifty feet above sea level and is visible from a vessel's deck in clear weather a distance of eleven miles. The Tower is painted white; the lantern red.[27]

Before the light station was completed, the keeper was chosen, but not by Meyer, who was directed to contact John Warren Burrows concerning charge of the light. Burrows, a seaman originally from Connecticut, arrived in the Islands about 1850 and became a naturalized citizen of Hawai'i in 1855. Burrows was in the service of the king, but when he showed an over-fondness for alcohol it was sug-

gested that he be sent as keeper to this isolated lighthouse to help him overcome his weakness.[28]

On November 21, 1881, J. A. Hassinger, chief clerk for the minister of the Interior, wrote Meyer stating that the keeper's salary would be sixty dollars per month and that part of Burrows' duties would be "to pack the oil for the Light House from the landing at Kaunakakai or elsewhere. Mr. Stirling will take a look among his papers for any instructions in regard to working of the lamps and if he can find anything useful he will promptly forward it to you."[29]

Meyer and Burrows needed some written directions, because the lamps and sections of the lens were scattered about all over the premises, needing to be assembled. The two men finally fitted the lens parts together. On December 8, 1881, Meyer reported that the light was functional and that the cottage was nearly finished "so far as to be habitable. . . . I have requested Mr. J. W. Burrows to take charge at once."[30]

Burrows' life as lightkeeper at Lā'au Point is revealed in part though the correspondence between Meyer, the Department of the Interior, and Burrows. It was a life of frustration, disappointment, severe hardship, and isolation. The lights that had been established—at Honolulu and Lahaina, as well as at Pauka'a Point and Kawaihae on the island of Hawai'i—were all harbor or anchorage lights. Ships could easily transport needed lighthouse and personal supplies to these places. Fresh water was available. Human companionship was always at hand. The light station at Lā'au Point had none of these advantages.

Keeping the light burning was a struggle for Burrows from the beginning. Lamps were a continual problem; transporting supplies to the light station was always laborious; a reliable water supply was never available. In March 1884 Meyer asked for new lamps "as the present ones have nearly all given out." Two months later he made the same request. In July the lamps he received from Honolulu would not work with the Fresnel lens. In August 1885 another lamp arrived, but it leaked much more than the old one. A replacement lamp was sent in December and after testing it Meyer once again wrote to the Interior Department, "I am extremely sorry to inform you that the new lamp . . . which Mr Julius Smith, Department of Public Works, sent up lately is found upon trial to be no better than all the others. . . . It leaks badly and I return the same herewith and would kindly ask you to have it tried at Honolulu before sending it up again."[31]

Burrows somehow managed, night after night, to keep the lamps working and the light burning, but an even more serious problem was developing. On May 15, 1886, Meyer reported that

> the long continued absence of rain on that part of the island where Mr. J. W. Burrows, the lighthouse keeper has to live, has caused his water supply to give out and he will be in need of drinking water. There is no water to be had for a good many miles. . . . Could not the *Mille Morris* or some other schooner coming from Honolulu land a few casks of drinking water for him at . . . Laau? He also wishes to know if a small distilling apparatus to obtain drinking water from the sea water would be expensive. There are no immediate prospects of rain. The whole country about there is drying up.[32]

No water was shipped to Burrows. Two weeks later Meyer again pleaded that Burrows was entirely out of water and the nearest waterhole to his place was four miles distant. It was not until July that the schooner *Mille Morris* delivered forty gallons of water.

Insufficient water and improperly functioning lamps continued to be problems for Burrows year after year. Added to these was the delay in the shipment of kerosene for the light. At one time Burrows was so desperate for kerosene that when he saw a

steamer about to round the point heading for Honolulu, he quickly scrawled a letter, corked it tightly in a bottle, and told his son to swim out from the west point to meet the steamer and to deliver the bottle to the captain. This letter contained a plea for more kerosene.[33]

Either because of bad weather or bureaucratic mismanagement, shipments of kerosene were seldom on schedule. Inflexible government procedures also resulted in delayed payment of wages. Although Burrows' salary was increased in 1882 to seventy-five dollars a month, he often had difficulty in collecting the money, and Meyer would write to the minister.

Meyer wrote many letters on Burrows' behalf. Over and over again he requested a "small but good water filter" to be shipped to Burrows, "The water sent him has been put in wine casks, without having been rinsed out and he thinks it is not wholesome to drink without being filtered. . . . The dry weather seems to become drier."[34]

The pleas from Meyer continued through the following year: "There has been no rain since March 1890 . . . wells have dried up . . . Burrows needs water and also again requests the lumber, etc. for repairs, and oil which was ordered some six or eight months ago and has not arrived."[35]

The most poignant letter is dated July 1891 and was written by Burrows to C. N. Spencer, minister of the Interior.

> I have been for nine and a half years Light Keeper at this place at a salary of $75 per month without rations. Out of this sum I have to pay an Assistant $25 per month including his board. I also have to bring all the oil (with the exception of 40 cases landed here) from Kaunakakai 20 miles each way, besides all my own food etc. For this purpose I am obliged to keep a large stock of pack animals. In former years I have been able to raise a few vegetables, which helped me out a little. But of late it has been so dry nothing would grow. My water still remains unfit for use. We are getting water (poor)

from Haleolono, 10 miles distant. I don't think there is a more out of the way, inconvenient place in the Kingdom than this. The landing is never to be depended on from one day to another. In consideration of the above disadvantages and inconveniences I humbly request Your Excellency to increase my Salary to $100 per month from July 1, 1891.[36]

Burrows' request was denied, and Meyer wrote to Spencer asking for an increase for the following year.[37]

Burrows did finally receive water filters; however, delays in shipments of oil and supplies continued. One letter informed Meyer that "the supply of oil was ordered May 6 and until we received your letter, supposed it had been promptly forwarded. The difficulty is in getting a vessel to touch at the point and save the long overland carriage."[38]

Burrows often had to pick up lighthouse and personal supplies shipped to Kaunakakai instead of to the lighthouse landing. George Cooke, a resident of Moloka'i, tells of seeing the Burrows family on these trips. "John married an Hawaiian woman, Koa by name, and raised a large family at the west end. It was a familiar sight to see him with them all in an open cart drawn by mules, coming across the wide plains to Kaunakakai for their . . . provisions. One of his sons, David, is purported to be the inventor of the 'steel guitar'."[39]

As Burrows grew older, his handwriting deteriorated and his letters become increasingly difficult to read. In 1895 he again wrote to request oil and an increase of his salary to $100. "In former years there were plenty of fish here but for the last two years there are no fish. So I have to buy Beef. Formerly I was able to raise corn, pumpkins, melons etc. but of late years we have had no rain . . . there is very little firewood."[40]

On January 4, 1896, Burrows received a raise! His joy was short lived, for soon afterward he was informed that he would be charged six dollars per head for every horse and mule he allowed to graze on ranch land belonging to the Bishop Estate. Burrows was no longer strong or well enough to write a letter himself, so the letter explaining his situation to the minister of the Interior was written by someone else.[41]

A few weeks later, Henry Holmes of the Bishop Estate wrote to James A. King, minister of the Interior. "I am instructed by the Trustees . . . to return to you the letter of the lighthouse keeper at . . . Laau, forwarded with yours of February 24, 1897. At their last meeting, the Trustees voted to exempt this official of the government from paying of pasturage on all animals required of him for transportation purposes."[42]

This was good news for Burrows. The "Old Captain," as he was called, was too sick to contend with either the Bishop Estate or the government. And his friend Meyer, who had written so many letters on his behalf, died June 12, 1897.

On March 4, 1898, the following letter was written to Minister of the Interior James A. King:

I am sorry to say that J. W. Burrows, the Light Keeper at this place is dead, he died on the 28th of February. Now dear Excellency, I am J. R. Burrows the Son of J. W. Burrows, age 26 years. And I have been with him for 15 years at this place and I know everything about keeping the Light. Now, if you please, let me have this light for the future. If you give me the Light, please let me know as soon as possible.[43]

No condolences were sent, but J. R. Burrows was "given the light." "We hope that you will perform the duties of Light House Keeper faithfully and conscientiously as your predecessor. Kindly inform this Department if you have taken the oath to support the Constitution and Laws of this Republic."[44] Lightkeepers and other government employees were required to take an oath of allegiance to the republic. Burrows complied and was appointed keeper of the Lā'au Point Light at a salary of seventy-five dollars a month.[45]

In the summer of 1898 President William McKinley signed a joint congressional resolution annexing Hawai'i to the United States. Even though the government of the Republic of Hawaii continued in power, the sovereignty of Hawai'i was formally transferred to the United States at ceremonies in Honolulu on August 12, 1898.

Burrows, though isolated at his station, must still have felt a part of these historic events. Shortly after the ceremonies took place, he requested an American flag for the lighthouse. "Several vessels passed by the Light House and gave salutes by their Whistle, but I have no flag to Salute with."[46] His request was granted, and the lighthouse at Lā'au Point was the first in Hawai'i to fly the American flag.

In 1902 the stone light tower was rebuilt and painted, and extensive repairs were made to the keeper's cottage. Soon after these improvements were completed, an attempt was made to remove Burrows as keeper. Mr. G. C. Munro, manager of the Molokai Ranch, wrote Alfred Carter, an attorney in Honolulu, explaining the situation. Munro believed that a man named Hugh Robertson was circulating a petition to have Burrows removed. Evidently Robertson had been promised the keeper's job, if it was vacated, as a political reward for election work. Munro wrote Carter:

> I could get up a petition and get every resident to sign if necessary to have Burrows retained. Burrows is not much use to the Ranch, but is a very harmless, peaceable fellow, careful of fire and careful to shut the gates . . . also he has lived all his life at the light and there has been no complaint of laxity of duty.[47]

Carter forwarded Munro's letter to Henry Cooper, superintendent of Public Works, adding this note, "Would you kindly do anything in your power for John Burrows, the Lightman at . . . Laau, as there

The Lā'au Point Light in 1906 was atop this wooden structure that was built adjacent to the original 1882 stone tower. The stones in the foreground are probably from the first tower, which had been torn down. (Courtesy of Carol Edgecomb Brown Collection)

seems to be a mean underhanded attempt to put him out."

Burrows remained the keeper of the Lā'au Point Light until it was automated in 1912. In 1906 the original stone tower was replaced by a thirty-five-foot wooden tower built in approximately the same location. Later, when the decision was made to automate the light, a new site was selected at the top of the 132-foot-high bluff at Lā'au Point. A nineteen-foot wooden pyramidal skeleton tower was built on the bluff, making the light 151 feet above sea level.

The characteristic of the light was changed from fixed white to "Group Flashing White, 10 seconds." The light could be seen eleven miles at sea.[48]

Today the light at Lā'au Point is still located on the bluff but is no longer displayed from a wooden tower. In 1972 a modern solar-powered light was installed on a twenty-foot steel pole that also displays a diamond-shaped dayboard. At night the light flashes white, but it can be seen only seven miles at sea.[49]

The isolation of Lā'au Point has not changed since John Burrows was the keeper of the first light. A reminder of the difficulties Burrows must have faced in transporting supplies by mule cart from Kaunakakai to the lighthouse can be found in Lieutenant D. T. Noviello's 1986 ANT report: "This light proved inaccessible with a rental car. In the future, either a Jeep should be rented or arrangements made with the local helicopter service to fly out to the site."[50]

And the road has deteriorated since 1986. In 1989 the ANT team reported that after driving through the last Molokai Ranch gates the road resembled a stream bed.[51] The Lā'au Point Light, however, is meticulously maintained. This once-important coastal light became a minor beacon when the tallest light tower in Hawai'i and the brightest light at the time in the Pacific was established in 1909, on the north coast of Moloka'i. This light is referred to by the Coast Guard as the Moloka'i Light, but it is more familiarly known as the Kalaupapa Light.

Kalaupapa (Moloka'i Light)

A need for a primary seacoast light on North Moloka'i was emphasized in the Hawaiian Investigation Report of 1902.

> The great bulk of the Pacific coast commerce passes through the channel between the islands of Oahu and

Molokai. Many hundred vessels now pass annually through this channel, and the number is rapidly increasing, and there are, with the single exception of the light-house at Diamond Head, no light-houses whatever on the exposed points of either of these islands. There is a small light on the further point of the island of Molokai, but it is not visible for more than about 5 miles at sea.[52]

In 1903 Lieutenant Hugh Rodman, U.S. Navy, made a careful investigation of possible lighthouse sites in Hawai'i, both in person and by questioning captains of vessels frequently calling at the various ports. Based on his study, he drew up a list of sites that in his judgment were necessary for the aid and protection of navigation among the Islands. One of the lights recommended by Rodman was a red light to be visible ten miles at sea, mounted on a trestle-type structure built at the "Leper Settlement on Moloka'i at a cost of $1,000."[53]

Leprosy, or Hansen's disease, was first reported officially in Lahaina on the island of Maui by Dr. Dwight Baldwin in 1857. On January 3, 1865, the legislature passed an act authorizing the acquisition of suitable land for an "isolation settlement and confinement for those afflicted." Godfrey Rhodes, president of the Board of Health, inspected various sites including land on Moloka'i. On September 20 Rhodes reported that he had bought a tract of land for about $1,800 and some government land in exchange. The area, consisting of over 6,000 acres, was located on a small peninsula called Makanalua or Kalaupapa. It was surrounded on the west, north, and east sides by ocean, and on the south side by cliffs that rose two thousand feet. The first group of Hansen's disease victims was landed on the east side of the peninsula at a place called Kalawao on January 6, 1866.[54]

In 1904 the settlement was still located at the Kalawao site when proposals were made for establishing a lighthouse. The Light House Board, after reviewing testimony and reports on navigational needs in the Hawaiian Islands, asked Congress for several appropriations, including $40,000 for a lighthouse at the "Leper Settlement" on Moloka'i. Congress did not appropriate the money. The following year the board again stated that a fourth-order light was needed at the "Leper Settlement," and again, appropriations for Moloka'i were turned down.[55]

In seeking funds for the Moloka'i light, the board explained that the Makanalua peninsula was an ideal location for a navigational aid because the land jutted out to sea for a considerable distance from the otherwise incurving and very steep north coast of Moloka'i. Still, many lawmakers remained opposed to the location of the light because it would be close to the leprosy settlement. At the time, Hansen's disease was greatly feared, and vessels took special precautions to give the island a wide berth.[56]

Whether or not Congress would eventually appropriate money, the Light House Board felt a lighted aid at this location was so important to navigation that it proceeded, without specially allocated funds, to make plans for the construction of a temporary light on the peninsula. In 1906 notice of the board's intention was published in the annual *Light List*—"Number 273: Molokai: Makanalua Light . . . To be established."

First Lieutenant J. R. Slattery, U.S. Army, assistant to the engineer of the Twelfth Lighthouse District, had designed a type of beacon that could be built for less than $500. Work on the temporary light began late in 1905, but stormy weather in mid-January 1906 delayed its completion. Slattery was in Honolulu awaiting the arrival of permits issued by the territorial Board of Health that would allow his work crew to go ashore at Kalaupapa. On January 22, 1906, L. E. Pinkham, president of the Board of Health, sent the required permits and wrote Slattery: "Superintendent J. D. McVeigh of the Leper Settlement . . . will do all the hauling you desire

and furnish clean labor. He advises you to delay sending material and men until the weather moderates and becomes settled. The storm has been quite severe and has done some damage."[57]

Slattery immediately replied. "Consulted the Weather Bureau and sea captains along the waterfront. They all seem to think that the weather has now settled and that the opportunity is favorable for sending men and supplies for the Light House at the Settlement by the *Likelike* tomorrow."[58]

A week later the first lighted beacon on the peninsula was completed. The Light House Board reported: "On March 1, 1906, a fixed red lens-lantern light was established on Makanalua . . . 64 feet above the water and 34 feet above the ground, on the top of a lead-colored mast, having at its base a small white house with lead-colored trimmings and a red roof." A shelter for the keeper was also built, with a catchment for rain water along with a water storage tank. James M. Keanu was placed in charge of the light.[59]

Although this was only a temporary light, it required inspection and maintenance, and each time anyone needed to go to the site, a special permit had to be issued by the Board of Health. Frustration over bureaucratic procedures is evidenced in letters from lighthouse engineers who pleaded for permanent passes to visit the station, so that they would not have to give long-term advance notice.[60]

For one year the temporary beacon marked the northern shore of Moloka'i before the Light House Board again requested funds. This time Congress complied and appropriated $60,000. Plans and specifications were drawn up for the station, and on October 27, 1908: "certain lands within the Kalaupapa Leprosarium" were acquired for lighthouse purposes by Executive Order 962, signed by President Theodore Roosevelt.[61]

The Board of Health, which controlled access to Kalaupapa, still had not devised an efficient procedure for granting permits to lighthouse personnel and those surveying the site. When work on the permanent concrete light tower began, emergency passes were sometimes issued before work parties could land. The ultimate frustration was expressed by Captain C. W. Otwell in a letter to the president of the Board of Health: "I have just learned that permits to leave as well as to visit the station are required."[62]

Arrangements were eventually made for regular passes to be issued to a number of people, including Eugene B. Van Wagner, who began working on the construction of the light station in June 1908.[63] Six months later he was made foreman. On March 12, 1909, Van Wagner wrote a friend that he had "fixed up the light at Oahu" as well as others in the Islands and was "now working on Molokai."

> This tower is 112 feet. Have the cement all in . . . and will begin putting up the iron work next week. Have raised one piece of the iron already. The light pedestal weighs 2200 pounds. Had to take it up on top. There are four other pieces each weighing 2,000 a piece. I snapped some pictures of the tower as men were lifting the large prism. . . . I wish I was through here, there is no place to go we are right in the leper settlement and of course are not allowed to go anywhere else, just like prison. . . . This life on the ocean wave isn't what it is cracked up to be.[64]

Before work on the station began, a source of fresh water had to be found. The catchment and water tank originally built were not sufficient for the needs of the new light station. "For construction purposes and for a permanent supply . . . the most feasible way to get water," Otwell wrote in a letter to Dr. C. E. Cofer, "seems to be through the mains already laid for the settlement." Water into the Kalawao settlement was piped from Waikolu Valley, southeast of the Kalaupapa peninsula. Otwell estimated the daily consumption for the station would

The Moloka'i Light was under construction from June 1908 to June 1909. When completed, it was the tallest light tower in the Islands and the brightest light in the Pacific. (Aids to Navigation, Fourteenth U.S. Coast Guard District)

be about 300 gallons, which "could be drawn off during the day or night as most convenient." Permission to tap into the settlement's water line was granted by the Board of Health, and one group of men began laying the water pipes to the station.

Other men worked on building a road that would extend over two miles from the boat landing at Kalaupapa (across the peninsula from Kalawao) to the station site.[65]

The lighthouse service in Hawai'i did not have its own tender at that time, and the vessels most used for transporting men and materials were the *Likelike,* the *James Makee,* and the *Iwalani.*[66] Arriving from Honolulu, ships anchored in the deep water of the bay off Kalaupapa. Cargo and men were off-loaded into small boats and rowed to the wharf, often through high seas and rough surf, for both bay and landing were open to strong and stormy north winds.

Once materials were ashore, they were carried by men, donkeys, and horses along the road from the landing to the construction site. Tons of cement, sand, lumber, ironwork, glass, machinery, tools, and so forth, were required to build the light station. In addition there were the food and the supplies needed by the workers who were camped at the site. The Board of Health allowed workmen to build a cement shed and a wooden building near the wharf for storing materials until they could be transported to the light station.[67]

The most significant cargo arriving at Kalaupapa had been shipped from halfway around the world. The lantern and lens, made by Chance Brothers and Company in England, were ordered by the Light House Board in September 1907. They were delivered to New York in July and arrived in Honolulu in November 1908. Both lens and lantern were originally intended for the Makapu'u Light on O'ahu, which when first proposed, was designated as a fourth-order light; but plans changed in 1907 when the Light House Board bought a hyperradial lens for the Makapu'u lighthouse and decided to use the second-order lens at Moloka'i.[68]

Once this decision was made, the tower for Moloka'i was designed specifically to house the second-order lens. The octagonal tower measured twenty feet in diameter at the base and tapered to a diameter of fourteen feet, four inches at the top. The octagonal reinforced concrete base was thirty-four feet in diameter and five feet, six inches thick. A molded concrete cornice supported the lantern at the top of the tower.[69]

The men began building the forms for the tower in September 1908. The tower was divided into two unequal vertical sections, with the first concrete section ending about five feet above the arched entrance door. Six windowlike openings in the remaining upper part of the tower shaft admitted light around the 189-step staircase. It took the workers six months to complete the concrete work. It was difficult, backbreaking, and sometimes dangerous work. As the tower was being readied for the ironwork, one workman fell from the top of the tower and was killed.[70]

The erection of the ironwork was started in April 1909. The stairs, up to and including the fourth landing, were built of concrete, but from this landing to the lantern floor they were of cast iron. The watch room floor was also cast iron, with steel I-beams beneath, supporting the lens pedestal. From the watch room to the third floor just below it, a hollow weight shaft was constructed for the clockwork.[71]

The clockwork and falling weight were designed to drive the revolving lens mechanically as it rotated around the lamp. A circular trough or vat containing liquid mercury supported the weight of the lens as it revolved. The vat could be lowered, with the lens temporarily braced, so that the keepers could examine the apparatus and also drain the mercury to clean it. Every six months the mercury would be filtered and then replaced in the vat. For some revolving lights, ball bearings on roller carriages were used, but the weight of the Moloka'i lens made this design unreliable—it weighed over three tons. The mercury ensured flotation and smooth revolutions at the speed required for the two-panel lens to revolve around the light and create a flash every twenty seconds.[72]

In June 1909 the lens and lantern were in place atop the tower. The total expenditure for the station, which included the light tower, keepers' houses, work and storage sheds, water and fuel tanks, and so forth, was $59,977.04, thus fulfilling Congress' requirement that the cost "not exceed $60,000."[73]

Thirty minutes before sunset on September 1, 1909, James Keanu, who had been the keeper of the temporary light, climbed the stairs to the watch room of the tower to prepare the lamp for lighting. Keanu checked the lamp to see if it was correctly focused within the lens. The illuminant was incandescent oil vapor (i.o.v.), which produced a light brighter than that of an ordinary oil lamp. When the lamp was lit, Keanu removed the clockwork weight from its rest and wound it, setting the revolving mechanism into operation. As the lens revolved around the lamp, the bright light flashed for the first time across the Kalaupapa peninsula, 213 feet above the water, and twenty-one miles out to sea.[74]

There was still work to complete at the station even though the light was in operation. Some outbuildings and one of the three keepers' homes were still under construction. The houses were one and a half stories high. Each had a living room, dining room, kitchen, two bedrooms, and a bathroom on the first floor, and high attic space above. Invitingly wide, covered verandas extended around three sides of each building. One of the houses was built with the dark blue volcanic rock found on the site; the other two houses were concrete. The frame roofs were covered with corrugated-iron sheathing. Each house had a view of ocean and *pali* (cliff). The keepers and their families would be living amidst the spectacular natural beauty of the Kalaupapa peninsula.[75]

The keepers' homes formed a tiny community on the tip of the isolated peninsula. Isolation is not unique for light stations, especially for landfall lights such as the one at Kalaupapa, which are often located on remote and almost inaccessible coasts. However, the men stationed at Kalaupapa did not suffer from loneliness. Three keepers and their families were usually in residence, and, though they were not supposed to have contact with the patients or even with released patients who chose to remain in the settlement, there were both friendliness and communication between the two groups. People from the settlement rode their horses or walked up to see the light tower; it was a place to go, something to do, a sight to share. It was the tallest lighthouse in the islands and a source of pride for both groups.

Most of the keepers stationed at Kalaupapa were dedicated men who had few illusions about the job. They showed a strong attachment to their work and liked the life-style. Many remained in the lighthouse service until they retired. Keanu, for example, served on the Moloka'i Light and also on the Kīlauea Light on Kaua'i until his retirement in 1939.[76]

Although living at each lighthouse in the islands had its own particular advantages and disadvantages, the Moloka'i Light differed in a dramatic way —access to the station was extremely restricted because of the leprosy settlement. Keepers and their families needed permission and passes from the Health Department every time they left or arrived at the station. Special permission was also required before any of the personnel from the lighthouse tender *Kukui* could come ashore.[77] The *Kukui*, assigned to duty in the islands in 1909, became a familiar sight at Kalaupapa.[78] It transported men and materials for maintenance work on the Kalaupapa Light tower and keepers' dwellings. It brought food and supplies for the keepers and their families. It carried lighthouse superintendents, inspectors, and personnel back and forth from Honolulu.[79] The *Kukui* was the life link between civilization and the remote light station.

The remoteness was not unusual for most of the keepers. Manuel Ferreira was the exception. Before his assignment to Kalaupapa, Ferreira had served for one year on the lighthouse in busy, bustling Honolulu Harbor. The Honolulu Harbor Light, which used a simple oil lamp with a wick, was discontinued in 1926, when an automated electric light was established at the top of Aloha Tower.

At Moloka'i, Ferreira tended a lamp that burned vaporized kerosene under an incandescent mantle. The light had a luminous intensity of 620,000 candlepower and could be seen twenty-one miles at sea. The characteristic of the Moloka'i Light had been changed in 1911 from flashing white twenty seconds to flashing white ten seconds. This meant that the light flashed on for a brief 0.3 seconds with an eclipse of 9.7 seconds.[80]

Other changes were made at the light station. In time, besides the 132-foot tower and the keepers' houses, there were several other buildings on the twenty-one-acre station. A wooden two-room storage and shop building was built east of the keepers' dwellings. In front of the middle house was a garage for the station's half-ton truck, and in back was a laundry and shower room. A concrete oil house was used for storing domestic oil in drums, alcohol in cans, paint, and so forth. The kerosene used for the light was stored in a 1,254-gallon cylindrical steel tank located on the southwest side of the tower; from there it was pumped by hand to a receiving tank on the first floor of the tower, and then to the oil tank in the watch room.

Northwest of the tower stood the 12,000-gallon water-storage tank built of reinforced concrete. Paths led between the tower, the keepers' homes, and the other buildings. Stone walls enclosed kitchen gardens. One inspector reported after his tour of the grounds: "The light station . . . is maintained efficiently by a lighthouse keeper and two assistants, all natives of Hawaii. The grounds are attractive with extensive well-kept lawns."

There were no school facilities within easy reach of the station, and school-aged children usually lived with relatives elsewhere in the Islands and came back to the light station on weekends and holidays. Medical attention for the keepers and their families was provided by the resident physician at the Kalaupapa settlement.[81]

"Extreme precautions were taken at all times to prevent the spread of leprosy," emphasized Ferreira. Subsistence supplies were purchased by the keepers in Honolulu and shipped, "double packed . . . the same as Territorial supplies for non-lepers at the settlement." As soon as supplies reached the boat landing, the cases going to the light station were "removed and brought immediately to the keeper. . . . All our food and other supplies came to Molokai in double cases."[82]

In spite of its disadvantages, of the many lights Ferreira served on, the Moloka'i Light held the most enjoyment for him. "Hunting was one of our favorite off-duty recreations," he said. "We used to go out frequently after wild pigs, goats, and deer. This meat came in mighty handy at times when food shipments were delayed because of bad weather at sea."[83]

The Kalaupapa peninsula, though isolated by ocean and high, steep cliffs, was populated in ancient times and important in Hawaiian religion. Historian Thomas G. Thrum in 1893 described two heiau located there, one at Pu'ukahi, at the foot of the pali, where Kahiwaka'apu, a famous priest, was in attendance, and another at the top of the pali at Kukuiohāpu'u, a place where signal fires to O'ahu were burned in time of war. In 1909 two other heiau were identified.[84]

Before Western contact, Kalaupapa was a place where leaders met to discuss warfare, jurisdictional disputes, land holdings, and other important matters. In the mid-nineteenth century, Hawaiians living on the peninsula used large areas of the land for pasture and agriculture. Kalaupapa was well known for the cultivation of a variety of vegetables and fruits. In 1857 a newspaper reported that "many sweet potatoes are being planted now. . . . Most of the crops are watermelons, and some small and big beans, and onions. Be on the watch, you traders, for Kalaupapa is the best in all the islands for good prices and fast work. All the California ships come to Kalaupapa."[85]

A description of the peninsula almost one hundred years later was given by Harry Franck in his book *Roaming in Hawaii*. Franck described the area around the lighthouse as being "covered with stones big and little, black sinister volcanic rocks, as if they had rained down upon it, as no doubt they did. The lighthouse in its fenced square quite separate from the leper settlement was until recently the last surviving kerosene lighthouse in the United States. . . . [It is] now . . . the largest single electric lighthouse, or the largest one with its own plant, on our coast."[86]

Moloka'i Light Station acquired its own electrical generating plant in 1934. Three fully automatic two-kilowatt engine generators had been purchased for the light and by 1935 the light tower and all the buildings at the station were wired for electricity.[87]

Shortly after electricity was introduced, Ed Marques became the second assistant keeper. James Keanu was once again head keeper, having returned when Ferreira was transferred to the Makapu'u Light Station. As far as Marques was concerned, "Keanu could do everything even though he lost his right hand." Keanu was using dynamite one day to blast out holes for fence posts when the stick of dynamite he was holding exploded. "All the jobs that needed to be done at the light station Keanu could do—he could use a shovel, a pick, an ax; he could

even wring out sheets! He was a good man and a good worker."[88]

Moloka'i was Marques' first light station assignment. He was working as a contractor, doing some dynamite blasting of his own, when he saw a notice on the bulletin board at the Federal Building in Honolulu listing an opening for a lightkeeper. He filled out the forms at once and then waited. "There were a lot of men who wanted the job, and I was surprised when the clerk called me. I guess my earlier job as seaman helped me. My salary as second assistant keeper was $125 a month and $20 was deducted for housing. Once a year we were given a 26 day leave."

Marques had been to Kalaupapa once before, in 1932—when he was shipwrecked! He was serving on the SS *Kaala* when it ran aground on the rocks off Kalaupapa. "It was a black night, but the light was right there in front of us. Some believe that the wreck occurred because of the great hatred that existed between the captain and the first mate." The captain, who was supposed to be on watch, had fallen asleep, and as the vessel approached the peninsula, the first mate denied the helmsman's request to change course. The vessel ran up on the rocks, ripping open the hull. With each wave the ship would lift and rock violently, then crash down on the jagged lava bed. Water rushed with powerful force over the deck, breaking loose the lashed-down barrels of gasoline. "Everything swung crazily and it was a great struggle to lower the skiffs." The timing had to be perfect or the skiffs would smash against the side of the vessel or be swamped in the waves; the men, lowering themselves down to the small boats, had to jump at just the right moment or they could be crushed between the skiff and the hull of the rolling vessel.

"We all made it safely to shore and the people at the settlement took good care of us. We stayed at Kokua House (helpers' quarters). The next morning we went out to look at the *Kaala* and we could see how the crude oil had spread out from the ship and killed all the fish.''

A ship to transport the stranded men back to Honolulu was sent to Kaunakakai Harbor, on the south side of Moloka'i. A three-mile trail, with twenty-six switchbacks, winds up the 1,664-foot steep cliff behind the settlement. The men hiked the trail to the top, where they were met by cars that took them to the harbor. "That is one of the most beautiful trails I've ever taken," remembers Marques, and he regrets that he seldom found time to hike while he was working at the station. "When I was shipwrecked off the Kalaupapa Light," Marques says, "I never dreamed I would someday be back as a keeper."[89]

The only way in or out of Kalaupapa, except for the precarious trail, was by sea until an airplane landing field was established on the northwest edge of the light station property in 1933.[90]

The road from the settlement to the light station was familiar to Fred Robins when he arrived at Kalaupapa in 1940 with his wife Annie Naua'ao, daughters Roselani and Anna Mae, and son Fred, Jr. As a youngster Robins had traveled the road many times when his father, Ed Robins, Jr., served as keeper at Kalaupapa from 1914 to 1916. Lightkeeping was a family tradition, and Fred Robins was returning to Kalaupapa as head keeper. In 1941 Robins joined the Coast Guard. For a while during World War II he left his lightkeeping duties to serve with navy units but later returned to the Moloka'i Light Station.

During the war there was a military atmosphere at the station, and Assistant Keeper Marques, who remained at the light until 1946, remembers that during the war years he had a Winchester "and carried a forty-five. We felt we were well protected—as long as we saw the enemy first!" The lights were off at night but still manned by the keepers and used as watchtowers to spot enemy shipping or submarines. Without any chores other than scanning the ocean through binoculars, it was sometimes difficult for the keepers to stay awake during their long night vigils. The Robins' daughter Anna Mae remembers her mother's evening routine: "She would finish up the dinner dishes, and then prepare a snack, perhaps some special treat. After she put us to bed, she would walk to the light tower, carrying the food and something to drink, and stay with our father on his shift at the light. Sometimes she would take us with her, and I would watch them as they sat together, and we would look out at that great ocean and the night sky."[91]

On April 1, 1946, nature gave a jolt to the idyllic scene. That was the day a tidal wave devastated many coastal areas in the Islands. Some of the houses along the beach at Kalaupapa were demolished. Henry Nalaielua, who lived at the settlement, remembers that several cottages were washed away. "One was lifted off its foundation and floated into the ocean. The main office was spun off its foundation . . . and faced in a different direction. Headstones from the graveyard . . . were strewn about. . . . The most severe damage for Kalaupapa was to our pipeline . . . the only source of water." The light station was on high ground, and the great thirty-five-foot wave did not engulf the lighthouse. But from this high and safe vantage point, Robins could see the destruction below him. "One minute the houses were there, and the next they were washing away in the wave." Robins rushed to help the people in Kalaupapa.[92]

Regulations may have required restricted contact between the leprosarium and those at the light station, but off the record, there was contact, not only in times of emergency, but for fun. The men in the settlement were enthusiastic baseball players and formed several teams. The men from the light station joined in the games. Gambling, not condoned at the settlement, found a less judgmental setting at the light station, and there was perhaps more than an occasional crap game at the site.[93]

Robins' favorite pastime was fishing—pole fishing, spear fishing, and throw-net fishing. One of his other hobbies was raising homing pigeons. The family also kept ducks and chickens. "We had quite a farm at Kalaupapa. We raised fruits and vegetables, goats and pigs," remembers Anna Mae. When the children reached school age they were sent to live with an aunt in Ho'olehua, where they attended Moloka'i Elementary School, and later they were sent off-island to high school. Anna Mae missed being at the lighthouse, but she returned on holidays and on some weekends. When Robins had leave, the whole family went to Honolulu or to visit relatives on one of the other islands. In 1964 he retired as keeper.[94]

One of Robins' assistants at the Moloka'i Light Station, beside Marques, was Boatswain's Mate Harry Kupuka'a, who spent twenty years in the lighthouse service and the Coast Guard. But career lightkeepers like Robins, Marques, and Kupuka'a were becoming history. In the 1950s as the civilian keepers (and those who had joined the Coast Guard) retired, they were replaced by younger Coast Guardsmen, or the lights they had tended were automated.

Realizing that it would be difficult to find younger Coast Guardsmen willing to serve at the remote station, Rear Admiral S. H. Evans, commander of the Fourteenth Coast Guard District, considered the possibility of hiring personnel from the Kalaupapa settlement. In 1959 he wrote to the director of the settlement:

For many years, civilian Lighthouse personnel who were transferred to the Coast Guard . . . have been available to maintain and operate Molokai Light Station. . . . We soon will be faced with no more "old timer" lighthouse personnel and are experiencing difficulty interesting the younger military generation in isolated duty assignments such as the Molokai Light Station.[95]

This letter was the beginning of plans to automate the Moloka'i Light. Newly developed equipment made it possible to modify the light so that it would operate automatically with very little supervision. Admiral Evans wanted to know if it would be possible for "locally available non-patient or released patient caretaker service . . . to perform lens and general cleaning; replace burned out lamps and make routine tests of standby equipment, with the Coast Guard responding in emergency situations." The Coast Guard at the same time wanted to investigate any possible health hazards and consulted with Clarence B. Mayes, medical director of the Public Health Service office in Honolulu. Dr. Mayes assured them: "Your Coast Guard personnel would not, in any way, be in danger. Hansen's Disease requires close and constant physical association in order to be contracted."[96]

While the "lamplighter service" was being investigated, plans were made for a standby light of lesser intensity, but with the same characteristic, to be mounted on the lantern gallery. This light would be battery powered and would switch on automatically in case the electricity to the main light should fail. Additionally, it was recommended that a "failure alarm system . . . be extended to the lamplighter's dwelling."[97]

During this time the Moloka'i Light continued to operate with Coast Guard personnel. Captain C. N. Daniel in a 1960 report commented: "Although family quarters are provided, it is not considered appropriate that men with their families be assigned and it is further recommended that this station be re-classified as an isolated unit and tour of duty be established at one year."[98]

Life sometimes takes an ironic twist. The victims of Hansen's disease, isolated at the settlement, could see that the young keepers of the light were the ones who felt alone and longed for companionship. "They were so lonesome we would sneak up to the light station and talk story with them," Rose Lelepali remembers. "There were still great restrictions and we were not supposed to visit the lightkeepers, but the men were thankful for the company." They took Lelepali to the top of the light. She had known earlier keepers and visited the station many times, but no one had ever taken her to the top of the light before. "To see that lens; to see the source of the light was something I will always remember." The brilliant light was part of her life as it swept over the pali, across the black lava rocks from which she sometimes fished at night, and rhythmically lit up her bedroom, "like a full moon's beam." It was a light that had shown through the darkness of the settlement from the time Rose arrived as a patient, leaving behind her home on the island of Hawai'i, her husband, and their six children, the youngest of whom was only two years old at the time.[99]

There is a well-known history of forced family separation among people who became patients at the settlement, but the lighthouse had always been a family station. Once the "old timers" retired from the service there was a change. At one time the Coast Guard officer in charge, M. F. Beeson, was alone at the station for over a month before a second man arrived. Because the station had not yet been classified as "isolated," the Coast Guard did not supply any books or magazines. Furthermore, because of the station's out-of-the-way location, Andrews Flying Service was charging the Coast Guardsmen six cents a pound for delivery of food and other personal needs, which were flown into the station. Captain Daniel recommended that the government pay this added expense "which it imposes on station personnel by assigning them to this duty

station," as well as supply "a reasonable number of magazines monthly and paper books occasionally."[100]

The inspection reports made during the 1960s reveal a picture of slow deterioration at the light station. With the exception of the light tower, which required only an occasional coat of paint, almost everything else needed repair. Roofs leaked and one building was infested with termites. The report noted that "a hit of the fist on the bulging bathroom wall will shake down termite dust in the tub." No one understood the plumbing, and because the quality of the water was dubious, the men used it only for cooking, resorting to soda pop for drinking purposes. The station had no telephone, and all paved roadways at the station were potholed and badly deteriorated. It was evident at this point that the light would eventually become automated, and the Coast Guard was understandably reluctant to pump money into facilities that were soon to be abandoned. A 1965 report estimated that conversion of this station to automatic operation would accrue an annual saving of $9,500 in operating expenses.[101]

In the summer of 1966, Daniel J. Bryson, Boatswain's Mate first class, and James R. Creighton, Engineman third class, were on duty at the Moloka'i Light Station. Bryson, who was from Jackson, Michigan, had served in the Coast Guard for twelve years and had been at Moloka'i for one year. Creighton, from San Antonio, Texas, joined the Coast Guard in 1964 and arrived at Moloka'i only four months before the light became fully automated. By August 1, 1966, the Moloka'i Light was operating on its own, and Bryson and Creighton, the last keepers of the light, departed.[102]

During the 1960s it was estimated that approximately eighteen hundred seagoing vessels a year passed the vicinity of the Moloka'i Light, as well as interisland fishing and pleasure boats. Of the vessels sailing to and from the west coast of the United

States, the Panama Canal, and the northern part of the west coast of South America, approximately five hundred used the Molokai Light as either their landfall light on the Hawaiian Islands or their departure light for the east. The remaining vessels used Makapu'u Light as their landfall/departure light. However, many of the vessels used both. If a westbound vessel from the mainland to Honolulu were even five to ten miles south of its track, the Moloka'i Light would be its landfall light rather than the Makapu'u Light. The seagoing vessels referred to ranged from small three-hundred-ton ocean-going tugs with tow, to tankers of twenty-nine thousand and above gross tons, to a few large passenger vessels. The Moloka'i Light, with an intensity of two million candlepower visible up to twenty-eight miles at sea, remained a crucial aid for these vessels, leading them through the narrow and tricky Kaiwi Channel between the islands of Moloka'i and O'ahu.[103]

The light was essential to navigation and the Coast Guard retained about three-quarters of an acre around the tower, but the rest of the land and buildings, "in excess to the needs of the Coast Guard," were released to the General Services Administration. The buildings and structures on the property were then in "run down" condition and presented a "poor appearance." Of the three keepers' homes originally built, only two remained. The one built of volcanic rubble was considered "restorable." The other dwelling, of concrete blocks, erected in 1951, was in fairly good shape, but the condition of the storehouse, garage, and fuel shed was poor.[104]

In 1971 the State of Hawaii expressed in writing their desire to have the area reconveyed to the state. Ten years later the General Services Administration transferred the light station property, not to the State of Hawaii, but to the Department of the Interior, National Park Service. The Kalaupapa Leprosy Settlement National Landmark District was listed on the National Register for Historic Places in January 1976, and the Moloka'i Light Station was included as part of this district, but the light tower with its unique lens was not listed as a separate entry on the Register until 1982.[105]

Almost as soon as the light was listed on the National Register for Historic Places, the lens and rotating mechanism became difficult for the Coast Guard to maintain because of age. The Coast Guard reported that the mercury created a significant health hazard to the personnel who maintain the light, and that mercury spills had occurred in the past, which required specially trained U.S. Navy teams to clean up.[106]

Accidents with the mercury had also occurred before the Coast Guard was on the scene. The lightkeepers, careful as they were (and before anyone knew that mercury created a health hazard), experienced spills while in the process of draining, straining, and cleaning the mercury. Tricky to pour and contain, the fluid is also known as "quicksilver" for good reason. One of the worst accidents occurred on December 25, 1923, when strong earthquake shocks occurred, "throwing and scattering the mercury from the vat." In 1933, as the keepers were cleaning the lens, earthquake tremors again shook the tower. The violent tremors caused so much mercury to spill out of the vat that the lens would not revolve. The emergency backup system for the light had to be used until the mercury could be replaced.[107]

Another spill due to earthquake shocks occurred on January 22, 1938, when Ed Marques was on duty.

> The mercury sloshed out all over and soon there was not enough mercury in the vat to support the weight of the lens and it stopped revolving. A supply of mercury was stored in cylinders on the floor below, and we carried two, hundred pound containers up the stairs and emptied them into the vat until the lens could revolve again. The next day, when we could see, we gathered

The Moloka'i Light Station, sans the second-order Fresnel lens and all but one small building, is part of the Kalaupapa Leprosy Settlement National Landmark District and is listed on the National Register of Historic Places. (Aids to Navigation, Fourteenth U.S. Coast Guard District)

the spilled mercury up by sweeping it, a little at a time, into dust pans, then we poured it through cheese cloth into containers. When it settled out clean and still it looked like polished silver and we could see the reflection of our faces in it.[108]

Marques and the other keepers acted so quickly after the spill that the light was out for only fifteen minutes. The only other damage reported at the station was the loss of five feet of stone wall, which was shaken down as a result of the quake.[109]

In 1984 there were no lightkeepers who would sweep the mercury into a dust pan if it spilled, and there was no local Coast Guard expertise on the handling and disposal of mercury. When spills occurred, personnel from the Navy Environmental and Preventive Medicine unit were called in. An inspection made on January 15, 1985, found that mercury was leaking from the vat.[110] It became necessary to dispose of the mercury, but once it was removed, the lens could no longer rotate. The Coast Guard decided to replace the entire illuminating apparatus with an optic that did not require a revolving Fresnel lens.

To prepare the tower for the new DCB-224 rotating beacon, six men from the Aids to Navigation team, including petty officers Aaron J. Landrum and Ralph Craig, were sent from their base at Sand Island, Honolulu, to Kalaupapa to disassemble the rotating mechanism. The men first removed the electric motor, gears, and shafts from the lens rotation mechanism. They removed the 1,000-watt lamp and the three-legged pedestal on which it was installed. All the wiring for the generators, the control panel, the battery charger, the alarm box, and the time clock were removed. A special contractor was given fourteen days in which to drain the mercury from the lowered vat and to decontaminate the float, vat, and tower surfaces. Fifteen gallons of mercury, weighing approximately two hundred pounds, were drained through a hose and sealed in containers to be disposed of at a designated site, along with all protective clothing and rags used in the decontamination process. The inside of the vat and float were painted with "Carbo mastic 15" and allowed to dry for two days, then silica sand was place in the vat, and the float platform and the gears were replaced in their original positions.[111]

The project, except for the decontamination, became a reenactment, but in reverse, of what workmen faced in 1909. The lens is six feet in diameter and has a framework of bronze. Each piece of hand-cut, ground glass is fitted at a precise angle into a section of the optic, and each section is fitted exactly into the whole framework. The position of individual pieces is noted by an engraved number. "The numbering system is so simple and clear," Landrum commented, "that anyone, even someone who had never seen a Fresnel lens before, can understand how the lens is assembled. There are Roman numbers as well as Arabic numbers, and on the bottom is stamped 'A go to A, 1 go to 1,' etc. The lens is so beautifully designed, once it is assembled the weight of the sections automatically makes the whole lens fit together tightly."[112] It had been planned to make video tapes of the disassembling process to facilitate reassembling, but the number and letter directions on the lens itself were all that were needed.

"There are 26 sections all together," explained Craig, "and each weighed about 264 pounds." As each section was removed from the lens it was lowered 138 feet down to the ground along the outside of the tower.

> We used this old truck—no brakes, only a hand brake, no doors, rusted out—and we tied a line to it. After we removed a section of the lens we'd wrap it up in two old mattresses and then attach it to the other end of the line. As the truck backed up towards the tower the lens was slowly lowered to the ground. You can imagine how tough it was getting every piece down. The road was rough and rocky, and the wind was blowing about 35 to 40 miles an hour.[113]

It took the men two and a half days to remove the lens from the tower. The sections were taken by truck and stored near the Kalaupapa boat landing until the Coast Guard Cutter *Mallow* arrived. The *Mallow* anchored offshore and each piece was loaded into a small boat and then off-loaded onto the *Mallow*. The lens was transported to Lahaina, Maui, where the Lāhainā Restoration Foundation assumed custodial care of it.

But this was not the end of the job for Landrum and Craig. The Lāhainā Restoration Foundation acquired a small building in the Wharf Shopping Complex in Lahaina that provided an excellent display area for the lens and was open to the public. Landrum and Craig were sent to Maui to reassemble the sections, which took five days. "Both of these men did a fine job putting the lens back together again," wrote Jim Luckey, general manager of the Lāhainā Restoration Foundation. "They overcame some difficult mechanical problems with ingenuity and dispatch."[114]

The completion of the Moloka'i lens exhibit in Lahaina does not, however, end the story of the light, the lens, and the Hansen's disease victims living at Kalaupapa. Landrum and Craig as Coast Guardsmen felt a satisfaction with the job accomplished by the ANT team, but as individuals they share a sadness for the people of Kalaupapa. From the day the dismantling of the lens began, people from the settlement began coming up the hill to the Light Station to watch. "They are the greatest people in the world," said Craig. "All of the people there are either victims of Hansen's disease or have something to do with its treatment. They love visitors. They don't get enough visitors. They treat everybody like royalty; they didn't want us to leave. They didn't want the lens to leave either."[115]

The people came up the hill to watch, not out of idle curiosity, but because something important in their lives was being slowly taken apart and taken away. "One of the things the people enjoyed doing was going up to the airport at night and watching the light," Landrum explained. "It was a romantic feeling the light created. There is so little the people have. There is so little they can do." The lens, a rare giant of a crystal-like jewel, was a source of pride to the people. It was something uniquely beautiful, perfect and functional. "They didn't want to see that Fresnel lens go," said Landrum. "A guy by the name of Richard Marks, who was a patient and is the Kalaupapa sheriff, really went to bat for those people." Marks, on July 17, 1986, told the *Maui News:*

> They talk about the Statue of Liberty, well, this light was the first thing that hundreds of thousands of immigrants to Hawaii saw when they came here. Everyone of our people . . . can remember this light looking over us. . . . Nobody gives a damn about the people here. . . . Maui is going to set up a building and put money into it. How willing are they going to be to give it (the lens) back? . . . We're not blaming the Coast Guard. They're doing their job . . . but the lens should be shown here. What does Lahaina have to do with the light?

Jim Luckey has said it will go back. "Several organizations were contacted concerning taking custody of the lens. We said we would take it only under the condition it be returned to Kalaupapa when some proper facility there becomes functional." Even with this reassurance Marks is skeptical.

> Times change. People change. Maybe the next guy won't want to give it up. . . . That light has been very special to the people here. . . . It has been here longer than any living person has. You could always look out and see it sweeping across the cliff. . . . It is the Kalaupapa Light.[116]

PART III

Lighthouses of Hawai'i County

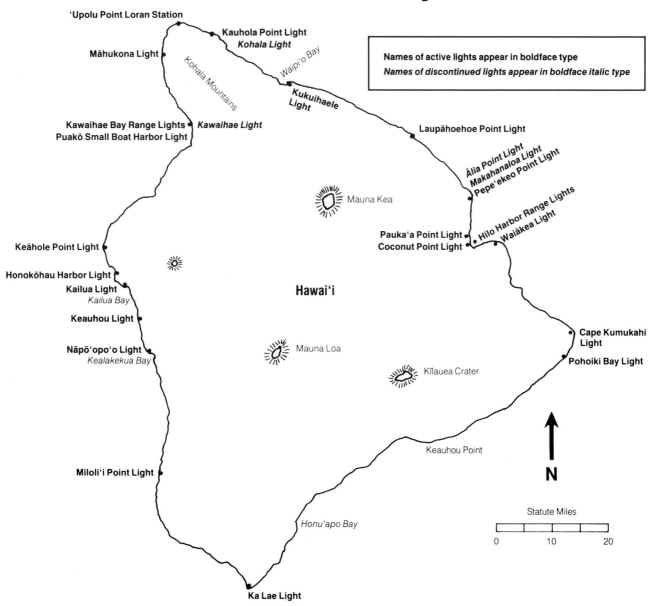

'Upolu Point Loran Station

Kauhola Point Light
Kohala Light

Māhukona Light

Kohala Mountains

Waipi'o Bay

Kukuihaele Light

Names of active lights appear in boldface type
Names of discontinued lights appear in boldface italic type

Kawaihae Bay Range Lights   *Kawaihae Light*
Puakō Small Boat Harbor Light

Laupāhoehoe Point Light

Ālia Point Light
Makahanaloa Light
Pepe'ekeo Point Light

Mauna Kea

Hilo Harbor Range Lights
Keāhole Point Light

Pauka'a Point Light   *Waiākea Light*
Coconut Point Light

Honokōhau Harbor Light

Hawai'i

Kailua Light
Kailua Bay

Keauhou Light

Cape Kumukahi
Light

Nāpō'opo'o Light
Kealakekua Bay

Mauna Loa

Pohoiki Bay Light

Kīlauea Crater

Keauhou Point

N

Miloli'i Point Light

Statute Miles

Honu'apo Bay

0   10   20

Ka Lae Light

Chapter 9

The Island of Hawai'i

In the Hawaiian language there are many specific words for "wind;" words describe the direction of the wind, its strength, and its association with places. According to historians there was a boy wonder named Kūa Pāka'a who could chant over two hundred wind names ranging from gentle breezes to wintry gales. One of the more fearsome winds was Ulumano.[1]

A story is told about the night when King Kamehameha and a group of men were fishing from their canoes off the west coast of the island of Hawai'i when Ulumano started to blow from the south. The villagers of Nawawa became concerned for the safety of their king. They knew that violent Ulumano could wreck the canoes and would blow the fishermen far out to sea. It was impossible to go out to help; the only aid that could be provided was lighting a fire on shore so that the men could be guided back to safety. The chief ordered the villagers to set their houses on fire—and the entire village of Nawawa was burned to light Kamehameha and his men ashore.[2]

There are few stories as dramatic as this in the annals of lighted beacons, and the incident vividly illustrates the need for navigational aids no matter how familiar the waters and coastline contours and landmarks are to local mariners. Hawaiians traditionally did not rely on headland fires for a landfall, but a light shining from shore was required at times, and a few permanent sites on the islands were selected. These sites for navigational fires were near

canoe landings and fishing areas and were usually associated with heiau. After the arrival of Westerners, who were familiar with lighthouses, open fires on shore were also occasionally used to direct foreign ships to anchorages. It was with the development of foreign trade that the need for established lighted aids at landings was realized.

The first important export from the Islands was sandalwood. Many of the exports to follow were not of native origin, but introduced. Foreigners brought cattle, horses, and sheep to the Islands, gifts that were to have a significant influence on the future development of harbors and navigational aids on all the Islands, but especially on the island of Hawai'i. By the late 1820s the sandalwood trees had been stripped from the land, but salt and salted beef were in demand by the whalers who were coming in increasing numbers to the island for provisions.

Later came two other products that profoundly influenced the development of commerce on the island of Hawai'i—coffee, introduced in Kona by missionaries in 1828, and sugar grown on the rapidly expanding plantations of the 1860s.[3]

Kawaihae

Kawaihae, on the northwest coast, was one of the anchorages that became widely used by foreign vessels. In pre-contact times it had been an important landing on the island. Accounts of ancient inter-island canoe voyages mention Kawaihae in connection with voyages throughout the Islands. It is also one of the places where fires were lit to guide fishermen home at night.[4]

When whaling ships first began coming to the Islands for supplies, they called most frequently at Honolulu and Lahaina, but by 1845 Kawaihae and the fast developing harbor town of Hilo were important sources for fresh food, water, beef, and salt. Cattle were also shipped from Kawaihae to Lahaina and Honolulu to supply the whaling ships anchored there.

With the increasing number of vessels anchoring off these landings on the island of Hawai'i, lighted aids at night were badly needed, but the government did not take any initiative in establishing them. A private firm, G. W. Macy and Company, planned to finance the building of a light tower at Kawaihae. According to the *Pacific Commercial Advertiser* of January 20, 1859, "The erection of a lighthouse will add to the safety of all vessels visiting that port."

It wasn't until 1869, when the private aid was in disrepair, that the government became involved in building a lighthouse at Kawaihae. Sam Chillingworth was chosen to erect the lighthouse, and on June 23, 1869, he wrote to Frederick W. Hutchinson, minister of the Interior, "I have framed in the stonework, and built a strong platform and protecting house and having whitewashed everything in connection with the light, it is now in a firm and complete state, and from this date the light will be attended to from sunset to sunrise without intermission."[5] Chillingworth was appointed keeper at a salary of four dollars a month.

In 1871 Kawaihae Bay was designated as one of six ports of entry in the Hawaiian Islands. It was also an important supply port for the products of the Waimea and Hāmākua inland districts.[6]

Although kerosene lamps were coming into use at other lighthouses, the lamp at Kawaihae continued to use sperm oil. The oil was delivered periodically by the schooner *Kilauea*. When the schooner was caught in a kona storm, as it was several times during the winter of 1874, the needed whale oil was not available to the keeper. On one occasion Chillingworth complained to the minister of the Interior, "I was compelled to use an ordinary kerosene lamp." This served well enough for several nights until November 24, "when about midnight the kerosene oil lamp, from some unexplained cause, exploded, completely destroying the Prism Glass of the lighthouse and rendering it entirely useless. I would respectfully inform your Excellency that an exactly similar light to the one destroyed here was originally sent to Hilo, but not finding it to suit that harbor it was replaced by a Kerosene lantern and that if that light is not at present in use it might be ordered to this port."[7]

A much more serious accident occurred on May 19, 1877, when the oil lamp exploded. Before the fire could be extinguished the lantern and the wooden frame upon which it rested were ruined. Chillingworth suggested that "a new stone rest can be built for $150, with a wooden hood for the light. A new lantern is needed. . . . If your Excellency will authorise it our Mr. Allen Stackpole will have a new light erected." In the meantime, a kerosene lantern was borrowed from neighbors and temporarily displayed from a wooden pole.[8]

The Kawaihae Lighthouse was either repaired or a new one was built in 1879. It was described in the *Hawaiian Annual:* "For the anchorage at Kawaihae a white light, about fifty feet above sea level, has been erected, at a point bearing from the N.E. corner of the reef. . . . The light can be seen at a distance of ten miles out to sea. With this light bearing E.N.E. there is a good anchorage in eight fathoms of water, about a quarter of a mile from shore." The description of the light remained the same for the next seventeen years.[9]

In 1896 the SS *Kinau* went aground off Kawaihae.

This Kawaihae Light served one of the most important landings on the island of Hawai'i from 1902 to 1916. As well as marking the anchorage, it warned of a dangerous reef about one-half mile offshore. (National Archives)

The agent for Wilder's Steamship Company complained that on the night of the steamship's mishap the light was not burning. "If such a light is not burning regularly," wrote the agent to the minister of the Interior, "it is worse than none at all." The

captain of the ship, when questioned, answered that he believed the light was burning that night, "but so dimly that it was impossible to distinguish it from the lights along the shore."[10]

A new light was built at Kawaihae sometime before 1902. The superintendent of Public Works in his annual report for that year stated that there was an entirely new light at Kawaihae, "the old light being low and shaded. The new one is a 40-foot tower placed on a bluff making the light 60-feet above high tide." The light was shown from a bay window in a small room built on top of the square wooden trestle tower. No keeper's house was built. A footpath led from the light to the village and the steamer landing, about one-quarter of a mile away.[11]

Māhukona

Sugar plantations were flourishing on the Big Island in the late nineteenth century. The six plantations or mills not far from Kawaihae in the North Kohala area needed the means to transport their products. Sugar from the Kohala District was at first carted over the hills to Māhukona, a landing north of Kawaihae. A railroad was eventually built to move both sugarcane and bagged sugar and also to haul freight. In 1889, C. L. Wight, president and manager of the Hawaiian Railroad Company, requested that a lighthouse be erected at Māhukona: "Foreign vessels call here about every three weeks and they often lose much time not knowing where to come in. In thick weather it is also hard for steamers to find the place. In addition it will be of material assistance to the vessels bound up the channel."[12]

Wight wanted the stone tower for the light to be built on the ridge toward Kawaihae. He estimated the cost would be about $250. He did not think keeper's quarters were necessary, because someone could be hired locally to tend the light at a salary of $12.50

The Mahukona Light, built in 1904, was the only tower in Hawai'i constructed with this unusual architectural design. The structure was described by the Light House Board as "a beehive-shaped solid stone tower 23 feet high." The vessel in the background is the *Lehua*. (National Archives)

a month. "The light," he wrote, "should burn every night." Wight agreed to do all that he could "to forward the building of the lighthouse. . . . I do not believe that it will be economy to send men from Honolulu. Wages are higher there and generally men coming from there are apt to make a holiday of a trip of that kind. I would accordingly suggest waiting till men from this district are available."[13]

The Māhukona Lighthouse was built on a solid stone ledge. It had an unusual shape, like a truncated cone, with a base twelve feet in diameter, tapering to three feet at the top. Mortar, one foot thick, was used for the sides from the base to a height of twelve feet. The inside of the cone was filled with rock. The remaining three feet was solid concrete. A platform was secured at the top with iron bars set into the concrete, and a ladder ran up the outside of the tower to the platform.

A nickel-plated brass stand held the one-hundred-candlepower lamp. The lantern, framed with oak and finished with redwood, had a pentagon shape with windows on four sides and a door in the fifth. The windows were three-quarter-inch glass, nineteen by twenty-two inches. The roof was sheet brass. Wight reported that "all the work was done in the most thorough manner."[14]

On August 5, 1889, W. D. Alexander, surveyor general, wrote to L. A. Thurston, minister of the Interior, "I have the honor to report that the new light house near Māhukona . . . is about 75 feet above sea level, and one third of a mile due south of the Māhukona anchorage. The bearing from the said light house to the Kawaihae Light House is south-east by south . . . and the distance is nine nautical miles. The light is visible 10 miles."[15]

Kohala Mill (Kauhola Point) and Makahanaloa

Two years later, in 1891, Wight requested a lighted beacon on the coast near the Kohala sugar mill east of Māhukona. After W. B. Godfrey and William C. Wilder, of Wilder's Steamship Company, agreed that an aid was needed in this area, the government authorized Wight to build one. Wight said he would accept the construction contract for $1,200 that was offered, but wanted to change the specifications. J. A. Hassinger, chief clerk with the Department of the Interior, replied that Wight would have to wait for appropriations.[16]

Wight also wanted another light near Makahanaloa, southeast of Kohala Mill and seven miles north of Hilo Harbor. Appropriations were not available for this light either, and it was not until 1897 that the two beacons were erected. Both beacons were built in the same design—open wooden-frame forty-foot towers surmounted by an enclosed lamp room painted white. The light was shown from a bay window constructed above the lamp room. Barbier and Benard of Paris built the lenses, with a reflector for both lights. A storeroom was built within each structure, but there were no keepers' dwellings. The lights could be seen a distance of ten miles.[17]

The light at Makahanaloa was tended by a worker from the Pepe'ekeo Sugar Company and John Hoopii was keeper for the Kohala Light. Both keepers received fifteen dollars a month.[18]

The Makahanaloa Light was located about one-half mile south of Ālia Point. In the 1904 report of the Light House Board it was described as a fixed white sixth-order light, estimated to be sixty-five feet above high water. "The tower and oil house are in a dilapidated and unsafe condition."[19]

The Kohala beacon was erected on Kauhola Point and in the 1904 report was called the Kauhola Point Light (see p. 122). It was in the same condition as the Makahanaloa Light, and the Light House Board was eager to make repairs. "The light marks a low point projecting into the sea from high cliffs on each side. . . . The light was established because of the wrecks on the point it marks."[20]

Hilo Harbor

The Hawaiian Railroad that carried freight and passengers between Kawaihae and Kohala was the only railroad on the island of Hawai'i in the late 1890s. Because there were few good roads, boats were the chief means of local and interisland transportation. Of the many boat landings on the island, Hilo Bay was the most important commercial anchorage.

Hilo Bay was also known as Byron's Bay in honor of Lord George Anson Byron, captain of HMS *Blonde,* the first man-of-war to anchor there. The bay was practically an open roadstead, with little protection from ocean swells. In 1824 the Reverend Charles Stewart was aboard the *Blonde* when the vessel made its way through the channel at the entrance to the bay; he wrote:

> The channel is formed by the cliff on the right, and a sunken coral reef on the left . . . making it necessary for ships to pass so close to the breakers, as to appear a dangerous situation. . . . The reef runs in a curved direction, from the point at the channel, about a half of mile to the east, where it joins a romantic little islet covered with cocoa-nut trees; from that fact called "Cocoanut Island."[21]

Hilo Bay was exposed to the north and northeast winds, but the reef, called "Blonde Reef," offered some protection. The entrance had a depth of thirty to forty feet. The bay became popular with whaling ships and vessels transporting coffee, arrowroot, and sugar.

In 1869 the town of Hilo was much larger and more developed than Kawaihae; there were many stores, blacksmith and cabinet shops, bakeries, schools, churches, framed dwellings, and thatched houses. In the center of Hilo stood a large building that housed courtrooms, the post office, the governor's office, and Sheriff J. H. Coney's office.[22]

When the lighted beacon was established at Kawaihae, the Hawaiian government also wanted one built at Hilo Harbor. Coney was requested to consult with the captains who frequently used the harbor. He reported that the preferred site "of Captain Sartani and other captains" was the small bay of "Onomea seven miles north of Hilo." But evidently not all the captains agreed. Several suggestions were made, including Pauka'a Point:

> The Pilot first said it was the best place and that the reef's extremity is nearly opposite the Honolii gulch and that vessels coming in always steer for the gulch. The Pilot now says that the proper place for the light is opposite his house on the beach, which is in between the town and the Government House. . . . Now if you can tell where the lighthouse ought to be erected you can do more than I can.[23]

In the end, after a lengthy correspondence, the decision was for Pauka'a. The lighthouse structure was built for $325 and the light was lit on August 13, 1869. Coney reported that the light could be seen only as a ship approached directly from seaward. "I moved the lamp farther out into the Bay windows, but it does not seem to improve it any. . . . The captains of the *Annu* and *Kate Lee* both say that the light shows well straight out."[24]

Coney, who had been sheriff of the island of Hawai'i for eighteen years, retired and L. Severance, who had arrived in the Islands from Maine in 1851, was appointed in his place. Fredrick W. Hutchinson, minister of the Interior, contacted Severance in 1871 because there was still a great deal of dissatisfaction with Hilo's lighthouse. Severance reported to Hutchinson that the "community and the Captains of Coasters" regarded the lighthouse at Pauka'a "of little use." The sperm oil lamp used with the lantern projected the "light only out in front." Severance substituted a small kerosene lamp "and found that it could be seen up and down the coast, a distance of ten or twelve miles."[25]

Even with this improvement the light was inadequate, and Severance considered the $144-a-year salary for the keeper a waste. He suggested taking "the same lamp and reflector and putting it up the Governor's flag staff." He thought another light on the wharf would give incoming vessels a "true course to steer by," and added that his "constable could attend to it and save the expenses of a light keeper."

After further debate, it was decided to retain the light at Pauka'a and place another light on the wharf. Both were kerosene lights, but there were still complaints. Severance investigated and reported: "I visited the lighthouse yesterday and find that the Chinaman in charge is very negligent in his duties, not trimming the light properly. I showed him the proper way and tonight it shows finely from here."

Two years later the Pauka'a Light needed repairs. Severance reported that the light "nearly blew over in the last strong wind we had. . . . This is a very valuable light to vessels coming into Hilo and it should not be allowed to go out of repair; $100 will put it in good condition. I have lately bought an excellent safety lamp for it, which throws a light visible at sea from 10 to 12 miles."[26]

In 1880 the Pauka'a Light was described as a plain fixed light, fifty feet above sea level. Severance urged the government to raise the elevation of the light to make it more easily identifiable to vessels approaching the harbor, especially since lighthouse dues of three dollars were collected from each vessel using Hilo Harbor. He reported: "One captain when charged for lights wanted to know where the lighthouse was and said he had not seen anything around that looked like a lighthouse." Severance agreed with the captain: "There is nothing about it to distinguish it as a lighthouse." His suggestion was favorably viewed by the minister of the Interior, who hoped "a move may be made for an improvement in your lighthouse as soon as the new appropriations are passed."[27]

Appropriations were not approved, though complaints about the light continued. Severance repeat-

The Pauka'a Light, photographed in 1904 and described in that year's *Light List* as a "white box on a white trestle," was similar in design to other early beacons constructed at Pepe'ekeo, Kawaihae, and Kauhola on the island of Hawai'i. (National Archives)

edly made specific suggestions for building a higher structure and increasing the light's intensity, but it was not until 1890 that he managed to have a new tower built for Hilo Harbor. It was located on Pauka'a Bluff, above the old beacon site. Two separate white lights atop the tower were set eighteen inches apart on a horizontal line parallel with the coast. The wooden tower was twenty-five feet high, placing the lights 159 feet above the sea. Sam Kapahua was appointed keeper and the pay was increased to $180 a year.[28]

In 1904 the Light House Board reported that the beacon on Pauka'a Point was a "fixed green light, of low power, composed of three small reflector lamps. The light is shown from the bay window of a small room constructed at the top of a wooden trestle tower 35 feet high." Because the tower was in unsafe condition, the Light House Board had it removed and a thirty-eight-foot mast erected in its place, which elevated the light to 170 feet above high water. A small white service house with a red roof was built at the base of the mast. The Pauka'a Light was fixed green.[29]

The board also reported on two other lights established by the Hawaiian government to aid vessels entering Hilo Harbor—Waiākea, on the southeast side of Hilo Bay, and Coconut Point, on the southwest point of the bay. The Waiākea aid was a city electric arc light with a red screen set in front. The Coconut Point light also used the city electric current and showed a fixed red light. These were the first lights on the island of Hawai'i to use electricity as the illuminant. Although the board installed a new lens lantern on the Coconut Point Light, it recommended that a new lighthouse be built in its place and justified this request by describing Hilo as the second port of importance in the Hawaiian Islands. "The present small fixed red lens lantern light, located on the old and dilapidated government wharf at the foot of Waiānuenue Street, is entirely inadequate for the requirement of the growing trade of Hilo." The old tower with the electric light was eventually replaced in 1915 by a reinforced concrete tower exhibiting a flashing acetylene light.

The Hāmākua Coast

Economically the island of Hawai'i was totally dependent on shipping. There was no local market for the island's cattle, sugar, or molasses, and the machinery and supplies needed by the islanders had to be shipped in. Landings on the leeward coast were so shallow that only lighters could be used to load and unload cargo, while Hilo and the entire windward coast, referred to as the Hāmākua coast, were open to treacherous winds and waves. For about fifty miles, from Hilo north to Kukuihaele, there is a coastal bluff from one hundred to four hundred feet above the sea. Many sugar plantations were located on top of the bluff. The water is deep along this shore, but the problem was how to anchor boats securely enough to load and unload cargo, and how to transfer cargo between the vessels and the cliff top.

The problem was ingeniously solved in the 1890s by using "wire landings." Four mooring buoys, to which the boats could be secured fore and aft, were located so that a vessel could be positioned, facing into the wind, below a hoist house on the bluff. It was a complicated procedure tying off to the buoys, dropping anchors, and attaching necessary wires for moving the cargo. The freight was loaded and unloaded by hoisting a trolley along a wire suspended from the top of the bluff and shackled to a sea wire that ran to an anchor on the seaward side of the vessel. At almost all of these landings there was also a derrick landing to handle cargo of more than two tons. The derrick landings were considered even more dangerous and precarious than the wire landings because they were so difficult to cast off from quickly in case the wind shifted.[31] Work at all of these landings was hazardous. Boats were frequently wrecked and minor accidents were common, but because the Hawaiian sailors were skilled surf swimmers there were few fatalities. Along this coast there were nine wire landings as well as several derrick landings. In 1905 lighthouses were established at two —Kukuihaele and Pepe'ekeo. The light at Pepe'ekeo was referred to as the Ālia Point Light and took the place of the 1897 Makahanaloa Light, which like the new one had been built about one-half mile south of Ālia Point.[32]

Another beacon on the Hāmākua coast had been built between Pepe'ekeo and Kukuihaele at Laupāhoehoe in 1890. The site selected for the beacon was a point of detached ledges of lava rock that projected seaward and on which the sea broke with considerable force. The landing was at the inner end of the point. The thirty-foot wooden trestle tower had been built on low, flat lava, five feet above the sea. An ordinary house lamp emitted a fixed white light of low power from a box on top of the tower. Neither an oil house nor a keeper's house had been built. In 1905 the Light House Board replaced the beacon with a thirty-four-foot mast that supported a lens lantern. The fixed red light was displayed forty-eight feet above high tide. A small service house, with a red roof and red trim, was constructed at the base of the mast.[33]

Ka Lae

When the Light House Board first assumed responsibility for the Territory of Hawaii's lighthouses in 1904, it was most concerned with repairing or rebuilding the beacons that had already been erected and did not have the funds for establishing lighthouses at new sites, even though they might be needed. There were twenty-two landings on the island of Hawai'i; seven had lights built by the Hawaiian government and seven had privately built and maintained aids, though the government did pay for oil and keepers at some of the latter. The Light House Board proposed taking over the private aids as well as improving all the existing government lights.

> Most of these stations are in such a dilapidated condition that they should be rebuilt; failing that, they should be thoroughly repaired, and in most cases the present old and poor illuminating apparatus should be replaced with new full-powered lights of proper orders. These coasts need to be strongly lighted, because of the many sugar plantations on which there are strong electric lights visible many miles at sea."[34]

After the existing beacons were initially improved, attention was given to establishing new lighted aids. The board anticipated that commercial shipping to Hawai'i and across the Pacific Ocean would increase as a result of the building of the Panama Canal. In particular, a seacoast light was needed to mark the southernmost point of the island at Ka Lae (South Point).

A beacon on South Point had first been proposed in 1883 to the Hawaiian government, but when appropriations were turned down, no further action was taken. In 1905 the Light House Board's request for an appropriation was passed, and the beacon was completed on March 5, 1906. The lens-lantern light was supported by a thirty-four-foot wooden mast painted a lead color. The fixed white light, illuminated by incandescent oil vapor, was seventy-five feet above the water and visible for nine miles. A small white service house with a green roof was built at the base of the mast.[35]

When repairs were made on this light in 1907, Captain C. W. Otwell, the army engineer with the Lighthouse Service in Hawai'i, reported:

> This station is isolated and desolate, the locality being only a waste of rough lava rock. No quarters have been

provided for the keeper. The only line of supply is over a rough trail, the nearest water and provisions being ten miles distant. To provide at least temporary relief from the hardship to which the keeper is exposed, $200 worth of materials were purchased for the construction of a shelter and a water tank. A suitable dwelling should be constructed at this . . . southernmost point of the Hawaiian Islands. The light is important, and the keeper should have this inducement to remain.[36]

The lightkeeper, John T. Nakai, could trace his family history back to two brothers who lived at Ka Lae and who were supposed to be the foremost fishermen for Kamehameha I.[37] The fishing has always been excellent off Ka Lae because of the converging currents that run just off shore. It is too deep to anchor a boat here, but Hawaiians of old fished from canoes tied off through holes they made in the rock ledges. Many of these holes can still be found in the rocks below the lighted aid.

When Nakai moved into the temporary keeper's house at Ka Lae, there were at least six other families living at the point. Kele Pinau first came to Ka Lae in 1890 and later built a home there. Iokewe Moi began fishing at the point in 1895 and after he was married he, too, built a house there. Some of the other residents were Haililani, Haloa Kuluipo, Charles Mokuhalii, and Maunalei. All of the houses were built of rock, but some had thatched roofs and some had metal ones. Besides fishing, the residents planted potatoes, pumpkins, and other vegetables in the 'a'ā (rough lava) flows about one-half mile above the lighthouse. Nakai raised watermelons and sweet potatoes near the lighthouse.[38]

This fishing settlement was not the first to exist at the point. Human habitation at Ka Lae may go back to A.D. 124, and the point is believed to provide one of the most important records of human occupation in the Hawaiian Islands.[39] When a new light was proposed for Ka Lae, Professor William Tufts Brigham of the Bishop Museum wrote to Governor Walter F. Frear requesting that particular care be taken not to destroy or injure the heiau, known as Kalalea, that was near the proposed lighthouse site. Professor Brigham wrote, "This venerable relic is the only heiau on Hawaii where the old religion is still in vogue and where it is possible for the right man to gather information of the ancient cult." Captain Otwell assured the governor that he would "make every effort to see that the relic was preserved."[40]

On December 4, 1908, slightly more than ten acres of land at Ka Lae were set aside for lighthouse purposes by a proclamation signed by President Theodore Roosevelt. The new light was exhibited from a thirty-four-foot-tall white mast and was sixty-three feet above the water. The light could be seen for nine miles. A keeper's house was also built at that time.[41]

Keāhole Point and Nāpō'opo'o

While the Ka Lae beacon project was underway, the Light House Board also investigated several sites for lighted aids along the west coast of the island of Hawai'i. One of the sites selected was Keāhole Point, southwest of Kawaihae Bay, where the first lighthouse on the island had been erected.[42] A fixed red lens-lantern light was established on the low black lava flow forming the westernmost point of the island.

The lens lantern was mounted on a thirty-six-foot white wooden mast. A service house, with a red roof and lead-colored trim, was built at the base of the mast. The fixed white light was sixty feet above high water. A one-story keeper's house was built about 550 feet east of the beacon. It was painted light gray and had a red roof and trim.[43]

A similar mast for a fixed white light and a keeper's house were also built on the west side of the island at Nāpō'opo'o in 1908. This light was located on the north side of Kealakekua Bay. The bay, which is about two miles wide, offered the best anchorage along the western coast of the island, and boats were fairly secure here except in strong southwest winds.[44]

The Nāpō'opo'o Light Station property, consisting of 2.93 acres, was turned over to the United States for lighthouse purposes by Governor Frear's proclamation on March 16, 1909. When the station was completed, Oliver Kua, a farmer living in Nāpō'opo'o, became the first keeper.[45]

Kauhola Point

During the next ten years constant lighthouse repair and construction work was in progress at sites all along the coasts of the island of Hawai'i. Reinforced concrete towers, pyramidal in shape, with automatic acetylene lights were built to replace the outdated lights at Keāhole Point, Kawaihae, and Māhukona on the west coast; and on the east coast at Kukuihaele, Laupāhoehoe Point, and Coconut Point. A new seventy-two-foot skeleton steel tower was erected at Ālia Point (Pepe'ekeo); and a temporary frame tower with an oil-vapor lamp replaced the old lens-lantern light at Kauhola Point on the north shore. By 1918 there were fourteen lighted aids on the island, all considered to be in good condition.[46] Yet funds were still needed by the Lighthouse Service—for example, $20,000 to improve the lights at Hilo Harbor, and $20,000 to build a primary seacoast light and a keeper's dwelling at Kauhola Point.[47]

The keeper of the Kauhola Point Light from 1910 to 1913 was Edward K. Moealoha. He lived with his family in his own house about one and a half miles from the light. When, as often happened, Moealoha was compelled to remain at the station overnight, he had to stay in the service shed at the base of the tower. In 1913 he resigned. The Bureau of Lighthouses reported that because of the lack of a house

The Kauhola Point Light in 1904, with service shed at right. The simple structure gives little hint of the importance of the beacon or that a future lighthouse on this site would become one of the primary seacoast lighthouses of Hawai'i. (National Archives)

for the keeper and his family it was difficult "to obtain satisfactory service, and therefore proper quarters were erected."[48]

The keeper's dwelling was built approximately 475 feet south of the tower. The one-story frame structure was erected on concrete piers. It had an asbestos shingled roof and the interior was plastered. The house was described as being "34 by 35 feet in plan, and consisting of a living room-dining room, kitchen, pantry, two bedrooms, a bath, storeroom, and two closets, and is provided with a veranda off the living room, and complete plumbing." It was completed January 12, 1914, at a cost of $2,833.43.[49]

Building the keeper's quarters was just the first step in the improvements the Bureau of Lighthouses wanted for the Kauhola Light Station. The bureau felt the light should be upgraded and in 1916 requested a $22,000 appropriation for a seventy-five-foot cast iron tower, a new fourth-order lens, and an assistant lightkeeper's dwelling.[50]

In 1917 the old lens-lantern light was discontinued and a temporary white pyramidal frame tower with a flashing fourth-order lens was erected. The illuminant for the light was incandescent oil vapor. The wooden skeleton tower placed the light sixty-six feet above high water and the light was visible fourteen miles. The "temporary" tower was not replaced, although requests for funds for a new tower were submitted annually to Congress for the next fourteen years.[51]

On the morning of September 26, 1931, Fred Edgecomb, superintendent of lighthouses for the Nineteenth District, received the news that the Kauhola Point Light was out. Keeper John Sweeney, who had been appointed in 1923, radioed the following message: "Last night at 9:45 P.M. the inside of the lantern was gutted by fire. I will try and continue light tonight until help arrives." Evidently the fire started when the thermostat failed to operate. The heat was so intense that all the lantern windows were broken and all the top prisms on both faces of the lens were cracked beyond saving. Sweeney said it was the worst accident that had happened in his eighteen years of lighthouse keeping. He was able to put out the fire before any damage was done to the tower or the clockwork. After the fire was out, Sweeney set up an emergency lamp so that a light

would remain showing from the Kauhola Light Station for the rest of the night.

The next morning the lighthouse tender *Kukui* brought all the materials needed for temporary repairs, plus a machinist and two laborers to help Sweeney repair the damage. The men installed seven new storm panes, overhauled the lens, checked the revolving apparatus, and put the machinery back in operating condition. One of the sailors remained at the light with Sweeney to help with the cleanup and to assist him in standing watch. Edgecomb had long objected to having only one keeper at this light. The only reason he had not recommended a second keeper was because of the plans under way to convert the light to electricity.[52]

Because the 1931 fire cracked the upper portion of the lens beyond permanent repair, Edgecomb recommended using thirty-six-inch airway beacons on the new tower in place of the fourth-order lens and lantern "to keep within the funds alloted." In addition, Edgecomb suggested adding "reinforcing iron in the foundation blocks and around openings in the tower shaft," because of the "numerous earthquake shocks experienced at the Kauhola Point Light Station."[53]

In 1933 funds were allocated for a new tower. The plans called for a duplication of the Nāwiliwili lighthouse on Kaua'i. The reinforced concrete walls were two feet thick. The structure was eighty-six feet high, placing the light 116 feet above water. The 105-step spiral staircase running through the center of the tower led to a trap door that slid back for entrance to the top of the tower. A welded superstructure supported two thirty-six-inch airway beacons. The glass lenses on the optic were thirty-six inches in diameter, with a central bulls-eye and twelve annular sectors. There were double inner lenses eighteen inches in diameter, one red and one green, so that the light would be distinguished by a characteristic of alternating flashing red and green

Architecturally a duplication of Nāwiliwili Lighthouse on Kaua'i, the Kauhola Point Lighthouse displayed an unusual (for Hawai'i) characteristic—alternating flashing red and green lights—from the time it was put into operation in 1933 until 1982, when the characteristic was changed to flashing white. (Aids to Navigation, Fourteenth U.S. Coast Guard District)

light. This was the first light in Hawai'i to use flashing red and green, although this characteristic was being used extensively on the Pacific coast. The duplicate second beacon was a standby light in case of failure of the first. The light was visible seventeen miles. Electric power for the light was supplied commercially, but on the first floor of the tower there was an emergency generator unit in case of power failure. The total cost for the lighthouse was $17,495.[54]

There were five buildings at the station besides the lighthouse: a keeper's dwelling, a paint locker, a covered 854-gallon iron gasoline storage tank, a laundry house, and a combination garage and workshop. The keeper's frame house had two bedrooms, a bath, kitchen, dining room, pantry, office, and large front and back porches. The house cost $4,000 to build.[55]

The gray tower was left unpainted for a year to allow the concrete to cure. In 1934 it was painted white to make it a more effective daymark.[56] John

Sweeney remained as keeper until the blackout on all Hawaiian lighthouses was imposed at the outbreak of World War II.

Cape Kumukahi

At the same time that airway beacons were placed on the Kauhola Point Light, they were also being considered for the Cape Kumukahi Light. This was a navigational aid that the Bureau of Lighthouses had fought for long and hard, just as they had for the Kauhola Point Light. The first request for a light on this most easterly point of the island of Hawai'i was made by the Light House Board in 1908.

> There is at present no landfall light for vessels bound to Hawaii by way of Cape Horn. Several vessels have within recent years gone ashore on Kumukahi Point. This is the first land sighted by vessels from the southward and eastward. The shipping from these directions now merits consideration, and with the improvement of business at Hilo and the opening of the Panama Canal, the necessity for a landfall light on this cape grows more urgent.[57]

The board considered the Cape Kumukahi Light essential, and appropriations for it were requested almost every year from 1908 until 1932.

In 1927 territorial delegate to Congress V. S. K. Houston restated the necessity of a light on Cape Kumukahi to guide vessels coming from the Panama Canal, South America, and the west coast of the United States, and added that the light was also needed by airplanes on trans-Pacific flights. "From San Francisco to Honolulu is 2,100 miles . . . one of the longest over-water flights to be found in the world," yet there was no prominent light southward and eastward other than Moloka'i.[58]

On December 31, 1928, the U.S. Government purchased fifty-eight acres of land at Cape Kumukahi for $500 from the Hawaiian Trust Company. The following year an automatic acetylene gas light was established at the cape. The 375-mm lamp, with 390 candlepower, was atop a thirty-two-foot wooden tower, elevating the focal plane to seventy-three feet. The light was visible twelve miles out to sea.[59] This was hardly the powerful primary seacoast light advocated by Representative Houston. It was barely adequate for interisland maritime needs and inadequate as an aid for trans-Pacific aviation.

It was four more years before appropriations were finally made for a primary seacoast light for Cape Kumukahi. In 1932 work began on improvements to the station. An asphalt macadam road was built from the paved state highway to the station at a cost of $10,797. The Bureau of Lighthouses reported: "A reinforced concrete tower foundation, two five-room dwellings, water tanks, outbuildings, sidewalks, etc. were constructed. Two 36-inch beacons, three 2-kilowatt engine-generator units and a 110-foot galvanized structural steel tower were purchased. Plans and specifications for completing this project are prepared."[60]

In 1934 a Honolulu builder, John Hansen, was awarded the contract to replace the old thirty-two-foot wooden tower with a square, pyramidal, steel skeleton tower, 125 feet high and 156 feet above sea level. When completed, it was the tallest structural steel tower in the Islands.

The airway beacon-type twin lamps were mounted one above the other, each lamp of 1,700,000 candlepower. The flashing, six-second light was visible nineteen miles seaward. Only one lamp was in operation at a time. If it failed during the night, the keeper had only to throw a switch at the bottom of the tower to start the other.

The two keepers assigned to the new Cape Kumukahi lighthouse were Charles K. Akana and his assistant, William J. Watkins. Akana, who was transferred from the position of "additional keeper," had been with the Lighthouse Service since 1911, serving on eight different lighthouses in Hawai'i. Watkins was transferred from the Makapu'u Point Light and Radio Beacon Station, where he had been second assistant keeper.

Two identical five-room dwellings were built for the keepers about three-fifths mile from the light. The reason they were located so far from the light was because the land surrounding the tower was absolutely barren—nothing but the hardened black lava flow of the 1700s. Other structures erected at the light station were a water tank, a small laundry house, a building for storing fuel, and a tool shed. The generators, which produced electricity for the station, were located in a building beneath the tower.[61]

Maintaining the two generators was only part of the keepers' job. The men were also responsible for the upkeep of all structures on the station, as well as maintaining the grounds in general. This particular station was completely barren until 1938, when Joe Pestrella was transferred from the light tender *Kukui* to the Cape Kumukahi Light as keeper. During his off-duty hours and at his own expense, he hauled loam, rich soil, and plantings to the reservation. He brought in fruit trees and ornamental trees—Tahitian lemons, mangos, litchis, Okinawan tangerines, and a rare bay leaf tree. In 1951 Sidney Estrella became assistant keeper. Estrella had worked for the Lighthouse Service since 1936 and had served on the Kauhola Point Light until it was automated. Estrella and Pestrella shared more than a similarity in names; both were meticulous in their work habits. The station was kept in superb condition. In 1955 the men received the Coast Guard's "Outstanding Performance Rating" award. Ludwig Wedemeyer, commander of Group Hilo, in his letter to the commander, wrote: "These two men have not only brought honor to the 14th Coast Guard District, but they have also brought honor to Hawaii." Wedemeyer requested a ceremony that would "knock the

keepers' eyes out." In regard to Pestrella, Wedemeyer observed, "To the best of my knowledge, this is the FIRST TIME IN THE HISTORY OF THE COAST GUARD that a native born (Island of Hawaii) U.S. Government civil service employee will be so honored."[62]

One extra on-duty job for the keepers was escorting visitors around the light station. Though tourists did not climb the tower as they did at Kīlauea lighthouse on Kaua'i, the Cape Kumukahi station was open during the 1950s from 1:00 to 3:00 P.M. on weekdays, 9:00 to 11:00 A.M. and 1:00 to 4:00 P.M. on Saturdays, Sundays, and holidays.[63]

One of the most constant and time-consuming duties for the keepers was scraping and painting the steel light tower to protect it against the corroding effect of the salt-laden trade winds. *Kumukahi* is one of the Hawaiian words for "east wind." It is also the name of a legendary "chief who pleased the goddess Pele, but who ridiculed her." In revengeful wrath, Pele "heaped lava over him, thus forming the cape."[64] And from time to time Pele has heaped more lava on Kumukahi.

In 1955 lava from Kīlauea volcano threatened to engulf the light station. Estrella was ordered to duty at an observation post manned by the U.S. Army and volcanologists, while Pestrella stayed on duty at the light. D. B. MacDiarmid, chief of the Personnel Division of the Coast Guard, later reported: "Keeper Pestrella remained on duty at the station . . . at the peril of his life as encroaching lava flows threatened the station. He kept Cape Kumukahi Light operating without interruption in the true tradition of keepers of lights." For his performance of light station duties "in outstanding fashion," Pestrella, in 1956, was selected "Civil Servant of the Year" for the Hawaiian Area.[65]

Four years later another eruption again caused lava to flow toward the light station. The eruption began immediately north of the town of Kapoho on

Cape Kumukahi Light, the tallest structural-steel light tower in Hawai'i, was twice threatened with destruction by lava flows, once in 1955 and again in 1960. The Coast Guard reported on February 2, 1960, that the light was extinguished and that the tower was "caught between the pincers of two widening streams of hot lava." The tower was left unscathed and the automated light remains one of the primary aids to navigation in the Islands. (Aids to Navigation, Fourteenth U.S. Coast Guard District)

the Puna coast about two miles west of the light-house, spilling lava from cracks that opened in the ground. On January 13, 1960, the Civil Defense Agency declared Kapoho a disaster area, and evacuation of the village was begun. That evening molten lava broke out in a sugarcane field northwest of Kapoho, and, as the fissure opened eastward, steam blasts and fountains of lava poured forth. The fiery lava began flowing eastward to the sea, spreading widely north and south.[66]

Civil Defense personnel tried to contain the flow using as many as twenty-five to thirty bulldozers working continuously day and night to build dikes on the southern side of the flow, in an effort to save the village and the light. The Coast Guard chief of Aids to Navigation, C. N. Daniel, reported on January 21 that Pestrella, his wife and child, and BM1 McDaniels were all at the light station "safe and sound," but that they were packed and ready to leave "in the event the need develops. The need is remote. . . . The lava has reached to about one-half mile of the dwellings and is now flowing northward away from the station towards the sea."[67]

Each day a map appeared in the *Honolulu Star-Bulletin* showing the path of the lava flow. When the mass of lava turned south and threatened to flank the station, Pestrella's wife Henrietta and their 21-month-old son Mike moved to safety. Pestrella's assistant was in the hospital, but Pestrella stayed on, saying, "When my backside feels hot, I'll move on. Not till then!!"[68]

But lava overflowed the dike protecting the light station. The gate to the station was set ablaze and lava moved down the road to the lighthouse. Pestrella placed the light on emergency power, raised the American flag, and left the automated light on January 28. His trees were devoured by flames, and the keepers' dwellings and all station access roads, together with power and telephone lines, were obliterated by lava flows ten to fifty feet or more deep.

The light continued operating until February 2, when the heat from the lava caused the fuel tanks to explode. A ten-ton temporary lighted radar reflector buoy that Pestrella had earlier helped the light tender CGC *Basswood* place 510 yards offshore of Kumukahi Point served temporarily as the Cape Kumukahi navigational aid.[69]

On the night of February 3, lava flowed into the sea at two points, one south of the lighthouse and one east, where it formed a new coastline. By the time the eruption ended on February 19, almost a square kilometer of new land had been added to the island.[70] Amidst all this devastation, and creation, the 115-foot tower still stood, its skeletal design looking especially delicate and vulnerable surrounded by the massive heaps of solid, smoking black lava. The lava had come within a few feet of the tower and then inexplicably divided into two red glowing streams that flowed on either side of the lighthouse. Before the streams widened enough to engulf the tower, the eruption stopped and lava ceased to flow. The light tower was unscathed and completely operable. All it needed was electricity to become a guiding light at night once again.

The Coast Guard determined that a trail could be made along the shore from the Kapoho Beach house lots along which electric power could be brought in to the light. A right-of-way was secured for the Hilo Electric Company to bring in commercial power for the light. Its intensity was increased to 1,800,000 candlepower and the light converted to permanent automation, so that resident personnel would no longer be needed.[71] Pestrella was transferred to the Makapu'u Light Station on O'ahu.

Around the Island with the ANT Team

The Coast Guard's goal was to automate all of the lighted aids in the Hawaiian Islands. Two serious problems emerged when lights became unattended —vandalism and dumping. The problem of vandalism is not as serious on the island of Hawai'i as it is on O'ahu, but abandoned cars, appliances, and litter began to appear on many of the lighthouse sites soon after the lights were automated. The Aids to Navigation Team now maintains and services twenty-three lights on the island of Hawai'i.

In 1989 Ralph Craig took Glenn Aikin, both Coast Guardsmen serving with ANT, on an orientation visit to the lighted aids on the island. Aikin, newly assigned to ANT, was an electrician specialist and knew how to service the lights. The difficulty was finding some of them. Many of the aids are located in unmarked areas far from main roads. The first lights the men examined were the front and rear range lights for Hilo Harbor. Both have rectangular red dayboards bearing a central white stripe, and show fixed green lights at night. The front range light is mounted on a seventy-five-foot steel pole and stands in the busy port area past the Coast Guard Station near the pier; it is usually surrounded by shipping containers awaiting loading. The rear range light is atop a 124-foot-square pyramidal skeleton tower in an isolated, heavily vegetated area on the south shore of the bay. A short, rough, potholed road off Kalaniana'ole Avenue leads to an even shorter dirt road that ends abruptly at the beacon site. "We spend a lot of time here cutting down the vegetation," Craig told Aikin. "It's a real lush area, lots of rain on this part of the island, and we try to keep the growth completely cleared away from the range. Also, when you come to work on this light bring lots of safety gear. It's one of the tallest ranges in Hawai'i."[72]

The Coconut Point Lighthouse is easy to find. It stands right off the main street in downtown Hilo on Route 19, which runs northwest from Hilo along the coast. It is a four-sided tapering concrete structure, the type of simple and practical lighthouse design used so successfully on all the Hawaiian Islands. The thirty-four-foot tower, built in 1975, stands at the edge of the water surrounded by coconut trees. Just offshore lies Coconut Island.

After inspecting the Coconut Point Light, the men continued on Route 19 around Hilo Bay. Between plantation houses on a street with no name, Craig found the turn-off for the Pauka'a Light. They parked in someone's driveway, walked through private property, and stepped through hedges to reach the light. Aikin felt like a trespasser; the light stands in someone's back yard! Dogs gave the "strangers are here" alarm, but their tails wagged and they stopped barking when they saw the familiar dark blue Coast Guard uniforms. Two golden retrievers have their fenced-in run behind the 145-foot concrete light tower, which was erected in 1929. The vegetation is lush along the shore and there are thriving tree ferns despite the close proximity of salt water. There is no litter here. The dogs guard the lighthouse as well as their own property.

Route 19 passes northwest through cane fields and over ravines and streams. The moist and rainy climate nurtures orchards of macadamia nut trees and keeps the roadside growth thick and green. Forty-five minutes out of Hilo, Craig pointed to a huge metal gear propped upright on the side of the road signifying the Hilo Sugar Processing Plant. "This is where you turn off for the Pepe'ekeo Point Light," he told Aikin. Then he turned right, drove down cane-field roads to the coast and turned left past the plant maintenance building. The bumpy dirt road finally ended, and there was a gate and a path through pandanus, ironwood, banana, and guava trees leading to an open cow pasture.

The Pepe'ekeo Point Lighthouse is a seventy-five-foot white pyramidal skeleton structure that was built at the most prominent point along the seventy-two-foot-high cliff line in this area. In 1907 the light replacing the original Makahanaloa Light was called the Ālia Point Light. David Kalili was keeper until 1913, when George Brockman took his place. After the light was automated in 1917, Brockman was transferred to the Nāpō'opo'o Light.

"This must have been a beautiful place for the keepers to live," observed Aikin as he and Craig climbed down from the top of the tower after checking the lamps. There are no signs of where the keeper's quarters once stood. The only other building on the site is a small white storage unit at the base of the tower. "Always keep the door on this cabinet closed," Craig warned. "Every time I've left it open a cow sticks her nose in. The cows are curious and they always want to know what's going on. Most of the time I have to push them out of the way. There are some bulls, too. We had a run in with a bull here. He wouldn't let one of our guys go back to the road. But they're usually no trouble, you just have to show them who's boss." A lively calf trotted alongside the men as they made their way back to their car.

The highway begins to wind as it goes northward past the road to 'Akaka Falls, the small village of Wailea, gulches, cane fields, and banana and coconut trees. After mile marker 27, there is a sign for Laupāhoehoe Park, and here Craig turned right toward the ocean. Steep cliffs form the backdrop for the park, and on the ocean side the waves crash impatiently and with great force against the jagged rocks. "The sea is very rough here, especially in winter," Craig told Aikin as he pointed north along the shore. "In 1985 a barge with Toyotas was coming into Hilo and it broke loose from the tug. The wave action shoved one car after another off the barge, and you can see what's left of the barge up on the black boulders."

The Laupāhoehoe Light is mounted on a twenty-foot pole that was erected in 1975. The pole also exhibits a red-and-white diamond-shaped dayboard.

The light is thirty-nine feet above the water at the outer end of a point of black lava rock that shelves out in detached ledges about 250 yards seaward of the light. The surf breaks over the ledges with powerful force that sends foam high in the air.

Offshore there is a submerged breakwater, and in front of a small cove another breakwater has been constructed with concrete pieces in the shape of jacks like the ones used in the children's game, but these are gigantic tetrahedrons, and the sea rumbles as it surges through the pieces. The breakwater light, constructed in 1989, marks the boat ramp, where only the most courageous or desperate boaters would attempt to launch or land. Yet in the early 1900s, the Laupāhoehoe landing was the only one besides Hilo that was used for passengers on this side of the island.

Laupāhoehoe was an important place in Hawaiian folklore and history. Rocks of the type found here were used in the construction of heiau; according to a 1913 guidebook: "Near the lighthouse site stood the heiau, Lonopuha, where a great and famous sacrificial stone is hidden. The Hawaiians claim that only one man today knows its hiding place, and he will not reveal it, fearing that the gods would punish him with death should he do so."[73]

Tragic deaths of recent time are commemorated by a plaque, which is almost hidden amidst the *naupaka*, ironwood, and palms. The plaque reads: "In memory of those who lost their lives in the April 1, 1946 tidal wave."

The heavy seas caused by the tidal wave undermined the concrete foundation of the lighthouse, and the thirty-four-foot pyramidal structure collapsed. It was replaced by a thirty-six-foot wooden skeleton tower, placing the light fifty-five feet above the sea. In 1975 the flashing white ten-second characteristic was changed to 2.5 seconds, and the light was mounted on a twenty-foot metal pole, thirty-nine feet above the water. The pole also exhibits a dia-

The lonely looking Laupāhoehoe Point Light replaced the original 1890 wooden trestle beacon in 1915. The photograph captures a time when the name Laupāhoehoe, meaning smooth lava flat, described the point well. Laupāhoehoe, though battered by winter storms and tidal waves, has since become lushly vegetated. (Courtesy of Carol Edgecomb Brown Collection)

mond-shaped dayboard with red sectors at the top and bottom corners.[74]

Farther along the northeast coast stands the Kukuihaele Lighthouse, another white concrete structure, similar to the original Laupāhoehoe lighthouse. It was built in 1937 and stands thirty-four-feet above the ground. The focal plane of the light is 120 feet above the water. This is the only concrete tower of this type in the Islands: constructed with an inside ladder leading to the lamp. The tower was designed this way because of the almost constant high wind that would have made climbing an outside ladder

dangerous. The light is reached by driving through cane fields. "It's obvious," Craig told Aikin as they bumped over the potholed dirt road, "you have to spend a lot of time four-wheeling it to get to this light; it's about two and a half miles from the paved road. Just find a cane road and keep trying to work your way down to the light. You have to get there any way you can. Every time I go it's a new way because they change the cane fields annually. I've gotten stuck many times getting to this light, but it's worth it. The view is one of the best."

To the northwest of the light is Waipi'o Gulch, the

largest ravine along this coast and about three miles southeast of Waipi'o Valley. Cliffs as high as thirteen hundred feet, sliced by deep gorges, drop into the sea along the ten-mile stretch of coast between Waipi'o Valley and 'Ako'ako'a Point to the northwest. Inland from the point rise the heavily wooded Kohala Mountains. North along the coast, waves break across the dangerous reef at Kauhola Point, marked by the lighthouse that warns vessels to give the point a wide berth of at least two miles.

According to Craig, the rough water is great for fishing, and on calm days he has "done some wonderful snorkeling right off the point." The lighthouse is set in the woods, about two miles off the main road. At the site there are pine and *koa* trees and some pastureland where cattle and horses graze. "I love working on this light," says Craig. "It is so beautiful here—unfortunately the area has become a dumping ground in the last few years. We try to clean it up, but it's impossible. Such a shame. And the lighthouse is so beautiful. The tower has been called one of the most picturesque in the Islands."

One navigational aid the members of the ANT team did not inspect was the Loran (LOng RAnge Navigation) station at 'Upolu Point on the northernmost extremity of the island. The 275-kilowatt navigational beacon is manned round-the-clock by Coast Guardsmen and is part of the Central Pacific Loran Chain. This chain consists of three transmitting stations. The "master" station is located on Johnston Atoll, nearly 1,000 miles southwest of the island of Hawaii; one secondary station, designated "Xray," is at 'Upolu Point; the other, designated "Yankee," is located on Kure Island in the Northwestern Hawaiian Islands. The master station transmits a series of nine pulses, then the secondary stations in turn transmit eight pulses each. This cycle is transmitted endlessly. The navigational signal reaches fifteen hundred miles at sea and enables users aboard vessels equipped with a Loran receiver to determine their positions quickly and accurately, day or night.[75]

Inland from the Loran station and the many low windswept bluffs along 'Upolu Point, cattle roam the Kohala mountainsides, and cane fields stretch for miles. South on Route 270, the road follows the coast to the Māhukona and Kawaihae lighthouses before joining Route 19 along the western shore. The uncultivated land between the lights is used for grazing, and the mountain slopes end as low cliffs along the coast, cut by ravines. The Māhukona Light is one of four concrete pyramidal towers that were built in 1915. The twenty-two-foot tower was erected on a forty-two-foot cliff above the sea. The lighted aid is within the boundaries of the Lapakahi State Historical Park, where there is a restored Hawaiian village. Offshore, snorkelers can explore the underwater life. The Lapakahi Marine Life Conservation District has been established to protect the wide variety of coral and brilliantly colored reef fish that abound in the area.

The Kawaihae Lighthouse, also built in 1915, is a thirty-six-foot pyramidal concrete tower in quite a different setting. It marks a commercial deep-water harbor in the northern part of Kawaihae Bay. Where once cowboys drove cattle into the water to be tied onto small boats and towed to waiting offshore vessels, there is now a barge wharf for the shipment of cattle and produce and for the receipt of cement and lumber. There are pipelines to petroleum and molasses storage tanks at the overseas terminal wharf, as well as a traveling bulk-sugar loading tower with conveyors. Military cargo is handled at the harbor on the southwestern side.

The Kawaihae range lights, also maintained by the ANT team, guide ships into the harbor, although use of the pilot boat is compulsory for all vessels of foreign registry. The range lights are mounted on poles seventy-eight and sixty-one feet high. "The difficulty in servicing these lights," Craig told Aikin, "is not only the height of the poles, but the wind. It's like climbing the mast of a ship, and there is lots of play in the poles. When two or more people are up there working you can feel every move anyone makes. Always use a safety belt. Sometimes the wind is so strong it will blow you right off the ladder if you aren't tied on!"

This is the hot, dry side of the island, and the black masses of lava that form the capes and cover the flat land seem to radiate heat. Keāhole Point Light was another one of the pyramidal concrete towers built in 1915. It marks the western extremity of the island of Hawai'i, but at night the rotating white-and-green aerobeacon atop the airport control tower is more prominent than the flashing white Keāhole Light. During the day, the low point of shore where the thirty-three-foot concrete tower is located is easy to identify. There is scant vegetation, and black lava alternates with white patches of sand. Coast Guard personnel inspecting and servicing the light in the 1940s noted that the light "could be approached from the land, but it is not recommended. . . . Five miles of the drive is only a trail and should not be attempted in a vehicle without four wheel drive and of the most sturdy sort; in any event the last five miles is directly over a lava bed and cannot be traveled except by walking." By 1988 the situation had changed. Paved roads made the light easily accessible. The area was developed by the state to attract laboratories researching ocean thermal energy conversion and large-scale commercial aquaculture projects.[76]

South of the Keāhole Point Lighthouse off Queen Ka'ahumanu Highway is the town of Kailua-Kona, a popular resort area and the home of the sport fishing fleet. Cruise ships and charter boats now use the docking facilities on the north side of Kailua Bay that was formerly the site of the barge terminal. Deep-draft vessels still must anchor offshore while the ships' tenders transport passengers and goods

The Keāhole Point Lighthouse, costing $2,365 to build, was one of four concrete towers with automatic acetylene lights built in 1915 on the island of Hawai'i; the others were at Laupāhoehoe, Kawaihae, and Māhukona. (National Archives)

ashore. The Kailua Light, another 1915 pyramidal concrete tower, is on Kūka'ilimoku Point at the northwestern side of the bay entrance. The light is in almost the exact place where the first fixed lens-lantern light was established in 1909, but now the area is developed and the Coast Guardsmen have to walk through someone's back yard to reach the light.

Craig calls the Kailua Bay Entrance Light "one of the most popular lights on the island." It is simply a lamp and dayboard mounted on a twenty-five-foot pole, but it is on the pier "right next to the fish weighing scale. This is where everybody congregates after the fishing tournaments, and there is always lots of activity by the light."

Keauhou Bay, like Kailua Bay, is merely a dent in the coastline. It lies between two lava flows and is one of the more protected little bays along the Kona coast. The entrance is marked by a dayboard mounted on a thirty-foot metal pole that was erected in 1967. The pole exhibits an unusual arrangement of lights. The lamp at the top of the pole has a characteristic of flashing white every four seconds; a three-color directional light is positioned 10 feet below on the same structure. When the fixed white light is seen from a vessel entering from seaward, the vessel is on the center line of the channel; if the red light is seen, the vessel is starboard of the center line, and the green light shows if the vessel veers to port of center. This type of directional light is used where it is too costly or for some reason impractical to build range lights.[77]

South from Keauhou Bay, Route 11 passes along the lower slope of Mauna Loa, an area famous for its coffee plantations. On the coast, Kealakekua Bay, a marine life conservation district and underwater park, is marked by a light on Cook Point where Captain James Cook was killed by natives in 1779. This is the Nāpō'opo'o Light. A twenty-two-foot, white pyramidal reinforced concrete tower was built for this light in 1922. "You don't have to worry about the Nāpō'opo'o Light," Craig told Aikin, "it's practically impossible to get to by land and so is serviced by boat."

"The next light we're responsible for," Craig continued, "is the Miloli'i Point Light, and that's a long drive from anywhere!" The area around the light is an almost totally barren mass of lava. The lava flow of 1926 from the southwest rift of Mauna Loa nearly engulfed the village of Miloli'i and did destroy the village of Ho'ōpūloa one mile north. "Once we leave the main road it's an eight or nine mile drive downhill on a curving trail through crushed lava. Some people actually live back there—no fresh water—don't know how they survive. The fishing is good, though, and the view is incredible. The water is so blue, so clear, and it's a great place for 'opihi. It's a treat to pick them right off the rocks and eat them. What you have to do," Craig explains to Aikin, who has never even heard of this edible limpet, "is to sneak up on them and when they're not looking, use a putty knife and get underneath them and flip them off the rock real fast. The ones at Miloli'i are the biggest I've ever seen, about three or four inches in diameter."

A twenty-foot concrete pyramidal tower was built in 1965 to display the automated Miloli'i Light. When the structure showed signs of deterioration, it was replaced. Today the lamp and dayboard are mounted on a twenty-foot white steel pole, forty-four feet above sea level. The light has been the victim of vandalism, but the Coast Guard report in 1987 had nothing but praise for the light's condition: "Paint looks fresh; dayboard unfaded; the battery box is on a platform and the whole thing looks outstanding. This light is easy to find . . . [but the drive] nearly killed the rental car—five miles of steep, poorly paved road."[78]

The road to Ka Lae Light, southeast of Miloli'i, is paved, but narrow. The light is exhibited sixty feet above sea level. "Talk about desert," Craig commented, "I'd describe the southernmost point in the United States as desolate, dry, dusty, and dirty. The wind blows all the time." Because of the constant wind, a forty-five-foot steel tower was constructed in 1929, and the Ka Lae Light was one of three lighthouses in the U.S. Lighthouse Service whose electricity was furnished by windpower. Electricity was produced by batteries charged by the wind-driven generator. Gasoline-engine-driven generators were used as backup power for the light, and generators also provided the electricity for the five-room keeper's dwelling and laundry building. The light station also included two wooden water tanks, an oil house, a combined workshop and storeroom, and a garage. A hoist house with a derrick built on a concrete platform was situated at the top of a cliff above a sheltered bight for unloading supplies that arrived by boat.[79]

In 1949 the Ka Lae Light was automated, and in 1972 the forty-five-foot steel tower was replaced by a thirty-two-foot concrete pole. The light, as with most automated secondary lights, was powered by batteries, which in the 1980s were charged by a solar panel. There is now little evidence of the buildings that were once part of the station.

"The Ka Lae Light seems so far from everywhere," Craig said, "but I like to go there. The view of the ocean is spectacular, the fishing is great, and it was a sacred place for ancient Hawaiians. The rocks from the ancient heiau are only about thirty feet from the light. We have to be real careful when we service this light; we don't want to disturb anything." The concrete pole is deteriorating in places, and there is evidence of corrosion. "It's due to weather conditions," Craig explained, "not neglect. We spend a lot of time on this light, but it's right next to the sea, and salt air is corrosive. There is only a little vegetation holding the sand down, and the wind is blowing all the time."

From Ka Lae the men take Route 11, called the Volcano Road, climbing northeast past Kīlauea caldera, then eventually southeast toward Cape Kumukahi. "We won't be going to the Pohoiki Bay Light this time," says Craig. "It's about twenty minutes down the road southwest from Cape Ku-

mukahi. The bay is just a tiny dent in the shoreline." The fishing is excellent in the offshore waters and Pohoiki Bay is popular for anchoring and launching fishing boats. In 1979, after the breakwater was built to give some protection to the small bay, the Pohoiki Light was established. "It's a real pretty place," said Craig. "Palm trees grow all along the tops of the wooded hills." The light is a flashing red four-second lamp mounted, along with a red triangle, on a metal pole. "We just recently sandblasted the pole and repainted it. The red lens was cracked, so the next time we service the light we'll bring a new one."

The light on Cape Kumukahi is right in the middle of a recent lava flow. According to Craig, "There is always a lot of scraping and painting to do on the metal work, but the top of the tower is new, put on a few years ago by the Field Construction Force. This is another tall structure, so we always use safety equipment when we are working on it." Cape Kumukahi's 115-foot light tower stands 156 feet above the ocean. The flashing white six-second light can be seen twenty-four miles at sea.

With the inspection of the lights complete, the men from the ANT team drove back across the desolate lava fields to the main roads and to Hilo, where they caught a plane back to Honolulu. Aikin spent most of the traveling time studying a chart of the island, visualizing where the turn-offs are for the lighthouses and trying to remember their names. Craig called out the name of a lighthouse and Aikin echoed him. They repeat the names over and over again like a litany, "Pauka'a, Pepe'ekeo, Laupāhoehoe, Kukuihaele, Kauhola, Māhukona, Kawaihae, Keāhole, Kailua, Keauhou, Miloli'i, Ka Lae, Pohoiki, Kumukahi."

PART IV

Lighthouses of Kaua'i County and Ka'ula

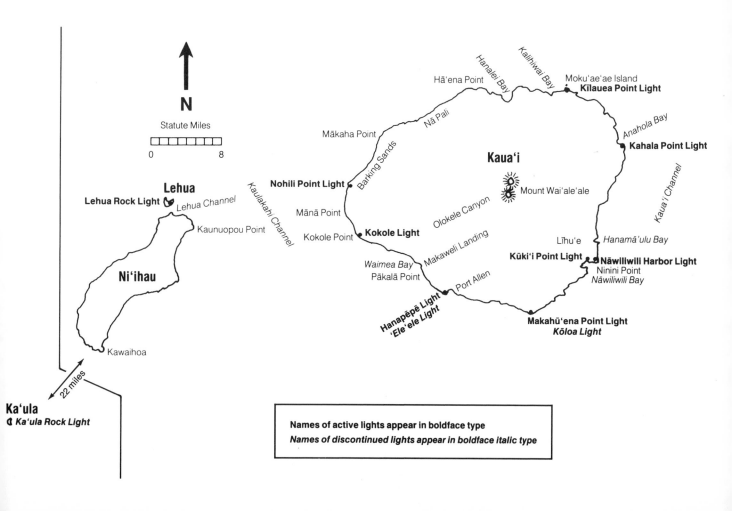

Names of active lights appear in boldface type
Names of discontinued lights appear in boldface italic type

Chapter 10

KAUA'I

Hurricane Fabio, with winds of over 100 miles an hour, was expected to hit Kaua'i within the first week of August 1988. This was the last weather report the Coast Guardsmen on the ANT team heard before they flew from Honolulu to Līhu'e, Kaua'i. It was August 1, 1988, time for the ANT's annual maintenance of lights on Kaua'i, and regardless of the weather the men were sticking to their schedule. "Hurricanes can be unpredictable," was Seaman Kenneth Savi's reaction, "and we can probably get quite a few lights painted before Fabio arrives. Besides, if the hurricane damages any of the aids we'll be on the spot to fix them."[1]

There are eight lights maintained by the ANT team on Kaua'i: two primary seacoast lights, Kīlauea on the north coast and Nāwiliwili on the east coast; and six other lights scattered along the east, south, and southwest shores. Many of these lighted aids are located near boat landings originally used during the period of rapid expansion of commerce in the late 1800s. Although Kaua'i is the only island in Hawai'i that has navigable rivers, there are no protected deep-water harbors at the mouth of the rivers nor indeed anywhere else along the coast. Two small bays, Nāwiliwili and Hanapēpē, which are little more than indentations in the coastline, have been made into ports by dredging and constructing breakwaters.

The lighted aids serving modern boat landings mark the same areas used by Hawaiians as canoe landings. Historical accounts of interisland canoe voyages made between A.D. 1400 and 1794 mention five places on Kaua'i used by Hawaiians: Hanalei on the north; Wailua on the east; Kōloa and Waimea on the south; and "Kona," literally meaning the leeward side or the south coast of Kaua'i. These were also the sites of the largest villages, such as Waimea, Hanapēpē, Nāwiliwili, Anahola, and Hanalei.[2]

To guide canoes at night, early Hawaiians set up their own "lighthouse" on the high land north of Hanapēpē Bay. The hill for the beacon fire was centrally located on the south coast, where much of the fishing activity took place. This fire was burned at a heiau dedicated to Lono, the god of agriculture, wind, cloud, and sea; it was called Kukui-o-Lono, meaning "light of Lono." Kukui-o-Lono may not have been the only beacon fire on Kaua'i. On the southeastern coast evidence was still visible in 1907 of a heiau called Kukui'ula, meaning "red light."[3] This heiau would have been an excellent location for a beacon fire and was the site chosen by the U.S. Light House Board for the Kōloa navigational light in 1908.

Kōloa was the location of the first permanent sugar plantation in the Hawaiian Islands. As early as 1838 the plantation reported obtaining 5,039 pounds of sugar and 400 gallons of molasses from one acre of cane. The success of this plantation gave encouragement to other planters on Kaua'i and the other islands. As the sugar industry grew, Kōloa became a busy landing, and in 1871 it was designated by the government as one of six official ports of entry in the Islands.[4]

It was not until the sugar industry became successful on Kaua'i that navigational lights were needed. But the first aids, with the exception of Nāwiliwili, were erected and maintained not by the government, but by private businesses. By 1884 there were eight sugar plantations, which shared the use of two mills, and six plantations with their own mills. These businesses needed to transport their produce to O'ahu, and boat landings in close proximity to the plantations were used. By the turn of the century there were twelve such landings with lights to guide approaching vessels. Eight of the locations were almost the same as the sites of today's navigational lights.[5]

When a vessel was expected at Kalihi Wai or Hanalei bays on the north shore of the island, the navigational aid used was nothing more than a red light emitted from a hand-held lantern, which could be seen about one and a half miles from the sand beach. Similarly, lanterns showing red lights to distinguish them from the lights of the plantations were attached to posts on the leeward side of harbor derricks on both sides of Hanamā'ulu Bay, at Kapa'a landing, and Anahola Bay on the east side of the island; and at Hanapēpē, Kaunuloa (now part of Makaweli Harbor), and Waimea bays on the south side of Kaua'i. These lights were exhibited fourteen to eighteen feet above sea level; some had reflectors and some did not. The lights could be seen about three miles at sea, and the posts on which the lights were exhibited could be moved about according to weather conditions.[6]

At 'Ele'ele Landing on Hanapēpē Bay, an ordinary steamer lamp with a reflector showed a red light. The lamp was raised thirty-six feet to the top of a "very weak tower frame of 1 x 3 battens." The only substantial tower on Kaua'i was at Nāwiliwili on Ninini Point. This light was established by the

government; all the others were built and maintained by either the sugar plantations or the Inter-Island Steam Navigation Company.[7]

The site for the Nāwiliwili Light was secured by the Hawaiian government in 1897 by a lease from the Lihue Plantation. Besides the light tower, a small dwelling for the keeper was built. The Department of Interior reported that the light did not have a lens, but did have a reflector that directed a light "directly to sea or towards the course of vessels coming from Oahu. The tower is an open wooden frame, forty feet high surmounted by a lamp room painted white. The light is seventy feet above sea level and is visible ten miles at sea."[8]

The increase of sugar production on Kaua'i justified the development of a port, but the shoreline offered few favorable locations. A port must offer not only a naturally or artificially sheltered harbor, but also facilities for handling cargo and cargo storage areas. Two landings were used in Nāwiliwili Bay, the government landing on the west side and a private landing on the north side. Between 1888 and 1890, the government had extended its wharf and installed a seven-ton derrick, but no plans were made for building a protective breakwater.[9]

Nāwiliwili was anything but a sheltered harbor. The only time it was calm enough for easy passenger or freight landings was during periods of kona, or southerly, winds; the rest of the year trade winds caused swells that made entering the bay hazardous. Nevertheless, it was the harbor closest to Honolulu and it was centrally accessible to many of the plantations on the island. Vessels came as far as possible into the harbor to load and unload passengers and freight. Ships would anchor about two thousand feet from the wharf and transport their passengers by rowboat. Even though the bay was sometimes too rough to transfer cargo and passengers, it remained the principal port of the island.[10] The lighthouse provided the needed navigational aid for these vessels, but breakwater construction and harbor dredging were desperately needed.

The first keeper of the Nāwiliwili Light, Manuel Souza, was described as a short, thick-set Portuguese man with a stubby, grizzled beard. Born in Massachusetts, Souza, as a youngster, had followed the sea and eventually settled in Hawai'i. In 1897 he secured the Nāwiliwili keeper's job. Each evening before sunset Souza climbed up to the lamp room. The small room looked like a large birdhouse raised high on wooden timbers. Inside, beneath a picture of President Dole of the Republic of Hawaii and several other colored prints, Souza lit the oil lamp. He placed the lamp with its reflector behind the glass window set in the corner of the building overlooking the channel in both directions.[11]

Souza tended the lamp during the night and extinguished it one-half hour after sunrise each morning. The reflector was then polished and the lamp cleaned and made ready for the evening lighting. Souza also maintained the tower and the keeper's house and grounds. For these services he received six dollars a month and a place to live.

Souza's wife Marie was also Portuguese and had come to Hawai'i with others from the island of Madeira as contract laborers to work on the sugar plantations. Souza had bought her contract, and they were married. The couple, though fairly isolated at the lighthouse, found some social life with the plantation workers who lived several miles away, but they were always happy to welcome a stranger to the lighthouse. When George De La Vergne was touring the island in the 1890s, he often visited Nāwiliwili.

The lighthouse was a delightful place to spend an afternoon, when the trade wind was blowing freshly down the channel, and the waves were tumbling and foaming over the black lava rocks, the green of the water marbled with the foam. Vines and thick grass covered the rocky coast and you could easily find some convenient place in the shadow of a rock to stretch out and read, or watch the moods of the changing sea. While landward you could see the great fields of sugar cane, like an inland lake of green, backed by the clear-cut mass of Waialeale. . . . The lighthouse keeper was the soul of hospitality and as soon as the visitor hove in sight . . . he would wave his hat and hurrah with much enthusiasm.[12]

By 1900 Souza's salary was raised to twenty dollars a month, but many times the money was late in arriving. The delays in payment caused Souza hardship, and he wrote to the superintendent of public works that "the salary is small and I must have it regularly in order to live." At one time he was unable to buy food, and M. F. Prosser, a friend of Souza's and a lawyer on Kaua'i, wrote to the superintendent on his behalf, "I know . . . that his credit has been stopped at the store, if there is any way in which you can help the old fellow out I am sure you will do so."[13] Two months later Souza wrote:

I have been working steadily for five years in a place that is about 3 miles from any house or supplies. . . . Can't my wages be raised for my present payment is too small to support my family. Besides my food, water costs me 50 cents a bucket and firewoods are the worst of all. I also spend my own money in preparing the lighthouse, such as painting it with white wash, etc. So with these few words I await your answer. P.S. Answer soon.[14]

In June 1903 Souza gave notice of his intended resignation as keeper of the Nāwiliwili Light. Carl Blum applied for and got the keeper's job and received, not twenty dollars a month, but eight. Blum, like Souza, was forced to buy fresh water not only because the water collected from the corrugated iron roof was often too salty to drink, but because the piping that supplied the rain water from the tank to the house was deteriorating. Indeed, when Blum became keeper, much at the light station needed repair or replacement. The situation became so serious that the sheriff of finally wrote to the superintendent of public works, "Nawiliwili is in very bad condition, send someone out to make repairs." When no action was taken, he wrote again a month later. "The keeper can not much longer venture to ascend the stairs leading to the top of the structure. The stairs are fast decaying and falling away. The roof is almost gone. The pipe which is supposed to supply the keeper with fresh water from the tower is gone."[15]

No repairs were made on the Nāwiliwili Light by the Hawaiian government, but the lighthouse was one of the first to receive attention when the U.S. Light House Board assumed responsibility for navigational aids in Hawai'i. It reported: "The lamp was out of repair, and the room on the tower needed to be rebuilt. The room . . . was removed, and a small box locker built in its place. On this locker was mounted a small lens lantern. The tower is dilapidated and unsafe. The dwelling is not fit for human habitation. There is no oilhouse."[16]

The Light House Board recommended that all the Islands' coasts "be strongly lighted, because of the many sugar plantations on which there are strong electric lights visible many miles at sea." Sometimes these plantation lights were not on the coast, as they appeared to be at night, but many miles inland. The board cited the experience of the USS *Iroquois*. "The vessel recently sighted a bright light on Kauai when 12 miles at sea. When 2 miles from shore the loom of the land was picked up, and after running 10 miles along the coast, the light was found to be some 3 miles inland." No light could be seen at Nāwiliwili, or Kōloa Point. "Suitable red lights on these points would have made it possible to tell that this light was not on the coast."[17]

The light at Kōloa Point, which was red, was maintained by the Inter-Island Steam Navigation Company and was displayed only when one of their vessels was expected. The company also operated lights on the east coast of Kaua'i at Ahukini, Hanamā'ulu Bay, and their private landing at Nāwiliwili Bay; at 'Ele'ele Landing on Hanapēpē Bay, on the south coast; and at the Makaweli plantation wharf and the Waimea Bay landing, both on the southwest coast. The Light House Board requested an appropriation large enough for purchasing these beacon sites, explaining, "These lights are necessary for the safe navigation of all vessels in their respective vicinities. There are many vessels using these lights, but being private they are only shown when their own vessels are expected."[18]

A light was also suggested for Mānā Point on the west coast of Kaua'i, but after further investigation the Light House Board decided it was more important to establish a first-order light on the north shore at Kīlauea Point.

> There is now no landfall light at the Hawaiian Islands for the large traffic from the Orient. . . . With a first-order light at Kilauea Point the trans-Pacific commerce would be accommodated, leaving only certain additional beacon lights of the island type . . . to be installed for the benefit of inter-island traffic.[19]

While a decision was being made on the Kīlauea location, the Nāwiliwili trestle tower was torn down and a lens lantern was established fifty-five feet above the water. The white mast supporting the light was $33\frac{1}{2}$ feet tall and had at its base a small, white house with lead-colored trimmings and a red roof. On December 22, 1906, the new light was put into operation.[20]

By 1908 the Light House Board had established lighted aids at Kokole, Waimea, 'Ele'ele Landing, Makahū'ena, and Kahala and had also approved an act appropriating money for the light proposed for the Kīlauea site. A general design for the lighthouse was submitted by the district officer, but specific architectural plans had not yet been decided upon; much would depend on the type of lens selected.[21]

The land for the light station was purchased in 1909 from the Kilauea Sugar Plantation Company for a token one dollar. In addition to the thirty-one acres acquired from the plantation, the Lighthouse Service also wanted the small islet of Moku'ae'ae. In 1910, R. W. Breckons, U.S. district attorney, wrote to Governor Walter Frear asking that he sign a proclamation "which sets apart for lighthouse purposes . . . an island lying (or laying, I don't know just which is the proper word) off Kilauea Point." Frear didn't help Breckons grapple with his grammar, but he did sign a proclamation "for the island off Kilauea Point." Moku'ae'ae Rock, black and flat-topped with an elevation of 104 feet, was a prominent landmark for coastal vessels passing the north shore of Kaua'i. No lighthouse use was ever made of the islet, however, and in 1962 the U.S. Government returned Moku'ae'ae to the State of Hawaii.[22]

Hawaiians have lived in the vicinity of Kīlauea Point since ancient times. Early Western travelers wrote about seeing taro and yam patches and clusters of habitations. The first foreigners to start a business in the area were two men named Standefer and Deeren, who raised beans, corn, and sweet potatoes to sell to the whalers anchored in Hanalei Bay.[23]

In 1863 Charles Titcomb, an ex-whaler, purchased the "ahupua'a of Kilauea," comprising over three thousand acres, from the Hawaiian government for $2,500. In 1877 Titcomb sold the *ahupua'a* to E. P. Adams and John Ross and leased them adjoining land, which they also devoted to sugarcane. The Kilauea Sugar Company experienced many financial ups and downs and management changes before A. B. Spreckels, the vice president of the company in 1910, conveyed the land at Kīlauea Point to the Lighthouse Service.[24]

The location chosen for the light station was a high, grass-covered bluff surrounded on three sides by the ocean's hard-pounding surf. Moku'ae'ae was once part of the point until eons of wave action eroded the connection away. The surf gouges deep cuts in the base of the cliffs, and in the winter months twenty- to thirty-foot swells have such power that they can toss boulders weighing several tons into the air.[25] Looking down on the tumultuous ocean surrounding the point and seeing and hearing the surf explode against the bluffs must have made the lighthouse engineers wonder how it would be possible to transport all the materials needed through these fierce waters and bring them ashore. But a plan was devised, and work began in August 1912.

In a small, funnel-shaped cove on the west side of the point, calmer waters could sometimes be found. No beach existed in the cove, only hard lava rocks at the ocean's edge. The lighthouse tender *Kukui,* anchored in deeper water, off-loaded supplies to smaller boats, which were then rowed into the shallower water in the cove. Cleats were cemented into the solid lava rocks so that the boats could tie off. The problem of unloading the cargo boats was solved by securing a boom derrick on a ledge approximately ninety feet above the water and hoisting the freight directly out of the boats and onto a landing platform built twenty feet above the derrick. Workmen climbed a trail up the side of the cliff to the landing platform and then followed a roadway that they had built from the platform to the building site farther up the hill, at an elevation of 165 feet. Later an incline railway ran from the platform to the site.[26]

Carol Edgecomb Brown, in writing about the Kīlauea Light, has this to say: "Assistant Superintendent Frank C. Palmer was in charge of construction on the site. My father, Fred Edgecomb, was directly involved in organizing and dispatching building materials, equipment, and supplies. He was also responsible for supervising their safe shipment from calm Honolulu Harbor to the rocky shores of Kilauea Point."[27]

Palmer faced two unexpected setbacks almost immediately. First, the rock at the site, which the men expected to crush and use for aggregate in the concrete, was found to be unsuitable. The plant set up for this work was abandoned, and suitable rock, which had to be purchased, was located in a quarry about five miles away. The more serious setback came when it was discovered that the bearing rock for the light tower was not solid, as had been indicated in the original survey. A good foundation of hard volcanic rock was not found until the men dug down eleven feet. The plans for the tower did not call for a basement—but improvisation is sometimes demanded by nature.[28]

While work progressed on the tower, the ironwork, including the spiral staircase and the lantern, was being built by the Champion Iron Company of Kenton, Ohio. The lens and all the parts needed for rotating the lens were designed and manufactured in Paris by Barbier, Benard, and Turenne; the cost was $12,000, including duty.[29]

The Lighthouse Service decided to use a second-order revolving lens that produced a group flashing characteristic. Its interior diameter is $55\frac{1}{8}$ inches. The lens is referred to as a "bivalve" or "clam shell," but this describes its shape rather than its beauty and its intricacy. There are twenty panels in the apparatus, five to each flash set. Each of the four flash panels contains seven refracting glass elements with eight reflecting glass prisms below and seventeen above. As the lens revolved, the arrangement and angle of panels produced a double flash alternating with a period of eclipse.[30]

This lens is so heavy that it could not be supported and rotated by ball bearing rollers on a track. Rollers were used for rotation, but the weight of the lens was supported by liquid mercury in a trough. The inside diameter of the trough was a little over six feet, with an inside depth of almost nine inches. The trough held $260\frac{1}{4}$ pounds of mercury.

The rotation of the lens was controlled by a clockwork mechanism that required winding every three hours and forty minutes. The clock weight hung down through a wrought iron shaft, $34\frac{1}{2}$ feet long and 20 inches in diameter, located in the center of the tower. The shaft terminated at the watch room floor and served as an additional support for three of the floors and the lens. The watch room contained the pedestal that supported the lens and lamp. The clockwork mechanism, as well as the tank and the pump for the incandescent oil-vapor lamp, were inside the base of the pedestal.[31]

All of these functional, complicated, and interrelated parts were dovetailed together in an architectural design that resulted in a tower of graceful proportions and aesthetic appeal. The lantern topping the tower and protecting the lens was itself a thing of beauty. It is called a "first order, cylindrical, helical bar" lantern; each curved, square plate of glass in the cylinder was held in place by iron bars running in a spiral path, creating a diamond pane pattern. Ten rows of glass panes, each two and one-half panes high, formed the cylinder, which shimmered in the sun and through which the group flashing light appeared in darkness. During the day a curtain was drawn around the inside of the lantern to protect the lens, and each pane of glass in the lantern was kept scrupulously clean by the keepers. The floor and roof of the lantern were of iron, and the roof was adorned with a bronze pinnacle, platinum-tipped, that was a lightning conductor spindle. A door from the lantern room led onto an outside gallery that encircled the lantern.

The directions for assembling the lantern were in English, but when the lens was unpacked Palmer discovered that the directions were in French. What happened next is described by Carol Edgecomb Brown.

My father received an urgent message in Honolulu—a request for him to get to Kaua'i as quickly as possible. . . . He was needed to help with the translation and installation of the lens. . . . He disembarked from an interisland ship near Nawiliwili Harbor . . . and rode about twenty miles by horseback to get to Kilauea Point. . . . It is interesting to speculate as to the complicated procedure involved in creating an efficient light out of glass prisms recently, and carefully, unpacked from a box shipped across two oceans! One can almost visualize an intense group of men gathered on that scenic point of land working together to accomplish one goal, to activate a light at Kilauea.[32]

All problems were surmounted and as the sun set on May 1, 1913, the Kīlauea Point Light flashed its signal 217 feet above mean high water. The light was visible twenty-one nautical miles at sea.[33] The Kaua'i newspaper, *The Garden Island,* on May 6, 1913, gave the occasion banner headlines and described the throngs of people that gathered along the cliffsides and shore to see the first gleam.

The Kilauea Point Lighthouse, like the Cyclops of old, which swept the sea with their one fierce eye, burst forth its shining eye of warning to the mariner . . . while hundreds of country people who had gathered to witness the wonderful sight made the shores and hills ring with astonished delight. . . . Palmer, under whose able direction this excellent piece of construction has come into existence, accompanied by Manager J. R. Meyers of the Kilauea Plantation, and other leading citizens, touched the button which set in motion the 250,000 candle power lamp, which responded as if by magic.

Although the light was operating, the station was not complete. The second assistant keeper's house was under construction, plumbing fixtures were still to be installed in all three keepers' houses, sewage disposal systems were not complete, the landing needed improvements, roadways were not yet graded, a guard rail had to be installed along the cliff, and the entire station was still to be fenced. On June 30, 1913, all work was suspended because of lack of funds. The additional cost of aggregate and sand, plus the unexpected foundation expense for the tower caused the cost of the project to exceed the original $75,000 provided, but in August 1914 Congress appropriated an additional $3,000, and work resumed on November 17, 1914.[34]

The first head keeper of the Kīlauea Light was Harry W. Flint; his assistants were David P. Haleamau and Luther K. Kalama. The keepers' houses were constructed of the volcanic rock found on the site. Each had a living room, two bedrooms, a bathroom, a kitchen, storeroom, and laundry. Porches were built at the front and back of the homes. Rain water, collected from roofs, was carried by leaders to cisterns. The leaders had a lever that allowed the rain water to first wash down the roof and drain off, before being collected and stored, and each house had its own reinforced concrete cistern. A supply tank for non-potable water was located at the southeast corner of the station, and the water was pumped two miles from Kilauea Plantation's irrigation ditches. There was also a barn at the rear of the dwellings and an oil house near the tower. Supplies were brought in by small boat from the *Kukui* and then hoisted with the steel derrick to the landing. A small shed was built on the cliff to house the derrick engine.[35]

The station was finally completed February 2, 1915, at a total cost of $77,982.07. Harry Flint left soon afterwards to become the keeper at Ka Lae Light on the island of Hawai'i. He was replaced by Samuel Apollo Amalu.

Amalu was greatly admired for his swimming ability. While stationed at Kīlauea his favorite swimming destination was Moku'ae'ae Rock, where the water was rough, the current strong, and sharks were not uncommon. Amalu liked challenges, and this swim was demanding. He said he enjoyed lightkeeping for the same reasons. To him the job was a challenge, where the keeper had to be a master of all trades.[36]

At Kīlauea Point, in addition to attending the light and maintaining the grounds and buildings, the keepers had special chores relating to the mercury lens float. The lighthouse service issued very precise directions for the handling and care of mercury and the cleaning and filling of mercury float vats. Keepers were warned that mercury vapor (produced by heating mercury to the boiling point) is deadly poisonous if inhaled, "therefore no piece of metal which has become coated with mercury . . . should ever be allowed to become heated." Keepers were given detailed instructions on how to empty the vat of all mercury at least once every six months, thoroughly clean the vat and float, and clean the mercury by straining it through cheesecloth before replacing it in the vat: "When the proper amount of mercury is in the vat the lens should float just high enough to make the chariot wheels clear the track about $\frac{1}{32}$" all around. . . . Too much mercury in the vat will cause the lens to ride too high and not operate properly." To achieve this delicate balance, an air pressure system was included in the float mechanism. Air pressure was not used with all mercury floats, but it was part of the float system for the Kīlauea lens.[37]

The keepers also followed specific instructions on the operation of the incandescent oil-vapor lamp. The lamp, manufactured at the Lighthouse Depot, Staten Island, New York, was supplied with oil from an air pressure tank. The tank held three gallons of oil, which was fed, under pressure, through the lamp. As the oil passed though the heated lamp it was vaporized. When the oil vapor came through the nozzle under the mantle of the lamp it was ig-

nited by the keeper. To keep the light burning steadily, the air pressure in the tank needed to be maintained, and the keeper pumped air into the tank every four hours.[38]

The duties of the keepers remained the same over the years at Kīlauea—the lamp was kept burning steadily, the mercury was strained and the vat cleaned, brass was polished, and glass was washed. There was only one important change. In 1927 when R. R. Tinkham, superintendent of the Lighthouse District, made his inspection of Kīlauea Light Station, he reported: "Old landing abandoned; derrick worn out and dismantled. Oil delivered in bulk by commercial tank truck. Other supplies delivered from Ahukini [a landing north of Nāwiliwili] by truck, or Kilauea steamer landing by wagon."[39]

Transportation was changing in other ways that would affect all the Islands and a few of the lighthouses—airplane flights were beginning between the mainland and Hawai'i. On June 28, 1927, army lieutenants Albert F. Hegenberger and Lester J. Maitland took off from Oakland, California, in a U.S. Army Fokker C-2-3 Wright 220 trimotor named *Bird of Paradise*. Their destination was Wheeler Field, O'ahu. The flight was reported to be a primary part of war games to test the operation and accuracy of the army's new beacon radio device, which had been perfected by Hegenberger. After takeoff, the Maui radio beacon guided the plane as planned, but only a few hundred miles off the coast of California the receiving set aboard the plane went out of commission. From that time on, Hegenberger navigated the *Bird of Paradise* the old-fashioned way—by celestial navigation and dead reckoning. During the day Hegenberger took sun shots, but as the weather deteriorated, he had to determine the plane's position by dead reckoning.[40]

When the men landed successfully on O'ahu they were interviewed by the *Honolulu Advertiser*. Both asserted that there was never a moment that they didn't know where they were. Maitland was quoted as saying, "Approaching the islands we knew we were north of our course, but that didn't worry us— and it was no surprise when we picked up a Kauai light just before daybreak. The island was covered with clouds and afforded us one of the most vivid spectacles at sunrise we have ever witnessed."[41]

Maitland expressed a slightly different version of his experience in a private conversation with Fred Edgecomb, as recorded by Carol Edgecomb Brown.

A community reception was held . . . in honor of the two pilots . . . and my father, Fred Edgecomb was invited to attend. . . . Lieutenant Maitland told him in detail how the Kilauea Lighthouse had saved his life. Apparently the men were extremely tired after about twenty six hours in the air, and as Lieutenant Hegenberger rested beside him, Lieutenant Maitland told of how he also started to doze with his head down. A flicker of light caught his eye and for an instant in his fatigued state he thought it was a cigarette. Immediately he realized that was an impossibility on his plane; the light he had seen was a flashing lighthouse beacon. . . . After circling the light of Kilauea, they checked their position and turned their plane back to O'ahu. They had overshot their destination in the dark . . . and by so doing had almost missed all of the Islands completely! By reestablishing their location in relation to the Kilauea Lighthouse signal they were able to continue their flight and then execute a perfect landing at Wheeler Field.[42]

The important navigational role of the Kīlauea Light in the successful conclusion of the flight was emphasized in the 1928 report of the Department of Commerce: "It is interesting to note that in this first flight by an airplane from the Pacific Coast to the Hawaiian Islands . . . the first landfall made was Kilauea Point Light . . . which was picked up at a distance of about 90 miles, and without which the aviators might have passed the Hawaiian Islands, missing them entirely." The Lighthouse Service was justly proud of the Kīlauea Lighthouse, and a model of the tower was included in the Lighthouse Service's exhibit at the Seville Exposition in 1929.

In 1930 Edgecomb was appointed superintendent of lighthouses for the nineteenth district. One of his goals was to establish a radio beacon station at Kīlauea Point similar to the one at Makapu'u Point, O'ahu. With $10,400 allocated for the project, building began on the 200-watt beacon station. Two eighty-foot structural steel towers were erected and a wooden house built as an operating center, containing all of the radio-transmitting equipment and the electrical generators required to run the radio beacon system.

Kīlauea Point now had its own generating plant. When electrical power was added for the radio beacon, it also became a source of power for the light. With the use of electricity, the light's intensity was increased from 250,000 to 540,000 candlepower. The oil-vapor system was retained and kept in working order in case of emergency.[44]

The operation of the Makapu'u and Kīlauea Point radio beacons was synchronized to give both ships and planes two reference points from which to obtain a fix on their positions. The Lighthouse Service considered radio beacons to be one of the most important improvements made in the development of aids to navigation.[45]

After the radio beacon station was in operation at Kīlauea, one of Edgecomb's next projects was to establish a new and better navigational aid for Nāwiliwili Harbor. On the north side of the harbor a spit of land, called Kūki'i Point, was the site of a light mounted on a twenty-two-foot pyramidal tower. The white flashing light, forty-seven feet above high water, was fueled with acetylene gas and operated automatically, but was maintained by the keeper from Nāwiliwili Lighthouse. The light could only be seen once the harbor was in view. To make sure vessels had a primary light guiding them to the harbor, Edgecomb wanted to improve the Nāwili-

After World War II Kīlauea Point Lighthouse and radio beacons were operational once again. This Coast Guard photograph was taken in 1945; Coast Guardsmen manned the station until 1975, when the light was automated. The light station is listed on the National Register of Historic Places and is part of the Kīlauea Point National Wildlife Refuge. (Aids to Navigation, Fourteenth U.S. Coast Guard District)

wili Lighthouse on Ninini Point farther north and east.[46]

The Nāwiliwili Lighthouse had been rebuilt in 1923 and repaired in 1926. The light, which could be seen nine miles at sea, was atop a thirty-four-foot wooden mast, placing the light sixty-five feet above high water. The keeper, Oliver Kua, climbed the mast by means of galvanized spikes set on the sides of the pole. He lowered the lamp each morning and serviced it in a small house next to the mast. The buildings on the station included an oil house, storage shed, privy, a laundry, and a four-room house for the keeper. In addition, Kua built a chicken house and a garage. Unlike early keepers, Kua no longer relied on rain water; water was fed to the station by gravity flow through a pipeline from the Lihue Plantation Company one and a half miles away.[47]

The importance of a new light at Nāwiliwili Harbor was emphasized in the December 9, 1930, edition of the *Honolulu Advertiser.* An article stated that the Nāwiliwili station and light were considered inadequate by the commissioner of lighthouses and that he had requested "an appropriation for $48,100, which would include costs for replacing the existing light with a high-powered long range light especially for west bound ships which have not heretofore been provided with the proper safety lighting. . . . Nawiliwili will be the principal port on Kauai."

It was not until 1932, however, that money was available and the E. E. Black Company was awarded the contract to build an eighty-six-foot cylindrical concrete tower to house a more powerful light. A new keeper's house was also built. The wooden keeper's quarters was set on concrete-block footings and contained three bedrooms, living room, kitchen, and bathroom. Electrical power was installed, concrete walkways joined the tower and other buildings, and a 490-foot-long roadway, eight feet wide, led from the plantation road to the light station. The focal point of the new Nāwiliwili Light, with 1,200,000 candlepower, was 118 feet above the sea and was visible for seventeen miles.[48]

Kua remained keeper of the Nāwiliwili Light until the Coast Guard took over the duties of the Lighthouse Service in 1939. Kua had been a farmer before he applied for a lightkeeping job. He was first assigned to the Nāpō'opo'o Light on the island of Hawai'i in 1910. In 1912 he was transferred to the Makapu'u Light on O'ahu. Six years later he became keeper of the Nāwiliwili Light, a job he retained until he retired in 1939 after twenty-nine years of lighthouse service.

During World War II no navigational aids were lit at night and the radio beacon system at Kīlauea Point was shut down. Just before midnight on December 31, 1941, a Japanese submarine surfaced off Nāwiliwili and began shelling the harbor. A direct hit was made on one of the large gasoline storage tanks near the pier, but the shell never exploded, nor did many of the other shells that were fired. A small cane fire was started and shrapnel hit one home, but total damages amounted to only about $500. The harbors at Hilo on the island of Hawai'i and Kahului on Maui were also attacked on the same night. There was considerable concern over possible invasion by the Japanese, and the Coast Guard stationed men at strategic places along the Kaua'i coast, including the Nāwiliwili and Kīlauea light stations.[49]

After the war, Coast Guardsmen continued to run the light stations, but new developments in optics and budgetary and manpower problems were pressing the Coast Guard toward automation of the lighthouses. In 1953 the Nāwiliwili Light was automated, but the Coast Guard continued the station as a Light Attendant Station. The man on duty was responsible for routine and emergency servicing of eight lights on Kaua'i, not including Kīlauea; these were Kahala Point, Nāwiliwili, Nāwiliwili jetty, Kūki'i Point, Makahū'ena Point, Hanapēpē, Hanapēpē breakwater, and Kokole lights.[50]

The Nāwiliwili Light Station was completed in 1933. In 1984 an aero-marine-type DCB-36 optic was installed on top of the tower. The fourth-order lens was no longer needed and was donated to the Hawaii Maritime Center. The lens is on display at the museum's Kalākaua Boat House. (Aids to Navigation, Fourteenth U.S. Coast Guard District)

Although the stations on Kaua'i were being automated, the Coast Guard still manned the Kīlauea
Light. In 1960 the light was increased to 4,700,000
candlepower and could be seen twenty-three miles at
sea. During the 1950s and 1960s many lighthouses in
the Islands, including Kīlauea, were open to the
public. Part of the Coast Guardsmen's duties was to
take visitors to the top of the light. The view at
Kīlauea was described in one of the guide books of
the day: "The emerald and lapis seas breaking at
the base of the bluffs, the small rocky islet a few rods
beyond, the cane fields leading to the mountains,
the shore line in the distance—are unforgetable.
Great frigate birds . . . skim by in effortless flight,
giving the visitor the curious eye."[51] Many hundreds of people were lured to the top of Kīlauea
Light to see the magnificent view and the lighthouse's unique clam-shell lens.

In 1974 the Kīlauea Light became part of the
Coast Guard's Lighthouse Automation Moderniza-
tion Program, known as LAMP. It took one year for
the automation to be accomplished. The Coast
Guard continued to maintain the tower and light,
but the thirty-one acres of the light station were
transferred to the Department of the Interior as part
of the national wildlife refuge system, with the U.S.
Fish and Wildlife Service in charge of protection,
conservation, and management programs.

The automation of the light was not successful,
and problems with the mercury flotation system
prompted the Aids to Navigation Branch to remove
the mercury from the vat and decontaminate the
surrounding area. Because the lens could not rotate,
the lighthouse could no longer function as a navigational light. In February 1976 a new light was
installed atop a ten-foot white concrete pole on the
seaward side of the tower. The light's characteristic
was changed from group flashing to a flashing ten-
second signal that could be seen by vessels twenty-
three miles at sea. Kīlauea Light Station, including
the tower with lens and lantern intact, was placed on

This automatic beacon was erected seaward of Kīlauea
Light tower when automation of the lens proved unsuc-
cessful in 1976 and Kīlauea Lighthouse was decommissioned. Visitors to the park are welcome to explore the
light tower, see the clam-shell lens, and enjoy the spectacular view 216 feet above the ocean. Offshore lies
Moku'ae'ae Rock, the favorite swimming destination of
Samuel Apollo Amalu, head keeper of the Kīlauea Point
Lighthouse from 1915 to 1924. (Photograph by the author)

the National Register of Historic Places on October
18, 1979.[52]

Once, a few hundreds of people a year visited
Kīlauea Point Lighthouse. Since it has become a
wildlife refuge, hundred of thousands of people
come to Kīlauea Point each year. They come not

only to see the lighthouse and the spectacular view, but to watch the humpback whales, spinner dolphins, monk seals, and green turtles offshore, and the seabirds of many kinds that abound in the area.[53]

Not many people visit the Nāwiliwili Lighthouse. The setting is not as spectacular as Kīlauea Point, nor are there as many birds. But often frigate birds hang motionless high above the tower along the shore, then glide away without a wing beat. Whales breach and blow offshore. Waves break against the rocky coastline and white foam swirls around the shiny, ever-wet black rocks. The roar of planes landing and taking off at the nearby Līhu'e Airport is the only sound loud enough to compete with the sound of the surf.

Around Kaua'i with the ANT Team

The road leading to the Nāwiliwili tower passes a plush resort, horse corrals and a carriage house, and part of a manicured golf course, before wind-shaped ironwood trees, tangled night-blooming cereus, and white-berried scaevola dominate the landscape. On August 3, 1988, the ANT team arrived at Ninini Point to work on the tower. Winds were strong, but there was no sign of the threatened hurricane. The sun was shining. The keeper's quarters alongside the tower have long since crumbled and been cleared away, but sections of the original stone wall along the cliffside were still standing.

When the ANT team arrived, they found that the barbed wire above the chain-link fence encircling the tower had been cut and the gate was ajar, but there were no signs of other vandalism. To further protect the tower, the first-floor windows have been concreted over and the glass in the windows above has been replaced with Plexiglas. The metal tower door, beneath the words "Erected in 1932," is kept securely locked.

The Coast Guardsmen, who had come to service the light and paint the inside of the tower, donned disposable white plastic coveralls over their dark blue uniforms. The light was serviced first. The optic had been changed from a DCB-36 to a DCB-24 Rotating Beacon. The characteristic of a flashing white light every fifteen seconds remained the same, but the range of the light had been increased from seventeen to twenty-four miles. When the DCB-36 was installed in 1984, the Fresnel lens was removed, as it was no longer needed.[54] The lens is now on display at Hawaii Maritime Center's Kalākaua Boat House in Honolulu.

After servicing the light, the ANT team prepared to paint the interior of the tower. It seems obvious that to accomplish this they would start at the top; the problem is that all of the windows in the tower are sealed and the only ventilation comes from the hatch at the top and the door at the bottom—a good draw for fresh air; but once the top floor is painted and the man painting the stairs starts down, the top hatch must be secured. From that point on paint fumes and hot air fill the tower with no place to escape. The men are forced to stop work occasionally and take a short break outdoors to cool off and breath fresh sea air. Inside the tower they chip rust away, seal cracks in the cement, and spread paint until the interior looks a pristine two-tone gray.

The next day the ANT team again passed through the plush resort and across the golf course, but in a different direction, toward Kūki'i Point. This time they could not drive to the light, but had to hike down a rough cliffside with all their supplies. The Kūki'i Point Light is atop a twenty-two foot pyramidal tower, forty-seven feet above the sea. The cliff is red clay. Here the waves, urged on by the strong winds, roll red until they break into peach-colored foam. In four hours, and before the fringes of Fabio brushed the island and sheets of rain closed in, the men serviced the light and painted the tower white.

The Kahala Point Light is not architecturally a romantic or even pleasing sight; it simply works. There is a metal storage cabinet for the battery, which is charged from a solar panel. There is a twenty-foot steel pole to support the light, with a ladder attached and a circular platform on which to stand to service the light. The men first cut down the growth in the area that might interfere with the light being seen; then the light was serviced and the cabinet and pole scraped and painted. On that visit, 250-watt lamps were installed that increased the range of the light from five to eleven nautical miles.

At Kahala, the small sandy beach twenty-two feet below the light is scattered with black, round lava rocks and white skeletal driftwood. Big black bees investigate the purple flowers of a morning glory vine. Covering the ground around the light are dried grasses, shrubby lantana, and shiny scaevola. Nature's growth is not enough to hide the human dumpings of old cars; garbage; beer bottles; fast-food containers; plastic plates, glasses, bottles, and six-pack holders; and miles of balled-up monofilament fishing line. As the men filled garbage bags with the litter, they heard a dog barking and a child crying. Two of the men took off to investigate. Thirty minutes later they reunited a lost child, a lost dog, and lost parents, who were grateful to the Coast Guard for this search-and-rescue mission.

Along the south coast of Kaua'i, the Makahū'ena Light is near Po'ipu Beach. This was also the setting of the Kōloa Light established by the U.S. Light House Board in 1908. Charlie Tanimoto is one of the people who remembered this light with nostalgia. Every year, the Fourth of July meant a great holiday for the Kōloa sugar plantation workers. Hundreds of people gathered on the beach, and there were games, plenty of delicious food, good conversation, and happy music. The holiday was a welcome break from the hard plantation work. As a child, Tanimoto watched the Kōloa Light shining at night during these celebrations. Long after the light had been

The Kahala Point Light on Kaua'i is nothing more than a light displayed from a pole, reminiscent of the first beacon established here in 1898 by the Hawaiian government. In 1908 the Light House Board replaced the ordinary kerosene lantern with a lens lantern. J. F. Rapozo was the keeper when the light was automated in 1913. During annual maintenance in 1989, the light, which was powered by commercial electricity, was serviced and given a new coat of paint by ANT team members *(top to bottom)* William Atkinson, Kenneth Savi, and Aaron Landrum. (Photograph by the author)

replaced and Tanimoto had moved to O'ahu, he could still close his eyes and see the Kōloa Light and feel the happiness of those Fourth of July celebrations. The light stood at an elevation of seventy-one feet. It was replaced in 1922 by the Makahū'ena Light, which was displayed on a twenty-foot pole, sixty feet above sea level and about fifteen feet north-northeast of where the Kōloa Light once stood.[55]

A similar light mounted on a twenty-foot metal pole marks Hanapēpē Bay. The choice oceanfront setting of the Hanapēpē Light was defiled with unidentifiable trash, soggy mattresses, discarded refrigerators, and rusting cars, which served temporarily as a home for two squatters. Graffiti marred the diamond-shaped daymarker. The black, pressure-sensitive reflective sheeting used on the top and bottom corners of the dayboard had been defaced. The Coast Guardsmen had to hurry to get the board papered and the aid painted before another rainstorm arrived.[56]

There were two more lights to service before the allotted week for inspection was over. The ANT team took the Kaumuali'i Highway west to the Pacific Missile Range Facility. Off the highway, the paved streets soon give way to sandy trails and then to unmarked beach and rolling dunes. Kokole Light, a skeleton-steel three-legged structure, fifty-eight feet above the sea, is easier to see than to get to. The lighted aid stands atop a sand dune on the southwest shore, in an area known as Barking Sands.

The Nohili Light is also located on Barking Sands, but farther north and on a hundred-foot-high dune. This is the area known as Mānā, that was first suggested in 1907 for a primary lighthouse; the idea was negated in favor of the Kīlauea Point location.

Barking Sands is probably the widest and longest beach on any of the Islands. The beach is flat for about five hundred or more yards landward of the

The Hanapēpē Light marks a small bay that was once an important canoe landing for ancient Hawaiians. The beacon shown here was built in 1902 and was one of the last lights to be established by the Hawaiian government. The modern automatic light is similar to the one that marks Kahala Point. (National Archives)

ocean; then the dunes begin. Some are small and rounded, some are giant mounds, others are high sand cliffs. As the dunes build in height, a rolling, sandy desert extends out behind them.

To get to the light at Nohili Point, at the top of a dune, one man drove the truck along a winding trail and the rest of the men walked, making their way straight up the side of the massive dune. At first the walking was easy, then the sand became looser and the incline steeper. The men's feet began sinking down two inches, then six. If they didn't keep up a fast momentum, they had to go down on all fours and try to crawl up faster then they slipped down.

Once at the top, the view from the sand cliff is well worth the scramble. Lehua and the "forbidden island" of Ni'ihau look purple in the distance and seem to be floating on the blue Pacific. To the northwest the sand gives way abruptly to the forest-green-covered cliffs of the Nāpali coast. Directly north are the rocket launchers on the Pacific Missile Range Facility.

Looking down the sand hills toward the ocean, the men watched the truck slowly make its way up a less-steep route through the dunes, its back wheels spinning ever faster. Finally, with the hubcaps almost buried in the sand, the driver let most of the air out of the tires and the truck slithered to the top. Sliding down the dune was easier for both truck and men.

With the completion of the work at the Nohili Point Light, the ANT's assignment on Kaua'i was complete. The rain had stopped and the threat of a hurricane was gone; Fabio simply skirted the island. The next day, as the men flew back to their base on Sand Island in Honolulu, the sun was shining from an almost-cloudless sky and the trade winds were blowing. As Seaman Savi said, "Hurricanes are unpredictable."

Chapter 11

LEHUA

AND KAʻULA

The island of Niʻihau lies approximately fifteen miles west of Kauaʻi. It is the only major island in the Hawaiian chain that does not have a lighthouse. The seventy-two-square-mile island is privately owned. During World War II a Loran-A tower was established on the island, but it was discontinued and removed after the war. At night vessels ascertain the position of Niʻihau by taking bearings on the Lehua Rock Light.[1]

The Lehua Rock Light and the Kaʻula Rock Light were among the navigational aids that were the most difficult to establish in the Hawaiian Islands. The light on the rocky islet of Kaʻula was discontinued in 1941, but the one on Lehua remains in service. Lehua is a small island about three-quarters of a mile north of Niʻihau and comprises about 291 acres. The highest elevation on the island is 710 feet, making it an obvious choice for a beacon site. The islet of Kaʻula is also high, with a maximum elevation of 540 feet. It lies twenty-two miles southwest of Niʻihau.[2] The problem with establishing navigational aids on these otherwise ideal lighthouse locations was that they were practically impossible to land on by boat. In the 1990s the Coast Guard does not attempt to put men on Lehua with anything but a helicopter. In the 1930s the Lighthouse Service had no choice but to use boats, and it took many years to put the Lehua Rock and Kaʻula Rock

lights in operation because landings could be made only in calm weather.

On August 10, 1928, Governor Wallace R. Farrington, by executive order, set aside Lehua for lighthouse purposes. Aerial and land surveys were made of the crescent-shaped islet to determine the best position for the light and to select a permanent landing location. It was determined to place the light at the crest of the island, almost 700 feet above sea level. Establishing a light at that elevation was effective because there were seldom low-hanging clouds and never any fog.[3]

A partially sheltered landing was found on the south side of the island across the channel from Niʻihau. The landing was at the inner end of a cut, about twenty-five feet wide and 105 feet long, through the wave-carved beach. A derrick, a small building to house the gasoline engine for the hoist, and an acetylene gas supply house were located about sixty feet above the landing on a rocky bluff. Instead of hoisting large acetylene gas cylinders to the top of the island to supply fuel for the light, it was decided to pipe the gas from the supply house to the light.[4]

The automatic gas control and the apparatus for turning the light off and on were designed in the San Francisco Lighthouse District especially for isolated stations where it was impossible to tend the light for

Helicopters are now used instead of boats to transport men and materials to the Lehua Rock Light. ANT team member Ralph Craig is being lowered to the island for the annual maintenance visit. (Aids to Navigation, Fourteenth U.S. Coast Guard District)

long periods of time. The lantern was manufactured by the New York Lighthouse District. The rest of the equipment was prepared and assembled at the Honolulu station at Pier 4. The light was designed to burn for a year without attention; nevertheless, it

would be inspected and serviced every six months, weather permitting. The construction project was completed in April 1931. The light was originally placed on top of a short concrete tower. Its characteristic was a one-second white flash every ten seconds, visible twenty miles. In 1989 the Lehua Rock Light was atop a ten-foot fiberglass pole, 704 feet above the sea. The characteristic had been changed to flashing white every four seconds and the range reduced to seven miles.[5]

The engineering problems associated with the establishment of Kaʻula Rock Light were more complicated than those encountered at Lehua. Since 1921 transpacific shipping companies had been requesting a light for Kaʻula because the island was regarded as a menace to ships en route to and from Midway Island, Guam, Manila, and Hong Kong. As a result of these requests, the *Kukui* tried to land survey teams on the island in 1921 and 1923, but rough seas prevented a close approach to the island each time.[6] On July 10, 1925, a survey team under the direction of Frederick Edgecomb was finally able to make a successful landing on the island.

In trying to gain information about Kaʻula, engineers with the Hawaiian Lighthouse District talked with George Gay, manager of the Niihau Ranch, who had been on the island. Gay had jumped from a boat and swam through the surf to get to Kaʻula. When he had tried to swim back to the boat, the water was so rough that he could not make it, and he had to remain overnight on Kaʻula. The next morning, Hawaiians in an outrigger canoe came to his rescue. Gay identified the spot where he had made his landing, and later two sailors from the *Kukui* landed at the same place and managed to climb almost one hundred feet up the face of the rock cliff, but they could not scale any higher.[7]

Edgecomb described the island's shape as being roughly like a boot, "the leg lying approximately in a north, northeasterly direction. A pronounced cres-

In 1931 Frederick Edgecomb *(far left),* lighthouse service workmen, and crew from the *Kukui* posed at the base of Lehua Rock Light, which they were completing. This beacon and the one on Ka'ula were two of the most difficult lights to establish, and for Edgecomb two of his greatest challenges and adventures. (Courtesy of Carol Edgecomb Brown Collection)

cent exists between the toe and leg of the boot that is open to the northeast trade wind," causing high seas and swells. "This is the condition," wrote Edgecomb, "that makes landing difficult as the full force of the sea breaks against the two points of the crescent, which are the north and east ends of the island and most accessible for landing and climbing to the top. . . . The south and west sides, which are the lee sides . . . are very precipitous, and while landings can be made on projecting shelves at many points,

the top of the bluffs are particularly inaccessible, due to the vertical and overhanging formations."[8]

Ancient Hawaiians somehow managed to build a heiau on the western edge of the summit. In his report of his first climb to the summit, Edgecomb wrote, "The only evidence of a visit to this island by man is the fact of three sets of stone walls at the top, near the north end. . . . It is related in myth that the ancient Hawaiians climbed to the top of the bluff, 350 to 400 feet, up sheer cliffs, by the unique

expediency of clinging to the backs of enormous opi-
hiis, which hold tenaciously to the rocks when
tapped lightly on the shell."[9]

There are many stories and myths connected with
Kaʻula. Ralph R. Tinkham, the superintendent of
lighthouses in 1925, believed that Hawaiians had frequently explored the barren islet. "There is a huge
cave on the waterline where the shark god (Kūhai-
moana) has his shrine, the Hawaiians say, and
before the natives will trust themselves in the water
—which is infested with thousands of sharks—they
go into the cave and talk to the shark god about it. If
the god is favorably inclined, they are then not
afraid to leap into the water and swim about the
place."[10]

Edgecomb reported his own experiences with
sharks and the cave when he was surveying the
island in 1925.

> On approaching the water cave on the northwest side of
> the rock, which is apparently a wave-cut tube about 125
> feet high and 150 feet wide at the entrance and tapers in,
> the Hawaiian sailors called out that a shark was on
> guard at the entrance. This appeared to be so to all in
> the boat, and if the cave had not been entered this
> would have been recorded as a positive fact and in
> accord with the old myth. Entering the mouth of the
> cave, however, this supposed shark proved to be only a
> light reflection in the water. The cave view from the
> small boat . . . was magnificent in grandeur and awe-
> inspiring. . . . The perfect arc of the entrance and
> dome above resembled the nave of a church and
> inspired one to reverence. . . . This may to a certain
> extent account for the old Hawaiian practice of enter-
> ing and praying before fishing or landing. It was
> believed that evil would befall one if this were not done.
> One old Hawaiian in our crew could not understand
> how no accidents befell us on our hazardous landings
> and scaling of the cliff because we had thus far failed to
> offer our devotions, but he finally concluded that the
> shark god was satisfied that our purpose was construc-
> tive and humanitarian and not destructive.[11]

Sharks abounded in the waters off Kaʻula, and
Edgecomb caught two soon after the *Kukui* arrived
at the islet. "Dire calamities were predicted," wrote
Edgecomb, "and bad luck was expected when the
first shark was caught, which, by the way, was sur-
reptitiously thrown overboard by the sailors in an
effort to ward off misfortune." For the next seven
days it was stormy and landings could not be made
on the northeast side of the island. The rough
weather was attributed to the fact that Edgecomb
had caught the sharks. There was even a rumor that
the first shark had a man's arm in its stomach, and
this "caused great consternation among the Hawaiian sailors."[12]

Although the seas were rough during the eleven
days the *Kukui* was stationed off Kaʻula, successful
landings were made on the southeast and the north
points. The southeast point was known to old
Hawaiians as an extremely bad landing. With great
difficulty, Edgecomb made his way from this landing
to the summit. From the summit he descended to
the west landing, where the small boat from the
Kukui picked him up. On another day he managed
to land on the north point, climb the bluffs to the top
and descend, once again to the west landing. Somehow or other, Edgecomb and the men working with
him managed to get ashore at some place on the
island every day from July 10 to July 21 to work on
the initial preparations for establishing the light.
Edgecomb used aerial reconnaissance photographs
as a guide for his survey of the island.[13]

Because it was not possible to camp on Kaʻula, the
men had to return each night to the tender. There
was good anchorage for the *Kukui* in twenty-eight
fathoms of water all around the islet about a thousand
feet offshore, but Edgecomb reported that the currents were strong. "The wind, which came up several
nights at 10 P.M. and lasted until 2 to 4 A.M., was
almost a gale. Several times the ship was moved to a
new anchorage due to wind and current."[14]

A trail to the selected site for the light had to be established before actual construction work could begin. Bronze handspikes were grouted into the rock about every four feet along the route chosen by Edgecomb. These handholds were a necessity, for without them the men would have been washed away by the waves, sometimes thirty feet high, that battered and often submerged the first 600 feet of trail before it ascended to an upper ledge. Most of the men were repeatedly drenched by the seas and tools were washed away, but no casualties or injuries occurred. One man was washed off the trail, according to the *Honolulu Star-Bulletin,* "but such an experience is not sufficiently unusual to be regarded as an incident by the men in the lighthouse service."[15]

With the survey work finished and the trail completed, the *Kukui* returned to Honolulu. Based on the knowledge gained from Edgecomb's survey of Ka'ula, plans were developed for landing men and equipment on the islet to build the light. Tinkham said that once a few men had effected a landing

a line will be shot to them from the lighthouse service vessel. Heavier lines will be made fast on the crags, and a party will be landed. Then will come supplies. A temporary haven will be constructed to protect the men and supplies from the weather, then the work of blasting a landing on the ledges on the western shore will proceed. When the landing has been made safe, the building materials and equipment for the lighthouse will be placed ashore.[16]

It was not until August 4, 1932, that a work crew once again arrived on Ka'ula to begin construction of the lighted aid. The lower trail was still in good condition but as precarious as ever. From the lower trail there was a nearly perpendicular climb of about eighty feet to an upper ledge. Along this part of the route, a line was made fast to the spikes that had been driven into the smooth face of the cliff up to the point where there was a small shelf. Here, one hundred feet above the sea, the men erected four struc-

tures. Edgecomb described them as a "stiff leg derrik; an 8' x 9' frame winch house, and two 5' x 5' tank houses."[17]

From this upper ledge a ladder was used to climb the remaining fifty-four feet to the rim. The unpainted wooden ladder built during the 1925 visit had been considered temporary, but when the men returned they found it still in place and in excellent condition.

"From the top edge of the cliff," Edgecomb wrote, "it is a steep climb of 1,100 feet, slope distance, to the highest point of the island and the locality of the light tower." At the summit a twelve-foot wooden skeletal tower was erected to hold the 375-millimeter lantern. The automatic acetylene light was lighted nightly by a constantly burning pilot flame and then doused in the mornings. This procedure was controlled by a uniquely designed sun valve that projected from the side of the light; called a thermo valve, it was developed in the Honolulu lighthouse shop.[18]

The construction field work was under the direct supervision of the assistant lighthouse engineer, N. W. Wetherby. Working with him were a carpenter, a machinist, and six laborers. The crew from the *Kukui* delivered all the supplies to shore and from there to the crest of the hill. They also helped with the construction work, which, owing to excellent weather conditions, was carried on every day from August 2 to August 13. The light was completed without any injuries or accidents, although almost everything about the project had been hazardous.

An allotment of $8,000 had been made for the light, and it was completed for $7,980. On the evening of August 18, 1932, the Ka'ula Rock Light was lit. The light, 562 feet above the water, was at the second highest elevation for a navigational light in the U.S. Lighthouse Service, exceeded only by the Lehua Rock Light. The Ka'ula Rock Light flashed white every five seconds and was listed as being visible for twelve miles, but Edgecomb observed it "for

The Ka'ula Rock Light was an automatic acetylene light with a backup light designed to turn on automatically in case the main light failed. The sun valve (upper right of lights), designed in the Honolulu Lighthouse Depot, turned the light off and on by responding mechanically to temperature. When the mechanism was heated by the sun, it closed, cutting off the light; after sunset the valve opened, allowing the fuel to be ignited. (*The Sales Builder,* March 1939, courtesy of the *Honolulu Star-Bulletin*)

a distance of 26 miles with the naked eye from the bridge of the tender *Kukui.*"[19]

One of things that fascinated Edgecomb the most while he worked on the island were the birds. "Approaching the island by steamer, one 'toot' of the whistle is sufficient to fill the air with flying, screaming birds of all colors and sizes." The terns covered the slopes of the hill so thickly that in places it was impossible for the men to walk "without hitting birds, nests, or eggs, so closely together were they nesting, right on the bare, steep sloping rock. . . . Higher up on the cliff the Bowswain or Tropic birds were found; pure white with red beaks and two long red tail feathers. Still higher and at the summit were found the Boobies. . . . On the east or windward slope and at the top were found the large frigate or Man-Of-War bird: the pirates and scavengers of the place and the only bird not possessing webbed feet."[20]

Edgecomb received a letter of commendation for his work on the Ka'ula Rock Light from George R. Putnam, United States Commissioner of Lighthouses. Everyone concerned with the establishment of this navigational aid received praise, for it was a great accomplishment. The memory that lingered for Edgecomb, though, "was the shrill, rancorous, piercing, and continuous screaming of the sea birds, never ending day or night, and which must be experienced to be fully understood."[21]

Once completed, it was a dangerous light to maintain. Getting on and off the island remained a challenge. While the *Kukui* anchored in the lee of the islet, oarsmen rowed the small boat to the established landing. One crewman crouched in the bow watching for his opportunity to jump on the rock ledge as the boat surged in on a high wave. The timing on everyone's part had to be exact. Once the crewman leaped ashore, the oarsmen pulled off to safety. Getting the other needed men ashore was easier. The crewman lowered a rope from a wooden derrick set at the beginning of the trail, and the men swung themselves up on the rope from the small boat to the rocky cliffside.[22]

Commenting on the difficulties of getting ashore, Edgecomb wrote, "While some of the landings were rather wet and difficult, they were not, in the judgement of the writer, extremely hazardous. . . . However, a landsman might differ in this opinion. . . . Landings have been made practically continuously on ten different islands of the group during the past fourteen years . . . and many more difficult ones have been made on the windward coasts of Hawaii and Maui (than on Kaula) by the crew of the lighthouse tender *Kukui*."[23]

The Kaʻula Rock Light was discontinued in 1948.[24] The development of radar and Loran made the need for a light on Kaʻula unnecessary. The island once again belongs to the birds and the shark god.

PART V
Lighthouse Tenders

The lighthouse tender *Kukui* at anchor off Lehua, awaiting the return of the men who were building the Lehua Rock Light. Frederick Edgecomb, on Lehua, took the photograph on May 21, 1931. The island of Niʻihau is in the background. (Courtesy of Carol Edgecomb Brown Collection)

Chapter 12

THE *KUKUI* AND OTHER

LIGHTHOUSE TENDERS IN HAWAI‘I

When, in 1904, the U.S. Light House Board took charge of the navigational aids in the Territory of Hawaii Light House Establishment, the aids were placed within the jurisdiction of the Twelfth Light House District. This district extended from the boundary between California and Mexico to the boundary between California and Oregon. Since the inspector and engineer of this district were stationed in San Francisco, two thousand miles from Hawai‘i, a subdistrict was established in Honolulu with offices in the Alexander Young Building. Two officers were placed in charge of the subdistrict: Lieutenant Commander A. P. Niblack, U.S. Navy, was assigned as assistant inspector, and Lieutenant J. R. Slattery, U.S. Army Corps of Engineers, became assistant engineer.[1]

Niblack also happened to be the officer in command of the USS *Iroquois,* and when his naval duties permitted, he was able to visit the Hawaiian aids to navigation aboard the *Iroquois.* Unfortunately, Slattery, who was in charge of construction and repair of these aids, did not have a ship at his disposal and was compelled to use commercial vessels to transport himself as well as the needed building materials and maintenance crews to the work sites on the various islands. This made it difficult for Slattery and expensive for the Light House Board to complete the

work planned for upgrading the existing aids and building new ones.[2]

The lighthouse tender assigned to the Twelfth District was unable to keep up with the immense lighthouse work on the California coast, and therefore it was impossible to assign the vessel additional duties in Hawai‘i. But the *Iroquois* could not serve as the light services' tender because it did not have enough storage capacity for carrying stores to the light stations. It was necessary to make many changes in the lighted aids in the Hawaiian Islands, and a specialized vessel was needed for this work. The Light House Board, in 1905, considered a tender "one of the first requisites" for Hawai‘i and requested $140,000 to build the ship. Congress turned down the request. One year later the Board recommended an appropriation of $150,000 for a "suitable steam tender"; however, no action was taken by Congress until March 4, 1907, when an appropriation was finally approved for $215,000 (the final cost of the *Kukui* was $213,879.99).[3]

The tender was designed as a schooner-rigged steel steamer of nine hundred tons' displacement. From bow to stern the ship measured 190 feet, with a thirty-foot beam and a twelve-foot draft. Two boilers provided steam under pressure to the two five-hundred-horsepower engines that drove twin bronze propellers, each measuring seven feet, six inches in diameter. With this machinery, the tender could attain a speed of twelve and a half knots, making it the fastest vessel in the Hawaiian Islands at the time. The vessel, according to the Light House Board, was "fitted throughout with all modern appliances, including electric lights and a search-light." Because the tender would also be responsible for navigational buoys, the deck was nearly fifty feet long, providing the space necessary for hauling buoys aboard. The steel foremast was part of a revolving steam derrick adapted for hoisting a load of twenty tons. This derrick was indispensable for handling the buoys and the building materials and supplies for the lighthouses.[4]

The only thing the tender lacked was a name. When the U.S. Lighthouse Service was first inaugurated, it was decided that all lighthouse vessels should be named after a shrub, flower, or tree common to a vessel's district—for example, those stationed in New York were named *Tulip*, *Larkspur*, *Pine*, and *Daisy*; the Alaskan tender was named *Cedar*; and *Sequoia* was the name of the Californian tender. For the new Hawaiian vessel the name *Kukui* was chosen by J. A. Combs, a stenographer-typist for Niblack. The name was even more appropriate than most tenders' names because the *kukui* is the native candlenut tree whose oily nuts were burned by the Hawaiians for light. The word *kukui* came to mean "light."[5]

The *Kukui* was one of eight sister ships built by the New York Shipbuilding Company at Camden, New Jersey, for the Lighthouse Service.[6] Launched in 1909, the tender arrived in Honolulu after a voyage of 16,493 miles around the Horn. The ship served continually in Hawai'i until 1946, except for a period between 1914 and 1917 when it was stationed in Alaska. Its peculiarly shaped, reinforced bow was built for ice-breaking, but it was never used in that capacity, even in Alaska, and it was an amusing fea-

ture for a vessel that served for thirty-four years in the tropics.

The *Kukui*'s job in the Hawaiian Islands included transporting building materials and crews to new lighthouse sites; maintaining existing navigational lights, markers, and buoys; supplying lighthouse equipment, including lamps and required illuminants, such as kerosene or acetylene; and carrying inspectors, relief keepers, and other lighthouse personnel and their families to the light stations. In its first year of service the *Kukui* steamed 8,876 miles.[7] In addition to its lighthouse duties, the *Kukui*, because of its speed, served at times in search-and-rescue missions, a service later assumed by the Coast Guard. The record of the officers and crews who served aboard the *Kukui* was outstanding. In over three decades of service only one tragic incident occurred that brought dishonor to the vessel.

On March 1, 1911, in the "Marine News" column of the *Pacific Commercial Advertiser*, there was a report that the schooner *Moi Wahine* had received a "glancing blow" from the *Kukui*, but had arrived in Honolulu on the following day without any signs of damage. On March 2, however, the same column noted that the *Moi Wahine* had not arrived and that relatives of those aboard were deeply concerned.[8] Three days later the implications of the tragic event became evident when Sam Manu, captain and owner of the *Moi Wahine*, related his story of the collision and his subsequent struggle for survival to the newspaper.

According to Captain Manu, the *Kukui* struck the *Moi Wahine* amidship, and the schooner sank almost at once; there wasn't even time for the crew to lower a lifeboat. The *Kukui* continued on course and then appeared to stop. Searchlights were turned on and directed over the surrounding sea. The eight men from the *Moi Wahine* were by this time in the water. "We yelled until we were hoarse," said Manu, "but the *Kukui* was far away and soon continued on course." Manu caught hold of two planks from the wreckage, took off his clothes in order to swim better, and headed toward Lānaʻi, for that was the direction the wind was blowing. For twenty hours he paddled and floated until he reached Kaʻena Point, the northwesternmost point of the island. Exhausted and without water, food, or clothes, Manu dragged himself overland to the deserted village of Awalu. The next morning, after improvising a covering for himself from an old mattress, he headed for Maunalei on the northeastern coast of Lānaʻi. There he found help. He was taken by boat to Lāhaina, Maui, where he boarded the steamer *Mauna Kea* and returned to Honolulu.[9]

Captain Frederick Kariger and those aboard the *Kukui* related a rather different version of the encounter. Kariger told a reporter, "I was in my room when the *Kukui* struck the schooner . . . second officer Shaw was in charge of the vessel. . . . I came on deck immediately and had the *Kukui* stand by while the search lights operated. We saw no one and we heard no one." It was noted in the *Kukui*'s log that the vessel remained in the area for one hour and twenty minutes. Shaw told the reporter that he "starboarded the helm when the schooner's sails came into view" and only struck the *Moi Wahine* a "glancing blow." He immediately stopped the engines, called the captain, and then ran aft, where he observed the schooner heading into the wind and saw a green light, which he assumed to be the schooner's starboard running light.

Lieutenant Leo Sahm, the lighthouse inspector who was aboard the *Kukui,* also reported that he had seen a green light and the sail of a vessel after the tender struck the *Moi Wahine*. "The light," he said, "was in view for some time after the two boats met."[10]

Testimony taken during the investigation conducted by the U.S. Inspectors of Hulls and Boilers indicated that after Manu observed *Kukui*'s lights,

he made the proper and required course changes to avoid collision, while the lookout on the *Kukui* was not on deck, but in the pilothouse looking at the Molokaʻi beach. This and other testimony indicated that the *Kukui* was responsible for the accident. A transcript of the inquiry was sent to the Lighthouse Bureau. The bureau reported that the Inspectors of Hulls and Boilers were unable to place responsibility for the collision "on account of conflicting testimony." Nothing further was done until Jonah Kūhiō Kalanianaʻole, Hawaiʻi's delegate to Congress, introduced a bill granting permission for Captain Manu, as owner of the *Moi Wahine,* to bring suit for the schooner and cargo against the United States.[11]

At the time of the accident Captain Manu was about seventy-five years old and no stranger to shipwreck. He had been serving aboard a vessel in 1881 when it sank in Island waters and he had to swim ashore. In 1899 the vessel he was on was wrecked off Oʻahu and he helped two companions swim to safety. When Manu was master of the *Lavinia,* the ship sank in a squall off Waikīkī, and once again he helped two men through the surf to shore. Unfortunately, Manu was unable to aid any of his crew from the *Moi Wahine*. It was presumed that all seven men drowned until 1913, when Han Duck Hyung showed up at a Honolulu police station claiming he was a survivor of the wreck.[12]

The shameful attempted cover-up of the *Moi Wahine* incident from its beginning to its end was not quickly forgotten, but the subsequent outstanding record of the *Kukui*'s officers and men, both in performing their lighthouse duties and in their search-and-rescue efforts, eventually brought respect for all those who served aboard the tender. In 1919 the *Kukui* towed the disabled schooner *Ida May* into Honolulu Harbor, pulled the steamer *Santa Cruz* off a reef outside the harbor, and assisted in floating the steamer *Cathana* when it was grounded on Sand Island. Later the same year, the *Kukui* searched for the schooner *Kitsap,* which had been wrecked in a collision with another vessel. The derelict was finally located, and the *Kukui* assisted in its destruction so that it would not be a danger to navigation.[13]

The following year, the *Annie E,* an old windjammer carrying a load of lumber from Honolulu to the island of Hawai'i, sprang a leak and took on so much water that only the lumber aboard kept the vessel afloat. Part of the crew took to a lifeboat and were picked up and brought to Honolulu. The captain and two of the crew remained aboard the drifting schooner, hoping for a tow. Ships and planes searched for several days, but there was no sign of the drifting vessel until about a week later, when the army transport *Madawaska,* on its way to the Philippines, sent a message to Honolulu that several flares from a vessel in distress had been spotted. The *Kukui,* under the command of Captain Ole Eriksen, proceeded to the area designated, but when it arrived there, the *Annie E* was nowhere to be seen. Being familiar with the winds and currents, Eriksen set a course in the direction he believed the *Annie E* would drift. By sunset one of the lookouts spotted a smudge on the horizon in the direction Eriksen had expected the *Annie E* to be found. The *Kukui* proceeded to investigate. With night came increasing winds and the seas began to build. Eriksen projected the searchlight toward the sky so that the unknown ship would know a vessel was approaching. Soon the men on the *Kukui* saw flares from the other ship and knew it was the *Annie E.*[14]

The men aboard the drifting vessel had been without food for five days. The two crewmen needed assistance to walk and were taken aboard the *Kukui,* but the captain insisted on remaining aboard his ship, while the *Kukui*'s crew tried to get towlines attached. The hawseholes in the *Annie E*'s bows were under water, and to get lines through them several men from the tender had to dive under water. Once under tow, the unbalanced cargo of lumber made the schooner yaw so badly in the high seas that the *Kukui* could not keep steerage way. Under the stress of towing, the old wood in the schooner's port bulkhead broke away. The captain of the *Annie E,* realizing his vessel could not be saved and would have to be burned, boarded the *Kukui.* Gasoline was poured over the lumber, and from a safe distance a torch was thrown aboard. The men watched the *Annie E* and her cargo of lumber disappear in smoke and ash; then the *Kukui* brought the survivors back to Honolulu. U.S. Secretary of Commerce J. W. Alexander wrote Eriksen, "This Department takes great pleasure in commending you and the officers and crew of the tender for their valuable service to the *Annie E.* . . . This commendation will be noted on the records as part of the official history of all concerned."[15]

Whenever the *Kukui* was hauled out for needed repairs, a relief lighthouse tender, *Columbine,* was sent to Hawai'i to take over the *Kukui*'s duties. This vessel also had an impressive record for rescue work. The *Columbine,* a 424-ton steel-screw steamship built in 1892 at a cost of $93,993, was 155 feet in length, twenty-seven feet in breadth, and fifteen feet in depth. The coal-burning steamer, although it did not have the speed of the *Kukui,* served proficiently as a relief tender for many years in Hawaiian waters. During 1916 alone, the *Columbine* covered a distance of 9,254 miles while on duty in Hawaiian waters.[16]

One of the assignments accomplished was a search-and-rescue operation. On January 17, 1916, the *Columbine* found the British bark *Yeoman* disabled in the breakers off Port Allen, Kaua'i. The bark was four times the size of the *Columbine,* yet the tender was able to tow the *Yeoman* through heavy seas for fifty-six hours and bring it safely into Honolulu Harbor. For their heroic efforts in saving the *Yeoman* and all aboard from almost certain destruction during the gale, President Woodrow Wilson expressed his appreciation to the officers and crew of the *Columbine*. The same year, the tender was commended by the Lighthouse Service for towing the grounded steamer *Mikahala* off a reef on the exposed shore of Moloka'i. The *Columbine* was also part of the search team for an army launch lost off O'ahu and was involved with the saving of the grounded schooner *Muriel*.[17]

The lighthouse tenders serving in Hawai'i have completed many other successful search-and-rescue missions—including some for airplanes and even errant buoys. One buoy that broke loose from its mooring off the California coast took seven years to drift over the Pacific to Hawai'i, where it was picked up by the *Kukui*. On June 22, 1922, the tender located a downed aircraft and saved both the pilot and the plane. On another occasion, one of the *Kukui*'s crewmen, William Jones, dived twenty-five feet under water to attach hoisting tackle to a sunken Army V-10 airplane so that it could be hauled to the surface and salvaged. The *Kukui*'s officers and crew were commended for this service on July 1, 1922, by Major General C. P. Summerall.[18]

During World War II, the *Kukui* became the first ship to land American troops. This came about, according to Lieutenant Commander Marcus B. Jacobson, commanding officer of the Coast Guard operations base at the time, when a Japanese fighter plane made an emergency landing on Ni'ihau on December 7, 1941. "Setting up two machine guns in the village the enemy flier fired wildly. The villagers hearing gunfire for the first time in their lives ran into the woods. With nobody left in the village the enemy proceeded to ransack it." A Ni'ihau cowboy, Hawila Kaleohano, managed to launch a whaleboat and, after hours of steady rowing across the rough channel, came ashore on Kaua'i where he notified officials of what was happening. When word reached Honolulu, the *Kukui* was dispatched with a

company of fully armed National Guardsmen aboard. The following morning the troops landed, but the danger was over. The Japanese pilot had been killed in a hand-to-hand battle with Ni'ihauan Benehakaka Kanehele. Kanehele, wounded in the fight, became an overnight hero. The unneeded troops returned with the *Kukui*.

But the *Kukui*'s most important function was as a lighthouse tender, a job that ranged from difficult to hazardous for the men and the vessel. Lighthouse personnel had to be taken on inspection tours to every light station on every island twice a year. The tender transported all the building materials and the work crews needed to maintain established lighthouses and erect new ones. Often the *Kukui*'s crew was directly involved with building many of the lighted aids. One of their greatest achievements was establishing the navigational light on the top of the almost insurmountable cliffs of Ka'ula, the rocky islet located twenty-two miles southwest of Ni'ihau.

The landing at Ka Lae Light Station on the southern tip of the island of Hawai'i presented another challenge. Rather than anchoring the *Kukui* off, a hawser was put aboard the small boat (also called the cargo boat). The oarsmen usually stood up as they pulled on the long oars and edged up to the ledge. Here, on calm days, the waves were sometimes only six feet high. As the bow lifted, a crewman jumped ashore and the hawser was passed to him. He took the heavy line and secured it to a ring bolt embedded in the ledge. The men aboard the *Kukui* then winched the hawser in, drawing the tender closer to the cliff. Those going to the light station still used the cargo boat, and they had to leap ashore at the correct moment—or end up in the sea. The oarsmen were experts at maneuvering the boat in rough seas. According to Frederick Edgecomb, oars were used instead of a motor because "we find oars more dependable in work like this. The motor might die at the wrong time. These sailors can edge the boat right up to the rocks with oars."[19]

The *Kukui* did carry a motor launch, but all difficult landings were made with the cargo boat, which resembled a double-ended lifeboat. Standing up, the men pulled on the oars with short powerful strokes. A seaman in the stern held the steering oar. If the boat was in danger of going aground or smashing into a rocky ledge, the oarsmen instantly backwatered with their oars or unshipped their oars to fend off.

In 1939 the captain of the *Kukui* was William J. H. Sietemeyer. Sietemeyer was born in the Netherlands and went to sea as a boy in 1887. He took command of the *Kukui* in 1925. Victor B. Gothe, the first officer, joined the *Kukui* in 1933. Born in Sweden, he also went to sea as a boy, serving on a windjammer in 1895. Gothe's hobby was making models of the many ships he had served on. Geoffrey Lloyd's hobby was collecting records of all types of music. Lloyd, who served as radio operator and was known by the traditional name of "Sparks," also published the ship's daily news sheet, except when he was seasick from the *Kukui*'s excessive rolling action. This uncomfortable motion was also noted by Second Officer William Wickman, who lived with his wife aboard a thirty-eight-foot ketch, the *Mundeamo*, in a slip at Ala Moana yacht basin (Ala Wai Harbor). Wickman claimed his ketch sailed better than the tender, and the *Kukui*'s crew agreed, for the ship, with its shallow draft and bulky shape, was well known for its rolling motion. Some of the crew claimed they had been aboard when the *Kukui* rolled so far over that the cargo boat, suspended above the side of the main deck from davits, almost dangled in the water. A jib sail was often flown in the hopes of steadying the vessel.[20]

One of the quartermasters aboard was Joseph Pestrella, who left the *Kukui* to become the lightkeeper at Kumukahi Point on the island of Hawai'i and later served on the Makapu'u Light. The other quartermaster, John C. Dyer, was studying to become an officer. The engine room force consisted of four oilers and four firemen. The total complement of the tender was thirty-one men.[21]

In 1940, after the *Kukui* went to the rescue of the sampan *Shinyo* off Moloka'i and saved the seven men aboard, the *Honolulu Star-Bulletin* ran the story under the headline, "There's Life In Old Boat Yet." But there were only a few more years of service left for the *Kukui*. On February 1, 1946, the *Kukui* was decommissioned. Lieutenant Alfred Anderson, U.S. Coast Guard, was the last to command the light tender and he was the officer who "broke down the flag and commission pennant." Old-timers were saddened when they no longer saw the familiar ship churning into port. They considered the lighthouse tender to be the most famous of any ship to sail Hawaiian waters.[22]

The vessels serving as buoy and lighthouse tenders after the *Kukui*, from 1947 to 1953, were the Coast Guard Cutters *Walnut* and *Basswood*. The *Buttonwood*, *Blackhaw*, *Planetree*, *Balsam*, *Ironwood*, and *Mallow* all served in the Fourteenth District at some time during the years 1954 to 1978. The cutters *Buttonwood* and *Sassafras* along with the *Mallow* have served in the district from 1978 to 1989. All of the tenders exhibit some of the same peculiarities that the *Kukui* was known for, but only the *Blackhaw* had an icebreaker bow. The incongruous bow on vessels serving in the tropics is explained by the fact that when the tenders were built their destination was not known, and it was thought prudent to equip some of them with the capacity for icebreaking, thus making them useful anywhere.

All tenders are famous for their rolling action, which is the direct result of the vessels' shallow

CGC *Mallow,* one of three multimission vessels serving in Hawaiian waters, is primarily a lighthouse tender. The 180-foot-long cutter establishes, maintains, and services buoys and is responsible for many lighted aids throughout the Islands that are not easily accessible to the ANT team by land. (CGC *Mallow,* Fourteenth U.S. Coast Guard District)

draft, a necessity for ships that must often work in shallow waters. The modern tenders have diesel engines and can make about thirteen knots (fifteen miles per hour), only one knot faster than the old *Kukui,* and their boom capacity of twenty tons matches that of the *Kukui*'s exactly.[23]

The tenders *Basswood, Sassafras,* and *Mallow* were all built to the same specifications and were first launched in 1944. They are 180 feet long with a thirty-seven-foot beam and a draft of twelve feet, eight inches when fully loaded.[24] Because the Fourteenth District covers nearly eighteen million square

miles of land and sea, making it geographically the largest command in the Coast Guard, the *Basswood* is stationed on Guam, and the *Sassafras* and the *Mallow,* although they are assigned duties elsewhere in the district, primarily service the buoys in Hawaiian waters, as well as the lighted aids not accessible by land to the ANT team.

Like the *Kukui,* all tenders are still given names of flowers, trees, or shrubs, but they are relocated so often that the name has little to do with their home port. The *Mallow*'s name, just by chance, is relevant to Hawai'i. Mallow is the name of a family of plants that includes the hibiscus, which is the state flower of Hawai'i.

The *Mallow* was assigned to the Fourteenth District in 1965, after serving two years in the Marshall Islands during World War II and nineteen years along the Washington and Oregon coasts. Like the *Kukui*, the *Mallow* has an impressive search-and-rescue record that includes saving many disabled fishing and sailing boats and their crews. The *Mallow* was part of fire-fighting operations off O'ahu during April 1989. Captain Steve Richmond, who deals with crises at sea within a fifty-mile radius of Honolulu, directed the fire-fighting force. A fire had broken out on a cargo barge that was being towed. The cargo was worth $3.5 million. Two salvage tugs went to its aid, but were unable to extinguish the blaze. The 286-foot barge was carrying cars, containers of household goods, paints, paint thinner, nitrogen in bottles, insecticide, diesel oil, and low-grade explosives. Even after the fire department's tug had fired four water cannons on the blaze, Richmond, aboard the *Mallow,* reported that the flames were intensifying. "She's glowing pretty red. You can put water on it and the flame goes out, but it doesn't take long for reflashes. What you have out there is hot mass and it will smolder for a long time, up to a couple of days." The smoke from the fire represented a serious health hazard, and Richmond made sure the barge was on a course that kept the smoke blowing out to sea. The fire was eventually subdued, and the *Mallow* escorted the barge to Barbers Point Harbor.[25]

Another mission for the *Mallow* included searching for the debris that was swept out of United Airlines Flight 811, along with nine passengers, when a hole opened up in the side of the Boeing 747 soon after takeoff from Honolulu on March 25, 1989. The *Mallow*'s assignments have always been varied and often unusual. Once, while on buoy-servicing duty, it carried two hundred seedling trees from O'ahu to

Johnston Atoll, for the residents to plant. In 1988 the *Mallow* and its crew were awarded the Special Operations Ribbon for participating in the largest marijuana seizure in the history of Hawai'i. "We are never bored," said Ensign Keith Russell. "We're involved in law enforcement, and search and rescue, as well as our primary mission of servicing aids to navigation."[26]

In Hawai'i, the *Sassafras* is responsible for buoys and breakwater lights on Lāna'i; Moloka'i; the windward side of the island of Hawai'i; Lāhaina Harbor, Maui; Port Allen Harbor, Kaua'i; and Honolulu and Pearl harbors, O'ahu. The *Mallow* is responsible for Kahului Harbor, Maui; Nāwiliwili Harbor, Kaua'i; Kāne'ohe Bay and Barbers Point Harbor, O'ahu; and the leeward side of the Island of Hawai'i.[27]

One of the aids Chief Warrent Officer Joe Neudecker is in charge of maintaining is the Nāpō'opo'o Light on the island of Hawai'i. "We take the small boat from the *Mallow* and dock at the landing near the Captain Cook Monument. From there we walk west across an area of mangrove trees that is crisscrossed by old rock walls." In the past, the light structure has suffered recurrent storm damage, but the men from the *Mallow* have repaired the concrete work, and the light is in good condition. The white pyramidal tower is twenty-two feet high, and the flashing white light can be seen seven miles at sea. The light, which functions automatically, was completed in 1922. It stands close to the bay waters on a low-lying ledge of black lava.

Kealakekua Bay is one of the most beautiful bays in the Islands. It was set aside in 1969 as a marine life conservation district and underwater park. The types of fish, coral, and seaweeds that are seen in the bay today are probably the same varieties that were seen by Hawaiians of ancient times. One hundred ten different species of fish have been identified in the bay, and there are types of coral and sea urchins that are found nowhere else in the Hawaiian chain.[28]

The Nāpōʻopoʻo Light is important as a day-marker as well as a lighted aid, for there is quite a bit of boat traffic in Kealakekua Bay. The Captain Cook Monument is a popular sight, attracting many private and charter boats, and the bay offers the best anchorage along the western shore of the island.

The other lighted aids maintained by the men from the *Mallow* are not on land, but on break-waters. When seven new aids were needed for the completed deep-draft harbor at Barbers Point, the *Mallow* was responsible for establishing them. Each year the crew spends about 160 days at sea just scraping, painting, and repowering buoys. Although the *Mallow* is considered a multi-mission vessel, it is primarily a lighthouse tender, just like the old *Kukui*.

EPILOGUE

The growth in number of lighthouses in Hawai'i from one small light marking Lahaina roadstead to 176 lighted aids marking all of the harbors and coasts of the Hawaiian Islands has been a remarkable achievement. New lights continue to be established; the most recent is a primary seacoast light erected in 1987 atop the Ka'ena Point Tracking Station on O'ahu. Lighted aids are continually being replaced and updated. In the future more efficient and effective optics will be displayed from structures built of steel, fiber glass, and perhaps some yet-to-be-discovered suitable material. The mariner benefits greatly from all of the technological and scientific advances made in the development of navigational aids.

In Hawai'i and the rest of the United States, every lighted aid is now automated. Modern electronics have practically eliminated the need for lighted beacons in the Islands, except as aids in interisland navigation. Many people lament the passing of the lightkeeper, but to me the tragedy of the unmanned lighthouse is the vandalism and deterioration that usually follows.

Vandalism of light stations in the Islands is a serious and costly problem, but deterioration of lighthouse structures in Hawai'i has not yet occurred because the Islands' lighted aids are serviced and maintained by the Coast Guard. As we move rapidly into a future of improved navigational aids, when the Islands' traditional lighthouses will become obsolete, it is hoped we will have the vision to preserve those that are part of the maritime heritage of Hawai'i.

LIGHTHOUSE KEEPERS
IN HAWAI'I

Ah Choy, George
Keeper, Kauhola Point, 1917–1920

Ah Foo (aka Ah Hu and Aho)
Keeper, Pauka'a Point, (18??) 1893–1898 (1899?)

Akana, Charles K.
Keeper, Kanahena Point, 1911–1913
Keeper, Ka'uiki Head, 1914
Keeper, Kanahena Point, 1915
First Assistant Keeper, Kīlauea Point, 1916–1919
Second Assistant Keeper, Moloka'i (Kalaupapa), 1920
Keeper, Kauhola Point, 1921–1922
Keeper, Makapu'u Point, 1923
Keeper, Diamond Head, 1924
Keeper, Makapu'u Point, 1925
Keeper, Barbers Point, 1926–1930
Lighthouse Service employee, 1931–1932
First Assistant Keeper, Kīlauea Point, 1932
Keeper, Cape Kumukahi, 1934

Ako, Samuel
Keeper, Lahaina, 1910–1921

Allen, J. C.
First Assistant Keeper, Kīlauea Point, 1940

Alona, A.
Keeper, Barbers Point, 1888

Amalu, Samuel Apollo
Keeper, Kawaihae, 1906–1910
Keeper, Barbers Point, 1911–1914
Keeper, Honolulu Harbor, 1914–1915
Keeper, Kīlauea Point, 1915–1924

Keeper, Makapu'u Point, 1925–1929
Keeper, Barbers Point, 1930–1939

Amara, Jesse
Keeper, Waialua, (1885?) 1893–(1899?)

Andersen, J.
Keeper, Kanahena Point, (1886?) 1893–1910

Anderson, J., Mrs.
Keeper, Kanahena Point, 1911

Anderson, Samuel
Assistant Keeper, Kīlauea Point, 1929–1940
Assistant Keeper and Keeper, Kīlauea Point, 1940–1942

Ano, John N.
Keeper, McGregor Point, 1913
Second Assistant Keeper, Kīlauea Point, 1914–1915

Bartels, Edward H.
Second Assistant Keeper, Moloka'i (Kalaupapa), 1918–1919

Beazley, George A.
Assistant Keeper, Makapu'u Point, (190?) 1909–1910
Keeper, Makapu'u Point, 1911–1924

Beeson, M. F.
USCG Engineman 2nd Class, Moloka'i (Kalaupapa), 1960

Blum, Carl
Keeper, Nāwiliwili, 1903–1910

Brockman, George
Keeper, Ālia Point (Pepe'ekeo Point), 1914–1917
Keeper, Nāpō'opo'o, 1918–1921

Bryson, Daniel J.
USCG Boatswain's Mate 1st Class, Moloka'i
(Kalaupapa), 1966

Burrows, J. R.
Keeper, Lā'au Point, 1898–1912

Burrows, John W.
Keeper, Lā'au Point, 1882–1898

Center, David
Keeper, Kaunakakai, 1899–1900

Chester, John
Keeper, McGregor Point, 1913–1914

Chillingworth, Samuel F.
Keeper, Kawaihae, 1869–1877 (18??)

Cianfarani, Ronald G.
USCG Boatswain's Mate, Makapu'u Point, 1972–1974

Conway, W. A.
Keeper, Mā'alaea, (18??)–1893 (18??)

Cornwell, James L.
Keeper, McGregor Point, (1906?)–1915

Creighton, James R.
USCG Engineman 3rd class, Moloka'i (Kalaupapa), 1966

Dooley, W. C.
Radio Operator, Lighthouse Tender *Kukui,* 1934
Second Assistant Keeper, Kīlauea Point, 1936–1937
First Assistant Keeper, Kīlauea Point, 1938
Keeper, Nāwiliwili, 1939–1941
USCG Boatswain's Mate, Kīlauea Point, 1942

Dunne, George H.
Keeper, Lahaina, 1895–1904

Edgar, John R.
Second Assistant Keeper, Kīlauea Point, 1917

Elgin, Robert R.
Keeper, Māhukona, 1909–1911

Enoka, William
First Assistant Keeper, Moloka'i (Kalaupapa), 1919–1924

Enos, John, Jr.
Second Assistant Keeper, (19??) 1930–1931
First Assistant Keeper, Makapu'u Point, 1932–1936
Keeper, Pa'uwela Point, 1937–1941

Estrella, Sidney
Assistant Keeper, Honolulu lighthouse depot, 1936–1941
Keeper, Kauhola Point, 1941–1951
Assistant Keeper, Cape Kumukahi, 1951–1956

Ezera, Fred
Keeper, Nāpō'opo'o, 1913

Ferreira, Manuel
Keeper, Ka'uiki Head, 1908–1913
Assistant Keeper, Barbers Point, 1914–1916
Keeper, Barbers Point, 1917–1926
Keeper, Honolulu Harbor, 1926–1927
Keeper, Moloka'i (Kalaupapa), 1927–1929
Keeper, Makapu'u Point, 1929–1942
USCG Petty Officer, Barbers Point, 1942–(1944?)

Flint, Harry W.
Keeper, Honolulu Harbor, 1910–1913
Keeper, Kīlauea Point, 1913–1915
Keeper, Ka Lae, 1916–1924
Keeper, Kīlauea Point, 1925–1931

Fredrick (first name unknown)
Second Assistant Keeper, Kīlauea Point, 1917

Gibson, James
First Assistant Keeper, Moloka'i (Kalaupapa), 1936

Gillespie, Ed
USCG Boatswain's Mate, Makapu'u Point, 1974

Haleamau, Daniel P.
Keeper, Kailua, 1910–1913
First Assistant Keeper, Kīlauea Point, 1913–1914

Haleamau, James K.
Keeper, Kailua, 1913–1923
Second Assistant Keeper, Moloka'i (Kalaupapa), 1923–1924
First Assistant Keeper, Moloka'i (Kalaupapa), 1925
Keeper, Ka Lae, 1925–1933

Hanuna, John M.
Keeper, Nākālele Point, 1910–1915

Hatton, W.
Keeper, Barbers Point, (18??) 1893–1905

Hearn, Robert
USCG Petty Officer, Pa'uwela Point, 1962–1964
Light Attendant, Maui, 1964–1967 (19??)

Heim, C.
Second Assistant Keeper, Kīlauea Point, 1925–1926
Keeper, Kaunakakai, 1927
Second Assistant Keeper, Moloka'i (Kalaupapa), 1928–1930

Hookuanui, William
Keeper, Kawaihae, 1901–1903

Hoopii, John
Keeper, Kahala Point (Kaua'i), 1898–1903
Keeper, Kohala Point (island of Hawai'i), 1903–1909

Huntington, Stanley
USCG Petty Officer, Kīlauea Point, 1949–1957 (195?)

Kahaule, John
Keeper, Makahū'ena Point, 1910–1913

Kahaunaele, David
Keeper, Kīlauea Point, 1957–1958

Kahinu, J. K.
Keeper, Kaunakakai, 1897

Kaiminaauao, D. P.
Keeper, Laupāhoehoe Point, 1914–1915

Kainali, Samuel
Keeper, Kaunakakai, 1889

Kaiwi
Keeper, Makapu'u Point, 1909 (before light was completed)

Kalama, Luther K.
Keeper, McGregor Point, 1911–1912
Second Assistant Keeper, Kīlauea Point, 1913–1915 (1916?)
Keeper, Nākālele Head, 1917–1922

Kaleimamo
Keeper, Kaunakakai, 1880

Kalili, David
Lighthouse Service employee, 1910
Keeper, Ālia Point (Pepe'ekeo Point), 1910–1913
Assistant Keeper, Diamond Head, 1914–1917

Kalili, P.
Keeper, Kaunakakai, 1900

Kamakoa, C. Moses
Keeper, Nāpō'opo'o, 1914–1917

Kamano, Peter
Keeper, Kanahena Point, 1916–1918
Second Assistant Keeper, Kīlauea Point, 1918–1919
Keeper, Kanahena Point, 1919–1920
Keeper, Makahū'ena Point, 1920–1921

Kanealii, Benjamin K.
First Assistant Keeper, Kīlauea Point, 1924–1925
Keeper, Makapu'u Point, 1925–1926

Kanekoa, John H
Keeper, Nāwiliwili, 1910–1912
Second Assistant Keeper, Moloka'i (Kalaupapa), 1913
First Assistant Keeper, Kīlauea Point, 1914–1918

Kanui, W. O.
Keeper, Kawaihae, (18??) 1893–(1899?)

Kaohimunu, John M.
Assistant Keeper, Kauhola Point, 1919–1921
Keeper, Kauhola Point, 1921–1922
Assistant Keeper, Makapu'u Point, 1923–1925
Assistant Keeper, Kīlauea Point, 1926–1927
Keeper, Barbers Point, 1927–1929
Lighthouse Service employee, 1930

Kapahua, Samuel
Keeper, Pauka'a Point, 1899–1913

Kaukaia
Keeper, Lahaina, (18??)–1893

Kaukaliu, John M.
Keeper, Diamond Head, 1899–1914
Keeper, Barbers Point, 1915–1916

Keanu, James M.
Keeper, Makanalua (first light at Kalaupapa), 1906
Keeper, Moloka'i (Kalaupapa), 1909–1926
Lighthouse Service employee, 1927–1928
Keeper, Moloka'i (Kalaupapa), 1929–1932
Keeper, Kīlauea Point, 1932–1936
Keeper, Moloka'i (Kalaupapa), 1937–1939

Kelsall, Emilia A.
USCG Boatswain's Mate, Kīlauea Point, (19??)–1975

Kepilino, Philip
Keeper, Pa'uwela Point, 1911–1921

Kua, Oliver (Oliva)
Keeper, Nāpō'opo'o, 1910–1912
Assistant Keeper, Makapu'u Point, 1913–1917
Keeper, Nāwiliwili, 1918–1939

Kukahiko
Keeper, Mākena, 1888

Kukaia (aka Kokaia)
Keeper, Lahaina, 1893

Kupukaa, Henry
Lighthouse Tender *Kukui,* 1924–1942
Assistant Keeper, Moloka'i (Kalaupapa), (19??)–1964

Leleo, Samuel
Keeper, Laupāhoehoe Point, 1911–1913
Assistant Keeper, Moloka'i (Kalaupapa), 1913
Keeper, Keāhole Point, 1914–1915

McCool, James F.
USCG Engineman 3rd Class, Kīlauea Point, 1957–1958

McGregor, Captain
Keeper, Honolulu Harbor Light, 1869–1871

McLaughlin, John
Keeper, Nāwiliwili, 1908–1909
Keeper, Makapu'u Point, 1909–1910

Madden, Edward
Keeper, Māhukona, 1913–1915

Mahoe, John K.
Keeper, Ka'uiki Head, 1914–1915
Keeper, Nākālele, 1915–1916

Makahi, John K.
Keeper, Keāhole, 1909–1913
Second Assistant Keeper, Moloka'i (Kalaupapa), 1914–1918
First Assistant Keeper, Kīlauea Point, 1919–1922
Keeper, Kīlauea Point, 1923

Mansfield, George
Assistant Keeper, Makapu'u Point, 1909–1911

Marques, Ed
Second Assistant Keeper, Moloka'i (Kalaupapa), 1936–1946
Keeper, Pa'uwela Point, 1946–1962

Martin, Charles L.
Second Assistant Keeper, Moloka'i, 1909–1910

Miller, Edward L.
Second Assistant Keeper, Moloka'i (Kalaupapa), 1910–1913
Keeper, Nāwiliwili, 1913–1915

Moealoha, Edward K.
Keeper, Kauhola Point, 1910–1913

Mosher, Ferdinand
Keeper, Coconut Point, 1911–1917
and Keeper, Waiākea (Hilo Harbor), 1912–1914

Nahinui, Joseph N.
Keeper, Kaunakakai, 1901–1904

Nakai, John T.
Keeper, Ka Lae, 1906–1907

Nihoa, Fredrick E.
Lighthouse Service employee, 1919
Second Assistant Keeper, Kīlauea Point, 1919–1922
First Assistant Keeper, Kīlauea Point, 1923–1924
Keeper, Kīlauea Point, 1925
Lighthouse Service employee, 1926
First Assistant Keeper, Moloka'i (Kalaupapa), 1928–1931
Keeper, Moloka'i (Kalaupapa), 1931–1936
Keeper, Cape Kumukahi, 1937–1942

Nihoa, William. K.
Second Assistant Keeper, Moloka'i (Kalaupapa), 1927–1934

Assistant Keeper, Makapu'u Point, 1935–1936
Lighthouse Service employee, 1936–1937

Pate, Frank
First Assistant Keeper, Makapu'u, 1930–1933
Lighthouse Service employee, 1933–1934
Second Assistant Keeper, Moloka'i (Kalaupapa), 1935–1936

Pele, D. K.
Keeper, Makahū'ena Point, 1914–1919

Pestrella, Joseph
Lighthouse Tender *Kukui,* 1933–1938
Keeper, Cape Kumukahi, 1938–1960
Keeper, Makapu'u Point, 1960–1962

Peterson, Frank A.
Keeper, Kauhola Point, 1914–1915
First Assistant Keeper, Makapu'u Point, 1916–1917

Platt, Claude E.
Second Assistant Keeper, Kīlauea Point, 1936–1937
First Assistant Keeper, Moloka'i (Kalaupapa), 1937–1940
Assistant Keeper, Kīlauea Point, 1941–1942

Rapozo, J. F.
Keeper, Kahala Point, 1910–1913

Reid, Robert I.
Keeper, Ka Lae, 1908–1911
First Assistant Keeper, Moloka'i (Kalaupapa), 1912–1913
Keeper, Barbers Point, 1914–1915
Keeper, Diamond Head, 1915–1917
Keeper, Barbers Point, 1917–1918
Keeper, Diamond Head, 1918–1919

Rickard, Harry S.
Keeper, Laupāhoehoe Point, 1890–1910

Robins, Edward E.
Keeper, Honolulu Harbor, 1914–1921

Robins, Edward E., Jr.
Second Assistant Keeper, Moloka'i (Kalaupapa), 1914–1916
First Assistant Keeper, Kīlauea Point, 1916–1918
Keeper, Honolulu Harbor, 1921–1925

Robins, Fred E. (Sr.)
Assistant Keeper, Barbers Point, 1922–1924
(Mariner, 1925–1929)
Assistant Keeper, Barbers Point, 1930–1933
Assistant Keeper, Kīlauea Point, 1934–1935
Keeper, Kīlauea Point, 1936–1940
Keeper, Moloka'i (Kalaupapa), 1940–1953
USCG Boatswain's Mate 1st Class, Barbers Point, 1953–1964

Souza, Manuel
Keeper, Nāwiliwili, 1897–1903

Sullivan, Steve
USCG Petty Officer, Makapu'u Point, 1974

Sweeney, John M.
First Assistant Keeper, Makapu'u Point, 1913–1915
Keeper, Honolulu Harbor, 1916–1917
(Mariner, 1918–1919)
Assistant Keeper, Makapu'u Point, 1920–1922
Keeper, Kauhola Point, 1923–1933
Assistant Keeper, Makapu'u Point, 1934–1935
Keeper, Kauhola Point, 1935–1941

Taylor, A. D.
Keeper, Nāpō'opo'o, 1922

Taylor, Captain David
Keeper, Lahaina, 1893–1895

Teves, Juan (Johan)
Keeper, Pauka'a Point, 1914–1923

Toomey, Alexander D.
Keeper, Kawaihae, 1908–1915
Keeper, Nāwiliwili, 1916–1917
Assistant Keeper, Makapu'u Point, 1918–1919
Keeper, Diamond Head, 1919–1924
Assistant Keeper, Makapu'u Point, 1924

Uahinui, Joseph N.
Keeper, Kaunakakai, 1903–1910

Watkins, William J.
Assistant Keeper, Diamond Head, (19??)–1931
Second Assistant Keeper, Makapu'u Point, 1932–1933

Assistant Keeper, Cape Kumukahi, 1934–1937
Assistant Keeper, Makapu'u Point, 1937–1940

Welsbarth, William
Keeper, Kauhola Point, 1916

Williams, Frank
Second Assistant Keeper, Moloka'i (Kalaupapa), 1921–1923
Lighthouse Service employee, 1924
First Assistant Keeper, Kīlauea Point, 1925–1932

Keeper, Kīlauea Point, 1932–1933
First Assistant Keeper, Kīlauea Point, 1933–1936

Williams, William ("Bill")
Keeper, Honolulu Harbor, 1871–1908

Williams, William F.
First Assistant Keeper, Moloka'i (Kalaupapa), 1909–1912
Keeper, Ka Lae, 1912–1914
Keeper, Honolulu Harbor, 1915

NOTES

Abbreviations used in the notes:

AH	Hawaii State Archives
DAGS	State of Hawaii, Department of Accounting and General Services
14th CGD, AtoN	U.S. Coast Guard, Fourteenth District, Honolulu, Aids to Navigation
Int. Misc.	Interior Department, Miscellaneous
Light List	*Light List, Pacific Coast and Pacific Islands* (Washington, D.C.: Government Printing Office)
Min. Int. Reports	Minister of Interior Reports, Honolulu
USDC	U.S. Department of Commerce
USDCL	U.S. Department of Commerce and Labor

Introduction

1. Alexander Pope, *Iliad of Homer,* eds. R. A. Brower and W. H. Bond (New York: Macmillan Publishing Company, 1965), p. 405. "So to the night-wandering sailors pale with fears, wide o'er the watery waste a light appears, which on the far-seen mountain blazing high, streams from a lonely watch-tower to the sky."

2. Paolo Curto, "The Pharos Lighthouse," *Oceans,* July 1981, p. 8.

3. Will Kyselka and George Bunton, *Polynesian Stars and Men* (Honolulu: Bishop Museum Science Center, 1969), p. 1. The Mediterranean Sea covers approximately 965 square miles. Polynesia includes some 15,000,000 square miles, mostly ocean with very little land area. The region in the Pacific known as the Polynesian triangle extends 4,000 miles from Ellice Islands on the west to Easter Island on the east, and more than 3,000 miles from New Zealand on the south to Hawai'i on the north.

4. Dudley Witney, *The Lighthouse* (Boston: New York Graphic Society, 1975), p. 14.

5. Elenor Loarie Schoen, "Beacons, Marks and Signs," *Sea Frontier,* May–June 1973, p. 156.

6. Francis Ross Holland, Jr., *America's Lighthouses, Their Illustrated History Since 1716* (Brattleboro, Vt.: The Stephen Greene Press, 1972), pp. 6, 26; Schoen, "Beacons, Marks and Signs," p. 156.

7. Schoen, "Beacons, Marks and Signs," pp. 159, 162.

8. Holland, *America's Lighthouses,* p. 155.

9. Kay Grant, *Robert Stevenson* (New York: Meredith Press, 1969), pp. 169–170.

Chapter 1. Honolulu Harbor

1. U.S. Coast Guard, *Coast Pilot* (Washington, D.C.: Government Printing Office, 1988), p. 385; U.S. Department of Transportation, *Light List,* 1989, pp. viii, x.

2. U.S. Coast Guard, *Coast Pilot,* p. 387.

3. Lieutenant George E. G. Jackson, Royal Navy, "Honolulu Harbor" (Registered Number 795), chart of harbor with drawing of the "Light House as seen from the entrance to Harbour," Survey Department, DAGS; Charles D. Sumner, letter to Department of Public Works, Honolulu, August 13, 1870, Int. Misc., Lighthouses, AH.

4. Interviews with David Lyman, Honolulu Harbor pilot, Honolulu Harbor, June 28, 1988 and June 28, 1989. By 1989 the channel had been widened to 500 feet and dredged to a depth of 45 feet.

5. Mary Kawena Pukui, Samuel H. Elbert, and Esther T. Mookini, *Place Names of Hawaii* (Honolulu: University of Hawaii Press, 1986), p. 175.

6. Mike Markrich, "Honolulu Harbor: Rude Beginnings—to World Port," *Historic Hawai'i News,* April 1984, p. 9; Thomas G. Thrum, "Honolulu 60 Years Ago," in *Hawaiian Annual 1913,* pp. 84–85; Pukui, Elbert, and Mookini, *Place Names of Hawaii,* p. 9. In modern times this ox path became Alakea Street.

7. *Honolulu Star-Bulletin,* May 27, 1939.

8. Mr. Crabb, Chamber of Commerce, Honolulu, letter to John Young, minister of Interior, March 12, 1851, Int. Misc. Correspondence, AH.

9. Min. Int. Reports, 1851, pp. 96–97, AH.

10. Privy Council Record, vol. 6, p. 316, file: Broadside, F. O. and Executive, 1863, AH.

11. "Cook's Monument at Kealakekua," in *Hawaiian Annual 1912,* pp. 62–63.

12. A. Grove Day, *History Makers of Hawaii* (Honolulu: Mutual Publishing, 1984), p. 37; Pukui, Elbert, and Mookini, *Place Names of Hawaii,* p. 65.

13. Thomas Hughes, Honolulu Iron Works, letter to Robert Sterling, superintendent of Public Works, Honolulu, February 17, 1869; L. L. Gilbert, letter to Sterling, July 15, 1869, Int. Misc., Lighthouses, AH.

14. *Pacific Commercial Advertiser,* May, August, 1869.

15. *Hawaiian Tariff and Digest of the Laws and Regulations of the Customs; Pilot and Harbor Regulations,* prepared by John A. Hassinger, Deputy Collector, port of Honolulu (Honolulu: Printed at the Gazette Office, 1871), pp. 24, 39, Hawaiian Mission Children's Society Library. By 1871 lighthouses had been established and light dues were collected at Honolulu Harbor, O'ahu; Pauka'a Point (Hilo Harbor) and Kawaihae on the island of Hawai'i; and at Lahaina, Maui.

16. Minister of Finance, *Annual Report,* 1870, p. 10, AH.

17. Ibid.

18. *Hawaiian Tariff and Digest,* p. 38.

19. Henry M. Whitney, *The Hawaiian Guide Book for Travelers; Containing a Brief Description of the Hawaiian Islands* (Honolulu: H. Whitney, 1875; Rutland, Vt., and Tokyo, Japan: Charles E. Tuttle, 1970), pp. 6–7.

20. Ralph S. Kuykendall and A. Grove Day, *Hawaii: A History, from Polynesian Kingdom to American State* (Englewood Cliffs, N.J.: Prentice-Hall, 1976), pp. 115–116, 160.

21. Charles W. Stewart, Jr., "Honolulu Harbor," *The Military Engineer,* vol. 28, no. 157, (January–February 1936), pp. 23–24.

22. U.S. Senate, *Hawaiian Investigation,* part 2, Fifty-seventh Congress, first session, 1902, p. 50.

23. "Jonah Kuhio Kalanianaole," Office Holder's Index, AH; Lori Kamae, *The Empty Throne, A Biography of Hawaii's Prince Cupid* (Honolulu: Topgallant Publishing Co., 1980), p. 114.

24. Kamae, *The Empty Throne,* pp. 114–115.

25. USDCL, *Annual Reports,* 1904, pp. 285, 288.

26. Kamae, *The Empty Throne,* p. 125.

27. Ibid., pp. 126–127.

28. USDCL, *Annual Reports,* 1905, pp. 254–256.

29. Ibid., 1906, pp. 222–223.

30. Ibid., p. 97; U.S. House of Representatives, Fifty-ninth Congress, first session, Report 4671, "Refund of Certain Moneys to Hawaii," June 4, 1906, p. 3; USDCL, *Annual Reports,* 1906, p. 97. The Light House Board requested an appropriation that would allow the annual salary of keepers to be raised to $52.38 a month.

31. USDCL, *Annual Reports,* 1906, p. 223.

32. Pukui, Elbert, and Mookini, *Place Names of Hawaii,* p. 26.

33. *Hawaiian Annual 1907,* pp. 148–149; U.S. Army Corps of Engineers, *Sand Island Shore Protection, Oahu, Hawaii* (Honolulu: U.S. Army Engineer District, 1978), pp. c-2, c-3.

34. USDCL, *Annual Reports,* 1909, p. 637.

35. Ibid., 1907, p. 609.

36. Ibid., pp. 636–637.

37. USDCL, *Annual Reports,* 1910, pp. 508–509. The final cost of the lighthouse was $39,998.62.

38. Kuykendall and Day, *Hawaii: A History,* pp. 236–239.

39. U.S. House of Representatives, Eighty-ninth Congress, first session, Document no. 93, p. 15.

40. Lucius E. Pinkham, member of Territorial Board of Harbor Commissioners, Report, 1916, Int. Misc., Lighthouses, AH.

41. Elinor A. Langton-Boyle, "Aloha Tower, A Welcome to Hawaii," *Paradise of the Pacific,* 1958, pp. 18–19; Jeri Bostwick, "Aloha Tower Rediscovered," *Historic Hawai'i News,* June 4–5, 1981, p. 4.

42. Ray Jerome Baker, *Honolulu in 1853* (Honolulu: R. J. Baker, 1950), p. 8; Pukui, Elbert, and Mookini, *Place Names of Hawaii,* p. 30. The fort was located near the harbor at the foot of what is now Fort Street.

43. Pukui, Elbert, and Mookini, *Place Names of Hawaii,* pp. 175, 208; Gorman D. Gilman, "Streets of Honolulu in the Early Forties," in *Hawaiian Annual 1904,* p. 81.

44. Bostwick, "Aloha Tower Rediscovered," p. 4.

45. Ibid.; *Honolulu Advertiser,* May 30, 1926.

46. *Honolulu Advertiser,* May 29, 1926.

47. Ibid., May 30, 1926.

48. Ibid.

49. *Mid Pacific Magazine,* October 1927, pp. 321–326; the fourth-order Honolulu Harbor Light lens is on display at Hawaii Maritime Center, Kalākaua Boat House, Honolulu.

50. Interview with William Mowat, Pilot Boat captain, Honolulu, June 28, 1988.

51. Ibid.

52. Display, Hawaii Maritime Center, Kalākaua Boat House, Honolulu.

53. *Honolulu Star-Bulletin,* May 7, 1934.

54. U.S. Department of Transportation, *Light List,* 1970, p. 273; interview with Petty Officer Rick McKersie, 14th CGD, AtoN, December 20, 1989.

55. U.S. Department of Transportation, *Light List,* 1989, p. 279; interview with Petty Officer Bill Souder, 14th CGD, AtoN, December 20, 1989.

Chapter 2. Barbers Point

1. Mary Kawena Pukui, Samuel H. Elbert, and Esther T. Mookini, *Place Names of Hawaii* (Honolulu: University of Hawaii Press, 1974), p. 72.

2. Elspeth P. Sterling, *Sites of Oahu* (Honolulu: Department of Anthropology, Bernice P. Bishop Museum, 1978), p. 40; F. W. Howay, "Captain Henry Barber of Barbers Point," in *Hawaiian Historical Society Annual Report 1938,* pp. 40–41.

3. Howay, "Captain Henry Barber of Barbers Point," pp. 40, 42.

4. Ibid., p. 45; *Honolulu Star-Bulletin,* September 6, 1968.

5. "Marine Casualties for the Hawaiian Islands," in *Hawaiian Annual 1882,* p. 34.

6. W. D. Alexander, letter to H. A. P. Carter, minister of Interior, Honolulu, November 15, 1880, Int. Misc., Lighthouses, AH.

7. A. Grove Day, *History Makers of Hawaii* (Honolulu: Mutual Publishing, 1984), p. 3; William Dewitt Alexander, *A Brief Account of the Hawaiian Government Survey, Its Objects, Methods and Results* (Honolulu: Bulletin Steam Press, 1889), p. 24.

8. Carl Bowers Andrews and William Dewitt Alexander, "Theories Concerning Artesian Wells," in *The Structure of the Southeastern Portion of the Island of Oahu* (Honolulu: Geology Department, Experiment Station, H.S.P.A., 1954), p. 1.

9. "Appropriation Bill for the Bienniel Period Ending March 31, 1880," in *Hawaiian Annual 1881,* p. 52.

10. W. H. Crossman & Brother, New York, letter to minister of Interior, Honolulu, February 11, 1881, Int. Misc., Lighthouses, AH.

11. W. H. Crossman & Brother to minister of Interior, May 28, 1881.

12. Min. Int. Reports, 1882, p. 21, AH.

13. J. A. Hassinger, chief clerk to minister of Interior, Honolulu, letter to John Ena, secretary of Inter-Island Steam Navigation Company, Honolulu, December 23, 1887, Int. Letter Book 33, p. 271, AH; Hassinger to James Campbell, Honolulu, December 23, 1887, p. 272.

14. John Ena, Inter-Island Steam Navigation Company, Honolulu, to Hassinger, chief clerk, December 24, 1887; Cecil Brown, Honolulu, to Hassinger, December 28, 1887, Int. Misc. Correspondence, AH.

15. J. A. Hassinger, chief clerk, to Peter High, Honolulu, February 3, 1888, Int. Letter Book 34, p. 225, AH.

16. L. A. Thurston, minister of Interior, Honolulu, to A. Alona, May 3, 1888, Int. Letter Book 35, p. 391, AH.

17. Min. Int. Biennial Report, 1888, pp. 28–29, AH.

18. Captain A. S. Baker, USS *Philadelphia,* letter to minister of Interior, Honolulu, February 12, 1894, Int. Misc., Lighthouses, AH.

19. USDCL, *Annual Reports,* 1904, pp. 285–286; U.S. House of Representatives, Fifty-ninth Congress, first session, Report 4671, June 4, 1906, p. 2.

20. Olof L. Sorenson, assistant government surveyor's report to Governor George R. Carter, December 7, 1903; Office of Assistant to Engineer of Twelfth Light House District, T.H., *Barber's Point Light Station*, prepared under the direction of Major E. Eveleth Winslow, Corps of Engineers, April 2, 1910, Survey Department, Lighthouses, Oahu, DAGS.

21. Bartell D. Davis, "Progress Report on Emergency Excavation at Barbers Point, Oahu," 3rd quarter (July–August) 1979 (unpublished manuscript, Hamilton Library, University of Hawaii), p. 5; Marie C. Neal, *In Gardens of Hawaii*, Bernice P. Bishop Museum Special Publication 40 (Honolulu: Bishop Museum, 1948), p. 362.

22. USDCL, *Annual Reports*, 1905, p. 255; 1908, p. 620; 1909, p. 678.

23. USDC, *Annual Reports*, 1914, p. 544.

24. Ibid., 1915, p. 652.

25. USDC, "Description of Barbers Point Light Station," February 15, 1916.

26. "Marine Casualities," in *Hawaiian Annual 1907*, p. 114.

27. Mifflin Thomas, *Schooner from Windward* (Honolulu: University of Hawaii Press, 1983), p. 130.

28. USDC, *Annual Reports*, 1919, p. 751.

29. *The Sales Builder*, vol. 12, no. 1 (January 1939), p. 21.

30. "Marine Casualties," in *Hawaiian Annual 1924*, p. 156.

31. Ibid., p. 166.

32. USDC, "Description of Barbers Point Light Station," September 30, 1930, p. 12; idem, *Annual Reports*, 1933, p. 106.

33. USDC, *Annual Reports*, 1934, p. 117.

34. Correspondence with Carol Edgecomb Brown, May 8, 1989.

35. USDCL, *Annual Reports*, 1911, p. 541; correspondence with Carol Edgecomb Brown, May 8, 1989.

36. George Remington, "Light House Keeping Is Robins Family Tradition," *Honolulu Advertiser*, August 5, 1956.

37. *Honolulu Star-Bulletin*, August 7, 1939.

38. Interview with Anna Mae Robins Ka'anehe, Honolulu, August 23, 1988.

39. Ibid.

40. U.S. House of Representatives, Eighty-ninth Congress, first session, Document no. 93, "Honolulu Harbor and Barbers Point Harbor, Oahu, Hawaii," February 25, 1965, pp. 17, 28.

41. Interview with Machinery Technician Aaron Landrum and Electrician's Mate Glenn Aikin, U.S. Coast Guard, Barbers Point Light, July 18, 1988.

42. U.S. Department of Transportation, *Light List*, 1989, p. 283.

Chapter 3. Diamond Head

1. Genie Pitchford, "Honolulu Waterfront Expands As the City Itself Grows," *Honolulu Star-Bulletin*, September 26, 1936.

2. Wai-Jane Char, "Three Chinese Stores in Honolulu," *Hawaiian Journal of History*, vol. 8 (1974), pp. 19–20.

3. *Pacific Commercial Advertiser*, October 23, 1856; "Marine Signals for the Port of Honolulu," in *Hawaiian Annual 1876*, p. 26.

4. *Pacific Commercial Advertiser*, July 4, 1908; "Marine Signals for the Port of Honolulu," in *Hawaiian Annual 1875*, pp. 44–45.

5. "Marine Signals for the Port of Honolulu," in *Hawaiian Annual 1875*, pp. 44–45.

6. *Hawaiian Gazette*, December 21, 1894; "James A. King," Office Holders Index, AH.

7. *Pacific Commercial Advertiser*, May 14, 1857.

8. Ibid.

9. C. N. Spencer, minister of Interior, Honolulu, to Charles Peterson, Honolulu, August 1, 1891, Int. Letter Book 51, p. 31, AH.

10. Nathaniel Portlock, *A Voyage Round the World: But More Particularly to the North-West Coast of America* (Amsterdam: N. Israel; New York: Da Capo Press, 1968), p. 69.

11. Charles Victor de Varigny, *Fourteen Years in the Sandwich Islands, 1855–1868* (Honolulu: The University Press of Hawaii, 1981), p. 4.

12. *Hawaiian Annual 1926*, p. 114; 1907, pp. 44, 58; Division of State Parks, *Diamond Head State Monument* (Honolulu: The Division, 1979), p. 21.

13. Division of State Parks, *Diamond Head State Monument*, p. 20.

14. Ibid, p. 21.

15. Captain A. S. Baker, USS *Philadelphia,* to James A. King, minister of Interior, Honolulu, February 12, 1894, Int. Misc. Correspondence, AH.

16. British Minister in Residence, Honolulu, to minister of Foreign Affairs, Honolulu, October 23, 1893, Int. Misc. Correspondence, AH.

17. *Hawaiian Annual 1894,* p. 135; *The Friend,* November 1893, p. 87; *Pacific Commercial Advertiser,* October 3 and 6, 1893.

18. British Minister in Residence, Honolulu, to minister of Foreign Affairs, Honolulu, October 23, 1893, Int. Misc. Correspondence, AH.

19. British Minister in Residence to minister of Foreign Affairs, April 20, 1894.

20. Min. Int. Reports, 1895, p. 55, AH.

21. *Pacific Commercial Advertiser,* December 4, 1897.

22. Min. Int. Reports, 1897, p. 205, AH.

23. Public Works, Lighthouses, 1899 [the invoice in this folder is dated 1897], AH.

24. C. H. Kluegel and John Ouderkirk, Honolulu, to Minister of Interior, Honolulu, August 8, 1898 and September 21, 1898, Int. Misc. Correspondence, AH.

25. Min. Int. Reports, 1895, p. 127, AH.

26. Int. Letter Book 91, p. 213, February 3, 1898, AH.

27. "Notice to Mariners," 1899, Int. Misc., Lighthouses, AH.

28. Public Works, Lighthouses, 1900–1903, Diamond Head, AH; U.S. House of Representatives, Fifty-ninth Congress, first session, Report 4671, p. 2.

29. Secretary George Cortelyou, USDCL, Washington, D.C., to Governor George R. Carter, Honolulu, December 30, 1903, Int. Misc. Correspondence, AH; USDCL, *Annual Reports,* 1904, p. 286.

30. George R. Carter, Executive Order, January 18, 1906 and Walter F. Frear, Executive Order, October 31, 1910, Int. Misc., Lighthouses, AH.

31. USDCL, *Annual Reports,* 1907, p. 609; 1910, p. 534; *Husted's Directory of Honolulu and the Territory of Hawaii,* 1908, p. 535; *Pacific Commercial Advertiser,* September 28, 1907.

32. USDC, "Description of Diamond Head Light Station," March 24, 1916, p. 12.

33. USDC, *Annual Reports,* 1918, p. 640; idem, *Light List,* 1918, p. 157.

34. USDC, *Annual Reports,* 1920, p. 710.

35. Ruth Youngblood, "Diamond Head Light Guards Sea Lane and It's a Home, Too," *Honolulu Star-Bulletin and Advertiser,* August 18, 1968.

36. Ibid.; USDC, *Annual Reports,* 1939, pp. 116–117.

37. *Honolulu Star-Bulletin,* February 6, 1930.

38. Diamond Head Light Station, "Historical Description," 14th CGD, AtoN.

39. *Honolulu Advertiser,* June 23, 1940; interview with Marine Controller Allen Sandry, Aloha Tower, Honolulu, January 12, 1990.

40. Diamond Head Light Station, Report, 1950, 14th CGD, AtoN. "This light was listed in the Light List as an unwatched light from 1924 to 1944, but appeared in the 1945 Light List as a watched light and has continued to be listed as such to date. . . . Headquarters authorized complement (1950) for Diamond Head Light Station is 1 BM2 [Boatswain's Mate], 1 SD2 [Signalman], and 1 TN [Steward]."

41. Youngblood, "Diamond Head Light."

42. Ibid.

43. Diamond Head Light Station, correspondence, 1987, 14th CGD, AtoN.

44. Interview with Machinery Technician Aaron Landrum, U.S. Coast Guard, July 18, 1988, at Diamond Head Light Station.

45. Interviews with ANT team at ANT Headquarters, Sand Island, August 26, 1988.

46. Department of Transportation, *Light List,* 1989, p. 278; interviews with ANT team and examination of Diamond Head Light Station, July 18, 1988.

Chapter 4. Makapuʻu Point

1. USDCL, "Description of Makapuu Light Station," September 14, 1910, p. 4.

2. Makapuu Light Station, "Historical Description," 14th CGD, AtoN.

3. *Hawaiian Annual 1889,* p. 84.

4. Petition to Lorrin A. Thurston, minister of Interior, Honolulu, October 9, 1888, Int. Misc. Documents, AH.

5. Min. Int. Reports, 1890, p. 273, AH.

6. Chance Brothers and Company, Smethwick, England, letter to W. E. Rowell, superintendent of Public Works, Honolulu, October 17, 1890, Public Works, Jumbo File 1, AH.

7. Report on Makapuu Light House, (no day), 1901, Public Works, Lighthouses, AH.

8. USDCL, *Annual Reports,* 1904, pp. 285, 288; 1905, p. 255.

9. U.S. House of Representatives, Fifty-ninth Congress, first session, Report no. 159, p. 1.

10. *Paradise of the Pacific,* September 1906, pp. 23–24; letter written by W. M. Gifford, president, Honolulu Chamber of Commerce, August 21, 1906, Historical Society of Hawaii, Makapuu; *Hawaiian Annual 1907,* pp. 113–114.

11. *The Friend,* September 1906, p. 3.

12. *Manchuria,* brief for claimant (Pacific Mail Steamship Company) in the District Court, pp. 3, 7, 25, Ships and Shipping, AH; *Hawaiian Annual 1907,* p. 114.

13. *Manchuria,* Pacific Mail Steamship Company, claimant, pp. 26, 132, Ships and Shipping, AH.

14. W. M. Gifford, president, Honolulu Chamber of Commerce, to Governor George R. Carter, Honolulu, August 21, 1906, Historical Society of Hawaii, Makapuu; *Paradise of the Pacific,* September 1906, p. 24.

15. George R. Carter, cablegrams, January 11, 14, 1907, AH.

16. USDCL, "Description of Makapuu Point Light Station," September 14, 1910, pp. 3, 16–17.

17. Kay Grant, *Robert Stevenson* (New York: Meredith Press, 1969), pp. 169–170.

18. Ibid., p. 170; USDCL and USDC, *Annual Reports,* 1904 through 1939.

19. USDCL, "Description of Makapuu Point Light Station," September 14, 1910, p. 13; *Pacific Commercial Advertiser,* October 18, 1908.

20. USDCL, "Description of Makapuu Point Light Station," September 14, 1910, pp. 4–5; idem, *Annual Reports,* 1909, p. 635.

21. *Pacific Commercial Advertiser,* October 18, 1908.

22. Theodore Kelsey, diary, July 3, 1909, Private Collection, AH.

23. Nathaniel Bright Emerson, *The Taste of Life and Death: Episodes from Pele and Hiiaka, a Hawaiian Mythological Romance* (Honolulu: Curriculum Research and Development Group, University of Hawaii, 1969), pp. 87–88; Abraham Fornander, *Hawaiian Antiquities and Folk-Lore,* Bernice P. Bishop Museum Memoirs (Honolulu: Bishop Museum, 1916–1920), no. 4, p. 114.

24. USDCL, *Annual Reports,* 1910, p. 508; Makapuu Light Station, Report, March 22, 1939, p. 3, 14th CGD, AtoN.

25. USDCL, *Annual Reports,* 1909, p. 635.

26. USDC, *Annual Reports,* 1939, p. 116.

27. *Pacific Commercial Advertiser,* October 2, 1909.

28. USDCL, "Description of Makapuu Point Light Station," September 14, 1910, pp. 7–10.

29. USDCL, *Annual Reports,* 1912, p. 604; USDC, "Description of Makapuu Point Light Station," February 18, 1916, pp. 2, 10; idem, *Annual Reports,* 1916, p. 744.

30. Rick Carroll, "Makapuu Lighthouse Flashback—Glowing Joy and Fade—out," *Honolulu Advertiser,* August 10, 1985.

31. *Honolulu Advertiser,* April 12, 1925; Carroll, "Makapuu Lighthouse."

32. USDC, *Lighthouse Service Bulletin,* May 1925.

33. Carroll, "Makapuu Lighthouse."

34. USDC, *Annual Reports,* 1925, p. 184.

35. Truman R. Strobridge, *Chronology of Aids to Navigation and the Old Lighthouse Service, 1716–1939* (Washington, D.C.: Public Affairs Division, U.S. Coast Guard, 1974), p. 31.

36. Doris Jividen, *Sammy Amalu: Prince, Pauper, or Phony?* (Honolulu: Erin Enterprizes, 1972), pp. 141–142.

37. Hans Christian Adamson, *Keepers of the Lights* (New York: Greenberg Press, 1955), p. 130; USDC, *Annual Reports,* 1921, p. 108; 1939, p. 117.

38. USDC, "Description of Makapuu Point Light Station," September 20, 1927, pp. 7–8, 8a–8c; "Light-oh! . . . Where Away?," *The Sales Builder,* vol. 12 (March 1939), pp. 6–7.

39. USDC, "Description of Makapuu Point Light Station," September 20, 1927, p. 5.

40. USDC, *Annual Reports,* 1927, pp. 203, 205.

41. USDC, "Description of Makapuu Point Light Station," September 20, 1927, p. 9.

42. Ibid., 1934, p. 10.

43. Makapuu Light Station, Report, March 22, 1939, p. 3, 14th CGD, AtoN.

44. Harry Albright, "Sentinels of the Sea Lanes," *Honolulu Advertiser,* August 14, 1938.

45. USDC, *Light List,* 1936, pp. 310–311.

46. Robert C. Schmitt, "Some Transportation and Communication Firsts in Hawaii," *Hawaiian Journal of History,* 1979, p. 106; Lieutenant Commander A. P. Scontras, "On a Wing and a Prayer," *Historic Hawai'i,* vol. 14, no. 7 (July 1988), p. 8; USDC, *Annual Reports,* 1928, p. 223.

47. USDC, *Annual Reports,* 1931, p. 212; idem, *Light List,* 1933, pp. 257, 261, 314, 320.

48. *Honolulu Star-Bulletin,* December 15, 1934.

49. Ibid., December 2 through 7, and December 26, 1934.

50. Ibid., December 15, 1934.

51. Makapuu Light Station, "Local Notice Makapuu/Kilauea Radio Beacon Discontinuance Reaction," 14th CGD, AtoN.

52. *Honolulu Star-Bulletin,* July 20, 1962.

53. Ibid., February 23, 1957.

54. Ibid., July 20, 1962.

55. Dick Paulicka, "Makapuu Light to End its Long Service," *Honolulu Advertiser,* October 21, 1972.

56. Bob Krauss, "The Last Keeper on Oahu," *Honolulu Advertiser,* January 4, 1974.

57. Makapuu Light Station, Monitoring Notice, Light officially automated February 15, 1974, 14th CGD, AtoN.

58. James Dooley, "A Weird Case of Security at Lighthouse," *Honolulu Star-Bulletin and Advertiser,* November 5, 1978.

59. U.S. Department of Transportation, *Light List,* 1989, p. 277.

60. Hawaii Maritime Center, Kalākaua Boat House, Honolulu. The *Hōkūle'a* is named for a navigational star used by Hawaiians, probably Arcturus, a zenith star above Hawai'i.

61. Makapuu Light Station, correspondence between U.S. Coast Guard and Tommy Holmes, a cofounder of the Hawaii Maritime Center, Honolulu, 14th CGD, AtoN; interviews with Tommy Holmes.

Chapter 5. Ka'ena Point and Other Lights along O'ahu's Shores

1. Governor J. O. Dominis, memo to minister of Interior, Honolulu, Int. Misc., Lighthouses, AH.

2. C. Bolte, agent for the Steamer *Waimanalo,* letter to L. Aholo, minister of Interior, Honolulu, May 18, 1887, Int. Misc., Lighthouses, AH.

3. Public Works, *Annual Reports,* 1902, pp. 42–43, 89, 202, AH; U.S. Treasury Department, *Post Office Sites in Honolulu and Hilo, Hawaii* (Washington, D.C.: Government Printing Office, 1903), p. 9.

4. USDC, *Annual Reports,* 1920, pp. 686, 750.

5. Correspondence with Carol Edgecomb Brown, May 8, 1988.

6. Mary Kawena Pukui, Samuel H. Elbert, and Esther T. Mookini, *Place Names of Hawaii* (Honolulu: University of Hawaii Press, 1986), p. 61.

7. Kaena Light Station: "National Register of Historic Places Registration Form," April 1988, 14th CGD, AtoN.

8. Ibid.

9. Abraham Fornander, *Hawaiian Antiquities and Folk-Lore,* Bernice P. Bishop Museum Memoirs (Honolulu: Bishop Museum, 1916–1920), no. 5, part 2, p. 270.

10. Nathaniel Bright Emerson, *The Taste of Life and Death: Episodes from Pele and Hiiaka, a Hawaiian Mythological Romance* (Honolulu: Curriculum Research and Development Group, University of Hawaii, 1969), p. 104.

11. Kaena Light Station, D. J. Fontaine, environmental specialist, letter to District Planning Officer, February 12, 1980; Lt. C. J. Conklin, letter to Chief, Aids to Navigation Branch, July 25, 1984; Commander R. W. Brandes, letter to Officer in Charge, ANT, September 16, 1985, 14th CGD, AtoN.

12. U.S. Department of Transportation, *Light List,* 1989, p. 284.

13. Ralph S. Kuykendall and A. Grove Day, *Hawaii: A History, from Polynesian Kingdom to American State* (Englewood Cliffs, N.J.: Prentice-Hall, 1976), pp. 115–116, 160.

14. S. E. Bishop, "Pearl Harbor As a Factor under Present Conditions," in *Hawaiian Annual 1898,* p. 85.

15. U.S. Senate, *Hawaiian Investigation,* part 1, Fifty-sev-

enth Congress, first session, 1902, pp. 49–50; "Retrospect for 1903," in *Hawaiian Annual 1904*, pp. 201–202.

16. Erwin N. Thompson, *Pacific Ocean Engineers* (Honolulu: Department of the Army, Fort Shafter, 1985), p. 64.

17. USDC, *Annual Reports,* 1920, p. 710; idem, *Light List,* 1989, pp. 280–282.

18. Jean McKean Grace and Lois S. Nishimoto, *Marine Atlas of Hawaii: Bays and Harbors* (Honolulu: Sea Grant College Program, University of Hawaii, 1974), p. 115.

19. Mary Kawena Pukui and Samuel H. Elbert, *Hawaiian Dictionary,* rev. ed. (Honolulu: University of Hawaii Press, 1986), p. 9. The land division usually extended from the uplands to the sea.

20. Pukui, Elbert, and Mookini, *Place Names of Hawaii,* pp. 119, 153, 154.

21. Dennis M. Devaney, *Kaneohe, A History of Change* (Honolulu: Bess Press, 1982), pp. 209–210, 221.

22. U.S. Department of Transportation, *Light List,* 1989, pp. ix, 276.

23. Interview with Petty Officer Ralph Craig, U.S. Coast Guard, ANT Headquarters, Sand Island, June 29, 1989.

Chapter 6. Maui

1. Mary Kawena Pukui, *The Echo of Our Song* (Honolulu: The University Press of Hawaii, 1973), pp. 104–105.

2. F. D. Bennett, *Narrative of a Whaling Voyage round the Globe from the Year 1833 to 1836* (London: R. Bentley, 1840), vol. 1, pp. 273–274.

3. J. C. Beaglehole, ed., *Journals of Captain James Cook on His Voyages of Discovery* (Cambridge: Published for the Hakluyt Society at the University Press, 1955), vol. 3, part 1, pp. 500–501.

4. Jean-Francois Galaup de La Pérouse, Louis Marie Antoina Destouff Milet de Mureau, *A Voyage Round the World Performed in the Years 1785, 1786, 1787, and 1788 by the Boussole and Astrolabe* (Amsterdam: N. Israel; New York: Da Capo Press, 1968), vol. 1, pp. 340–345.

5. George Vancouver, *A Voyage of Discovery to the North Pacific Ocean and Round the World* (London, 1801), vol. 3, pp. 292–294.

6. H. G. Purcell, "Hawaii and the Whaling Fleet," *Nautical Research Journal,* vol. 7, p. 3; Ralph S. Kuykendall, *The Hawaiian Kingdom,* vol. 1, *1778–1854, Foundation and Transformation* (Honolulu: University of Hawaii Press, 1968), p. 307.

7. Mary Kawena Pukui, Samuel H. Elbert, and Esther T. Mookini, *Place Names of Hawaii* (Honolulu: University of Hawaii Press, 1986), p. 104.

8. A Roving Printer, *Life and Adventure* (New York: Harper & Brothers, 1861), p. 321.

9. J. Kapena, Lahaina, to P. Kanoa, Honolulu, November 14, 1840, Int. Misc. Correspondence, AH. Kapena served in the House of Nobles 1845–1866. Kanoa became the governor of Kaua'i in 1847.

10. Kuykendall, *The Hawaiian Kingdom,* vol. 1, p. 307.

11. Lāhainā Restoration Foundation, *Story of Lahaina* (Lahaina: Lāhainā Restoration Foundation, 1974), p. 23.

12. Harriet Baldwin Damon, "A Sister's Tribute to Henry Perrine Baldwin," Windley Research Collection, Lāhainā Restoration Foundation. Drawn from original material held by the Hawaiian Mission Children's Society.

13. *The Friend,* June 1, 1844, p. 60; *Sandwich Island News,* vol. 1, no. 23 (February 3, 1847); H. I. W. F. Allen, Collector General, Honolulu, letter to F. W. Hutchison, minister of Interior, Honolulu, August 14, 1869, Int. Misc. Lighthouses, AH. In 1869, when the Honolulu Harbor Light was established, lighted aids were also established at Hilo and Kawaihae on the island of Hawai'i, and light dues were raised to three dollars.

14. Sereno Edwards Bishop Letters (1889–1908), September 19, 1906, Hawaiian Historical Society. "That light on Duvauchelle's shop was a beginning of lighthouse improvement. Of course it was fed with whale oil, as indeed were all the light-houses of that period. . . . I remember E. P. Bond bringing the first petroleum lamp to Honolulu in 1856. It was a dark, ill smelling oil. I bought our first kerosene lamp when in Hana in 1864."

15. *Pacific Commercial Advertiser,* December 25, 1856; February 26, 1857.

16. Receipts and Expenditures for the Island of Maui, July 29, 1846; March 31, 1850, Finance, AH. Finance Department records show an expenditure of $83.60 in 1846 for "Harbor lights," and $279.60 in 1849 for "new Lamp, oil wicking, and native attendance."

17. P. H. Treadway, Lahaina, letter to F. W. Hutchison, minister of Interior, Honolulu, June 10, 1865, Int. Misc., Lighthouses, AH.

18. Ibid., June 10, 1865; January 24, 1866; September 17, 1866.

19. P. H. Treadway, Lahaina, letters to H. A. Wiedemann, chief clerk, Department of Interior, Honolulu, October 20, 26, and 30, November 7 and 8, 1866, Int. Misc., Lighthouses, AH.

20. *Hawaiian Gazette,* November 17, 1866.

21. Account Sale by Auction of the Lease of the Store House under the Lahaina Lighthouse, November 21, 1866, Int. Misc., Lighthouses, AH.

22. *Pacific Commercial Advertiser,* March 26, 1864.

23. Minister of Finance Reports, April 18, 1868, AH.

24. P. H. Treadway, Lahaina, letters to chief clerk, Department of Interior, Honolulu, February 14, 19, and 23, and March 29, 1870, Int. Misc., Lighthouses, AH.

25. Thomas C. Forsyth, Lahaina, letter to S. G. Wilder, minister of Interior, Honolulu, March 8, 1879, Int. Misc., Lighthouses, AH.

26. Abraham Fornander, acting governor of Maui, Lahaina, letter to Charles Gulick, minister of Interior, Honolulu, January 17, 1884, Int. Misc., Lighthouses, AH; Min. Int. Reports, 1886, p. 130; DAGS, Drawer 13(9): Lahaina Road, Island of Maui, 1841, corrected 1872, R. H. Wyman, Commander, U.S. Navy, Hydrographer to the Bureau of Navigation. Chart also shows government buildings and a small settlement north of Pu'unoa Point.

27. Captain David Taylor, Lahaina, letters to James A. King, minister of Interior, Honolulu, February 27 and March 8, 1893, Int. Misc., Lighthouses, AH.

28. Captain David Taylor, Lahaina, letter to James A. King, minister of Interior, Honolulu, December 28, 1893; George H. Dunne, Lahaina, to J. A. Hassinger, chief clerk, Department of Interior, Honolulu, February 21 and March 29, 1895, Int. Misc., Lighthouses, AH; U.S. House of Representatives, Fifty-ninth Congress, first session, Report 4671, p. 2. George H. Dunne's last name was also spelled "Dunn" in some of the Light House Board's reports.

29. George H. Dunn, notary public, Lahaina, letter to J. A. Hassinger, chief clerk, Department of Interior, Honolulu, April 25, 1900, Public Works, Lighthouses, AH.

30. USDCL, *Annual Reports,* 1904, p. 286.

31. *Hawaiian Gazette,* January 16, 1906.

32. USDCL, *Annual Reports,* 1906, p. 254.

33. USDC, *Light List,* 1917, pp. 54–55; idem, *Annual Reports,* 1917, p. 749.

34. *Maui News,* September 8, 1937.

35. "Light Houses, Hawaiian Islands," in *Hawaiian Annual 1890,* pp. 110–111.

36. J. Andersen, Makena, letter to James A. King, minister of Interior, Honolulu, February 5, 1896, Int. Misc., Lighthouses, AH. In reports and letters from the Department of Interior the keeper's name is sometimes spelled "Andersen" and sometimes "Anderson."

37. Minister of Interior to Wilder's Steamship Company, Honolulu, March 8, 1886, Int. Letter Book 27, p. 464, AH.

38. P. W. Simeona, Makena, letters to Department of Interior, March 24 and April 6, 1888, Int. Misc., Lighthouses, AH.

39. J. Andersen, Makena, letter to James A. King, minister of Interior, Honolulu, February 5, 1896, Int. Misc., Lighthouses, AH.

40. Hawaii Department of Public Works, *Report* (Honolulu: The Bulletin Publishing Company, 1901–1903), p. 90.

41. USDCL, *Annual Reports,* 1904, p. 286.

42. Ibid., 1905, p. 254.

43. Interview with Warrant Officer John Haley, 14th CGD, AtoN, January 25, 1990; USDC, *Annual Reports,* 1918, p. 590.

44. USDC, *Annual Reports,* 1918, p. 640; idem, *Light List,* 1923, p. 7.

45. McGregor Point Light Station, 14th CGD, AtoN, Survey Report; USDCL, *Light List,* 1906, pp. 58–59; 1908, pp. 70–71.

46. John R. K. Clark, *The Beaches of Maui County* (Honolulu: The University Press of Hawaii, 1980), pp. 51–52; USDCL, *Annual Reports,* 1906, pp. 222, 224.

47. USDCL, *Annual Reports,* 1906, p. 224; *Maui News,* April 14, 1906.

48. USDCL, *Light List,* 1908, pp. 70–71.

49. USDCL, *Annual Report,* 1915, p. 658.

50. USDCL, *Light List,* 1908, pp. 70–71; 1912, pp. 90–91; 1917, pp. 54–55.

51. Pukui, Elbert, and Mookini, *Place Names of Hawaii,* pp. 40, 92.

52. Thomas G. Thrum, "Maui's Heiaus and Heiau Sites Revised," in *Hawaiian Annual 1917,* pp. 52–53; Document Ceding Land, Island of Puuiki, signed by James W. Pratt, commissioner of Public Lands, T.H., and Marston Campbell, superintendent of Public Works, T.H., January 8, 1909, Walter Francis Frear, U.S. Departments, Lighthouse Establishment, 1907–1908, AH; USDCL, *Light List,* 1908, pp. 70–71; 1912, pp. 90–91.

53. Harold W. Kent, "The Story of Pharology," speech delivered to the Social Science Association, December 5, 1949, Kent Papers, Social Science Association Collection, AH. Hula translated by Carlton Keauʻi Reichel, Maui, November 1988.

54. Jan Jabulka, "Manuel Ferriera, Lighthouse Keeper," *Honolulu Star-Bulletin,* May 12, 1934.

55. USDC, *Light List,* 1923, p. 7.

56. Hawea Point Light Station, Survey Report, 14th CGD, AtoN; USDC, *Annual Reports,* 1917, pp. 54–55; USDCL, *Annual Reports,* 1912, p. 586. The Hāwea Point Light was one of four "acetylene lens lantern" lights established in the Hawaiian Islands in 1912. The others were Pauwalu Light, Maui; Hanapēpē Light, Kauaʻi; and Kukuihaele Light on the island of Hawaiʻi.

57. *Hawaiian Annual 1882,* p. 31; George E. Gresley Jackson, R. N., *Kahului Harbor, North Coast Of Maui, 1881,* Map File no. 190, AH.

58. L. A. Thurston, minister of Interior, Honolulu, to W. G. Irwin, W. G. Irwin and Company, Honolulu, April 19, 1889, Int. Letter Book 38, p. 381, AH; S. B. Rose, secretary, Wilder's Steamship Company, Honolulu, to Thurston, April 21, 1889, Int. Misc. Correspondence, AH.

59. Captain James A. King, Honolulu, to L. A. Thurston, minister of Interior, Honolulu, May 9, 1889, Int. Misc. Correspondence, AH.

60. W. E. Rowell, superintendent of Public Works, Honolulu, letter to L. A. Thurston, minister of Interior, Honolulu, April 5, 1889, Public Works, Lighthouses, AH.

61. Min. Int. Reports, 1890, p. 38, AH.

62. Chance Brothers and Company, Smethwick, England, letter to W. E. Rowell, superintendent of Public Works, Honolulu, October 17, 1890, Public Works, Jumbo File 1, AH.

63. U.S. Treasury Department, Office of the Light House Board, Washington, D.C., letter to W. E. Rowell, superintendent of Public Works, Honolulu, October 15, 1890, Public Works, Jumbo File 1, AH.

64. U.S. Senate, *Hawaiian Investigation,* part 2, Fifty-seventh Congress, first session, 1902, p. 49.

65. USDCL, *Annual Reports,* 1905, pp. 255–256.

66. Ibid., 1911, p. 569; idem, *Light List,* 1912, pp. 90–91.

67. Benjamin Franklin Rush, *History of the Construction and Development of Honolulu Harbor, Hilo Harbor, Kawaihae Harbor, Kahului Harbor, Kaunakakai Harbor, Nawiliwili Harbor, Port Allen Harbor* (Honolulu: Territorial Board of Harbor Commissioners, 1957), pp. 41–42; USDC, *Light List,* 1917, pp. 54–55.

68. U.S House of Representatives, "Kahului Harbor," Sixty-second Congress, third session, Document no. 1330, 1912, pp. 5–6.

69. Pauwela Light Station, Proceedings of a Board of Survey, June 16, 1972, p. 4, 14th CGD, AtoN; USDCL, *Annual Reports,* 1910, p. 519.

70. USDCL, "Description of Pauwela Point Light Station," December 10, 1914, pp. 1–12.

71. Ibid., May 10, 1912, p. 1.

72. Ibid., pp. 1–12; idem, *Light List,* 1919, p. 9.

73. USDC, *Light List,* 1936, pp. 306–309.

74. USDC, *Annual Reports,* 1937, p. 11; *Maui News,* June 19, 1937.

75. *Maui News,* June 18, 1945, p. 6.

76. Pauwela Light Station, Description, 1985, 14th CGD, AtoN; interviews with Ed Marques, Kīhei, Maui, November 12, 14, and 26, 1988.

77. Pauwela Light Station, Job Description, Keeper, 14th CGD, AtoN.

78. Interviews with Ed Marques, Kīhei, Maui, November 12, 14, and 26, 1988.

79. Pauwela Light Station, Commander, Fourteenth District, Honolulu, letter to Ed Marques, USCG Light

Station Pauwela Point, Maui, March 17, 1960; "Aids to Navigation Operation Request," Project Number 14-60-09, "Light Equipment: Single DCB-36 Airway Beacon rotating 2RPM with 120V., 1500W., C-13D fil., clear lamps," July 28, 1959, 14th CGD, AtoN.

80. Pauwela Light Station, Commanding Officer, CGC *Planetree,* Fleet Post Office San Francisco, letter to Commander, Fourteenth District, Honolulu, July 12, 1960, 14th CGD, AtoN; interviews with Ed Marques, Kīhei, Maui, November 12, 14, and 26, 1988.

81. Pauwela Light Station, Robert F. Hearn, EN2, letter to Commander, Fourteenth District, Honolulu, January 29, 1962; Commander, Fourteenth District, Honolulu, to Commandant, Fourteenth District, Honolulu, April 3, 1964, 14th CGD, AtoN.

82. Pauwela Light Station, Commander, Fourteenth District, Honolulu, letter to Commandant, Fourteenth District, Honolulu, April 3, 1964, 14th CGD, AtoN.

83. Pauwela Light Station, Commander, Fourteenth District, Honolulu, letter to Officer in Charge, Pauwela Point Light Station, Maui, August 14, 1964, 14th CGD, AtoN.

84. Pauwela Light Station, Operational Planning Proposal, Commander, Fourteenth District, Honolulu, to Commandant, Fourteenth District, Honolulu, July 19, 1965, 14th CGD, AtoN.

85. Pauwela Light Station, AtoN Inspection for Molokai and Maui, June 10–13, 1986, 14th CGD, AtoN.

Chapter 7. Molokini, Kahoʻolawe, and Lānaʻi

1. Interview with Petty Officer Kenneth Savi, U.S. Coast Guard, ANT Headquarters, Sand Island, August 30, 1988.

2. Ibid.

3. Interview with Petty Officers Kenneth Savi and Ralph Craig, U.S. Coast Guard, ANT Headquarters, Sand Island, August 30, 1988.

4. USDCL, *Annual Reports,* 1905, p. 255; Governor's Proclamation, September 13, 1910, Walter Francis Frear File, AH.

5. William Ellis, *A Journal of a Tour Around Hawaii, or Owhyhee* (London, 1827; Honolulu: Hawaiian Gazette Co., 1917), p. 6; Henry M. Whitney, *The Hawaiian Guide Book for Travelers; Containing a Brief Description of the Hawaiian Islands* (Honolulu: H. Whitney, 1875; Rutland, Vt., and Tokyo: Charles E. Tuttle, 1970), p. 53.

6. USDC, *Light List,* 1922, p. 7; Jim A. Gibbs, *Lighthouses of the Pacific* (West Chester, Penn.: Schiffer Publishing Co., 1986), p. 221; *Paradise of the Pacific,* vol. 38 (December 1925), pp. 73–74.

7. *Maui News,* November 7, 1925.

8. Interview with Petty Officer Ralph Craig, U.S. Coast Guard, ANT Headquarters, Sand Island, July 24, 1989.

9. Hawaii Legislature, Committee on Kahoʻolawe, *Kahoʻolawe: Aloha No: A Legislative Study of the Island of Kahoʻolawe* (Honolulu: n.p., 1978), p. 35.

10. Ibid., pp. 39, 55.

11. J. Gilbert McAllister, *Archaeology of Kahoolawe,* Bernice P. Bishop Museum Bulletin 115 (Honolulu: Bishop Museum, 1933; New York: Kraus Reprint Company, 1971), p. 6.

12. U.S. Department of the Navy, "Kahoolawe Cultural Study. Part I: Historical Documentation." Prepared by Environment Impact Study Corporation, April 1983, p. 135.

13. Mary Kawena Pukui, Samuel H. Elbert, and Esther T. Mookini, *Place Names of Hawaii* (Honolulu: University of Hawaii Press, 1986), pp. 101, 120, 127. The names Kuikui Cape, the most northerly point of Kahoʻolawe, and Laeokuikui on northeast Kahoʻolawe both suggest that these places were sites for ancient navigational fires. *Kuikui* is a variant of *kukui,* meaning candlenut, torch, or light; Hawaii Legislature, *Kahoʻolawe,* p. 55; McAllister, *Archaeology of Kahoolawe,* p. 7.

14. Governor's Executive Order No. 308, December 19, 1927, and Presidential Proclamation No. 1827, February 3, 1928, Survey Department, Maui County File, DAGS; Hawaii Legislature, *Kahoʻolawe,* p. 44.

15. Hawaii Legislature, *Kahoʻolawe,* p. 45; interview with Petty Officers Kenneth Savi and Ralph Craig, U.S. Coast Guard, ANT Headquarters, Sand Island, August 30, 1988.

16. Pukui, Elbert, and Mookini, *Place Names of Hawaii,* p. 61; Kenneth P. Emory, *The Island of Lanai,* Bernice P.

Bishop Museum Bulletin 12 (Honolulu: Bishop Museum, 1924), pp. 18–19.

17. *Hawaiian Annual 1882*, p. 31; Emory, *The Island of Lanai*, p. 8.

18. *Maui News*, November 7, 1925.

19. *Honolulu Star-Bulletin*, February 6, 1930.

20. *Hawaiian Annual 1924*, p. 62; USDC, *Light List*, 1926, p. 9.

21. Manele Bay Light Station, Aids to Navigation Service Report, November 1965, 14th CGD, ANT Headquarters, Sand Island.

22. Interview with Petty Officers Kenneth Savi and Ralph Craig, U.S. Coast Guard, ANT Headquarters, Sand Island, August 30, 1988; Pohakuloa Point Light Station, Light Inventory and Check List, 14th CGD, ANT Headquarters, Sand Island.

23. Interviews with Chief A. P. McAdams, U.S. Coast Guard, ANT Headquarters, Sand Island, February 6, 1989 and March 15, 1989.

24. Pohakuloa Point Light Station, Light Inventory and Check List, 14th CGD, ANT Headquarters, Sand Island; Pukui, Elbert, and Mookini, *Place Names of Hawaii*, p. 176. The word *palaoa* means whale.

25. Kaumalapau Light Station, Light Inventory and Check List, 14th CGD, ANT Headquarters, Sand Island; interview with Chief A. P. McAdams, U.S. Coast Guard, ANT Headquarters, Sand Island, March 15, 1989.

Chapter 8. Moloka'i

1. Jean McKean Grace and Lois S. Nishimoto, *Marine Atlas of Hawaii: Bays and Harbors* (Honolulu: Sea Grant College Program, University of Hawaii, 1974), p. 86. Moloka'i is about thirty-four miles long from east to west and seven miles from north to south. Of the eight major islands, it is the fifth largest in size, containing 261 square statute miles.

2. Robert J. Hommon, *Use and Control of Hawaiian Inter-Island Channels, Polynesian Hawaii, A.D. 1400–1794* (Honolulu: Office of the Governor, 1975), pp. 174, 233–234; Mary Kawena Pukui, Samuel H. Elbert, and Esther T. Mookini, *Place Names of Hawaii* (Honolulu: University of Hawaii Press, 1986), p. 95.

3. Grace and Nishimoto, *Marine Atlas of Hawaii*, pp. 86, 88–89.

4. R. W. Meyer, Molokai, letters to H. A. P. Carter, minister of Interior, Honolulu, October 21, 1880 and December 31, 1881, Int. Misc., Lighthouses, AH.

5. Meyer, letter to minister of Interior, May 24, 1889, Int. Misc., Lighthouses, AH; U.S. House of Representatives, Fifty-ninth Congress, first session, Report 4671, p. 2.

6. U.S. Treasury Department, *Post Office Sites in Honolulu and Hilo, Hawaii* (Washington, D.C.: Government Printing Office, 1903), p. 9.

7. USDCL, *Annual Report*, 1904, p. 286; idem, *Light List*, 1906, pp. 58–59.

8. USDCL, *Light List*, 1912, pp. 90–91.

9. Ibid., 1917, pp. 54–55.

10. *Maui News*, December 25, 1937.

11. USDC, *Light List*, 1917, pp. 154–155; 1923, p. 8; 1926, p. 9; 1970, p. 268; 1988, pp. xx, 274.

12. Molokai Light Station, AtoN Report made by Lieutenant D. T. Noviello, June 24, 1986, p. 2, 14th CGD, AtoN.

13. U.S. Department of Transportation, *Light List*, 1989, pp. xx, 274.

14. G. Peabody, "Development of Kaunakakai Beach and Lighthouse Park Proposed by County," *Molokai News*, October 1, 1988.

15. Eileen Tamura, Cornelia Anguay, and James Shon, *The Shaping of Modern Hawaiian History: Databook and Atlas* (Honolulu: Curriculum Research and Development Group, University of Hawaii, 1983), p. 185.

16. *Hawaiian Annual 1879*, pp. 68–69.

17. U.S. Senate, *Hawaiian Investigation*, part 2, Fifty-seventh Congress, first session, 1902, p. 49.

18. *Hawaiian Annual 1881*, p. 52; R. W. Meyer, Molokai, letter to H. A. P. Carter, minister of Interior, Honolulu, November 20, 1880, Int. Misc., Lighthouses, AH.

19. Pukui, Elbert, and Mookini, *Place Names of Hawaii*, p. 72.

20. Philip Spalding III, *Moloka'i* (Honolulu: Westwind Press, 1984), p. 12.

21. Meyer, letter to Carter, February 22, 1881, Int. Misc., Lighthouses, AH.

22. Ibid.

23. Carter to Meyer, March 8, 1881, Int. Letter Book 19, p. 187, AH.

24. Carter to Louis Richard, Honolulu, November 4, 1880, Int. Letter Book 18, p. 336; Carter to Joseph Bishaw, Honolulu, November 4, 1880, Int. Letter Book 18, p. 336½; Carter to Benjamin Macy, Honolulu, February 21, 1881, Int. Letter Book 19, p. 187; Meyer, letters to Carter, February 22, 1881 and December 31, 1881, Int. Misc., Lighthouses, AH.

25. Meyer, letter to Carter, March 14, 1881, Int. Misc., Lighthouses, AH.

26. Carter to Meyer, April 18, 1881, Int. Letter Book 19, p. 282; W. N. Armstrong, minister of Interior, Honolulu, to minister of Foreign Affairs, Honolulu, December 8, 1881, Int. Letter Book 20, p. 215, AH.

27. Molokai: Notice, December 1881, Int. Misc., Lighthouses, AH.

28. George Paul Cooke, *Moolelo o Molokai* (Honolulu: Honolulu Star-Bulletin, 1949), p. 132.

29. J. A. Hassinger, chief clerk for minister of Interior, Honolulu, to Meyer, November 21, 1881, Int. Letter Book 20, p. 192, AH.

30. Meyer, letter to Hassinger, December 8, 1881, Int. Misc., Lighthouses, AH.

31. Meyer, letters to minister of Interior, Honolulu, March 2, May 6, and June 15, 1884, August 10 and December 18, 1885, Int. Misc., Lighthouses, AH.

32. Meyer, letter to W. M. Gibson, minister of Interior, Honolulu, May 15, 1886, Int. Misc., Lighthouses, AH.

33. Cooke, *Moolelo o Molokai,* p. 132.

34. Meyer, letters to minister of Interior, Honolulu, May 24, 1889 and June 23, 1890, Int. Misc., Lighthouses, AH.

35. Meyer to minister of Interior, June 8, 1891.

36. J. W. Burrows, Lae o ka Laau, letter to C. N. Spencer, minister of Interior, Honolulu, July (no day), 1891, Int. Misc., Lighthouses, AH.

37. Meyer, letter to minister of Interior, Honolulu, July 15, 1891, Int. Misc., Lighthouses, AH.

38. Hassinger to Meyer, May 27, 1893, Int. Letter Book 61, p. 181, AH.

39. Cooke, *Moolelo o Molokai,* p. 132.

40. Burrows, letter to minister of Interior, Honolulu, December 30, 1895, Int. Misc., Lighthouses, AH.

41. Ibid., March 8, 1897.

42. Henry Holmes, Bishop Estate, letter to minister of Interior, Honolulu, April 1, 1897, Int. Misc., Lighthouses, AH.

43. Burrows, letter to James A. King, minister of Interior, Honolulu, March 4, 1898, Int. Misc., Lighthouses, AH.

44. James H. Boyd, first assistant clerk to minister of Interior, Honolulu, to Burrows, March 7, 1898, Int. Letter Book 97, p. 75, AH.

45. Burrows, letter to James A. King, April 1, 1898, Int. Misc., Lighthouses, AH.

46. Ibid., August 26, 1898.

47. John A. McCandless, *Second Annual Report of the Superintendent of Public Works, Year Ending June 30, 1902* (Honolulu: The Bulletin Publishing Company, 1902), p. 91; G. C. Munro, manager of Molokai Ranch, Molokai, letter to Alfred Carter, minister of Interior, Honolulu, December 9, 1902, Int. Misc., Lighthouses, AH.

48. USDCL, *Light List,* 1906, pp. 58–59; 1923, p. 8. Group Flashing White, ten seconds: the first flash was one second, the eclipse lasted two seconds; the second flash was one second, and then there was an eclipse of six seconds.

49. U.S. Department of Transportation, *Light List,* 1989, pp. xx, 274.

50. Molokai Light Station, AtoN Report made by Lieutenant D. T. Noviello, June 24, 1986, p. 2, 14th CGD, AtoN.

51. Interview with ANT team members, ANT Headquarters, Sand Island, June 26, 1989.

52. U.S. Senate, *Hawaiian Investigation,* part 2, Fifty-seventh Congress, first session, 1902, p. 49.

53. U.S. Treasury Department, *Post Office Sites,* pp. 8–9.

54. Hawaii Board of Health, *The Molokai Settlement* (Honolulu: Hawaiian Gazette Co., Ltd., 1907), p. 7. Hansen's Disease is the official term used in Hawai'i, but the term leprosy is universally used. The word leper is inappropriate and I use this term only when it is quoted.

55. USDCL, *Annual Reports,* 1903, p. 255; 1907, p. 609.

56. Molokai Light Station, "Historical and Current Descriptions," 14th CGD, AtoN; Hans Christian Adamson, *Keepers of the Lights* (New York: Greenberg Press, 1955), p. 285.

57. L. E. Pinkham, President, Board of Health, T.H., letter to J. R. Slattery, U.S. Army, Honolulu, January 22, 1906, Board of Health, U.S. Lighthouse Establishment, AH. Permits were issued to Frank Palmer, John F. Hunt, and Robert Gillespie.

58. Slattery, letter to Pinkham, January 22, 1906, Board of Health, U.S. Lighthouse Establishment, AH.

59. USDCL, *Annual Reports,* 1906, p. 224.

60. Lieutenant Commander A. P. Niblack, U.S. Navy, assistant to inspector of Twelfth Light House District, Honolulu, letter to Pinkham, March 3, 1906, Board of Health, U.S. Lighthouse Establishment, 1906–1913, AH.

61. USDCL, *Annual Reports,* 1907, p. 608; Theodore Roosevelt, Executive Order 962, October 27, 1908, Survey Department, Honolulu, Lighthouses, Molokai, DAGS.

62. Captain C. W. Otwell, letters to Mark P. Robinson, president, Board of Health, Honolulu, July 6 and 15, 1908, Board of Health, U.S. Lighthouse Establishment, AH.

63. Otwell to Robinson, August 17, 1908 and December 28, 1908. Others receiving "regular permits" were David Alama, blacksmith and receiver of materials; Ah Lee and Wong Fat, cooks; Joe Sylva, teamster; John Perry, Antone Nunus [Nunes?], Joseph Gomez, Peter Johnson, Manuel Fernandez, Manuel Olivierra, Henry Wegesend, laborers; Manuel Dias, mason; Joe Rawlins, donkey man; and Dick Davenport, carpenter. Men who received permits but whose jobs were not identified were F. H. Kales, M. S. Dutra, H. H. Allen, A. M. Ormiston, Daniel Boone, Thomas Sorenson, Frank Schonenbert, Joe Lopis, and Kaluea Paulo.

64. Eugene Van Wagner, Kalaupapa, Molokai, letter to Darr Perry, Caro, Michigan, March 2, 1909, Private Collection, AH.

65. Captain C. W. Otwell, Honolulu, letter to Dr. L. E. Cofer, Honolulu, April 28, 1908; Cofer to Otwell,

June 9, 1908, Board of Health, U.S. Lighthouse Establishment, AH.

66. Otwell, letter to Mark P. Robinson, Honolulu, July 6, 1908, Board of Health, U.S. Lighthouse Establishment, AH.

67. Robinson, letter to Otwell, July 6, 1908, Board of Health, U.S. Lighthouse Establishment, AH.

68. USDCL, *Annual Reports,* 1909, p. 636; 1910, p. 508.

69. Ibid., 1909, p. 636.

70. Eugene Van Wagner made a note regarding the accident on one of the photographs sent with a letter he wrote from Kalaupapa, Molokai, to Darr Perry, Caro, Michigan, March 2, 1909, Photographic Collection, Molokai, AH.

71. USDCL, *Annual Reports,* 1909, p. 636.

72. USDC, "Description of Molokai Light Station," November 9, 1927, p. 5; USDCL, *Annual Reports,* 1909, p. 636; interviews with Paul Morioka, maintenance mechanic foreman, 14th CGD, Sand Island, Honolulu, August 30, 1988 and September 1, 1988.

73. USDCL, *Annual Reports,* 1910, p. 508.

74. Ibid., 1910, p. 517.

75. USDCL, *Annual Reports,* 1909, p. 636.

76. *Polk-Husted Directory* (Honolulu: Polk-Husted Directory Company, 1924).

77. Letters, December 30, 1910, January 5, and April 28, 1911, Board of Health, U.S. Lighthouse Establishment, AH. Permit requests were made for the following members of the *Kukui's* crew: second officer Aubrey D. Shaw; machinists Charles Kort and Walter Jarret; seamen Robert Makaema, William Needham, Henry Au, David Kupukaa, and Joseph Kaimana.

78. USDCL, *Annual Reports,* 1910, pp. 508, 520; 1907, p. 611.

79. Captain C. W. Otwell, Honolulu, letters to Mark P. Robinson, Honolulu, April 28, 1911, May 12, May 20, June 16, and June 23, 1913, Board of Health, U.S. Lighthouse Establishment, AH. Letters list the following men who were transported by the *Kukui:* foreman Leslie E. Bailey; painters Thomas Kalawai, David Henry, William Kau, and William Haleole; carpenters A. F. Cook and Gene Gomard; pipefitters Robert Weber and Charles

Marse; mason J. C. Picanco; plumber's helpers K. Iwa-naza; tinsmith T. Omori; laborers George Kahapula and Joe Morse.

80. USDCL, *Light List,* 1912, pp. 90–91; 1926, p. 10.

81. USDC, "Description of Molokai Light Station," November 9, 1927, pp. 7, 12.

82. Ted Randolph, "36 Years of Memories," *New Pacific Magazine,* vol. 2 (May 1944), p. 8.

83. Ibid.

84. *Hawaiian Annual 1893,* p. 40; Catherine C. Summers, *Molokai: A Site Survey* (Department of Anthropology, Bernice P. Bishop Museum, 1971), p. 194.

85. U.S. House of Representatives, Ninety-fourth Congress, prepared statement of Lynette Roy Akana, researcher, "Oral Tradition," H.R. 11180, April 26, 1976, pp. 15–16; John Wesley Coulter, *Population and Utilization of Land and Sea in Hawaii, 1853,* Bernice P. Bishop Museum Bulletin 88 (Honolulu: Bishop Museum, 1931), p. 20; E. S. C. Handy and E. G. Handy, *Native Planters in Old Hawaii: Their Life, Lore, and Environment,* Bernice P. Bishop Museum Bulletin 233 (Honolulu: Bishop Museum, 1972), p. 518.

86. Harry Franck, *Roaming in Hawaii* (New York: Frederick A. Stokes Company, 1937), pp. 189–191.

87. USDC, *Annual Reports,* 1934, p. 117; 1935, p. 127.

88. Interview with Ed Marques at Kīhei, Maui, November 12, 1988.

89. Ibid.

90. Interviews with Ranger Neil Borgmeyer, National Park Service, and Henry Nalaielua, resident, Kalaupapa, November 17, 1988.

91. Interviews with Anna Mae Ka'anele, Honolulu, August 16 and 23, 1988; interview with Ed Marques at Kīhei, Maui, November 12, 1988.

92. Henry Nalaielua, "Tidal Wave," *Kalaupapa Historical Collection Project & Newsletter* (Kalaupapa, Hawaii: Kalaupapa Historical Collection Project, May 1985), vol. 4, no. 3, p. 2; Elaine Fogg, "Molokai Lighthouse," *Honolulu Advertiser,* August 2, 1948.

93. Interview with Dr. Alfred Morris regarding John Cambra, Honolulu, October 1988. Cambra has been a resident of Kalaupapa Settlement since the 1930s.

94. Interviews with Anna Mae Ka'anele, Honolulu, August 16 and 23, 1988.

95. Molokai Light Station, Rear Admiral S. H. Evans, commander of Fourteenth Coast Guard District, letter to Ira D. Hirschy, M.D., director, Division of Hansen's Disease, Honolulu, January 20, 1959, 14th CGD, AtoN.

96. Ibid.; Molokai Light Station, Clarence B. Mayes, medical director, U.S. Department of Health, Education, and Welfare, Public Health Service, letter to Captain A. C. Unger, Fourteenth Coast Guard District, Honolulu, April 15, 1959, 14th CGD, AtoN.

97. Molokai Light Station, Form CG-3213, DP 14-59-12, March 3, 1959, 14th CGD, AtoN.

98. Molokai Light Station, Captain C. N. Daniel, office memorandum to chief of staff, August 12, 1960, 14th CGD, AtoN.

99. Interview with Rose Lelepali, Kalaupapa, Moloka'i, November 17, 1988.

100. Molokai Light Station, Captain C. N. Daniel, report to chief of staff, January 18, 1960; ibid., office memorandum, August 12, 1960, 14th CGD, AtoN.

101. Molokai Light Station, Daniel, office memorandum to chief of staff, August 12, 1960; "Aids to Navigation Operation Request," Project Number 14-65-17, March 1965, 14th CGD, AtoN.

102. Molokai Light Station, "Notice to Mariners," August 1, 1966, 14th CGD, AtoN.

103. Molokai Light Station, Form CG-3213, DP 14-65-17, August 1965, 14th CGD, AtoN.

104. Molokai Light Station, Proceedings of a Board of Survey, May 17, 1971, 14th CGD, AtoN.

105. Molokai Light Station, U.S. Coast Guard Logistics and Property Division, letter to G. Bryam Harry, director, Pacific Area, National Park Service, Department of Interior, Honolulu, March 13, 1981; notification from Aids to Navigation to Commander L. Graham, controller, Fourteenth District, May 6, 1976, 14th CGD, AtoN; National Park Service, *Kalaupapa National Historic Park: Land Protection Plan* (Washington, D.C.: U.S. Department of Interior, National Park Service, 1986), p. 22.

106. Molokai Light Station, Captain B. D. Lovern,

chief, 14th CGD, AtoN, letter to Louis Wall, Western Division of Project Review, Advisory Council on Historic Preservation, Honolulu, January 11, 1983, 14th CGD, AtoN.

107. USDC, *Lighthouse Service Bulletin,* No. 3, March 1, 1924; Linda Greene, *Exile in Paradise* (Washington, D.C.: U.S. Department of Interior, National Park Service, 1985), p. 379.

108. Interview with Ed Marques at Kīhei, Maui, November 12, 1988.

109. USDC, *Lighthouse Service Bulletin,* No. 27, March 1938.

110. Molokai Light Station, officer in charge, Navy Environmental and Preventive Medicine Unit No. 6, letter to commander, Fourteenth District, March 7, 1985, 14th CGD, AtoN.

111. Molokai Light Station, Data Sheet 6-D(15), 14th CGD, ANT Headquarters, Sand Island; Molokai Light Station, Work Order Number 9105-86, March 27, 1986, 14th CGD, AtoN. Cost to replace classical lens with DCB-224 beacon: labor and overhead, $11,400; materials, $1,300; travel/per diem, $5,200.

112. Interview with Petty Officer Aaron J. Landrum, U.S. Coast Guard, ANT Headquarters, Sand Island, August 30, 1988.

113. Interview with Petty Officer Ralph Craig, U.S. Coast Guard, ANT Headquarters, Sand Island, August 30, 1988.

114. Molokai Light Station, Jim Luckey, Lahaina, Maui, letter to E. Neil Erickson, chief, Logistics and Properties, Fourteenth District, Honolulu, March 24, 1987, 14th CGD, AtoN.

115. Interview with Petty Officer Ralph Craig, U.S. Coast Guard, ANT Headquarters, Sand Island, August 30, 1988.

116. *Maui News,* July 17, 1986.

Chapter 9. The Island of Hawai‘i

1. Mary Kawena Pukui and Samuel H. Elbert, *Hawaiian Dictionary,* rev. ed. (Honolulu: University of Hawaii Press, 1986), pp. 370, 560.

2. *Hawaiian Annual 1891,* p. 104.

3. George Vancouver and John Vancouver, *A Voyage of Discovery to the North Pacific Ocean and Round the World* (Amsterdam: N. Israel; New York: Da Capo Press, 1967), vol. 2, p. 53; Richard Jeffry Cleveland and Horace William Shaler Cleveland, *Voyages of a Merchant Navigator of the Days That Are Past, Compiled from the Journals and Letters of the late Richard Jeffry Cleveland* (New York: Harper and Brothers, 1886), pp. 96–97; John Wesley Coulter, *Population and Utilization of Land and Sea in Hawaii, 1853,* Bernice P. Bishop Museum Bulletin 88 (Honolulu: Bishop Museum, 1931), p. 30; Eileen Tamura, Cornelia Anguay, and James Shon, *The Shaping of Modern Hawaiian History: Datebook and Atlas* (Honolulu: Curriculum Research and Development Group, University of Hawaii, 1983), pp. 180–181, 184.

4. Robert J. Hommon, *Use and Control of Hawaiian Inter-Island Channels, Polynesian Hawaii, A.D. 1400–1794* (Honolulu: Office of the Governor, 1975), pp. 174, 232–233; James Atwood Gibbs, *Shipwrecks in Paradise* (Seattle: Superior Publishing Company, 1977), p. 131.

5. Sam Chillingworth, Kawaihae, letter to Fredrick W. Hutchinson, minister of Interior, Honolulu, June 23, 1869, Int. Misc., Lighthouses, AH.

6. *Hawaiian Tariff and Digest of the Laws and Regulations of the Customs; Pilot and Harbor Regulations* (Honolulu: Printed at the Gazette Office, 1871), p. 27, Hawaiian Mission Children's Society Library. The other ports of entry were Kealakekua and Hilo, Hawai‘i; Honolulu Harbor, O‘ahu; Lahaina, Maui; and Kōloa, Kaua‘i.

7. Chillingworth, letter to Hutchinson, December 4, 1874, Int. Misc., Lighthouses, AH.

8. Chillingworth, letter to J. Watt Smith, minister of Interior, Honolulu, July 5, 1877, Int. Misc., Lighthouses, AH.

9. *Hawaiian Annual 1880,* p. 58.

10. H. Hackfeld and Company, agents for the underwriters of SS *Kinau,* Honolulu, letter to James A. King, minister of Interior, Honolulu, October 5, 1896; T. K. Clarke, Master, SS *Kinau,* Honolulu, letter to C. L. Wight, president, Wilder's Steamship Company, Honolulu, October 7, 1896, Int. Misc., Lighthouses, AH.

11. John A. McCandless, *Second Annual Report of the Superintendent of Public Works, Year Ending June 30, 1902* (Honolulu: The Bulletin Publishing Company, 1902), p. 90.

12. *Hawaiian Annual 1875,* p. 36; *Hawaiian Annual 1884,* pp. 38–39; *Hawaiian Annual 1887,* p. 73; C. L. Wight, Hilo, letter to L. A. Thurston, minister of Interior, Honolulu, March 19, 1889, Int. Misc., Lighthouses, AH.

13. Wight, letters to Thurston, April 15 and 25, 1889, Int. Misc., Lighthouses, AH.

14. Wight to Thurston, July 28, 1889.

15. W. D. Alexander, surveyor general, Honolulu, letter to Thurston, August 5, 1889, Int. Misc., Lighthouses, AH.

16. Wight, letter to C. M. Spencer, minister of Interior, Honolulu, January 16, 1891, Int. Misc., Lighthouses; J. A. Hassinger, chief clerk, Department of Interior, Honolulu, to W. B. Godfrey and William C. Wilder, Honolulu, January 27, 1891, Int. Letter Book 48, p. 165; Hassinger, letter to Wight, February 4, 1891, Int. Letter Book 48, p. 182; Wight to Hassinger, March 18, 1891, Int. Misc., Lighthouses; Hassinger to Wight, April 2, 1891, Int. Letter Book 49, p. 30, AH.

17. Min. Int. Reports, 1897, pp. 207–208, AH.

18. U.S. House of Representatives, Fifty-ninth Congress, first session, Report 4671, p. 2.

19. USDCL, *Annual Reports,* 1904, p. 287.

20. Ibid. The Kauhola Point Light was listed as the Kauhala Point Light until the spelling was corrected in the 1906 *Light List,* p. 56.

21. Mary Kawena Pukui, Samuel H. Elbert, and Esther T. Mookini, *Place Names of Hawaii* (Honolulu: University of Hawaii Press, 1986), p. 19; Charles Samuel Steward, *Journal of a Residence in the Sandwich Isles During the Years 1823, 1824, and 1825* (London: H. Fisher, Son, and Jackson, 1828), pp. 362–363.

22. Henry M. Whitney, *The Hawaiian Guide Book for Travelers; Containing a Brief Description of the Hawaiian Islands* (Honolulu: H. Whitney, 1875; Rutland, Vt., and Tokyo: Charles E. Tuttle, 1970), pp. 75–77; Ralph S. Kuykendall, *The Hawaiian Kingdom,* vol. 1, *1778–1854, Foundation and Transformation* (Honolulu: University of Hawaii Press, 1968) pp. 306–308. More than 120 vessels were reported arriving at Hilo in 1845; *Hawaiian Annual 1877,* p. 36.

23. J. H. Coney, Hilo, letters to Fredrick W. Hutchinson, minister of Interior, Honolulu, February 27 and July 12, 1869, Int. Misc., Lighthouses, AH.

24. Coney, letter to Hutchinson, August 30, 1869, Int. Misc., Lighthouses, AH.

25. *The Friend,* November 1, 1880, p. 85; *The Advertiser,* July 12, 1917; L. Severance, Hilo, letter to Hutchinson, January (no day), 1871, Int. Misc., Lighthouses, AH.

26. Severance, letters to Hutchinson, February 14, 26, and 27, March 15, 1871, and March 8, 1873, Int. Misc., Lighthouses, AH.

27. *Hawaiian Annual 1885,* p. 61. "There shall be levied upon all vessels arriving from abroad at any port of this Kingdom where a lighthouse may be established, the sum of three dollars, which shall be paid before departure to the Collector General of Customs."; Severance, letter to L. G. Wilder, chief clerk, Department of Interior, Honolulu, March 18, 1880, Int. Misc., Lighthouses, AH; Minister of Interior, Honolulu, to Severance, September 21, 1882, Int. Letter Book 21, p. 260, AH.

28. Joseph Nawahi, Hilo, letter to Joseph E. Bush, minister of Interior (letter in Hawaiian translated by E. H. Hart), Honolulu, September 21, 1882; Severance, letter to J. A. Hassinger, chief clerk, Department of Interior, Honolulu, October 11, 1882, Int. Misc., Lighthouses, AH; *Hawaiian Annual 1890,* p. 111.

29. USDCL, *Annual Reports,* 1904, p. 287; Assistant to Inspector of Twelfth Light House District, Honolulu, letter to A. L. C. Atkinson, acting governor of Hawaii, Honolulu, July 25, 1905; report by C. W. Otwell, U.S. Engineer, June 3, 1907, George Robert Carter, Misc., Lighthouses, AH.

30. USDCL, *Annual Reports,* 1904, p. 287; 1908, p. 620; USDC, *Annual Reports,* 1916, p. 744.

31. Richard Nelson, "Notes on Wire Landings Along the Hamakua Coast on the Island of Hawaii," *Hawaiian Journal of History,* vol. 8 (1974), pp. 138–142.

32. *Hawaiian Annual 1904,* p. 58; USDCL, *Light List,* 1906, pp. 56–57.

33. USDCL, *Annual Reports,* 1904, p. 287; idem, *Light List,* 1906, pp. 56–57.

34. USDCL, *Annual Reports,* 1904, p. 287; 1905, p. 255. The lights established by the Hawaiian government were Mahukona (northwest coast), Kawaihae (northwest coast), Waiakea (southeast Hilo Bay), Cocoanut Point (southwest Hilo Bay), Paukaa Point (north entrance to

Hilo Bay), Makahanaloa (east coast), Laupahoehoe (northeast coast), and Kohala (Kauhola, north coast). The private aids were Punaluʻu (south coast), Honuapo (south coast), Hoopuloa Landing (southwest coast), Hookena (southwest coast), Kealakekua Bay (west coast), and Kailua Bay (west coast).

35. USDCL, *Annual Reports,* 1906, p. 224. The Ka Lae Light was completed March 5, 1906.

36. Report by Captain C. W. Otwell, U.S. Engineer, June 3, 1907, George Robert Carter, Misc., Lighthouses, AH.

37. Ka Lae, Claim of Annie Moi Mukini to Samuel W. King, delegate to Congress, October 21, 1935, Survey Department, Honolulu, Lighthouse Sites, Folder 292, DAGS.

38. Pukui and Elbert, *Hawaiian Dictionary,* p. 472; Ka Lae, Claim of Annie Moi Mukini to Samuel W. King, delegate to Congress, October 21, 1935, Survey Department, Lighthouse Sites, Folder 292, DAGS.

39. Jean McKean Grace and Lois S. Nishimoto, *Marine Atlas of Hawaii: Bays and Harbors* (Honolulu: Sea Grant College Program, University of Hawaii, 1974), p. 7.

40. Governor Walter Francis Frear, Honolulu, letter to Captain C. W. Otwell, assistant engineer, Twelfth Light House District, Honolulu, April 18, 1908; Otwell, letter to Frear, April 30, 1908, Walter Francis Frear, U.S. Departments, Lighthouse Establishment, AH.

41. Ka Lae, Copy of Proclamation and survey map, Survey Department, Lighthouse Sites, Folder 292, DAGS; USDCL, *Annual Reports,* 1908, p. 624.

42. USDCL, *Light List,* 1906, pp. 56–57. *Light List* states "Keahole Point, To be established."

43. USDCL, *Light List,* 1908, pp. 70–71.

44. Captain C. W. Otwell, Honolulu, letter to Governor Walter Francis Frear, June 30, 1908, Walter Francis Frear, U.S. Departments, Lighthouse Establishment, AH; USDCL, *Annual Reports* 1909, p. 654.

45. Napoopoo, Copy of Governor's Proclamation and survey map, Survey Department, Honolulu, Lighthouse Sites, DAGS; USDCL, *Annual Reports,* 1908, p. 600.

46. USDC, *Light List,* 1917, pp. 150–153. Lights listed in 1917: Laupahoehoe Point, Alia Point (Pepeekeo), Paukaa, Coconut Point, Waiakea, front and rear range lights at Kuhio Bay, Ka Lae, Napoopoo, Kailua, Keahole Point, Kawaihae, Mahukona, Kauhola Point, and Kukuihaele.

47. USDCL, *Annual Reports,* 1908–1913; USDC, *Annual Reports,* 1914–1928.

48. USDC, *Annual Reports,* 1914, p. 567.

49. Ibid., p. 526.

50. USDC, *Annual Reports,* 1916, p. 733.

51. Ibid., 1918, p. 640; idem, *Light List,* 1926, p. 7; idem, *Annual Reports,* 1918–1931.

52. Kauhola Point Light Station, F. A. Edgecomb, superintendent of lighthouses, Honolulu, letter to Commissioner of Lighthouses, Washington, D.C., October 3, 1931; F. A. Edgecomb, office memo, "Kauhola Lantern and Lens Destroyed by Fire," January 21, 1937, 14th CGD, AtoN.

53. USDC, *Annual Reports,* 1930, p. 42; Kauhola Point Light Station, Edgecomb, to Commissioner of Lighthouses, October 30, 1931, 14th CGD, AtoN.

54. William Walker, "New Light for Kauhola," *Honolulu Star-Bulletin,* April 8, 1933; USDC, *Annual Reports,* 1932, p. 21; 1933, p. 106; Kauhola Point Light Station, J. M. Peoples, CBOSN, Inspectors Report, 1948, 14th CGD, AtoN.

55. Kauhola Point Light Station, Title "A" Property Record, prepared by Ludwig Wedemeyer, Commander, Group Hilo, February 11, 1954, 14th CGD, AtoN.

56. USDC, *Annual Reports,* 1933, p. 106; U.S. Bureau of Lighthouses, *Annual Report,* 1932, p. 21; Kauhola Point Light Station, Project Number 208, from C. N. Elliot, assistant superintendent, Honolulu, to Edgecomb, March 9, 1934, 14th CGD, AtoN.

57. USDCL, *Annual Reports,* 1908, p. 620.

58. V. S. K. Houston, delegate to Congress, Honolulu, letter to Milton W. Shreve, chairman, Sub-Committee on Appropriations, Department of Commerce, House of Representatives, Washington, D.C., December 10, 1927, Int. Misc., Lighthouses, AH.

59. Cape Kumukahi Light Station, Title "A" Property Record, Deed dated May 31, 1928; "Historic Cape Kumukahi Light Station," 1929, 14th CGD, AtoN.

60. USDC, *Annual Reports,* 1933, p. 106.

61. Ibid.; 1934, p. 117; *Honolulu Advertiser,* March 17, 1934.

62. Cape Kumukahi Light Station, Ludwig Wede-

meyer, commander of Group Hilo, letter to Commander, Fourteenth District, Honolulu, November 20, 1955, 14th CGD, AtoN.

63. "The Islands' Lights," *Sunset Magazine,* November 1958. Makapuu Light Station was also open the same hours; however, visitors were not allowed on the trail down the cliff or on the light tower. Barbers Point and Pauwela Point lighthouses could be visited by making arrangements with the Coast Guard in Honolulu. Tourists wishing to tour the Molokai Light and also visit Kalaupapa made arrangements with the airline, who secured permission from the Board of Health.

64. Pukui, Elbert, and Mookini, *Place Names of Hawaii,* p. 124.

65. Cape Kumukahi Light Station, D. B. MacDiarmid, chief, Personnel Division, report to chief of Operations Division, December 26, 1956, 14th CGD, AtoN.

66. Gordon A. Macdonald, Agatin T. Abbott, and Frank L. Peterson, *Volcanoes in the Sea: The Geology of Hawaii,* 2d ed. (Honolulu: University of Hawaii Press, 1983), pp. 97–99.

67. Cape Kumukahi Light Station, C. N. Daniel, AtoN, "Report of Volcano Near," to Chief of Staff, January 21, 1960, 14th CGD, AtoN.

68. Shurie Hirozawa, "Bulldozer Drivers Turn Lava Tide," *Honolulu Star-Bulletin,* January 25, 1960; Alton Slagle, "Lightkeeper at Kumukahi Not Yet Ready To Leave," *Honolulu Star-Bulletin,* January 25, 1960.

69. Cape Kumukahi Light Station, "Aids to Navigation Operation Request," "Convert Light to Automatic Unattended Operation," June 9, 1960, 14th CGD, AtoN.

70. Macdonald, Abbott, and Peterson, *Volcanoes in the Sea,* p. 103.

71. Cape Kumukahi Light Station, Captain R. D. Dean, chief, Engineering Division, letter to Hilo Electric Company, March 15, 1960, 14th CGD, AtoN; U.S. Treasury Department, U.S. Coast Guard, "Local Notice to Mariners," March 22, 1961.

72. I accompanied the ANT team on this inspection tour.

73. Henry Walsworth Kinney, *The Island of Hawaii* (Copyright Henry Walsworth Kinney 1913, authorized by Hilo Board of Trade, n.p.), p. 31.

74. Laupahoehoe Light Station, Aids to Navigation Service Report, 14th CGD, AtoN; interview with Petty Officer Rick McKersie, U.S. Coast Guard, December 19, 1989.

75. U.S. Department of Transportation, *Light List,* 1989, pp. xxiv, xxxi.

76. Keahole Point Light Station, John M. Peoples, officer in charge, Hilo, letter to Commander, Fourteenth District, Honolulu, July 22, 1948, 14th CGD, AtoN; 1949 Report, "This aid should, if at all possible, be at all times serviced from seaward."; 1953 Report, "Light can only be reached by water."; Barbara Hastings, "Keahole Point Aquaculture Projects Bloom," *Honolulu Star-Bulletin and Advertiser,* August 14, 1988.

77. Keauhou Bay Entrance Light, "General Description of the P.E.L. Sector Light," 14th CGD, ANT Headquarters, Sand Island.

78. Milolii Point Light Station, Aid Inspection, September 21, 1984; October 2, 1987, 14th CGD, ANT Headquarters, Sand Island.

79. USDC, *Annual Reports,* 1930, p. 233; idem, "Description of Ka Lae Light Station," January 3, 1933, pp. 1–2, 5, 9.

Chapter 10. Kaua'i

1. Interview with Petty Officer Kenneth Savi, U.S. Coast Guard, ANT team, Kaua'i, August 2, 1988.

2. Wendell Clark Bennet, *Archaeology of Kauai,* Bernice P. Bishop Museum Bulletin 80 (Honolulu: Bishop Museum, 1931), p. 9; Robert J. Hommon, *Use and Control of Hawaiian Inter-Island Channels, Polynesian Hawaii, A.D. 1400–1794* (Honolulu: Office of the Governor, 1975), pp. 174, 234; Mary Kawena Pukui, Samuel H. Elbert, and Esther T. Mookini, *Place Names of Hawaii* (Honolulu: University of Hawaii Press, 1986), p. 117.

3. *Hawaiian Annual 1907,* pp. 37, 41; Pukui, Elbert, and Mookini, *Place Names of Hawaii,* pp. 122, 123.

4. Eileen Tamura, Cornelia Anguay, and James Shon, *The Shaping of Modern Hawaiian History: Datebook and Atlas* (Honolulu: Curriculum Research and Development Group, University of Hawaii, 1983), p. 181; *Hawaiian Tariff and Digest of the Laws and Regulations of the Customs; Pilot and*

Harbor Regulations (Honolulu: Printed at the Gazette Office, 1871), p. 27, Hawaiian Mission Children's Society Library.

5. "Sugar Plantations and Mills," in *Hawaiian Annual 1884,* pp. 38–39; Public Works, Lighthouses, *List of Lights on Kauai,* AH; *Hawaiian Annual 1904,* p. 58; U.S. Department of Transportation, *Light List,* 1989, pp. 284–286.

6. Public Works, Lighthouses, 1900–1903, *List of Lights on Kauai,* AH.

7. Ibid.; Pukui, Elbert, and Mookini, *Place Names of Hawaii,* p. 27. ʻEleʻele Landing was renamed Port Allen in 1909 in honor of Honolulu merchant Samuel Cresson Allen.

8. Min. Int. Reports, 1893–1899, 1897, p. 206, AH.

9. Benjamin Franklin Rush, *History of the Construction and Development of Honolulu Harbor, Hilo Harbor, Kawaihae Harbor, Kahului Harbor, Kaunakakai Harbor, Nawiliwili Harbor, Port Allen Harbor* (Honolulu: Territorial Board of Harbor Commissioners, 1957), p. 52.

10. Ibid., pp. 66–67, 76.

11. George H. De La Vergne, *Hawaiian Sketches* (San Francisco, Calif., 1898), pp. 90, 104–105.

12. Ibid., pp. 90, 101.

13. M. Souza, Lihue, letters to superintendent of Public Works, Honolulu, December 13, 1900, September 14, 1901, and August 23, 1902; M. F. Prosser, Lihue, letter to superintendent of Public Works, Honolulu, September 18, 1902, Public Works, Lighthouses, AH.

14. Souza, letter to superintendent of Public Works, Honolulu, November 22, 1902, Public Works, Lighthouses, AH.

15. G. N. Wilcox, Lihue, letter to H. E. Cooper, superintendent of Public Works, Honolulu, June 10, 1903; Public Works, Lighthouses, AH; U.S. House of Representatives, Fifty-ninth Congress, first session, Report 4671, p. 21; letters from the sheriff's office, Lihue, to superintendent of Public Works, Honolulu, October 17, 1903 and December 11, 1903, Public Works Lighthouses, AH.

16. USDCL, *Annual Reports,* 1904, p. 285.

17. Ibid., pp. 287–288.

18. USDCL, *Annual Reports,* 1905, pp. 255–256.

19. Ibid., 1907, pp. 609–610.

20. Report filed June 3, 1907, Hawaiian Light House Establishment by C. W. Otwell, U.S. Engineer, Twelfth Light House Subdistrict, Int. Misc., Lighthouses, AH.

21. USDCL, *Annual Reports,* 1908, p. 654; 1910, p. 516.

22. Governor Walter Frear, letters to U.S. Department of Interior, Lighthouse Establishment, January 11 and 22, 1910, AH; Ross R. Aikin, *Kilauea Point Lighthouse* (Kilauea Point Natural History Association, 1988), p. 31.

23. "A Change for Kilauea," *Historic Hawaiʻi News,* July 1979, p. 4.

24. Hawaii Department of Land and Natural Resources, Royal Patent No. 2896, Survey Department, Lighthouses, DAGS; Mary Kawena Pukui and Samuel H. Elbert, *Hawaiian Dictionary,* rev. ed. (Honolulu: University of Hawaii Press, 1986), p. 9. *Ahupuaʻa* is a land division usually extending from the uplands to the sea; "A Change for Kilauea," *Historic Hawaiʻi News,* p. 4.

25. David Boynton, "Kilauea Point: A Wilderness Sanctuary," *Maui News,* January 10, 1988.

26. USDCL, "Description of Kilauea Point Light Station," June 28, 1913; Jan Tenbruggencate, "Lighthouse Begins Its Lonely Vigil," *Honolulu Advertiser,* December 20, 1974.

27. Correspondence with Carol Edgecomb Brown, "Kilauea Light, A Personal Perspective" (unpublished), March 1989.

28. USDCL, *Annual Reports,* 1913, p. 415.

29. Kilauea Point Light Station, Report, March 23, 1939, 14th CGD, AtoN.

30. USDCL, *Annual Reports,* 1913, p. 415.

31. USDCL, "Description of Kilauea Point Light Station," June 28, 1913, pp. 3, 5; idem, *Annual Reports,* 1914, p. 415.

32. Brown, "Kilauea Light, A Personal Perspective," p. 2.

33. USDCL, *Annual Reports,* 1913, p. 415; U.S. Department of Treasury, *Light List,* 1951, p. 403; 1960, p. 295; U.S. Department of Transportation, *Light List,* 1988, p. 284. The original characteristic of the group flashes was every ten seconds. The timing has changed several times over the years.

34. USDC, *Annual Reports,* 1915, p. 612; U.S. House of Representatives, Document 855, March 23, 1914, p. 2.

35. USDC, "Description of Kilauea Point Light Station," June 28, 1913, pp. 9–10, 12.

36. "Light-oh! . . . Where Away?" *The Sales Builder,* vol. 12 (March 1939), p. 17.

37. Kilauea Light Station (Historic): "Directions for the Handling and Care of Mercury and the Care, Cleaning and Filling of Mercury Float Vats at Lightstations With Mercury Float Apparatus," pp. 1–3, 14th CGD, AtoN.

38. Kilauea Light Station (Historic): "Instructions For The Operation of the Incandescent Oil Vapor Lamp," p. 1, 14th CGD, AtoN.

39. USDC, "Description of Kilauea Point Light Station," August 31, 1927, p. 12.

40. Lieutenant Commander A. P. Scontras, "On a Wing and a Prayer," *Historic Hawai'i,* vol. 14, no. 7 (July 1988), pp. 8–9.

41. *Honolulu Advertiser,* June 30, 1927.

42. Brown, "Kilauea Light, A Personal Perspective," p. 3.

43. USDC, *Annual Reports,* 1928, p. 223; 1930, p. 236.

44. Ibid., 1931, p. 206; idem, *Lighthouse Service Bulletin,* August 1930.

45. William Norwood, "Mechanical Devices Change the Lighthouse Keepers' World," *Honolulu Star-Bulletin,* February 15, 1936.

46. USDC, *Light List,* 1917, pp. 158–159; the original lantern for the Kūki'i Light was donated in 1966 by the U.S. Coast Guard to the Kaua'i Museum, Līhu'e.

47. USDC, "Description of Nawiliwili Light Station," August 30, 1927, pp. 2–10.

48. Nawiliwili Harbor Light Station, Proceedings of Board of Survey, May 25, 1978, pp. 1–2, 14th CGD, AtoN; *Honolulu Advertiser,* February 16, 1932.

49. Tim Klass, *World War II on Kauai* (Portland, Ore., n.p., 1970), p. 20.

50. Nawiliwili Harbor Light Station, Petty Officers G. F. Zych and J. L. Brantley, "Nawiliwili Light Attendant Station," (no date), 14th CGS, AtoN; *The Garden Island,* October 31, 1966.

51. Kauai Writers Group, *Hawaii's Garden Isle* (Lihue, Kauai, T.H.: The Garden Isle Publishing Company, 1951), p. 29.

52. Kilauea Point Light Station, National Park Service, Site Number 30-04-300, TMK 5-2-04:17, 14th CGD, AtoN.

53. Lois Taylor, "Kilauea Point," *Honolulu Star-Bulletin,* August 24, 1984.

54. Kilauea Point Light Station, Commander to Commandant (G-EOE), "Rotating Optics for 1984 Phase II LAMP Projects, 1983, 16510.2/AF/SF, Serial 32280, 14th CGD, AtoN.

55. Interviews with Charlie Tanimoto (author of *Return to Mahaulepu,* self-published, 1982) during 1988, Kailua, O'ahu; Makahuena Point, Survey Department, Honolulu, Lighthouses, DAGS.

56. Interview with Chief Charles Womack, U.S. Coast Guard, ANT Headquarters, Sand Island, February 1, 1990. The dayboards in Hawai'i are hand-papered with sheets of fluorescent film that reflects light. The colors of the "paper" used in Hawai'i are red, green, black, and white.

Chapter 11. Lehua and Ka'ula

1. Interview with Petty Officer Rick McKersie, 14th CGD, AtoN, February 5, 1990.

2. Mary Kawena Pukui, Samuel H. Elbert, and Esther T. Mookini, *Place Names of Hawaii* (Honolulu: University of Hawaii Press, 1986), pp. 93, 131. Lehua is part of Kaua'i County, but Ka'ula is part of the City and County of Honolulu.

3. Lehua Rock Light, Governor Wallace R. Farrington, Executive Order, August 10, 1928, Survey Department, Lighthouses, DAGS.

4. USDC, *Annual Reports,* 1931, p. 206.

5. Ibid.; U.S. Department of Transportation, *Light List,* 1989, p. 286.

6. Frederick A. Edgecomb, "Memorandum: Kaula Construction," August 17, 1932, p. 1, private collection, Carol Edgecomb Brown.

7. *Honolulu Advertiser,* February 10, 1925; July 14, 1925.

8. Frederick A. Edgecomb, "Kaula Island; Memo of Visit to Island," July 10–21, 1925, p. 2, private collection, Carol Edgecomb Brown.

9. Pukui, Elbert, and Mookini, *Place Names of Hawaii*, p. 93; Edgecomb, "Kaula Island," p. 3.

10. *Honolulu Advertiser*, May 22, 1925.

11. Edgecomb, "Kaula Island," pp. 3, 5.

12. Ibid., p. 8.

13. Ibid.; USDC, *Annual Reports*, 1925, p. 182.

14. Edgecomb, "Kaula Island," p. 5.

15. *Honolulu Star-Bulletin*, August 15, 1925.

16. *Honolulu Advertiser*, May 22, 1925.

17. Frederick A. Edgecomb, "Kaula Rock Light, New Secondary Light Station for the Hawaiian Islands," p. 1, private collection, Carol Edgecomb Brown.

18. Ibid., pp. 2–3.

19. Edgecomb, "Memorandum: Kaula Construction," pp. 1–2; idem, "Kaula Rock Light," p. 3.

20. Edgecomb, "Kaula Island," p. 7.

21. USDC, Bureau of Lighthouses, George R. Putnam, Washington, D.C., letter to F. A. Edgecomb, Honolulu, October 18, 1932, private collection, Carol Edgecomb Brown; Edgecomb, "Kaula Island," p. 9.

22. Edgecomb, "Kaula Rock Light," p. 1.

23. Ibid., p. 8.

24. USDC, *Light List*, 1949, p. 390.

Chapter 12. The *Kukui* and Other Lighthouse Tenders in Hawai'i

1. USDCL, *Annual Reports*, 1906, p. 212; *Old Honolulu; A Guide to Oahu's Historic Buildings* (Honolulu: Historic Buildings Task Force, 1969), p. 43. The Alexander Young Building, which extended between Bishop and Hotel Streets, was completed in 1903. Though primarily a hotel, it did have some stores and offices.

2. USDCL, *Annual Reports*, 1906, p. 212; 1905, pp. 256–257.

3. U.S. House of Representatives, Document 127 (53-3) 4830, 1905; USDCL, *Annual Reports*, 1906, p. 226; 1910, p. 530.

4. USDCL, *Annual Reports*, 1907, p. 611.

5. W. K. Basset, "Towers of Light," *Pacific Commercial Advertiser*, March 28, 1920; Mary Kawena Pukui and Samuel H. Elbert, *Hawaiian Dictionary*, rev. ed. (Honolulu: University of Hawaii Press, 1986), pp. 177–178, 474.

6. USDCL, *Annual Reports*, 1908, p. 631.

7. Ibid., 1910, p. 530.

8. *Pacific Commercial Advertiser*, March 1, 1911; Mifflin Thomas, *Schooner from Windward* (Honolulu: University of Hawaii Press, 1983), p. 117.

9. *Pacific Commercial Advertiser*, March 4 and 5, 1911.

10. Ibid., March 11, 1911.

11. Thomas, *Schooner from Windward*, p. 118; USDCL, *Annual Reports*, 1911, p. 596; *Pacific Commercial Advertiser*, September 21, 1911.

12. *Pacific Commercial Advertiser*, April 2, 1913; Thomas, *Schooner from Windward*, p. 120.

13. USDC, *Annual Reports*, 1919, p. 751.

14. *Honolulu Advertiser*, August 19, 1920; Hans Christian Adamson, *Keepers of the Lights* (New York: Greenberg Press, 1955), p. 53.

15. Adamson, *Keepers of the Lights*, pp. 54–55; Bernard and June Perkins, 1973.49, J. W. Alexander, secretary of USDC, Washington, D.C., letter to Captain Ole Eriksen, Honolulu, September 20, 1920, Bernice P. Bishop Museum, Visual Collection, Scrapbook on Honolulu Harbor, Ships, and Lighthouse Tender *Kukui*.

16. USDC, *Annual Reports*, 1917, p. 696.

17. Ibid., 1916, pp. 673, 712; 1917, p. 714.

18. *Honolulu Advertiser*, August 14, 1938; Bernard and June Perkins, 1973.49, Ralph R. Tinkham, superintendent of lighthouses, Honolulu, letter to Frederick A. Edgecomb, Captain Ole Erikson, and William Jones, Honolulu, June 28, 1922, Bernice P. Bishop Museum, Visual Collection; Major General C. P. Summerall, U.S. Army, letter to Tinkham, July 1, 1922.

19. Richard Weinberg, "Lighthouses! 150 Years of Service," *Honolulu Star-Bulletin*, May 27, 1939.

20. Ibid.

21. Ibid.; "Light-oh! . . . Where Away?," *The Sales Builder*, vol. 12 (March 1939), pp. 14–16. Other men known to be part of the crew in 1939 were Joe Manasey Hatori, Albert Castro, James Aukai, Douglas Keahi Sproat, Ed

Davis, Henry Kupukao, David Kawailoa Ahia, Philip Aaka, Joseph Kahoai Kipahulu, Kun Ung Chun, Charles H. Y. Liu, John C. Allen, and John Priestley.

22. Correspondence with Carol Edgecomb Brown, August 1989; *Honolulu Star-Bulletin,* January 2, 1940 and February 4, 1946.

23. Interview with Ensign Keith Russell and Ensign John Boynewicz, U.S. Coast Guard, aboard CGC *Mallow,* July 11, 1989.

24. *Jane's Fighting Ships* (London: Jane's Publishing Company Limited, 1984–1985), p. 119.

25. Rod Ohira, "Barge Still Afire," *Honolulu Star-Bulletin,* April 21, 1989, p. 1.

26. Ibid.; interview with Ensign Keith Russell, U.S. Coast Guard, aboard the *Mallow,* July 11, 1989.

27. Interview with Ensign John Boynewicz, U.S. Coast Guard, aboard the *Mallow,* July 11, 1989.

28. Thomas Hawk Creighton, George S. Walters, and Hawaii Department of Land and Natural Resources, *The South Kona Coast Historic and Recreational Area, Island of Hawai'i* (Honolulu: Hawaii Department of Land and Natural Resources, 1969), p. 12.

GLOSSARY

Acetylene A highly flammable gaseous hydrocarbon used as an illuminant for lamps. The acetylene, in gaseous form, was contained under pressure in metal tanks. Copper tubing led from the tank to the lamp enclosed by a glass prismatic lens cover. A mechanically operated timing mechanism in the lamp automatically lit the flame by igniting a pilot light and also automatically extinguished the flame. Acetylene was first used in the Hawaiian Islands in 1911 for the Kahului Harbor Breakwater Light, Maui, and the lighted aid established on the islet of Molokini.

Aid to navigation Any device external to a vessel or aircraft specifically intended to assist navigators to determine their position or safe course, or to warn them of dangers or obstructions to navigation.

Beacon A lighted or unlighted fixed aid to navigation attached to the earth's surface. Lights and day beacons both are "beacons." In the early 1900s the Light House Board gave the designation of "beacon lights" to certain types of aids to navigation that cost less than $500 to construct. Any navigational aid that cost over $500 was designated as a lighthouse and required a special appropriation from Congress. Beacon lights could usually be seen at night for a distance of eight or nine miles and were established for interisland use. Lieutenant J. R. Slattery, U.S. Army Corps of Engineers, designed a particular type of beacon and service house, which became recognized as distinctly Hawaiian. This type of beacon light was first built in 1906 at Makanalua, Moloka'i, and at Laupāhoehoe and Ka Lae, island of Hawai'i.

Bearing The horizontal direction of a line of sight between two objects on the surface of the earth.

Buoy A lighted or unlighted floating aid to navigation that is secured to the seabed or riverbed by a mooring.

Bureau of Lighthouses In 1910 the nine-member U.S. Light House Board was replaced by the Bureau of Lighthouses headed by a commissioner under the direction and control of the U.S. Department of Commerce and Labor. Civilian inspectors replaced the army and naval officer inspectors, but a Corps of Engineers officer, who was responsible for repairs and new construction, was assigned to each district. The number of districts was increased from the original twelve to nineteen. Under Franklin D. Roosevelt's Reorganization Plan of 1939, the Bureau of Lighthouses was transferred to and consolidated with the Coast Guard, administered by the Treasury Department. Lighthouse Service employees were given the option of retaining their civilian status or joining the Coast Guard.

Characteristic The specific audible, visual, or electronic signal displayed by an aid to navigation that assists in the identification of the aid. Characteristic refers to lights, sound signals, radio beacons, and day beacons. Types of characteristics of lights: (1) Fixed (F): a characteristic in which the light shows continuously and steadily; (2) Occulting (Oc): a characteristic in which the total duration of light in a period is longer than the total duration of darkness, and the intervals of darkness (eclipses) are usually of equal duration; (3) Flashing (Fl): a characteristic in which the total duration of light in a period is shorter than the total duration of darkness, and the appearances of light (flashes) are usually of equal duration.

Commission The action of placing a previously discontinued aid to navigation back in operation.

Daybeacon An unlighted fixed structure that is equipped with a daymark for daytime identification.

Daymark The daytime identifier of an aid to navigation presenting one of several standard shapes (square, triangle, rectangle) and colors (red, green, white, orange, yellow, or black).

DCB Directional Code Beacon: a standard optic used

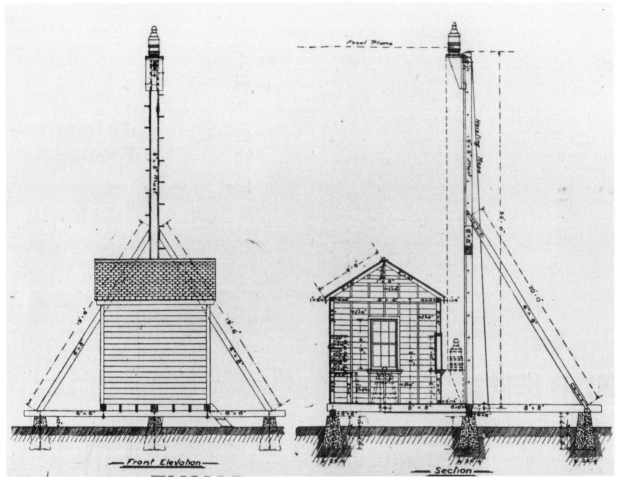

Type of Hawaiian beacon designed by Lieutenant J. R. Slattery. (*Pacific Commercial Advertiser,* reprinted with permission of the *Honolulu Advertiser*)

by the Coast Guard for landfall lights that must have a minimal range greater than 18 nautical miles. The DCB-24 (with a 24-inch diameter) and the DCB-224 (two DCB-24s) emit one and two pencil beams, respectively, which sweep the horizon at a predetermined number of revolutions per minute, creating the specific characteristic that identifies the aid.

Discontinue   To remove from operation (permanently or temporarily) a previously authorized aid to navigation.

Establish   To place an authorized aid to navigation in operation for the first time.

Flasher-regulator for acetylene lamps   A gas-operated device that provided a light of adjustable characteristics. The regulator contained two chambers, one set upon the other. In the top flasher chamber, gas previously burned was replenished. The duration of the eclipse was determined by the amount of time it took to expand a diaphragm to the point of tripping a valve, allowing gas to

DCB-224. (Courtesy of The Carlisle & Finch Company, Cincinnati, Ohio)

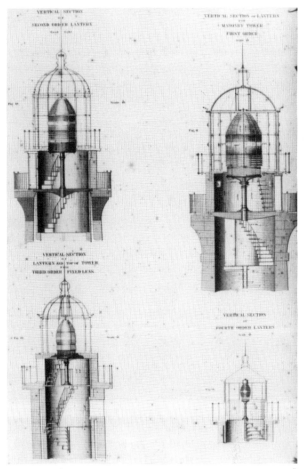

First- through fourth-order Fresnel lenses showing vertical sections of lantern and tower mountings. (National Archives)

enter once again. The duration of the flash was determined by the time it took for the gas to burn sufficiently for the pressure to drop. The duration of these intervals could be adjusted for providing various light characteristics.

Focal plane   A plane that is level with the plane of light that passes through the principal focus of the lens measured by the distance above mean high sea level.

Fresnel lens   (fra-nel′) A type of lens designed by Augustin Jean Fresnel in 1823. The lens collected and focused the light rays into a horizontal beam; it was known as the dioptric system (Greek *dioptrikos,* to see through) which was more efficent than the reflector system. An experiment conducted in the nineteenth century measured the percentage of the light shown from a lighthouse that actually reached an observer on the deck of a ship. The results revealed that 3.5% of the light from an open light of candles or fire reached a ship; 17% of the light from a reflector lamp reached it; and 83% of the light from a Fresnel lens lamp could be seen.

The lenses were originally manufactured by two French companies and later by one company in England. The firms produced a specific range of lights that were standardized. The Fresnel lenses were available in seven sizes or orders:

	Inside Diameter	Height
First	72 $^{7}/_{16}$ "	7' 10"
Second	55 $^{1}/_{8}$ "	6' 1"
Third	39 $^{3}/_{8}$ "	4' 8"
Three-and-a-half	29 $^{1}/_{2}$ "	3' 8"
Fourth	19 $^{11}/_{16}$ "	2' 4"
Fifth	14 $^{3}/_{4}$ "	1' 8"
Sixth	11 $^{3}/_{4}$ "	1' 5"

Usually the fourth, fifth, and sixth orders were used for channel navigational lights, while lights of the third order were either major harbor or minor coastal lights. First- and second-order lenses were generally used on primary lights.

Illuminant   The material used to produce a light, such as wood, oil, acetylene, electricity. In Hawai'i sperm oil was first used, then, occasionally, colza oil. Kerosene came into use in Hawai'i about 1877. By 1885 kerosene was the principal illuminant. In 1904 electricity became the illuminant for two Hawaiian aids. Incandescent oil vapor (i.o.v.) came into wide use after 1910.

Incandescent oil vapor (i.o.v.)   The i.o.v. lamp used kerosene that was forced, under pressure, into a vaporizing chamber. When the kerosene struck the hot walls of the chamber it was vaporized. The vapor then passed through a series of small holes where it was ignited on a Bunsen burner. The mantle, which was placed over the flame, became white-hot and gave off a bright light. The illuminating power of the light was eight to ten times greater than that achieved with the use of an ordinary kerosene wick lamp. Equipment for the i.o.v. system included the lamp; one high-pressure tank with reducing valve attached, and gauge; one oil-and-air tank, with connections to the lamp; a spirit lamp for the initial heating of the vaporizing chamber; and the implements required to clean, adjust, and repair the various parts. Incandescent oil vapor was first used in the Hawaiian Islands at Diamond Head and Makapu'u Point lighthouses in 1910.

Lantern   The top portion of the lighthouse tower. This section of the lighthouse was sometimes constructed by the same companies that manufactured Fresnel lenses.

The lantern was transported in sections to the lighthouse site. It contained a service room where the clockwork for rotating optics, fuel tanks, lamps, and so forth, were located. This was where the keepers cleaned the lamp chimneys and prepared the lamps for lighting. Above the service room was the lantern room. Here the lens was enclosed and protected from the weather by storm panes, which were glass windows set in metal frames. The lantern was usually topped with a metal dome. A door led from the lantern room to an outside balcony, called gallery, which encircled the lantern room.

Lens lantern   A glass protective cover for a lamp that consisted of prismatic rings of glass, which focused the light rays into a horizontal beam.

Light   (1) The signal emitted by a lighted aid to navigation. (2) The illuminating apparatus used to emit the light signal. (3) A lighted aid to navigation on a fixed structure.

Light House Board: A nine-member board formed in 1852 to administer the navigational aids of the United States. Congress authorized the board to divide the coasts of the United States into twelve districts and assign an army and naval officer to each district as engineer and inspector. In 1904 the U.S. Department of Commerce and Labor, through the Light House Board, was charged with all the administrative duties relative to the lighthouse service of the Territory of Hawaii. The board ordered that the boundaries of the Twelfth U.S. Lighthouse District be extended to include within it the Hawaiian Islands. The district previously extended from the boundary between California and Mexico to the boundary between California and Oregon. The Light House Board was replaced by the Bureau of Lighthouses in 1910.

Lighthouse Service   The term Lighthouse Service had official status during the period when the Bureau of Lighthouses was functioning. Although no agency with this name ever existed, the term is often used to designate America's lighthouse system.

Light station   The station included the lighted beacon (as well as other navigational aids such as radio beacon towers) and all other buildings relative to the particular navigational aid, such as the keepers' homes.

Loom   The glow of a powerful light often seen beyond the limit of visibility of the actual rays of the light. The loom may sometimes appear sharp enough to provide a bearing.

Primary light or major seacoast aid A lighted aid to navigation established for the purpose of providing assistance in making landfalls and coastwise passages. Hawai'i has ten primary lights: Kauhola Point and Cape Kumukahi lights on the island of Hawai'i; Pa'uwela Point Light, Maui; Moloka'i Light, Moloka'i; Diamond Head, Makapu'u Point, Ka'ena Point, and Barbers Point lights, O'ahu; and Kīlauea Point and Nāwiliwili Harbor lights, Kaua'i. There are 65 other lighted navigational aids that can be seen over five nautical miles at sea, and 101 lighted navigational aids that can be seen under five nautical miles at sea.

Radiobeacon Electronic apparatus that transmits a radio signal for use in providing a mariner with a line of position.

Range A pair of beacons, lighted or unlighted, commonly located to define a line down the center of a channel.

Reflectors Used with a lamp to gather rays from the available light, the bowl-like shape of the reflector both reflected and directed the beams of light in a desired direction. The arrangement came to be known as the catoptric system (Greek *katoptron,* mirror).

Secondary light A major light other than a primary seacoast light established at harbor entrances and other locations where high intensity and reliability are required.

Sun valve for acetylene lamp A device that automatically extinguishes the light during daylight hours. Movement of the mechanical part that controls the flow of gas to the burner is obtained by the difference in expansion of certain of the structural members that absorb light. The minute difference in temperature is multiplied by mechanical linkage to provide the necessary valve opening or closing.

INDEX

Acetylene, 203; at Cape Kumukahi, 125; at Coconut Point, 122; at Hanamanioa, 68; at Hāwea Point, 72; at Ka'ena Point, 54; at Kaho'olawe, 83; at Kahului Harbor, 73, 133; at Kailua, 133; at Kauhola Point, 122; at Ka'uiki Head, 71; at Ka'ula Rock, 158, 159; at Kawaihae, 122; at Keāhole Point, 122, 133; at Kūki'i Point, 146; at Kukuihaele, 122; at Lahaina, 66, 67; at Lehua Rock, 154-155; at McGregor Point, 70; at Māhukona, 122; at Makanalua, 98; at Molokini, 73; at Nākālele Point, 70; at Palaoa Point, 87; at Pauwalu Point, 75; at Pa'uwela Point, 74, 75

Ahukini, 141

'Ai'ai, 86

Aids to Navigation (ATON), 36

Aids to Navigation Team (ANT), 168; at Diamond Head Light, 35; on island of Hawai'i, 129-135; on Kaho'olawe, 83, 85; at Kāne'ohe Bay, 58; on Kaua'i, 138, 150-153; on Lāna'i, 88; on Lehua Rock, 154; at Makapu'u Point Light, 51; on Maui, 81; on Moloka'i, 108-110; on Molokini, 84

Aikin, Glenn, 35, 36-37, 52, 129-135

Akana, Charles K., 68, 125-126, 173

Alderman Wood, 86

Alexander, William Dewitt, 18, 116

Ālia Point, 116, 120, 122

Ālia Point Light, 120, 122. See also Makahanaloa Light; Pepe'ekeo Point Light Station

Aloha Tower, 6, 13-16, 34. See also Honolulu Harbor Light Station

Alona, A., 19, 173

Amalu, Sammy, 40

Amalu, Samuel Apollo, 23, 46, 144-145, 173

American Sugar Company, 90

Anahola Bay, 138, 139. See also Kahala Point Light

Andersen, J., 67, 173

Andersen, Mrs. J., 68, 173

Annie E, 165. See also *Kukui*

Archaeological sites, 55-56, 85, 86, 121. See also Heiau

Arthur. See Barber, Henry

Atkinson, William, 151

Automation: of Barbers Point Light, 24; of Cape Kumukahi Light, 128; of Diamond Head Light, 33, 45; of Honolulu Harbor Light, 14; of Ka Lae Light, 135; of Kauhola Point Light, 124; of Kīlauea Point Light, 149; of Makapu'u Point Light, 50; of Moloka'i Light, 105; of Nāwiliwili Light, 148; of Pa'uwela Light, 75, 80. See also Acetylene; Electricity; Solar power

Aviation (trans-Pacific), 48, 125, 145-146

Baker, A. S., 19-20, 29. See also Barbers Point Light Station; Diamond Head Light Station

Barber, Henry, 17

Barbers Point (Barber's Point), 17, 31

Barbers Point Harbor, 169, 170

Barbers Point Light Station, 18, 20, 22-25, 30, 31

Barbier and Benard, 30, 116; as Barbier and Company, 42; as Barbier, Benard, and Turenne, 74, 143. See also Fresnel lens; Lantern

Barking Sands, 152. See also Kokole Light Station; Nohili Point Light

Basswood, CGC, 128

Beazley, George A., 44, 173

Beeson, M. F., 106, 173

Bennett, F. D., 60

Bernice Pauahi Bishop Estate, 41, 58, 95

Bianca, 21-22

Bird Island, 40

Black Company, E. E., 147. See also Nāwiliwili Light Station

Blonde, HMS, 117. See also Hilo Bay

Blum, Carl, 140-141, 173

Board of Harbor Commissioners (Territory of Hawai'i), 13

Board of Health (Territory of Hawai'i), 97, 98

Brigham, William Tufts, 121. See also Ka Lae Light Station

Brockman, George, 130, 173

Brown, Carol Edgecomb, 23, 55, 142, 144, 146

Bryson, Daniel J., 106, 174

Bureau of Lighthouses (U.S.), 45, 125, 203; commendation by, 21; goals of, 75; reports of, 33, 54, 87, 122, 123, 125, 146

Burrows, John Warren, 93-96, 97, 174

Burrows, John R., 95-96, 174

Byron, Lord George Anson, 117

Byron's Bay. See Hilo Bay

Campbell, James, 19, 63

Cape Hanamanioa. See Hanamanioa Light Station

Cape Kumukahi Light Station, 125-128, 135

Carter, George R., 11, 41

Carter, H. A. P., 89, 91, 92, 93, 96

Cattle industry, 90, 113, 119

Champion Iron Company, 143. See also Kīlauea Point Light Station

Chance Brothers and Company, 39, 72, 100. See also Fresnel lens; Lantern

Chillingworth, Sam, 113, 174

China, 30. *See also* Diamond Head Light
    Station
Chinese: in Hawai'i, 91
Cianfarani, Ronald, 50, 174
Clark Company, Howard, 14
C. M. Ward, 27. *See also* King, James A.
Coast Pilot, 6
Coconut Point Light Station, 119, 129
Coffee industry, 112
Columbine, 165–166
Coney, J. H., 117. *See also* Pauka'a Point
    Light Station
Cook, James, 60, 134; monument to, 8, 169
Cooke, George, 95
Coolidge, Calvin, 85
Cornwell, James L., 70, 174
Craig, Ralph, 58, 82; at Moloka'i Light,
    108–109, 129–135, 155
Creighton, James R., 106, 174
Crossman & Brother, W. H., 18

Daniel, C. N., 105, 106, 128
Davies & Co., T. H. *See* Lloyds of London
DCB (Directional Code Beacon), 203–204;
    on Barbers Point Light, 25; on Cape
    Kumukahi Light, 125; on Ka'ena Point
    Light, 56; on Kauhola Light, 123; at
    Kīlauea Point, 148–149; for Makapu'u
    Point Light, 52; on Moloka'i Light, 108;
    on Nāwiliwili Light, 148, 150
Department of Commerce (U.S.), 165
Department of Commerce and Labor
    (U.S.), 11, 32, 41, 44
Department of Public Works (Territory of
    Hawai'i), 18, 40, 57; Henry Cooper as
    superintendent of, 96; 1902 report of, 54,
    68, 114; Robert Sterling as superinten-
    dent of, 8; W. E. Rowell as superinten-
    dent of, 30, 39, 72
Department of the Interior (Territory of
    Hawai'i), 6, 8. *See also* Department of
    Public Works
Diamond Head Charlie. *See* Peterson,
    John Charles
Diamond Head crater, 8, 27–29, 91
Diamond Head Light Station, 6, 31–36;
    early proposals for, 8, 29

Diamond Head Lookout Station, 26, 27,
    30, 34. *See also* Pilots' watchman
Dole, James, 86
Dominis, J. O., 54
Dowsett, J. I., 8
Dowsett, W. James, 92
Dunne, George H., 64, 174
Duvauchelle, Edouard, 61. *See also*
    Lahaina Light Station

Earthquake, 107, 123. *See also* Hurricane;
    Tidal wave; Volcano eruption
Edgecomb, Frederick: as assistant super-
    intendent, 23; background of, 33–34; on
    Ka'ula Rock, 155–160; as Lighthouse
    Service engineer, 20, 32, 75, 142–144, 146;
    at Makapu'u Point Light Station, 46,
    49; as superintendent, 33, 49, 55, 86,
    123
Electricity, 81; for Barbers Point Light, 22;
    for Cape Kumukahi Light, 126, 128; for
    Coconut Point Light, 119; for Diamond
    Head Light, 30, 32, 33; for Hanamanioa
    Light, 78; for Hāwea Point Light, 78;
    for Honolulu Harbor Light (Aloha
    Tower), 14; for Kahala Point Light, 151;
    for Kahului Range Lights, 78; for Ka
    Lae Light, 134–135; for Kauhola Light,
    124; for Kīlauea Point Light, 146; for
    Lahaina Light, 67; for Makapu'u Point
    Light, 47, 50; for Mānele Bay Light, 87;
    for Miloli'i Point Light, 134; for Molo-
    ka'i Light, 103; for Molokini Light, 84;
    for Pa'uwela Light, 80; for Waiākea
    Light, 119. *See also* Solar power; Wind
    power
'Ele'ele Light, 139. *See also* Hanapēpē Bay
Ellis, William, 83. *See also* Molokini
Emory, Kenneth, 86. *See also* Lāna'i
Engel, Benjamin, 34. *See also* Diamond
    Head Light Station
Engel, Mrs. Benjamin (Ruth), 34
Enos, John, 46, 76, 174
Eriksen, Ole, 165
Esplanade, 13; light tower on, 9
Estrella, Sidney, 126, 174
Evans, S. H., 105

Farrington, Wallace R., 154
Ferreira, Manuel, 21–22, 46–47, 71, 102, 174
Ferreira, Mrs. Manuel, 21
Flint, Harry W., 12, 144, 174
Forsyth, Thomas C., 64
Fort Ruger, 32
Franck, Harry, 103
Frear, Walter Francis, 83, 121, 122, 142
Fresnel lens, 42, 205; on Barbers Point
    Light, 18, 19, 22, 25; on Diamond Head
    Light, 30, 33, 35; on Honolulu Harbor
    Light, 9, 12; on Kauhola Point Light,
    123; on Kīlauea Point Light, 143–144; on
    Kohala Light, 116; on Lā'au Point
    Light, 93, 94; on Lahaina Light, 66; on
    Makahanaloa Light, 116; on Makapu'u
    Point Light, 42–43, 100; on Moloka'i
    Light, 100, 101, 108–110; proposed for
    Kahului Harbor, 72–73. *See also* Hyper-
    radiant lens
Fur trade, 17, 60

Gay, George, 155
Gifford, W. M., 41
Gilbert, L. L., 8
Gillespie, Ed, 50, 174

Hackfeld and Company, H., 93
Haiku Sugar Company, 74
Haleakala. See Loncke, Captain
Haleamau, David P., 144, 174
Hale'iwa Harbor Range Lights. *See*
    Waialua navigational lights
Hāmākua Coast, 119
Hāna Bay, 70
Hanalei Bay, 138, 139
Hanamanioa Light Station, 67, 68, 75, 81
Hanamā'ulu Bay, 139, 141
Hanapēpē Bay, 138, 139
Hanapēpē Light, 148, 152
Hansen, John, 125
Hansen's disease, 97–98
Hanuna, John M., 70, 175
Harbor pilots, 7, 16, 26–27, 34
Harbor Wink, 7, 9, 12. *See also* Honolulu
    Harbor Light Station
Hassinger, J. A., 19, 93, 116

Hatton, W., 20, 175

Hawai'i (island), 169

Hawaiian Investigation Report. *See* Light House Board

Hawaiian News Company, 26

Hawaiian Pineapple Company. *See* Dole, James

Hawaiian Railroad Company, 114, 117

Hawaii Maritime Center, 52, 150

Hāwea Point Light, 72, 75, 77, 78, 81

Heiau: Ahi, 28; Honua'ula, 70; Kalalea, 121; on Kalaupapa peninsula, 102; in Kāne'ohe area, 58; on Ka'ula Rock, 156–157; Kukui-o-Lono, 138; Kukui'ula, 138; Lonopuha, 130; Pahu-o-Māui, 29. *See also* Archaeological sites

Hearn, Mrs. Robert (Elizabeth), 80–81

Hearn, Robert, 80–81, 175

Hegenberger, Albert F., 145–146

High, Peter, 19

Hilo, 113, 117, 119

Hilo Bay (Harbor), 117, 118, 122, 148

Hilo Harbor Range Lights, 129

Hilonian, 44

H. N. Carleton (Carlton), 91, 92

Holmes, Henry, 95

Honolulu, 6; Custom House light in, 9

Honolulu Harbor, 6–16, 26, 39, 69

Honolulu Harbor (entrance) Light, 6, 16

Honolulu Harbor Light Station, 6–10, 12, 16

Honolulu Iron Works, 8, 13, 30

Hoopii, John, 116, 175

Hospital Point, 57. *See also* Pearl Harbor

Houston, V. S. K., 125

Hua a Pohukaina, 70. *See also* Ka'uiki Head

Hughes, Thomas. *See* Honolulu Iron Works

Hurricane, 138. *See also* Earthquake; Tidal wave; Volcano eruption

Hutchinson, Frederick W., 62, 63, 113, 117

Hyperradiant lens, 42–44, 100. *See also* Fresnel lens

Incandescent oil-vapor (i.o.v.), 12, 20–21, 32, 42, 44, 101–102, 120–123, 145, 206;

directions for use of, 145; report on, 44

Inter-Island Steam Navigation Company, 19, 21; lights maintained by, 139, 141

Iroquois, USS, 21, 141, 162

Iwalani, 100

James Makee, 100

Jordon, Fred, 75

Kaala, 103–104. *See also* Kalaupapa peninsula; Marques, Edward

Ka'amola Point Light, 90. *See also* Kamalō Harbor

Ka'ena Point (on Lāna'i), 86

Ka'ena Point (on O'ahu), 54, 55

Ka'ena Point Light Station, 54–56

Ka'ena Point Passing Light, 55, 56. *See also* Ka'ena Point Light Station

Kahala Point Light, 141, 148, 151

Kaho'olawe, 82, 85

Kaho'olawe Point Light, 83, 85

Kahoolawe Ranch Company, 85. *See also* Cattle industry

Kahului Harbor, 72, 73, 148, 169

Kahului Harbor lights, 73, 75, 77, 78

Kailua Bay Entrance Light, 133–134

Kailua Light Station, 133

Kaimuki Lookout Station, 26

Kainali, Samuel, 89, 175

Kaiwi, 43, 175

Ka Lae (South Point), 120, 121

Ka Lae Light Station, 120–121, 134–135, 166

Kalaeloa (point), 17. *See also* Barbers Point

Kalaeokalā'au Point Light. *See* Lā'au Point Light Station

Kalama, Luther K., 70, 144, 175

Kalaniana'ole, Prince Jonah Kūhiō, 10–11

Kalaupapa Light. *See* Moloka'i Light Station

Kalaupapa peninsula, 89, 97–98, 100, 102–103

Kalawao, 97, 100

Kaleimamo, 89, 92

Kalili, David, 130, 175

Kalihi Wai (Kalihiwai Bay), 139

Kamalō Harbor, 89, 90

Kamehameha I, 58, 112, 121

Kamehameha III, 8, 67

Kanahena Point Light, 67–68

Kanaloa. *See* Kaho'olawe

Kāne'ohe Bay, 39, 57–58, 169

Kanoa, Paulo, 61

Kaohimaunu, John, 45, 175

Kapa'a landing, 139

Kapahua, Sam, 119, 175

Kapalama (Reserved) Channel, 13, 16. *See also* Honolulu Harbor

Kapena, Jonah, 61

Kapueokahi Bay. *See* Hāna Bay

Kariger, Frederick, 164

Kaua'i, 17, 138

Kauhola Point Light Station, 116, 122–125, 132

Ka'uiki Head, 70, 75

Ka'uiki Head Light Station, 70–71, 77–79

Kaukaliu, John M., 32, 175

Ka'ula, 154, 156, 157

Ka'ula Rock Light, 154, 155–160

Kaumalapau Harbor Light, 86, 88

Kaunakakai Harbor, 89–90, 104

Kaunakakai Harbor Range Lights, 89, 92

Kaunuloa, 139. *See also* Makaweli Harbor

Kawaihae, 112–113, 114, 117

Kawaihae Light Station, 113–114, 132–133

Kawelo, 86. *See also* Lāna'i

Keāhole Point Light Station, 121, 133

Kealaikahiki Point, 85

Kealakekua Bay, 122, 134, 168. *See also* Nāpō'opo'o Light Station

Keanu, James M., 101, 103, 176

Keauhou Bay Entrance Light, 134

Keawaiki Light, 61. *See also* Lahaina Light Station

Kelsey, Theodore, 43

Kepilino, Philip, 75, 176

Kerosene, 44; for Barbers Point Light, 19; for Ka'uiki Head Light, 71; for Kaunakakai Range Lights, 89; for Kawaihae Light, 113; for Lā'au Point Light, 93; for Lahaina Light, 62, 63, 64; for Nāwiliwili Light, 140; for Pauka'a Point Light, 117; for Pa'uwela Point Light, 74. *See also* Incandescent oil-vapor

Kilauea, 12, 89, 113

Kīlauea, 126–128

Kīlauea Point, 142

Kīlauea Point Light Station, 48, 101, 138, 147, 148–150, 152. *See also* Aviation; Lightkeepers; Radio beacon

Kilauea Sugar Plantation Company, 142

Kinau, 113–114

King, James A.: as minister of the Interior, 29, 30, 31, 32, 64, 95; as ship captain, 27, 72, 74

Kluegel, C. H., 31

Kohala, 114, 116

Kohala Light, 116. *See also* Kauhola Point Light Station

Koko Head, 6, 26

Kokole Light Station, 141, 148, 151

Kōloa, 138–139, 151. *See also* Makahū'ena Point Light; Sugar industry

Kōloa Light, 138, 141. *See also* Makahū'ena Point Light

Kua, Oliver, 122, 147–148, 176

Kualoa Point Range Lights. *See* Kāne'ohe Bay

Kukaia, 64, 175

Kūki'i Point Light Station, 146, 148, 150

Kukui, 83, 86, 126, 161; Alaskan service of, 162; crew of, on Ka'ula Rock, 155, 157–160; decommissioning of, 167; description of, 162–163; Ka Lae Light supplied by, 166–167; Kauhola Light supplied by, 123; Kīlauea Point Light supplied by, 142, 144; Moloka'i Light supplied by, 101; officers and crew of, 167; Palaoa Point Light supplied by, 87; search and rescue operations of, 163, 164–165, 167; World War II service of, 166. See also *Columbine; Moi Wahine*

Kukuihaele Light Station, 119–129, 131

Kulikolani, 93. *See also* Lā'au Point Light Station

Kumukahi, 126

Kupukaa, Harry, 105, 176

Lā'au Point, 91–92, 93

Lā'au Point Light Station, 91–97

Laewahie Point, 86. *See also* Pōhakuloa Point Light Station

Lahaina, 60–61, 63, 66, 169

Lahaina Light Station, 61–67, 72, 75, 77

Lāhainā Restoration Foundation, 109–110. *See also* Moloka'i Light Station

Lāna'i, 81, 86–88, 89, 164, 169

Landrum, Aaron, 35, 36–37, 52, 108–110, 151

Lantern: on Barbers Point Light, 19, 25; on Diamond Head Light, 30, 35; on Honolulu Harbor Light, 7; on Kīlauea Point Light, 143–144; on Lā'au Point Light, 93; on Lahaina Light, 66; on Makapu'u Point Light, 43–44; on Moloka'i Light, 100

La Pérouse, Jean-Francois Galaup de, 60

La Pérouse Bay, 60, 67, 69

Laupāhoehoe Point Light Station, 120, 130–131

La Vergne, George De, 140

Lē'ahi, 8, 29. *See also* Diamond Head Light Station

Lehua, 153, 154–155

Lehua Rock Light, 154, 156, 158, 161

Lelepali, Rose, 106

Lemonnier, L. Santter, 18. *See also* Fresnel lens; Lantern

Leprosarium. *See* Kalaupapa peninsula

Leprosy. *See* Hansen's disease

Light dues (fees), 9, 61, 118

Light House Board (U.S.), 10, 11, 32, 40, 74, 162, 206; display at 1893 Chicago World's Fair, 42; 1902 Hawaiian Investigation Report to, 97; 1903 report of, 54; 1904 report of, 11, 64, 68, 115, 116, 119, 141; 1905 report of, 68, 72, 73, 83, 120; 1908 report of, 70, 125; 1909 report of, 57. *See also* Department of Commerce and Labor

Lighthouse tenders, 80, 162, 165, 167–170. See also *Columbine; Kukui;* U.S. Coast Guard

Lighthouse Week, 76

Lightkeepers: of Barbers Point Light, 19, 20, 21, 23, 32; benefits for, 45–46; of Cape Kumukahi Light, 125–126; of Diamond Head Light, 32; of Honolulu

Harbor Light, 7, 11, 12, 102; of Ka Lae Light, 121, 144; of Kanahena Light, 67, 68; of Kauhola Point Light, 122; of Ka'uiki Head Light, 71; of Kaunakakai Range Lights, 89; of Kawaihae Light, 113; of Kīlauea Point Light, 101, 144; of Kohala Light, 116; of Kūki'i Point Light, 146; of Lahaina Light, 64; of McGregor Point Light, 70; of Māhukona Light, 114; of Makahanaloa Light, 116; of Makapu'u Point Light, 33, 44–47, 50; of Moloka'i Light, 101, 103–105; of Nākālele Point Light, 70; of Nāpō'opo'o Light, 130; of Nāwiliwili Light, 140–141, 146; of Pauka'a Point Light, 117–118, 119; of Pepe'ekeo Point Light, 130; salary of, 11, 67

Light List, 47, 98, 118

Likelike, 72, 100. *See also* King, James A.; Moloka'i Light Station

Lloyds of London, 27. *See also* Pilots' watchman

Loncke, Captain, 83

London, 86

Lookout Station, 26. *See also* Diamond Head Lookout Station

LORAN, 49, 154. *See also* 'Upolu Point LORAN Station

Lucas, George: Lucas tower built by, 26. *See also* Honolulu Harbor

Luckey, Jim, 109–110

Lyra, 72

Lyra Bay. *See* Kahului Harbor

Mā'alaea Bay, 69. *See also* Wilder's Steamship Company

McAllister, J. Gilbert, 85

McGinni, Knefler, 48. *See also* Aviation; Makapu'u Point Light Station

McGregor, Daniel, 7, 9, 12, 176. *See also* McGregor Point

McGregor Point, 69

McGregor Point Light, 69–70, 75, 80

McKinley, William, 96

McLaughlin, John, 44, 176

Macy and Company, G. W., 113

Mahoe, John K., 70, 176

Māhukona landing, 114

Māhukona Light, 114–116

Maitland, Lester J., 145–146

Makahanaloa Light, 116. *See also* Ālia Point Light

Makahū‘ena Point Light, 138, 141, 148, 151

Makanalua. *See* Kalaupapa peninsula

Makanalua Light, 98. *See also* Moloka‘i Light Station

Makapu‘u Point, 42

Makapu‘u Point Light Station, 6, 38–39, 42–43, 46, 50–52, 100. *See also* Aviation; Radio beacon

Makaweli Harbor, 139, 141. *See also* Inter-Island Steam Navigation Company

Makee Sugar Company. *See* Mākena; Sugar industry

Mākena, 67

Mākena Light, 67

Mallow, CGC, 167, 169–170. *See also* Lighthouse tenders

Mānana Island. *See* Bird Island

Mānā Point, 141. *See also* Nohili Point Light

Manchuria, 39, 40–41, 52. *See also* Makapu‘u Point Light Station

Mānele Bay, 87, 88

Mānele Bay Light, 87

Mansfield, George, 44, 176

Manu, Sam, 163–164

Marks, Richard, 110

Marques, Edward (Ed), 76–80, 103, 104, 107–108, 176

Marques, Helene, 79–80

Marques, Mrs. Edward (Helen), 76

Marquis de Turenne, 17–18. *See also* Barbers Point

Māui (demigod), 56, 70

Maui (island), 60, 82, 89

Mercury (for revolving lenses): use of, 100–101, 107–109, 143, 145, 149

Metcalf, John, 41

Meyer, Rudolph William, 89, 91–95

Mikahala, 166. See also *Columbine*

Mille Morris, 94. *See also* Lā‘au Point Light Station

Miloli‘i Point Light Station, 134

Miowera, 29. *See also* Diamond Head Light Station

Moealoha, Edward K., 122, 176

Moi Wahine, 163–165

Moku‘ae‘ae Rock, 142, 144, 149

Moloka‘i, 86, 89, 97, 169

Moloka‘i Light Station, 98–103, 106–110

Molokini, 73, 82, 83, 85

Molokini Light, 82–84

Munro, G. C., 96

Nakai, John T., 121, 176

Nākālele Point Light Station, 70, 75, 77, 81

Nalaielua, Henry, 104. *See also* Kalaupapa peninsula

Nāpō‘opo‘o Light Station, 121, 134, 169–170

National Construction Company, 13

National Park Service (U.S. Department of the Interior), 107. *See also* Kalaupapa peninsula; Moloka‘i Light Station

National Register of Historic Places, 52, 56, 107, 149

National Wildlife Refuge, 149. *See also* Kīlauea Point Light Station

Nāwiliwili Bay (Harbor), 139–140, 141, 146, 148, 169. *See also* Inter-Island Steam Navigation Company

Nāwiliwili Light Attendant Station, 148

Nāwiliwili Light Station, 123, 138, 139, 147–148, 150

Neudecker, Joe, 169

New York Shipbuilding Company, 163

Niblack, A. P., 162

Nielsen, Niels C., 32

Ni‘ihau, 154, 161, 166

Nineteenth U.S. Lighthouse District, 33, 83, 86, 123, 146. *See also* Twelfth U.S. Lighthouse District

Ninini Point. *See* Nāwiliwili Light Station

Nohili Point Light, 152–153

Noviello, D. T., 90, 97

Otwell, C. W., 42, 99, 120–121

Ouderkirk, John, 31

Pacific Mail Steamship Company. See *Manchuria*

Pagoda Building, 26. *See also* Diamond Head Lookout Station; Lucas, George

Pākākā, 7, 13

Palila, 91. *See also* Lā‘au Point

Palmer, Frank C., 142–144

Panama Canal, 12, 120, 125

Papa, 85

Pate, Frank, 46, 177

Pauka‘a Point Light Station, 117–119

Pauwalu Point Light, 75

Pa‘uwela Point Light Attendant Station, 80

Pa‘uwela Point Light Station, 74, 75, 77, 80, 81

Pearl, 26–27. *See also* Honolulu Harbor

Pearl Harbor, 6, 57; Japanese attack on, 14; naval air station at, 48; navigational lights in, 56–57, 169; U.S. treaty rights to, 56

Pearl River, 56. *See also* Pearl Harbor

Pele, 43, 126

Pepe‘ekeo Point Light Station, 120, 129–130

Pepe‘ekeo Sugar Company, 116

Pestrella, Joseph, 50, 126, 128, 167, 177

Peterson, John Charles, 27, 28, 31, 32

Peterson, Melika, 27

Philadelphia. *See* Baker, A. S.

Pilots' watchman, 27, 32

Pineapple industry, 12, 86, 90

Planetree, CGC, 80. *See also* Lighthouse tenders

Pōhakuloa Point, 86, 87

Pōhakuloa Point Light Station, 87–88

Pohoiki Bay Light, 135

Point Rose, 27. *See also* Diamond Head crater

Port Allen Harbor, 169. *See also* Hanapēpē Light

Portlock, Nathaniel. *See* Point Rose

Punchbowl Crater (Hill), 6, 26

Putnam, George R., 159

Pu‘uki‘i (islet). *See* Ka‘uiki Head Light Station

Pyramid Rock Light, 58. *See also* Kāne‘ohe Bay

Quarantine Island, 12

Rabbit Island, 40, 52
Radio beacon, 46–49, 146
Rapozo, J. F., 151, 177
RDF (Radio Direction Finder), 50. *See also* Radio beacon
Reciprocity Treaty: of 1875, 9, 91; of 1887, 56. *See also* Sugar industry
Reid, Robert I., 32, 177
Revolving mechanism, 21, 44, 100–101, 143
Reynolds, Arthur. *See* Aloha Tower
River and Harbor Act, 13
Robins, Anna Mae, 23–24, 104–105
Robins, Ed, Jr., 104
Robins, Fred, 23–24, 104–105, 177
Robins, Fred, Jr., 104
Robins, Mrs. Fred (Annie Naʻauao), 23, 104
Robinson, James, 13
Rodman, Hugh, 97. *See also* Light House Board; Molokaʻi
Roosevelt, Franklin, 76
Roosevelt, Theodore, 11, 32, 41, 98, 121
Russell, Keith, 169

Sacred temples. *See* Heiau
Sahm, Leo, 164
Salvi, Kenneth, 82–83, 138, 151, 153
Sampan Channel Range Lights, 58. *See also* Kāneʻohe Bay
Sandalwood trade, 7
Sand Island, 12
Sassafras, CGC, 167, 168, 169, 170. *See also* Lighthouse tenders
Saunders, J. W. *See Manchuria*
Severance, L., 117–118
Sharks, 157
Sheridan, 21. *See also* Barbers Point Light Station
Shipwreck Beach. *See* Lānaʻi
Simeona, P. W. *See* Kanahena Point Light
Slattery, J. R., 98, 162
S. N. Castle, 38. *See also* Makapuʻu Point Light Station
Solar power, 55, 84, 88, 90, 97, 134–135, 150–152. *See also* Wind power
Souza, Manuel, 140, 177
Souza, Mrs. Manuel (Marie), 140

Spalding, Z. S., 64. *See also* Lahaina Light Station; Sugar industry
Spencer, C. N., 27, 94
Spreckels, A. B., 142. *See also* Kīlauea Point Light Station; Sugar industry
Star of Australia. *See* Ulm, C. T. P.
Stevenson, Charles and David, 42. *See also* Hyperradiant lens
Stevenson, Thomas, 42. *See also* Fresnel lens
Stewart, Charles, 117
Sugar industry, 9, 12, 90, 91; on island of Hawaiʻi, 112, 114, 119; on Kauaʻi, 138–139; on Maui, 63. *See also* Reciprocity Treaty
Sullivan, Steve, 50, 177
Sumner, J. K., 8
Sweeney, John, 123, 125, 177

Tanimoto, Charlie, 151–152
Taylor, David, 64, 177
Territory of Hawaii, 10, 70. *See also* Department of Public Works
Thomas, E. B., 31
Thrum, Thomas G., 102
Thurston, Lorrin A., 19, 38, 39, 72, 116
Tidal wave, 91, 104, 130–131. *See also* Earthquake; Hurricane; Volcano eruption
Tinkham, Ralph R., 83, 86, 145, 157
Toomey, Alexander, 33, 45, 177
Toomey, Julia, 33, 45
Transpac Yacht Race, 34–35
Treadway, P. H., 62–63
Turton, Harry, 63. *See also* Lahaina Light Station; Sugar industry
Twelfth U.S. Lighthouse District, 11, 162. *See also* Nineteenth U.S. Lighthouse District

Uahinui, Joseph N., 70, 177
Ulm, C. T. P., 48–49. *See also* Aviation; Makapuʻu Point Light Station
Union Hotel, 61
ʻUpolu Point LORAN Station, 132
U.S. Coast Guard, 34, 50, 52, 85, 87, 148; Coast Guard cutters of, 80, 167–170; fourteenth district of, 49, 80, 105; LAMP program of, 149; Lighthouse

Service consolidated with, 23, 148; light station duty of, 50, 76, 105–106, 148. *See also* Aids to Navigation Team
U.S. Lighthouse Service, 11, 23, 154, 158, 163; radio beacon development by, 46; Seville Exposition exhibit by, 146

Vancouver, George, 60, 85
Van Wagner, Eugene B., 99
Varigny, Charles Victor, 28
Volcano eruption, 50, 126–128, 134. *See also* Earthquake; Hurricane; Tidal wave

Waha, 86
Waiākea Light Station, 119. *See also* Hilo Bay
Waialua navigational lights, 54
Waikiki Beach, 6
Wailua, 138
Waimanalo. *See* Waialua navigational lights
Waimānalo Landing, 40, 42, 44. *See also* Makapuʻu Point Light Station
Waimānalo Sugar Company, 41. *See also* Sugar industry
Waimea Bay, 138, 139, 141
Wākea, 85
Watkins, William J., 125–126, 177–178
Wedemeyer, Ludwig, 126
West Eldura, 21. *See also* Barbers Point Light Station
Wetherby, N. W., 158
Whale oil, 9, 62, 113, 117
Whaling ships: in Honolulu Harbor, 7–8, 61; in Kawaihae anchorage, 113; in Lahaina Roadstead, 60–61, 63
Whitney, Henry, 9, 83
Wichman & Company, H. F., 14
Wight, C. L., 114, 116
Wilder, Samuel G., 64
Wilder's Steamship Company, 67, 69, 73, 114, 116
Williams, William ("Bill"), 11, 12, 178
Wind power (wind-driven generator), 134. *See also* Solar power
Winslow, E. Eveleth, 57
Wire landings, 119–120

Yeoman, 165–166